DEATH, DYING
── AND ──
BEREAVEMENT

Health, Welfare and Practice: Reflecting on Roles and Relationships
edited by J. Walmsley, J. Reynolds, P. Shakespeare and R. Woolfe

Youth in Society
edited by J. Roche and S. Tucker

Changing Experiences of Youth
edited by D. Garratt, J. Roche and S. Tucker

Working for Health
edited by T. Heller, R. Muston, M. Sidell and C. Lloyd

Critical Practice in Health and Social Care
edited by A. Brechin, H. Brown and M. Eby

Changing Practice in Health and Social Care
edited by C. Davies, L. Finlay and A. Bullman

Using Evidence in Health and Social Care
edited by R. Gomm and C. Davies

Evaluating Research in Health and Social Care
edited by R. Gomm, G. Needham and A. Bullman

All eight books are Course Readers for the Open University Diploma in Health and Social Welfare.

Details of the Diploma and the related courses are available from The Information Officer, School of Health and Social Welfare, Horlock Building, The Open University, Walton Hall, Milton Keynes MK7 6AA, UK.

DEATH, DYING
— AND —
BEREAVEMENT

2nd edition

Edited by
Donna Dickenson, Malcolm Johnson
and Jeanne Samson Katz

The Open
University

in association with

Los Angeles • London • New Delhi • Singapore

the hospice and palliative care movements and in recognition that this area needed both academic study as well as practical application. Dr Gillian Ford and Professor Norman McKensie were influential in ensuring that The Open University was able to meet this need and we are immensely grateful for their endeavours. Recognition is due to the roles played by Professor Malcolm Johnson and Dr Donna Dickenson in preparing the original manuscript, other members of the original course team who commissioned, selected and edited contributions were Alyson Peberdy, Dr Jeanne Katz and Dr Moyra Sidell. Margaret Allott as course manager and Rae Smyth as secretary co-ordinated this complex undertaking.

The *Death and Dying* course is very successful, with annual figures at over 1,000 students. This second edition of the reader accompanies the remake of that course and reflects the changes in this field that occurred in the last decade of the century. I have had the privilege to chair the remake of the course and edit the new edition of this reader. Thanks are due to Alyson Peberdy and Dr Moyra Sidell who have continued their academic involvement in the course, and to Carol Komaromy who joined the course team. Particular thanks are also due to Dr Louise de Raeve, Dr Stephen Wilkinson and Eve Garrard who, as consultants to the course component which relates to Part 3 of this Reader, thoughtfully selected most of the new contributions for this part. Without the remarkable efficiency of Claire Edwards the course manager and our secretary Val O'Connor, who have had the unenviable task of piecing together newly selected and commissioned articles as well as making sense of those articles that have been updated from the first edition, the task would have been almost impossible. Giles Clark of The Open University Co-publication unit and Karen Phillips of Sage have continued to provide valued support throughout the production of both these editions and I express my gratitude to them both.

I should like to acknowledge academic colleagues from other institutions, practitioners in the field and those who wrote first-person accounts for generously agreeing to write specially commissioned articles for both editions of this book, and particularly to those who agreed to update what they wrote eight years ago. Their commitment to the field and willingness to share their experiences has ensured that this book remains one of the most comprehensive collections of articles on this subject.

Jeanne Samson Katz

PART 1

LIFE AND DEATH

Introduction

Addressing the eternal questions of life and death presents a daunting prospect. World literature, philosophy, religion and history provide us with an endless source of material which is necessarily inconclusive. Fortunately our task is not to present our readers with a digest of this vast body of work. It is more focused and instrumental. So this first part offers a selection of contributions which contextualize the *contemporary* experience of dying and death. It provides powerful sketches of the awesome struggle human-kind has with the reality of mortality, whilst concentrating on the ways in which the past and the present influence the attitudes, rituals and practices which operate in modern societies at the end of life.

David Clark's beautifully observed anthropological account of death in Staithes at the turn of the century provides an evocation to add to the current debate about 'the world we have lost'. Its precise descriptions of the complex religious, metaphysical and folk beliefs about death and the associated rituals, public and private, are not confined to a seaside town in the staunchly traditional north-east of England. It offers a universal picture of the interweaving of fear, hope, respect, celebration, mourning, cere monial and petty concerns which have surrounded death everywhere and in every age. As an opening piece it stimulates many of the questions and debates which follow in the rest of the book.

From the local and the particular we move to the great canvas of history addressed by Phillipe Ariès in his monumental survey of death. Here we can only offer a taster of a huge scholarly work which has excited much con-troversy and debate since it was first published in French in 1977. In a characteristically Gallic review Ariès does not hesitate to interpret history or to make judgements. The passage reproduced here propounds the view that modern societies are death-denying societies which are unwilling to face the inescapable facts of death. He argues that this attitude explains the professionalizing of death and its sanitization by the funeral industry.

Tony Walter, Jane Littlewood and Michael Pickering's article picks up several themes from Ariès. In subjecting the question of public invigilation of private emotion to critical scrutiny, they note the powerful position of journalists in constructing the images of bereaved people. One significant change not alluded to in the first articles of this book is the increasing ethnic and religious diversity to be found in the United Kingdom. Shirley Firth addresses an important dimension of this newly acknowledged mix, as she examines the religious, cultural and family patterns of Sikh and Hindu communities in Britain. Attention is drawn to the distinctive attitudes to health, illness and dying which require reactions from health professionals quite different from those predominant in the host culture. The need of Hindus to die lying on the floor, in the midst of their family, to the accompaniment of ritual chanting is juxtaposed with the clinical atmosphere of typical hospital wards.

The next group of chapters are of a much more practical nature, exploring the demographic reasons for the dramatic changes in the contemporary experience of death and ways in which society provides services for dying people. Clive Seale, in a specially written article, demonstrates how the dramatic rise of life expectancy and the shift from infectious diseases to degenerative diseases during the twentieth century changed experiences of dying. Drawing on official statistics as well as national surveys he demonstrates contrasts in gender in both the experiences of old age and dying. Also in a specially written and updated article Christina Victor provides further demographic data, taking a macro view of mortality rates and the causes of death, placing them in the broad context of social policy and provision. She identifies a range of challenges to health and social care systems, if they are to provide an adequate response to the needs of dying people.

Taking the particular case of sudden death by suicide, Stella Ridley continues the practical approach by mapping the incidence of self-inflicted death and the limited services which relate to it. But she also raises more philosophical questions about the meaning and the taking of life which are treated more fully in Part 3. In a similar vein, Mary Bradbury's questioning of what constitutes a good or a bad death combines anthropological and theological considerations with observations about the medical management of terminal illness. These two updated specially commissioned pieces act as valuable links between the global subjects at the start of this part and much of the rest of the book.

The selection of poetry and prose in this part reflects the ideas, concerns, practices and beliefs uncovered by the preceding articles. The extracts from the mid-Victorian *Child's Own Magazine* portray a middle-class Christian version of death designed to comfort children and likely to incur the wrath of Ariès. John Donne, Philip Larkin and Dylan Thomas, however, have no illusions about death, although they respond to it in characteristically different ways: Donne with a comforting romanticism, Larkin with clinical realism and Thomas with exuberant defiance – such a contrast with Kahlil Gibran's calm spirituality.

Jane Martin's brief but arresting personal story of the experience of someone else's death reminds us of the emotional strength that professional carers need if they are to work well in the midst of dying and grief. At the close of this part we explore the meanings of life and death. Alyson Peberdy's specially rewritten article considers what we mean by spirituality and the need for spiritual care of dying people. She examines some of the philosophical questions that people ask themselves and also ways in which carers can 'accompany the person going through the journey of dying'. This resonates with the earlier statements by Martin which reflect the same, universal concerns which captured the imagination of the great Russian writer Leo Tolstoy, whom we present twice in this volume. The mixture of philosophical reflection and literary anguish he displays in this first piece is a marked contrast in style and analysis.

1

Death in Staithes

David Clark

Death in Staithes in the early twentieth century

With the exception of accidental fatalities, death in Staithes in the early part of the century almost invariably took place in the home, where the sick and the dying were the immediate responsibility of the family, to whom also befell the task of laying the dead to rest in an adequate and befitting manner. In the midst of their bereavement, therefore, the kinsfolk were kept busy by funeral preparations and various related tasks. The first duty was that of laying-out the body, known in Staithes as 'the lying-out'. As one old man put it, 'When a person passed away the first thing they did was go for the board – the lying-out board'. This board, upon which the corpse was stretched out was kept in the workshop of the village joiner, who also performed the duties of undertaker. 'Lying-out', however, was the charge of a handful of women who were recognized in the village as qualified to carry out the work and who, from their painstaking attention to detail, appear to have taken considerable pride in their task.

The process began with the washing of the body and the tying-up of the jaw; the corpse was then wrapped in a white sheet and laid on the board in the centre of a double bed. White woollen stockings were used to cover the feet, a pillow was placed on each side of the head and another sheet, meticulously folded in a series of horizontal pleats which ran down its entire length, was laid over the body. Finally, a large white handkerchief covered the face. The linen used in the laying-out was of the finest quality and that edged with Maltese lace was particularly popular. In common with the practice in many other areas and classes of society, the material was usually purchased well in advance. [. . .]

Thus laid out, the corpse became the object of formalized visits on the part of kin and friends, who upon calling at the house would be invited to go upstairs to see the dead person for the last time. 'Would you like to have a look at him?', was the usual question asked of visitors, who would then be escorted upstairs. The person watching over the corpse would then lift the face cloth for a few moments to allow a final view of the deceased, at which point the visitor was expected to touch the body as an expression of sympathy or, as one man put it, 'to show that they always held out goodwill

Extract from *Between Pulpit and Pew*, Cambridge: Cambridge University Press, 1982, pp. 128–38 (abridged).

while the person was alive'. Following a few moments of silence the visitor would return below to the other members of the family.

After the initial separation of the dead person, the stage leading up to the burial had all the aspects of liminality associated with the middle phase of the rite of passage; we see therefore the suspension, not only of normal conventions and patterns of behaviour, but also, one feels, of time itself. The progression of day and night became meaningless as clocks were stopped and members of the family sat up throughout the night, dozing in chairs and taking it in turns to go to sit by the body. Mirrors and pictures were carefully covered over with white napkins and curtains remained drawn.

Meanwhile, funeral preparations continued to occupy various individuals – the joiner, in the construction of the coffin, and the women, in the baking of the special funerary foods. One woman, known as the 'bidder', was specially employed at this time to announce the day and time of the funeral throughout the village. Her task took her to every house in Staithes, at each of which she would knock at the door and 'bid', or invite, the household to attend. Sunday was the preferred day for funerals, despite the charging of double burial fees. Since sabbatarian observance prohibited working on the Sabbath, all who wished to attend were free to do so. [. . .] Coffin bearers were usually recruited from close kin; as one old lady put it, the rule was that 'you always went as near as you could'. The bearers were always of the same sex as the deceased. The servers at the funeral tea, known locally as 'waitresses', were usually neighbours.

On the day of the funeral itself, and at the appointed hour, a group of villagers would congregate outside the house of the deceased. Inside, when all members of the immediate family were present they would gather around the open coffin (or 'box' as Staithes people habitually refer to it), whereupon the minister or priest placed one hand upon it, and delivered a short extempore prayer of thanks for the life of the dead person and the comfort of the mourners. [. . .] At the conclusion of the prayer the coffin lid was fixed in position and at this point special sweet 'funeral biscuits', along with glasses of port, or occasionally spirits, were taken to the people outside. Clay pipes and tobacco were passed around among the men on a special black patterned funeral plate which each family kept for such occasions. The bearers also received food and drink for, as one man put it, 'they used to like a glass before the lifting'. [. . .] As members of the family left the house, care was taken to leave the door open in the belief that this facilitated the departure of the dead person's soul. Then, with the coffin resting on the chairs, all present would sing the first verse of a funeral hymn. Still singing, the bearers took the coffin and began moving away in the direction of the chapel. [. . .]

Behind the bearers in the funeral procession came the women who would later serve at the tea. Six or eight in number, they wore black hats with white crocheted shawls and black silk sashes. With characteristic meticulousness, the women walked in pairs, one wearing her sash diagonally from the left shoulder and the other wearing hers from the right in order to form an inverted V pattern. The minister followed, then came a separate group made up of the bereaved family and finally the rest of the company. [. . .] After the service had taken place in the chapel it was necessary to carry the coffin some one-and-a-half miles to the graveyard of the parish church at Hinderwell. Even today Staithes has no cemetery of its own. In the days before motor transport this meant a steep climb out of the village followed by a tiring walk along the cliffs. [. . .]

At the foot of the hill, and before returning to prepare the funeral tea, the serving women stepped to one side and watched as the others left the village. The processions were evidently a spectacular sight. Male coffin bearers wore small white bows or rosettes in their lapels – three men with them on the right side and three on the left side. The bows had to be worn on the side nearest to the coffin. Women bearers wore black skirts, white shawls and white hats. Behind the bearers came the men, wearing seal-skin caps or bowler hats, dark blue jerseys and serge trousers. Then came the women, all in black. [. . .]

At the committal it was the duty of the grave-digger to throw soil down onto the coffin during the final obsequies and when the prayers were completed a hymn would be sung at the graveside; 'Gather at the River' was a popular choice. The company then set off back to the village where they were met at the top of the bank by the serving women who divided them into small groups for the funeral tea. [. . .] Large attendances at funerals, coupled with the smallness of the fishermen's cottages, made a collective meal impossible and gave rise to the practice of holding the meal in several different households. Very often a neighbour having a slightly larger house would offer assistance by putting it at the disposal of the waitresses. In later years the problem was overcome by holding the funeral tea in the relevant chapel Sunday Schoolroom. Smoked ham, fruit cake (known as 'funeral bread') and Madeira cake were the traditional foods for the tea, which was manifestly an expensive affair. During one funeral I attended, I was told by a man in his early seventies that in the past, 'the poorer class o' person often had to spend his last penny paying for everything', whilst in an interview another man remarked, 'nearly everyone had a small insurance out to cover the cost of the fees and the funeral tea'. There were also funeral clubs into which weekly subscriptions were paid. [. . .]

The funeral tea may be seen as the first in a series of rites of incorporation, bringing the group together in a final acknowledgement of the death, whilst at the same time preparing the bereaved for their return from the fraught liminal phase and their subsequent re-entry into the regulated pattern of group life. Consequently, when the family returned to their home after the funeral, the white napkins would be removed from the mirrors and pictures and the curtains partially opened. While it was true that the bereaved family had to follow a host of mourning rules and injunctions for many weeks, there was a steady divestment and relaxation of sanctions, which progressively admitted the re-entry of the mourner into a normal role in the community. The emphasis throughout this re-admission, however, was on a *gradual* progression. [. . .] For women in particular, mourning represented a protracted period wherein onerous restrictions on movement and dress were only gradually removed during subsequent months. For example, women frequently ceased to attend chapel for as much as a whole year; indeed, one old lady told me that 'some never went for five or six years – they used to think it wasn't reverent'. Not only attendance at chapel, but any appearance outdoors in the early weeks and months after the death was considered improper and gave rise to unfavourable comment. [. . .]

More permanent reminders of the death were kept in the house for years to come. Throughout the Victorian period and on into the early twentieth century it was common to have special mourning cards printed to commemorate the death of a member of the family. The cards were solemnly funereal in design and style and contained various biographical details of the dead person.[1] [. . .] Large cards such as this (some seven inches by nine) were framed and hung on the walls, whilst smaller ones were often tucked behind picture frames or mirrors. Grim reminders they must have been to a community where death was such a frequent and untimely visitor.

Death in Staithes today

Whilst listening to old people talking of the beliefs and ritual surrounding death in the early part of the century I was continually impressed by their detailed and highly specific accounts. These displayed a remarkable internal consistency and few differences appear to have existed between funerals taking place at the different religious institutions in the village. Even funerals at the parish church differed from those in the chapels only in so far as the company had to walk to the church at Hinderwell beforehand. When we turn to the subject of death in the contemporary situation, however, a number of important changes are immediately apparent and various traditional practices appear to have been abandoned or modified. I could find no evidence, for example, for the continuance of the custom of covering up mirrors and pictures in the death house. Similarly, bearers are no longer of the same sex as the dead person; in fact, to have bearers at all is now rather exceptional, since the duty frequently falls to the undertaker's staff. Curtains are still drawn in the house of the dead, but now only on the day that death occurs and then again immediately before the funeral. The practice of printing special death cards ended in the 1940s. Perhaps the most significant innovation is the emergence of a number of specialist organizations which increasingly concern themselves with the processes of death and dying. It is a transformation which has stripped the family of one of its traditional functions, so that some of the familial and communal rituals previously associated with the death of a villager have disappeared beneath a general trend towards standardization. [. . .]

The professionalization of death

In Staithes today, and in contrast to the situation in the early part of the century, the immediacy of death as a communal event has been considerably attenuated. For most villagers contact with death takes place at a distance or through intermediaries, in the form of bureaucratically organized agencies which perform the duties and tasks once held to be the responsibility of the family or community. We may call this process the professionalization of death since it perpetrates the notion that competence to deal with the practical matters associated with death is vested solely in specially trained professionals, who in conducting their work seek to emphasize the ascendancy of their skills in this matter over any related ones held by the family. Professionalization has thereby resulted in a vastly different set of responses to the problem of death.

First of all, it is important we recognize that the home is no longer the only setting in which death is likely to take place. Other alternatives exist, such as hospitals, residential homes and geriatric units, which in assuming responsibility for care of the dying have taken death not only out of the home, but also out of the village. At the same time the duties of the undertaker, transferred from village joiner to local Co-operative Society and then aggrandized in the role of 'funeral director', have been made to include many of the responsibilities formerly borne by relatives and neighbours. Thus, when death occurs in one of these institutions it is common for the body to be removed to the funeral director's memorial house rather than to the individual's home, and for the preparation of the corpse and laying-out to be done by the funeral director rather than by the traditional female specialists in the village. [. . .] Formal announcement of the death and notification of the date and time of the funeral have ceased to be jobs for the 'bidder' and whilst news of the death still travels quickly, it is usual for the funeral director to arrange for publication of details in the death and obituary column of the local evening newspaper. [. . .] Similarly, making the coffin, once a task for the local joiner, is now arranged by the funeral director, who in addition to ordering flowers and wreaths also makes provision for the preparation of the funeral tea by outside caterers. One woman summed the changes up thus, 'Now the Co-op has it all – tea, flowers, box – he'll put it in t' paper and everything'. Even the laying-out board itself has become the property of the North Eastern Co-operative Society, and hangs on a gate next to the village store.

Burial and cremation

Perhaps the greatest innovation coming from those professional agencies who now concern themselves with death has been the introduction of cremation as an alternative form of disposal of the dead. Its implications for any analysis of death in the village are considerable. During the period of fieldwork in Staithes there were thirty-five funerals. Three of these took place entirely at the crematorium and two were at the Roman Catholic Church. Of the remaining thirty, twenty-two were held in one or other of the three chapels and eight took place in the parish church. Six out of ten funerals were burials, whilst the remainder were cremations. These figures almost reverse those for the country as a whole, which show that in 1974 approximately 60 per cent of all deaths in Britain were followed by cremation.[2] What interpretation can we give to this local phenomenon? Two possibilities exist. The first is that, in common with the situation in many other areas, a considerable distance must be travelled to the nearest crematorium, thereby creating undue expense and making the funeral itself a lengthy and tiring affair. Practical considerations may therefore militate against the choice of cremation among villagers. Alternatively we might consider whether or not there are to be found in the village any indication of values and attitudes *vis-à-vis* cremation which might prevent it from being regarded as an acceptable means of disposal of the dead. [. . .]

In fact a far more satisfactory explanation can be found. As should become increasingly apparent, the people of Staithes have never allowed considerations of time or cost to interfere with what they consider to be the right and proper way of bidding farewell to the dead. Popular though the notion of the parsimonious Yorkshireman may be, it is not confirmed here; indeed cremation, which requires no grave-plot or headstone, is cheaper than interment. The high figures for burial are rather, we suggest, the product of a particular aversion to cremation, combined with a deep-seated preference for the traditional ritual.

Notes

1. Similar cards were used by Roman Catholics, especially on the Continent.
2. From *Resurgam* – the Journal of the Federation of British Cremation Authorities, 1975: 19–22.

Death denied

Philippe Ariès

In the early twentieth century, before World War I, throughout the Western world of Latin culture, be it Catholic or Protestant, the death of a man still solemnly altered the space and time of a social group that could be extended to include the entire community. The shutters were closed in the bedroom of the dying man, candles were lit, holy water was sprinkled; the house filled with grave and whispering neighbours, relatives and friends. At the church, the passing bell tolled and the little procession left carrying the *Corpus Christi*.

After death, a notice of bereavement was posted on the door (in lieu of the old abandoned custom of exhibiting the body or the coffin by the door of the house). All the doors and windows of the house were closed except the front door, which was left ajar to admit everyone who was obliged by friendship or good manners to make a final visit. The service at the church brought the whole community together, including latecomers who waited for the end of the funeral to come forward; and after the long line of people had expressed their sympathy to the family, a slow procession, saluted by passersby, accompanied the coffin to the cemetery. And that was not all. The period of mourning was filled with visits: visits of the family to the cemetery and visits of relatives and friends to the family.

Then, little by little, life returned to normal, and there remained only the periodic visits to the cemetery. The social group had been stricken by death, and it had reacted collectively, starting with the immediate family and extending to a wider circle of relatives and acquaintances. Not only did everyone die in public like Louis XIV, but the death of each person was a public event that moved, literally and figuratively, society as a whole. It was not only an individual who was disappearing, but society itself that had been wounded and that had to be healed.

All the changes that have modified attitudes toward death in the past thousand years have not altered this fundamental image, this permanent relationship between death and society. Death has always been a social and public fact. It remains so today in vast areas of the Latin West, and it is by

From *The Hour of Our Death*, London: Allen Lane, 1981, London: Peregrine Books, 1983, pp. 559–63. This brief extract from Ariès's large and important volume contains one of his principal theses, but all too little of the elaborate argument contained in the book. It is included here as a sampler of an impressive if controversial contribution to the historical and cultural analysis of death.

no means clear that this traditional model is destined to disappear. But it no longer has the quality of absolute generality that it once had, no matter what the religion and the culture. In the course of the twentieth century an absolutely new type of dying has made an appearance in some of the most industrialized, urbanized and technologically advanced areas of the Western world – and this is probably only the first stage.

Two characteristics are obvious to the most casual observer. First is its novelty, of course, its contrariness to everything that preceded it, of which it is the reverse image, the negative. Except for the death of statesmen, society has banished death. In the towns, there is no way of knowing that something has happened: the old black and silver hearse has become an ordinary grey limousine, indistinguishable from the flow of traffic. Society no longer observes a pause; the disappearance of an individual no longer affects its continuity. Everything in town goes on as if nobody died anymore.

The second characteristic is no less surprising. Of course, death has changed in a thousand years, but how slowly! The changes were so gradual and so infinitesimal, spread out over generations, that they were imperceptible to contemporaries. Today, a complete reversal of customs seems to have occurred in one generation. In my youth, women in mourning were invisible under their crepe and voluminous black veils. Middle-class children whose grandmothers had died were dressed in violet. After 1945, my mother wore mourning for a son killed in the war for the twenty-odd years that remained to her.

The very rapidity and suddenness of the change have made us take stock of it. Phenomena that had been forgotten have suddenly become known and discussed, the subjects of sociological investigations, television programmes, medical and legal debates. Shown the door by society, death is coming back in through the window, and it is returning just as quickly as it disappeared.

The change is rapid and sudden, there is no doubt of that; but is it really as recent as it appears to the journalist, the sociologist, and to ourselves, dazed as we are by the acceleration of pace?

The beginning of the lie

After the second half of the nineteenth century, an essential change occurred in the relationship between the dying man and his entourage.

Obviously, the discovery that one's end was near has always been an unpleasant moment. But people learned to overcome it. The Church saw to it that the doctor carried out the role of herald of death. The role was not a coveted one, and it required the zeal of the 'spiritual friend' to succeed where the 'earthly friend' hesitated. When the warning did not happen spontaneously, it was part of the customary ritual. But in the later nineteenth century it became more and more problematical, as we see from a story in Tolstoy's 'Three Deaths', which appeared in 1859.

The wife of a rich businessman had contracted tuberculosis, as happened so often at that time. The doctors have pronounced her condition hopeless. The moment has come when she has to be told. There is no question of avoiding it, if only to allow her to make her 'final arrangements'. But here is a new element: the distaste of the entourage for this duty has increased. The husband refuses 'to tell her about her condition', because, he says, 'It would kill her. . . . No matter what happens, it is not I who will tell her.' The mother of the dying woman is also reluctant. As for the dying woman, she talks about nothing but new treatments; she seems to be clinging to life, and everyone is afraid of her reaction. However, something has to be done. Finally the family enlists an old cousin, a poor relation, a mercenary person who throws herself into the task. 'Sitting beside the sick woman, she attempted by a skilfully manoeuvred conversation to prepare her for the idea of death.' But the sick woman suddenly interrupts her, saying, 'Ah, my dear! . . . Don't try to prepare me. Don't treat me like a child. I know everything. I know that I haven't much longer to live.' Now they can begin the classic scenario of the good death in public, which has been momentarily disturbed by the new reluctance regarding the warning.

Behind this reluctance, even when it grates under the satirical pen of Tolstoy, there is the love of the other, the fear of hurting him and depriving him of hope, the temptation to protect him by leaving him in ignorance of his imminent end. No one questions the idea that he ought to know, yet no one wants to do the dirty work himself; let someone else take care of it. In France the priest was all ready, for the warning had become part of his spiritual preparation at the last hour. Indeed, the priest's arrival will be interpreted as the sign of the end, without it being necessary to say anything else.

As for the patient, and Tolstoy describes this very well, he does not really need to be warned. He already knows. But his public acceptance would destroy an illusion that he hopes to prolong a little longer, and without which he would be treated as a dying person and obliged to behave like one. So he says nothing.

And everyone becomes an accomplice to a lie born of this moment which later grows to such proportions that death is driven into secrecy. The dying person and those around him continue to play a comedy in which 'nothing has changed', 'life goes on as usual' and 'anything is still possible'. This is the second phase in a process of domination of the dying by the family that began among the upper classes in the late eighteenth century, when the dying man chose not to impose his last wishes in a legal document but entrusted them directly to his heirs.

A new relationship had been established that brought the dying man and his entourage closer on an emotional level; but the initiative, if not the power, still belonged to the dying. Here the relationship persists, but it has been reversed, and the dying man has become dependent upon the entourage. It is useless for Tolstoy's heroine to protest that she is being treated like a child, for it is she who has placed herself in that position. The day will come when the dying will accept this subordinate position, whether he simply submits to it or actually desires it. When this happens – and this is the situation today – it will be assumed that it is the duty of the entourage to keep the dying man in ignorance of his condition. How many times have we heard it said of a husband, child or relative, 'At least I have the satisfaction of knowing that he never felt a thing.' 'Never felt a thing' has replaced 'feeling his death to be imminent'.

Dissimulation has become the rule. These feats of imagination inspired Mark Twain to write a story about the tissue of lies maintained by two nice old maids in order to conceal from each of the two invalids they are taking care of, a mother and her 16-year-old child, the fact that the other is dying.

This dissimulation has the practical effect of removing or delaying all the signs that warned the sick person, especially the staging of the public act that once was death, beginning with the presence of the priest. Even in the most religious and churchgoing families, it became customary in the early twentieth century not to call the priest until his appearance at the bedside of the patient could no longer come as a surprise, either because the patient had lost consciousness or because he was unmistakably dead. Extreme Unction was no longer the sacrament of the dying but the sacrament of the dead. This situation already existed in France by the 1920s and 1930s, and became even more widespread in the 1950s.

Gone are the days of the solemn procession of the *Corpus Christi*, preceded by the choirboy ringing his bell. Gone, long gone, the days when this procession was welcomed sadly by the dying man and his entourage. It is clear that the clergy finally had had enough of administering to cadavers, that they finally refused to lend themselves to this farce, even if it was inspired by love. Their rebellion partly explains why, after Vatican II, the Church changed the traditional name of Extreme Unction to the 'anointing of the sick', and not always the terminally sick. Today it is sometimes distributed in church to old people who are not sick at all. The sacrament has been detached from death, for which it is no longer the immediate preparation. In this the Church is not merely recalling the obligation to be fully conscious when one receives the unction. It is implicitly admitting its own absence at the moment of death, the lack of necessity for 'calling the priest'; but we shall see that death has ceased to be a moment.

In the nineteenth century the disappearance of pious clauses from the will had increased the importance of the final dialogue: the last farewells, the last words of counsel, whether in private or in public. This intimate and solemn exchange has been abolished by the obligation to keep the dying man in ignorance. Eventually he left without saying anything. This was almost always the way the very old, even the conscious and the pious, died during the 1950s and 1960s in France, before the influx of new modes of behaviour from America and northwestern Europe. 'She didn't even say good-by to us,' murmured a son at the bedside of his mother. He was not yet accustomed to this stubborn silence, or perhaps to this new modesty.

3

Death in the news
the public invigilation of private emotion

Tony Walter, Jane Littlewood and Michael Pickering

The 'public abuse – private presence' thesis

The conventional sociological wisdom that has emerged in the past decade is that, in Mellor's 1993 phrase, death is publicly absent but privately present. Variations on this theme have been proposed, each identifying the structural location of people who are dying or who have been bereaved within contemporary Western society.

The most influential writer on this theme has been the historian Philippe Ariès. He originally claimed that death is 'forbidden' in modern society because of the high value placed by twentieth century Western culture on happiness and on romantic love, both of which are profoundly undermined by the death of someone you love, (1974: chapter 4). At the same time Ariès noted that in the USA social scientists and 'grief therapists' were encouraging the public to speak of death and were encouraging people who had been bereaved, and people who were dying, to speak about their feelings.

Only a few years later, however, Ariès (1981 [1977]) was speaking of death more as 'invisible' or 'hidden' – hidden in particular from public view. People know they are dying or that their loved one has died; the sin is to let this awareness penetrate the public realm or even in some cases to mention it to their intimates. People who are dying are relegated to a side ward so as not to disturb the other patients and so as to maintain the idea that hospitals cure. In the third book, on images of death, Ariès claims that the twentieth century is the first in Western civilisation to have abandoned a public visual icononography of death: 'Relegated to the secret private space of the home or the anonymity of the hospital, *death no longer makes any sign.*' (1985: 266, his emphasis).

The idea of death being hidden was taken up by Norbert Elias (1985 [1982]), who noted how we rarely observe death and dying. Moreover, death threatens the modern individualist more than members of more collectively oriented societies. Elias criticises Ariès for romanticising the past, but agrees that death and dying were once spoken of more frequently and people who were dying were not isolated. The result is that: 'everything goes on as if nobody died anymore' (Ariès 1981: 560).

From *Sociology*, November 1995, 29(4): 579–96 (abridged).

Giddens has touched upon this subject only briefly (1991: 161–2, 203–4), but continues the theme that death is hidden in modern society, though he prefers the word 'sequestered'. Phenomena such as madness, criminality, sexuality, nature, sickness and death, all of which threaten the rationality and social management of modernity, are institutionally repressed – not psychologically repressed, but removed from the major arenas of modern life. Hence the prison, the mental hospital, the wilderness nature reserve, the old people's home and the hospice are relegated to the shadows and recesses of the public domain.

Expanding on Giddens' theory of self-identity in high modernity is the work of Mellor (1993) and Mellor and Shilling (1993), who argue that death is increasingly being privatised, not least because of the demise of a generally accepted religious language in which the symbolic meanings of death can be articulated. The research in which one of us has been engaged (Walter 1994: 98–103) indicates that, even when the hospital chaplain is called to the bedside, s/he is concerned to elicit the patient's personal meaning system as a resource for coping with death rather than to proclaim or affirm a traditional religious 'sacred canopy' under which the dying may shelter (Berger 1967). No longer able to find comfort in authoritative dogma, the patient is alone with his or her own values, which may or may not be up to the task of preparing the person for their own demise.

Against this dominant sociological view that death has been dismissed to the private sphere is the argument that death is very much present in the public sphere. Parsons and Lidz argue that 'American society has institutionalized a broadly stable, though flexible and changing, orientation to death that is fundamentally not a "denial" but a mode of acceptance appropriate to our primary cultural patterns of activism' (1967: 134). We eat a healthy diet, go to exercise classes, take out medical and life insurance, and take active steps to try to ensure that we live fully until we die as peacefully as possible in old age. Much of public life, from the actuarial basis of pension funds to health care planning, to the local aerobics class, is premised not only on an acceptance of human mortality but also on scientific assessments of the mortality risk of specific populations. This is public life based on a realistic assessment of when death is likely to come.

Prior's work (e.g. see 1989; Prior and Bloor 1992) on the rationalisation and bureaucratisation of death leads to a similar conclusion. Since the invention of the mathematics of probability in the late seventeenth century, and medicine's subsequent ousting of the church as comforter at the deathbed and as guardian of the dead (with public health rather than religious considerations coming to determine the disposal of the Victorian dead), death has increasingly become the domain of public officials. Family members who used to care for the dying now hand them over to the public hospital; and families and neighbours who used to care for the dead now hand them over to the commercial funeral director and to the municipal crematorium. These data suggest the exact opposite of Mellor's thesis: with most of us getting through many years without either ourselves being seriously ill or someone we love dying, death is generally absent from private personal experience yet is very much institutionalised in public institutions. Death is publicly present, but privately absent.

In this article, we suggest that this alternative thesis offers an important corrective, but misses the obvious challenge to the 'public absence of death' thesis. Just because municipal officials and commercial funeral directors are concerned with disposal of the dead does not mean that death is made public: to the contrary, funeral parlours (or at least the 'working' parts of them) and crematoria are tucked out of the way. Nor does the preoccupation of pension fund and health policy actuaries with accurate statistical prediction of mortality mean that death has gone public: it simply means that the actuarial profession focuses on mortality, while the rest of us sign up for a pension plan or life insurance and promptly forget about it as the bank takes care of the monthly standing order. Certainly there are actuarial and medical discourses about death, but these are not exactly public; in fact, these discourses are usually highly arcane. But there is one arena that is very public and in which death makes a more-than-daily appearance: the mass media. In this article, we argue that this is what really challenges the 'public absence of death' thesis.

Death in the media

Death regularly appears in various informational and entertainment media, and in specific media genres and narratives. For example, in a number of film genres ranging from Westerns and thrillers to the recent fashion for ghost movies such as *Truly, Madly, Deeply*, as well as in movies such as *Flatliners* which make near-death experience the narrative focus, death in some form or other is a familiar presence and a common fictive device. In television drama series such as *Casualty*, death or its imminent possibility are central to its pathos, attributions of blame, moments of suspense and so on, while in television programmes that reconstruct either criminal acts (as, for example, in *Crimewatch*) or life-threatening accidents (as in *999*), death is a key element of the entertainment.[1] Other examples could be cited, but in order to avoid facile generalisations it is important to look at particular areas of media output, and with this in mind we wish to focus on daily news reporting in British national media. We do so because of the salience of both print and broadcast news in our contemporary media environment, and because of the rhetoric of factuality through which news stories gather much of their force and authority.

The week in which we first talked about writing this article was not untypical: it contained the school minibus crash on the M40 in which a teacher and eleven children were immolated, and the trial of the two boys who murdered the infant James Bulger. The first story dominated the front pages and several of the inside pages of both tabloids and broadsheets on

19 November 1993; the second did likewise on the 25th. Meanwhile, the carnage in Northern Ireland and the former Yugoslavia continued to receive prominent coverage. Most days, it seems, it is impossible to read the papers on the train to work, or to eat tea with the children after school without death being present. And this is what one might call 'normal times'. Yorkshire in the period of the Ripper, or the USA during the Vietnam War, or several countries during the Gulf War experienced not so much a series of one-off 'accidents' but a daily realisation that one's daughter or wife or the soldier son of the man next door were at risk of their life. A smaller proportion of the population of contemporary Western societies dies in any one day than in any society at any time in the history of humankind, yet through the news media death is now extremely visible.

Still, only a tiny minority of deaths hits the news. These appear to be of two kinds. First, there are the deaths of public figures – the underlying journalistic principle here being that those who live in public cannot expect to die in private. Obituaries, photographs and personal stories are filed and continually updated by the press, radio and TV as soon as a 'personality' or 'star' is made, as soon as a national leader is elected, and even as soon as a relatively central member of the royal family is born. Just occasionally such deaths occur when the people concerned are on a duty so public that it is actually being televised, the classic and perhaps most memorable cases being the assassination of John F. Kennedy and the blowing up, soon after take-off, of the Challenger space shuttle. The Kennedy assassination revealed for the first time the awesome immediacy of television over all other forms of news media (Jameson 1991: 355), and this medium has the potential on such occasions to bring the reality of violent death home to millions in an unprecedented way. But in more general terms, the reporting of the deaths of politicians, television personalities, rock stars, and so on, uses well-worn criteria of newsworthiness, and extrapolates already existing affective themes of celebrity discourse. It would appear that the appeal to the news consumer in these cases is relatively distinct from that involved in the second kind of death that receives prominent coverage in national media.

These are the public deaths of private individuals. An ordinary person dying of a heart attack at home is not news, but one who is murdered or dies in a fire will certainly make the local news, and those who die in a major air crash will have the cause of their death raked over in fine detail by the national media. The public salience of such reported deaths is proportionate to their extraordinary features, and these features are deemed story-worthy because their dramatic immediacy and high threshold as events, their potential for sensationalist treatment, and their extreme negativity as interruptions to the smooth flow of the daily round, accord closely with well-known news values. The commercial orientation of such news values exists in uneasy tension with the creative and investigative practices of journalism; but from one perspective at least it could be argued that newspapers need to sell their product and TV channels to maintain their ratings, that competition between papers and between channels is becoming more intense, and that violent death has always sold well, particularly when sex crime is involved, or can be salaciously dragged in. The more intense the competition, the more shocking must be the portrayal of violent deaths; and the more used we get to violence in the news, the more explicitly it must be portrayed if we are to take notice.

This is, of course, a reasonable argument, and visual images of death and grief certainly seem to have become more explicit in recent decades. However, our sociological concern is not just with the volume and explicitness of such portrayals but also with their content, meaning and function. It is surely clear that Ariès is wrong when he says that 'everything goes on as if nobody died any more' and that 'death no longer makes any sign'. But what kind of signs do the media make and how are they interpreted? One of the most significant features of representations of death in the news is their reversal of the discursive imperatives of the documentary. [. . .]

As we shall see, death has to be viewed, in terms of established news values, as way out of the ordinary for those who are closely related or involved with the dead to be given a public voice, albeit of course one mediated by the discourse of news reporting itself. The peculiar corollary of this is that people's psychological distress and emotional pain when caused by the death of a private citizen intimately known to them only becomes publicly visible, and thereby publicly authenticated, when that death is extraordinary, or when the circumstances in which it has occurred are extraordinary.

This outline of the ordinary/extraordinary, private/public inversions that routinely characterise death's signs in the news sets the stage for our discussion of the public (that is, publicised) presence of death in contemporary Western societies. In this paper, we concentrate on the reporting in national newspapers and television of the peacetime deaths of private UK citizens who were not, prior to their deaths, public figures, since these are the people and the deaths that readers and viewers are most likely to identify with – in contrast, say, to the deaths of Cambodian peasants or American service personnel. The former publicised deaths are typically the result of accident or murder, and we shall argue that their reporting typically contains, as a major theme, the public invigilation of private emotion.

Private emotion, public invigilation

In 1955, Geoffrey Gorer published a short but much-cited article entitled 'The Pornography of Death'. Gorer argued that when something as central to the human condition as sex or death becomes taboo its portrayal does not disappear but goes underground – to re-appear, in literate societies, as pornography. Such, he argues, is what has happened to death in the twentieth century: 'While natural death became more and more smothered in prudery, violent death has played an ever-growing part in the fantasies offered to mass audiences – detective stories, thrillers, Westerns, war stories, spy stories, science fiction, and eventually horror comics' (1965: 173). Gorer goes on to say that a chief characteristic of pornography is its exclusion of emotion or humanity; there is no sense that the 'Page 3 girl' or the 'dead Hun in the war comic' is, or was, a sentient person. Giddens (1991: 204) and Mellor and Shilling (1993: 422) likewise claim that current talk about death rarely deals with its subjective and existential aspects.

If one thing is clear about recent reporting of violent and accidental death it is that it is not pornography in Gorer's sense. Far from being averse to portraying the humanity of those killed and the emotions of those who grieve, reporters actually home in on emotions like flies to a glowing light. A cursory content analysis of the press reports on the M40 crash and the Bulger trial reveals that up to a half of both pictures and text concern the emotions of the chief actors. After the M40 school minibus crash, several papers carried a dramatic picture (by Dylan Martinez of Reuters) of two weeping school friends comforting each other, plus a picture and a report of the headmaster who broke down in the course of his press interview. Eamonn McCabe, picture editor of the *Guardian*, defended his decision to print the dramatic photographs of the two schoolfriends crying and hugging each other on the grounds that: 'It was surely better to run that picture than one of the mangled wreckage or of the bodies. The grief on those two faces touched hearts and people shared, albeit briefly, the tragedy of loss' (*The Guardian*, 31 December 1993).

Other papers covered their front pages with pictures of each of the twelve and thirteen year-olds who died, followed inside with idealised accounts of them and their academic and creative potentials. [. . .] Both incidents prompted a wave of press inquiry into what kind of people were involved in these two tragedies, and how those still alive might feel now. This is not emotional avoidance but emotional invigilation, not de-personalisation but an active reporting of the personal. [. . .]

Did Gorer fail to notice this? It is that for some unknown reason he chose to ignore the news? Or is it that today's intense emotional invigilation did not characterise press reports of the 1950s? This last question requires extensive, longitudinal empirical research if it is to be answered in any comprehensive manner, and in this article we are concerned primarily with the *current* phenomenon of press invigilation of emotion.

Puzzles of identification

By emotional invigilation we mean the simultaneous arousal of, and regulatory keeping watch over, the affective dispositions and responses associated with death. The dispositions and responses manifest in relation to particular events are those immediately associated with the events reported, but in representing them in definite ways it is clear that appeals are being made to news consumers such that certain dispositions are mobilised and certain responses encouraged. This does not mean, of course, that reader/viewer identifications can openly or directly be 'read off' from news texts. The range of possible identifications is obviously broad, particularly bearing in mind that the deaths reported are usually violent.

It may well be, for instance, that the prominence of this kind of death in the news engenders for some certain voyeuristic pleasures, and perhaps facilitates the response of *Schadenfreude* or some such similar macabre enjoyment of the misfortunes of others. It would, however, be a gross travesty to claim that journalism – even of the 'gutter' press – routinely and actively encourages this type of response; if this were the case, there would be little differentiation between death in news discourse and death in horror comics or sadistic pornography, and even for the latter examples we can make no easy assumption about moral or other 'effects'. If, however, there is encouragement to engage in some soft of identification with characters whose emotional intensity and social vulnerability are being displayed, news audiences are likely to experience not so much personal pleasure as vicarious pain on behalf of those suffering and/or anxiety that this could happen to them or to their children. Without this identification, news reports would imply that death does not happen to people like us; with it, they worryingly reveal our own mortality even at the tea-table. There are good reasons for thinking that identification does take place, or at least often enough for it to be untrue that for media audiences death is 'hidden'.

First, though reports of disasters outside the UK may contain horrifying explicit pictures (the more culturally removed from us are the victims, the more explicit the pictures), written text about overseas disasters rarely contains extensive personalisation or emotional invigilation. After the M40 crash, for example, the nation was treated to detailed accounts of the grief-torn state of the school (involving teachers as well as children); such detailed accounts rarely characterise overseas disasters. After the Armenian earthquake or during an African famine there might be accounts of a general state of shock, but not column after column about personal shock; there might be one representative personal story, but not story after story. [. . .]

Second, every now and then there is criticism from some members of the public that the press have been too intrusive, usually through pictures rather than text, into the private grief of survivors or the death throes of victims. Two examples (both colour front page pictures) that come to mind are the already mentioned photograph of the two weeping schoolgirls after the M40 crash (*Daily Mirror* and several other papers, 19 November 1993), and the picture of two teenage girls seemingly in their death throes as they were crushed against the fence in the Hillsborough stadium disaster (*Daily Mirror*, 17 April 1989). Another example was the anger on Merseyside at *Sun* photographers gaining access to post-Hillsborough funerals on the pretence that they were from the locally trusted *Liverpool Daily Post and Echo* (Walter 1991: 602). Such criticisms always concern victims or survivors who are British citizens, again suggesting a high measure of individual projections – 'how would I feel if that were my daughter portrayed in hysterics on the front page?', 'how would I feel if that were the horribly injured body of my husband shown on the television just hours before he died?'

One (rare) questionnaire and small group discussion study found that British viewers overwhelmingly felt that television close-ups of the dead were not acceptable; 73 per cent of these objectors gave as their reason that relatives of the victims might be watching and be upset (Docherty 1990). Regardless of its complex psychological dynamics, this implies some measure of identification between viewer and survivor, which clearly does not apply to overseas and especially 'Third World' survivors who are less likely to consume British media.

Within the UK, there are significant ethnic and regional variations in what are considered to be appropriate ways of responding to those dead, dying or mourning, especially over what counts as 'respect' for the dead and what counts as 'intruding into grief'. In England, for example, funerals tend to be private, and press and TV cameras at a funeral may be seen as intruding into the grief of the family. In the much more traditional communities of Northern Ireland, where respect for the deceased is measured by how many attend the funeral, to have the funeral televised can be interpreted as a mark of respect. Such variations are not appreciated by most viewers, who may as a result feel uneasy about such portrayals on TV – 'I wouldn't like that if that were my husband's funeral'. This lack of awareness of cultural relativity implies, if anything, not under- but over-identification with survivors, or at least a projection onto them of one's own culturally relative feelings.

The other common reason given by viewers for not wanting pictures in their living rooms of the dead and injured was that children might be watching. To quote the report, significantly titled 'A Death in the Home':

> In three out of every ten British homes the early evening news will be watched in a room in which children are present and in which, in many cases, the family will be eating the main meal of the day. This simple, almost humdrum, fact is nevertheless the foundation for the strong reactions expressed by viewers about the way in which real-life violence enters into their house. To face a horrified child who asks: 'Why is that man bleeding, Mummy?', requires considerably more courage and insight than more parents feel that they are able to muster night after night. (Docherty 1990: 91)

Not only do parents identify with those suffering on the screen, they are aware that their children identify too, and ask such questions because those suffering are ordinary human beings, like themselves, and not ants or cattle.

We may also note that Docherty's (1990) survey evidence contradicts the claim of Elias (1985: 19) that children nowadays are protected from awareness of death. The survey also contradicts Mellor and Shilling's comment on this claim:

> The difficulties of helping children reach such an awareness are made particularly intense by the fact that they are growing up in a culture which continues to repress, systematically, this awareness. Given such a situation, the consciousness of their own finiteness would tend to remain a personal, private experience with very little support and encouragement from other social sources. (1993: 421–2)

It may be true that parents do not provide such support, but which parents, in which social locations; and in any case, how can we know? This is to stray into areas of unwarranted speculation and generalisation. By contrast, what is certain is that there is support available, if not from parents and guardians, then certainly, in a massive although troublesome way, from news media which *foster, rather than repress*, an awareness of death.

The third good reason for supposing that audiences do identify with the suffering they see when fellow UK citizens are killed is that news editors are aware that their pictures can shock and give offence. Whereas some critics assume that editors deliberately choose to publish the most shocking pictures, the reality is that editors are very aware that there are many pictures too shocking to print. (This was a point made by Andy Warhol in his exhibition of American news photographs of violent death that were too shocking to publish, and also by the publication in 1993 of some pictures of the Kennedy assassination deemed at the time too gruesome.) Some tabloid editors may print a picture with as much brutal impact as they believe they can get away with, but in so doing they recognise that their readers do identify and can be upset and offended. In 1988 the Home Secretary set up the Broadcasting Standards Council to establish standards in this and similarly delicate areas, a move not unwelcome among some news editors, and a year or so later commissioned the research into viewers' responses to death and suffering on TV news (reported by Docherty 1990) on which we have drawn. Given the absence of a moral panic on this issue (contrasting with the recurrent waves of concern over the portrayal of sex and violence in TV and cinematic fiction), it seems unlikely that editors would be concerned and this kind of research commissioned if there were not some evidence that some viewers identify with the suffering they witness.

Displaying 'proper grief'

Emotional invigilation in press reports of UK deaths focuses primarily on the grief of survivors. Despite claims of bereavement counsellors that grief is a 'natural' and universal reaction, press portrayals of grief are clearly structured by social factors such as gender, age, status, and relationship to the deceased. After the M40 crash, teenage girls were shown out of control in their grief, while the male headmaster was shown hiding his grieving face with his hand: theirs was a shared abandonment to their emotions, his a solitary and stoical attempt at control. More than one newspaper reported the advice of the leader of the team of ten psychological counsellors brought into the school that day: 'I TOLD THE CHILDREN THEY'VE ALL GOT TO CRY' was a headline in the *Daily Mirror* (19 November 1993: 7). 'They are quite devastated. I tried to make the point, to the boys in particular, that it is not silly to cry. It is important to cry, to show their feelings' (*Daily Mail* 19 November 1993: 3). Here then we find not just pictures in words and text of appropriately grieving people, but outright advice on the proper way to grieve. [. . .]

We cannot assume that either the news narrative or the gloss which our reading has put on it bears anything other than an approximate resemblance to the episode of emotional suffering in the lives of the family represented; but if we do assume that this kind of close detail about such suffering is welcomed by readers, why should they be interested in the intimate anatomy of others' grief? Why should they be interested in the differences, subtle and not so subtle, between the grief of schoolgirls and of headmasters, between boys and girls, between mothers and fathers? Why should they want to read about advice from psychologists about the proper way to grieve? We suggest three hypotheses, each concerning cultural uncertainty in the UK as to how to grieve and how to respond to grieving people.

Hypothesis 1. Following Gorer (1965), bereavement experts have often suggested that with the demise of Victorian mourning rituals, British people no longer know how to behave both as a griever and toward grievers. We distrust ritual ('it's only a form, it doesn't express how I really feel') and we value informality, yet 'Anglo-Saxons' remain reserved about expressing their feelings (Elias 1985: 26–7), so neither people who have been bereaved nor their would-be comforters know what to say or how to behave. It is, therefore, not surprising if readers show intense interest in press reports of how the grief of their fellow citizens is handled; though it may sound somewhat glib, we could characterise this as the thanatological equivalent of reading an article in a woman's or teenage magazine about the sexual behaviour of the British, particularly those like 'you and me'.

Hypothesis 2. A different view observes that there *is* a culturally accepted norm for proper grief in (white, mainstream) Britain. This is that you should feel deeply about your loss, that you should give off cues to indicate how deeply you are feeling, but you should affirm the cultural value of stoicism and show consideration for others by not actually expressing your feelings in their presence. The relative who reads the lesson at the funeral and who momentarily has a catch in his or her voice but masters this and continues to read the lesson perfectly, the funeral attender who dabs at a tear but who doesn't break down, the widow who, on answering a telephone call of condolence, has the occasional halt in her voice but continues to enjoy the conversation – all these have mastered the British art of grief. But it is not an easy act. There is always the danger that you will break down uncontrollably in public (breaking down in the privacy of your own home, and not in front of the children, is, of course, fine and expected); and there is the danger that you are so stoical that others wonder if you cared for the deceased at all (Littlewood 1992). It is not that there are no shared norms about how to grieve in Britain, but that the shared norms are very difficult to enact. Detailed accounts and telling pictures of how others pull off this delicate act are therefore a useful resource for us all.

Hypothesis 3. Experts on bereavement are increasingly telling us to 'let out our grief', 'to express our feelings'. Expressivism (Martin 1981, especially chapter 2) has become nowhere more trendy than in the expression of negative feelings, especially those associated with loss. Since the expression of grief is seen in this view not as social but as natural, little if any distinction is made by its promoters between private and public situations. The counsellor who encourages bereaved clients to show emotions during the privacy of the counselling session rarely suggests that this might not be appropriate in the supermarket or at work. Press reports of the psychologist who counselled the schoolmates of the children killed on the M40 made no distinction between expressing grief in private and in public. If expressing grief is 'natural', then it must be harmful to repress the tears – whatever the situation. Public situations, however, are not natural but governed by socially constructed rules. This is recognised in all traditional societies in which, contrary to what is suggested in some 'pop' psychology, the public display of the tears of grief is not free expression by a feeling individual but a display that is strongly governed by cultural norms. [. . .]

A general lack of reference to emotional relativism cannot but leave millions of would-be expressivists rather confused. They are told to cry, and are aware that encounters with others are rule-governed and that breaking down spontaneously in supermarket or filling station will disturb others who are unlikely to know the person is bereaved, yet they are given no guidelines as to which situations are appropriate for expressing grief. They want to be more expressive about their grief, but are offered no ground rules as to when, how, in what manner, or with whom. In many ways the old norm, that you grieve alone and keep a stiff public upper lip, is much easier. For the new norm to take hold, the emphasis on tears as natural and psychologically healthy must be complemented by social guidelines on when and where is the best place to do this. Otherwise the anxiety level of people who are bereaved, not to mention everybody else, cannot but rise. The new norm may yet emerge as but a variation of the old – grieve in private (private being extended to include one-to-one encounters with a trusted friend or counsellor) but not in public. But this is not yet clear. In the meantime, would-be-expressivists read the press accounts of grief looking eagerly for clues. [. . .]

Which of these hypotheses (if any or in combination) accounts for the invigilation of the emotions of the survivors of UK tragedies would require further research. Each of them, however, suggests that the needs of editors to become ever more gripping in their accounts of tragedy if they are to sell newspapers and maintain programme ratings, engages, however problematically, with the needs of the audience to observe how others handle grief. In this complex interaction of representation and response, death in the news is nothing if not overdetermined.

Conclusion

In this article we have criticised both the thesis that death in modern society is privately present but publicly absent and the thesis that a new public discourse, that of medicine, has taken over from the old authority of religion. In reply to Berger's observation that 'legitimations of the reality of the social world in the face of death are decisive requirements in any society' (1967: 43–5), Mellor and Shilling comment that 'a major feature of contemporary society is that such public legitimations are becoming increasingly *absent*' (1993: 414). This is clearly not true of the mass media, whose treatments of disaster are surely an attempt at a sustained legitimation of our social world in the face of death.

By looking, albeit briefly, at the reporting of tragedies involving private UK citizens, we have sought to show that the media are generating a very public discourse of death, far more public and more accessible than that of medicine. This discourse not only affects the personal feelings of readers and viewers, and doubtless those of the survivors whose emotions are reported, but also has a political effect. It is through the media reporting of deaths and disasters that there is public pressure to change seating arrangements at football stadia, that politicians find ammunition to attack one-parent families, that reviews of police methods are initiated. In the USA, TV pictures of dead, dying and injured GIs helped turn public opinion against the Vietnam War. Moreover, the concerns of parents about death being portrayed in front of their children on the early evening news indicates not a death that is acknowledged within the family but banned in public discourse, but a public discourse that invades families who would either prefer to exclude awareness of death or are ambivalent and uncertain about it, and remain troubled by the stark presence of its signs in prime-time or front-page news.

The deaths boldly headlined and portrayed by the news media are extraordinary deaths. That is why they are so eminently story-worthy as news. They are also types of death which, unlike the majority of deaths, typically occur in a public place. We have suggested that the focus of these stories, once the drama of tragic mortality has been staged, is upon the emotional invigilation of the survivors. Whilst we do not presume that the emotions narratively represented accord with the suffering of particular individuals in anything other than broad terms, we do base our analysis on the assumption that this suffering is of interest to readers. Consequently, we have offered three hypotheses in an attempt to account for this interest.

Neither media researchers nor sociologists interested in death have looked at its portrayal in the media; careful content and textual analysis, comparing changes in the style and content of reporting over time – even over the post-war decades – has not been done, and little research has been conducted into the social and psychological complexities of the reception of such reporting by viewers and readers.[2] Given the centrality, we argue, of the media for any understanding of death in modern society, the new sociologists of death should speedily put cultural representations and responses on their research agenda, as should media researchers, given the importance of mortality to the human condition and the key symbolic work which media images and discourses of mortality may be said to perform. Until such research is done, theoretical assertions by Ariès, Elias, Giddens, Mellor and Shilling on the repression of death in modernity should be treated with considerable caution.

Notes

1   In movies, there may well have been a major shift to encourage identification with the dead, dying or grieving over the past four decades. Back in 1950 Wolfenstein and Leites observed that Hollywood movies did not characteristically permit audiences to develop much emotional identification with a character who will subsequently die or be killed. In such murder movies, the slain person is not deeply mourned but instead someone close to him or her and apparently unaffected by grief pursues the slayer; death serves as a convenient catalyst for other action, not as an emotional reality in itself. Twenty years later, however, movies such as *Butch Cassidy and the Sundance Kid, Midnight Cowboy*, and the Vietnam movies induced massive identification with either the about-to-be-killed and/or the bereaved. A more recent example from another visual medium is the British TV drama-documentary about a woman with ME (myalgic encephalomyelitis) in which the final death scene was apparently as harrowing for the actors as for the viewers (*Wide-Eyed and Legless*, BBC 1, 5 September 1993). [. . .]
2   For a review of sociological work on death and dying, including grief and bereavement, up to the early 1980s, see Riley 1983. This and more recent work is also covered by Walter 1993.

References

Ariès, P. (1974) *Western Attitudes Toward Death: From the Middle Ages to the Present.* Baltimore: Johns Hopkins University Press.
Ariès, P. (1981 [1977]) *The Hour of Our Death.* London: Allen Lane.
Ariès, P. (1985) *Images of Man and Death.* Cambridge: Harvard University Press.
Bauman, Z. (1992) *Mortality, Immortality and Other Life Structures.* Oxford: Polity.
Berger, P. (1967) *The Social Reality of Religion.* London: Faber.
Docherty (1990) 'A Death in the Home.' *Sight and Sound* 59: 90–3.
Elias, N. (1985 [1982]) *The Loneliness of the Dying.* Oxford: Blackwell.
Giddens, A. (1991) *Modernity and Self-Identity.* Oxford: Polity.
Gorer, G. (1955) 'The Pornography of Death', *Encounter*, October (reprinted in Gorer 1965).
Gorer, G. (1965) *Death, Grief, and Mourning in Contemporary Britain.* London: Cresset.
Jameson, F. (1991) *Postmodernism: Or, the Cultural Logic of Late Capitalism.* London: Verso.
Littlewood, J. (1992) *Aspects of Grief: Bereavement in Adult Life.* London: Routledge.
Martin, B. (1981) *A Sociology of Contemporary Cultural Change.* Oxford: Blackwell.
Mellor, P. (1993) 'Death in High Modernity', in D. Clark (ed.), *The Sociology of Death.* Oxford: Blackwell.

Mellor, P. and Shilling, C. (1993) 'Modernity, Self-Identity and the Sequestration of Death', *Sociology*, 27: 411–32.

Parsons, T. and Lidz, V. (1967) 'Death in American Society', in E. Shneidman (ed.), *Essays in Self Destruction*. New York: Science House.

Prior, L. (1989) *The Social Organisation of Death*. London: Macmillan.

Prior, L. and Bloor, M. (1992) 'Why People Die', *Science as Culture*, 3: 346–74.

Riley, J.W. (1983) 'Dying and the Meanings of Death: Sociological Inquiries', *Annual Review of Sociology*, 9: 191–216.

Walter, T. (1989) 'Deathwatch', *Third Way*, 12: 6.

Walter, T. (1991) 'The Mourning After Hillsborough', *Sociological Review*, 39: 599–625.

Walter, T. (1993) 'Sociologists Never Die: British Sociology and Death', in D. Clark (ed.), *The Sociology of Death*. Oxford: Blackwell.

Walter, T. (1994) *The Revival of Death*. London: Routledge.

Wolfenstein, M. and Leites, N. (1950) *Movies: a Psychological Study*. New York: Free Press.

4

Approaches to death in Hindu and Sikh communities in Britain

Shirley Firth

Hindus and Sikhs live in many parts of Britain and most try to maintain their own religion and culture as far as possible. However, living in a country with a different culture, belief systems and family patterns can create problems for Asians because they may not be able to follow their traditional practices at a time when they would most wish to. Those who have come from rural areas may have little experience of Western medical techniques and intensive care units. Ignorance and lack of sensitivity on the part of medical or social work personnel about the religious beliefs and cultural outlook of patients can make an already frightening situation worse, particularly in hospital, where language may be an additional barrier. There are rituals which need to be done at the moment of death, which make it essential for at least family members to be present; failing to do this can have long-term consequences.

Hindu beliefs

Hindus have emigrated from India, East Africa, the West Indies, Fiji or Malaysia, and speak Hindi, Gujarati, Panjabi and other regional languages. Different classes and castes reflect ancient social and occupational divisions and form the basis of marriage alliances. Priests, from the highest class, the Brahmins, are required for funeral and post-mortem rituals (Burghart, 1987; Sulivan, 1989).

There is an immense diversity of religious and cultural beliefs and practices. Many Hindus follow 'Sanatan Dharma', the eternal religion, code

My gratitude to all those who advised me on the current paper: Dr Tanaji Acharya, Prof. S.N. Bharadwaj, Dr Amrit Bening, Dr Desai, Ram Krishan and Eleanor Nesbitt, Dr Kanwaljit Kaur Singh, Dr Yashvir Sunak, Dr Harcharan Sanir, Darshan Singh, Piara Singh Sambhi and many members of the Hindu and Sikh communities.

Material for this article has appeared in Firth, 1988, 1989, 1991, 1997 and Berger, 1989.

or law. They may worship God in one form, such as Shiva, Krishna, or Mataji (the Mother), or in many forms, believing that underlying these is one Ultimate Reality. There are also a number of devotional sects in Britain, such as Swaminarayan, Dushtimarg, and Pushtimarg, Sathya Sai Baba and 'Hare Krishna' (The International Society for Krishna Consciousness, ISKCON).

Certain commonly held beliefs are important in understanding Hindu approaches to death. Hindus believe that we are reborn many times as part of a cosmic cycle involving all living things. During this lifetime our good and bad thoughts and actions generate good or bad *karma*, which determines what happens to us after death. A truly holy soul will be with God in heaven or, according to other beliefs, merges with Ultimate Reality. Less perfect souls are reborn as humans or as animals or even insects. Unexplained suffering and handicaps may be understood as a person's previous *karma*. It is important to prepare for death by scripture reading, meditation, prayer and fasting so that when the time comes there is no attachment to family or possessions and one is ready to go. Such a death in old age is a good death and may be anticipated to the exact day and time. It should take place on the floor, with God's name or the scriptures being chanted and holy Ganges water and *tulsi* (basil) leaf in the mouth (Firth, 1989, 1991, 1996, 1997).

Sikh beliefs

Sikh men are recognizable because of their turbans and beards, although some wear neither; women usually wear a trouser suit, *salvar kameze*. Initiated Sikhs wear the five Ks, symbols of the faith, at all times. These are uncut hair, *kesh* (spirituality); the comb, *kangha* (discipline, neatness and cleanliness); the sword, *kirpan* (readiness to defend the faith, the poor and the oppressed); the steel circle, *kara*, on the right wrist as a reminder to use the hands only for good and as a symbol of divine unity and infinity (Cole and Sambhi, 1978: 128); and shorts, *kachh* (restraint, modesty and purity). The latter are worn in Britain as an undergarment. The turban is a mark of identity. Women cover their heads in the *gurdwara*, the place of worship, and may do so in the presence of men.

Sikhism arose out of Hinduism in the sixteenth century. Although caste is rejected as a religious ideology, it is still important in marriage arrangements. As a symbol of the equality of all people there is a shared meal (*langar*) in the *gurdwara*, available to everyone. There is no hereditary or ordained priesthood, although in *gurdwaras* there is a knowledgeable man, *granthi*, who is paid to read the sacred text, the *Guru Granth Sahib*, and lead services. However, anyone may do this, including women, who have equal status (Cole and Sambhi, 1978: 64).

Sikhs also believe in *karma* and reincarnation. After death those who are rid of their self-centredness and spiritual blindness come into God's presence, but those who are not spiritually ready are reborn according to their karma. A truly spiritual person who meditates is said to know of his approaching death and prepares for a good death. Life should be lived in such a way that death does not take one unawares.

Talking about death

Although Hindus and Sikhs believe in principle that it is important to know about death in advance in order to be prepared, death in Britain is a less familiar part of life than it would be in India where life expectancy is much lower and where more deaths would occur at home in the extended family situation. In Britain there are greater expectations that doctors and modern medicine will be able to do something.

> Asians like the idea of symptom clearance. If you can stop a cough or fever the person is cured. It is difficult to say the effects are of an underlying disorder. There is a feeling that you should be able to keep people alive. Indians find it harder to accept that illness is terminal, they may feel that one says so out of malice. I have a relative of 50 with motor neurone disease who can't accept that nothing can be done medically. More and more people want to blame someone. (Sikh doctor)

According to the doctor quoted above, the death of the elderly in the Asian community in Britain occurs in a very different context to India, because there

> the elderly in villages have more of a sense of preparation for death. Here there is a feeling that one can keep the old alive, without any preparation for death. Many people feel, 'Now we are wealthy, let's bring the old folks here'. It is making a mistake because the elderly are uprooted from the familiar environment where they had a role to play and a sense of continuity. Here they are lost and lonely, and the [younger] women work, whereas there they did not. In India the older generation would keep old folks at home because they would have had the experience of supporting the dying at home, but here people expect health care professionals to do it.

Telling a person she or he has a terminal illness or telling the relatives is felt to be necessary, yet it should be done in a way which does not lead to the patient's loss of hope, particularly in the case of a premature death, where the belief that this is due to bad *karma* may make it difficult to come to terms with (Neuberger, 1987: 25). Hindu and Sikh doctors may also be in a dilemma because sometimes the patient or relative collapses emotionally on being told that an illness is terminal, yet they are also aware of the longer-term emotional and spiritual needs of the family: 'The majority of patients don't want to know – the relatives may have an inner idea, but they don't want to know. They may cry or become hysterical'. One Hindu doctor told a man, on the basis of reports from the hospital, that his father was not likely to live more than six months. Having been reassured by the hospital that the father would be alright, the son did not believe the doctor and was not prepared for or present at his father's death, which was emotionally shattering for him.

Lack of communication between Asians and medical staff may cause great frustration, especially in hospital, if they are kept in the dark about the prognosis and miss actually being present at the point of death. Sometimes it is felt that lack of sensitivity on the part of doctors and nurses borders on racism, particularly when assumptions are made about the patient's or relative's capacity to understand what is going on, because of real or perceived language difficulties. This is well illustrated in the case of a graduate Panjabi woman who had a heavy accent. She did not understand the implications of her husband's treatment and was not told, so kept demanding more help and care and came to be thought of as a nuisance. It was also assumed incorrectly that the father could not understand English, although his problems of communication were due to partial paralysis of his throat. Their 15 year-old daughter ended up as an interpreter and was expected to pass messages on to him.

Caring for the dying

In spite of the difficulties involved in informing relatives, they want to know when death is imminent so that they can make the right preparations.

> In hospitals, when someone is near death he must have his next of kin with him because there are a few religious rituals to be performed. When we know he is near death we start reciting the *Bhagavad Gita* or religious books. The only people who can perform this service for the dying patient are their own. The nurses and doctors won't do it, so obviously we must be told (death is imminent) rather than keeping this news away, and only being told after the death has happened. I know it's not easy to say, 'Look, he is going to die.' It's easier to say, 'He's alright, nothing to worry about', and then you are given a telephone call, 'Sorry we couldn't save him.' But there are rituals to be done before the person dies, and chanting the Gayatri Mantra is evergreen and gives you power, strength, satisfaction and peace. (Panjabi Brahmin)

Sikhs have similar views about being present, but for Hindus it is especially important because there is a belief that unless the rituals at the time of death are performed properly the dying person will not pass on to the next life but will remain a ghost. This spells disaster not just for the patient but also for the family subsequently. In one Gujarati family the death of an aunt was complicated by the fact that the family were not permitted to place Ganges water on the patient's lips. This is so holy it washes away the sin of the dying.

> An aunt was dying, everybody knew she was dying, the doctors told the family, and the whole family was present at the death. But when the doctors switched off the life-support machine they wouldn't let the family give Ganges water or perform any last rites to this lady, and even today after ten years it still affects the

family that they weren't able to do this. If they want to have a social occasion like a wedding in the family or something, they must do some penance first, because they say she died without water, therefore her soul is still not free, and her family is not free, and they've got to keep performing all these rites that they weren't able to during her death, until the soul is free . . . for at least seven generations. (Gujarati woman)

Even without such an extreme situation, the failure of the family to be present can have long-term consequences for the family.

Nurses should let the family be present when the soul leaves, because if the person dies without the family there, then that person will not be thinking of God but of his family who weren't there. Not only would the family be affected, but the dying person, who would have to take rebirth. The family couldn't take part in any social occasions or anything because it would always be hanging over them that they hadn't been present at the death, so no good omen will occur for them to perform auspicious rituals for a very long period. The whole extended family would be affected, uncles, aunts, distant cousins. (Gujarati woman)

The moment of death

The idea of death at home and on the floor is recognized by most Indians to be impractical in Britain, although elderly Hindus have been known to get out of bed and lie on the floor.

The belief is that you should die on the floor. Here a lot of people die in hospitals and a lot of us families are very shy to [ask for what we want]. We feel out of place, like a Muslim praying on the factory floor. (Panjabi Brahmin)

Clearly, the needs of Indian patients may conflict with the needs of the ward as a whole and the chanting or singing can be very disruptive unless a separate room is made available. A Sikh doctor, having observed disturbances by Sikh families around dying patients, made sure in the case of his own dying niece that visitors were restricted to the immediate family and then the *granthi* was called: 'He sang hymns and we asked him to leave when the machine was switched off. The nursing staff left us for a good hour'.

Ending or prolonging life

Hindus and Sikhs believe life should never be artificially ended, although the boundaries between active 'killing' or euthanasia and 'allowing to die' are acknowledged to be hard to draw at times. A Panjabi doctor said that on principle he would always treat aggressively (to prolong life):

I can't dream of a Hindu considering euthanasia; one would want to know that everything had been done, because of one's attachment, and because of guilt that one hadn't done one's duty. There would be enormous pressure from others that not enough is being done, so that doesn't allow you to do anything but treat aggressively . . . I can't imagine a Hindu signing something like a living will. That is far too intellectual.

However, switching off a life-support machine when it is clear that death is imminent or the person is brain-dead is acceptable in principle, if difficult to accept in practice.

After death

Because there are fewer taboos against women weeping or against men showing emotion than in Anglo-Saxon society, a great deal of distress may be shown on the death of a Hindu or Sikh relative and this may disturb staff and other patients. A Sikh nurse described another Asian woman who had a stillbirth in the maternity unit. The English nurses thought she was being very extreme because she was expressing her grief very loudly. A couple of her relatives and her mother-in-law were also wailing and 'making a scene' in a way which would be regarded as quite normal and the 'done thing' in a village setting at home but was regarded as abnormal here. The nurses, not surprisingly perhaps, kept telling them to 'keep your voices down' but the Sikh nurse said they needed to get it out of their system and work it out.

The family may wish to wash and dress the body in the hospital, although it will have to be done again immediately before the funeral, so many families prefer to leave this until later when they can obtain help from more experienced members of the community. Most Hindus and Sikhs will allow the nurses to help lay out the body and remove tubes, etc., but there are taboos against women touching men, apart from a husband, and vice versa, so men may prefer to deal with the body of a male member of the family. Post-mortems are disturbing, but often they will be accepted if the reasons are adequately explained and they help to explain the death. Sikhs wish to wear the five Ks at all times, even in hospital, and these should not be removed at death.

If for any reason the family are not present at the moment of death this will be particularly traumatic (see above) and they may want to know what the last words of the patient were. These give an indication of the mental state of the dying person. If positive they are treasured, giving a great deal of hope and comfort to the bereaved. They also become part of family lore and an important way of passing on religious beliefs.

Conclusion

From the point of view of the patients and their families what is wanted is sensitivity: 'Carers don't have an idea about cultural diversity – but they only need to listen for a few minutes to be sensitive' (Sikh doctor). This sensitivity needs to be manifested from the outset – over the details of nursing care, such as ensuring there is plenty of water for washing after bedpans and before prayers; allowing Sikhs to keep the five Ks on or within reach and understanding their intense feeling about these; respecting strict dietary rules and the intense modesty of Asians, particularly of women patients regarding male doctors and nurses; and finally showing openness and willingness to communicate with patients and relatives so that mutual compromises can be made and no one dies alone.

Indians, particularly those from the subcontinent, are members of a family first and individuals second: this fact needs to be recognized in helping people deal with death and bereavement. It is this which also provides mechanisms for coping with the loss in a social context, providing an ongoing support system.

Bibliography

Berger, A. (ed.) (1989) *Perspectives on Death and Dying*. Philadelphia, PA: Charles Press.

Burghart, R. (ed.) (1987) *Hinduism in Great Britain: the Perpetuation of Religion in an Alien Cultural Milieu*. London: Tavistock.

Cole, W.O. and Sambhi, P.S. (1978) *The Sikhs, their Religious Beliefs and Practices*. London: Routledge and Kegan Paul.

Firth, S. (1988) 'Hindu and Sikh approaches to death and bereavement'. Unpublished paper, Panjab Research Group, Coventry.

Firth, S. (1989) 'The good death: approaches to death, dying and bereavement among British Hindus', in A. Berger (ed.), *Perspectives on Death and Dying*. Philadelphia, PA: Charles Press.

Firth, S. (1991) 'Changing patterns of Hindu death rituals in Britain', in D. Killingley, W. Menski and S. Firth, *Hindu Ritual and Society*. Newcastle upon Tyne, S.Y. Killingley. pp. 52–84.

Firth, S. (1993) 'Cultural issues in terminal care', in David Clark (ed.), *The Future for Palliative Care: Issues of Policy and Practice*. Buckingham: Open University Press. pp. 98–110.

Firth, S. (1996) 'The Good Death: Attitudes of British Hindus', in Glennys Howarth and Peter Jupp (eds), *Contemporary Issues in the Sociology of Death, Dying and Disposal*. Basingstoke: Macmillan. pp. 96–110.

Firth, S. (1997) *Dying, Death & Bereavement in a British Hindu Community*. Peeters: Leuven.

Kalsi, S.S. (1996) 'Change and continuity in the funeral rituals of Sikhs in Great Britain', in Glennys Howarth and Peter Jupp (eds), *Contemporary Issues in the Sociology of Death, Dying and Disposal*. Buckingham: Macmillan. pp. 30–43.

Neuberger, J. (1987) *Caring for Dying People of Different Faiths*. London: Lisa Sainsbury Foundation, Auston Cornish Publishers.

Sulivan, L.E. (1989) *Healing and Restoring: Health and Medicine in the World's Religions*. New York: Macmillan.

5

Demographic change and the experience of dying

Clive Seale

In this article I review the effect of changing patterns of disease, population structure and living arrangements on the experience of dying, focusing in particular on the United Kingdom. I show that rising life expectancy and the shift from infectious disease to degenerative disease as causes of death has meant that the experience of dying merges with the more general experience of being old. I draw upon official statistics as well as national surveys which I and others have done, to describe patterns of symptoms and the prevalence of disability towards the end of life. The effect of changes in the living circumstances of elderly people is shown to be related to the sources of care on which people can draw at this time, with particularly marked contrasts between men and women being evident. Finally, I show how these demographic changes, as well as cultural factors that are typical of the kind of society that experiences such changes, are related to an increasing desire to control the timing and manner of death, through various methods of human intervention.

Life expectancy and causes of death

The expectation of life at birth varies widely between countries and in most has increased dramatically during the twentieth century. In the UK, life expectancy at birth 1995–2000 was 75 for males and 80 for females, compared with figures for this period in all African countries of 52 and 55 respectively (ONS, 1998a). A century ago (1891–1900), life expectancy in the UK was lower than these African levels, being 44 for males and 47 for females (ONS, 1998b). Previous to this rise, life expectancy in England had hovered between 30 and 40 years since the mid-1500s, which is as far back as records can be reconstructed (Wrigley and Schofield, 1989).

Underlying this trend are dramatic reductions in the infant mortality rate (IMR) which in the UK stood at six per thousand births in the period 1995–2000 (ONS, 1998a), compared to 105 per thousand in 1910 (Drever and Whitehead, 1997). Before the Second World War this figure had never dropped below 30 (ONS, 1998a), and the decline is generally understood to be the result of better nutrition and living conditions, although the role of antibiotics in reducing mortality from childhood infections has also played a part. In pre-industrial times, once childhood had been survived, mortality then began to rise as people entered adulthood, leaving relatively few survivors into what we now understand to be old age. The causes of the decline in infant mortality, however, have now also reduced the death rates in early adulthood and in the middle-aged. This then concentrates contemporary experience of death in the older years of the life course, so that in 1997 83 per cent of deaths in the UK occurred to people aged over 65, compared to a figure of 24.5 per cent in the years 1900–1902 (ONS, 1999).

Changes in medically-defined causes of death reflects a general decline in mortality from infectious diseases in the UK, to be replaced by mortality from the so-called degenerative diseases, for example cancer, heart disease and stroke. Thus, in 1997 25 per cent of deaths in England and Wales were caused by neoplasms (cancers); 22 per cent were caused by ischaemic heart disease; and 10 per cent by cerebrovascular disease. A further 17 per cent were assigned to diseases of respiratory system, of which a large proportion were caused by pneumonia, a cause of death which commonly affects very elderly people who are physically frail for a variety of other reasons. Only 0.6 per cent of deaths were assigned to infectious and parasitic diseases, such as tuberculosis (ONS, 1999). Historically, of course, deaths from TB, diptheria, influenza, cholera, typhoid and so on have been major causes of death. Indeed, in some other countries infectious diseases remain a prominent cause of death. In 1997 17.3 million (33 per cent) of an estimated 52.2 million deaths worldwide were due to infectious and parasitic diseases, with respiratory infections, TB, diarrhoea, HIV/AIDS and malaria accounting for the largest proportions of these (WHO, 1998).

While these changes in age at death and in disease patterns have been occurring steadily throughout the century in the UK and many other 'developed' countries, social inequalities in mortality have not reduced in the UK since the Second World War, so that social class as a 'cause of death' remains a relatively constant, or even increasing influence (Drever and Whitehead, 1997). The effect of social inequality on death has been relatively poorly addressed in the United Kingdom when compared internationally, this being exacerbated by rising income inequalities from the 1980s onwards (Wilkinson, 1996).

Gender also plays a part in 'causing' death. In most countries, women live longer than men and the UK is no exception, there being a five year gap in life expectancy at birth at the end of the twentieth century (see above). From age 60 onwards, the proportion of females to males in the population therefore begins to increase dramatically, so that there are roughly twice as many females as males after the age of 80 (Craig, 1995). Females are more likely than men to die from cerebrovascular disease (strokes, largely) or to have pneumonia recorded on their death certificates. Additionally, breast cancer (the main site of cancer for women) and cancer of the uterus are specific to women. Males are more likely to die from cancer of the stomach and lung, ischaemic heart disease and bronchitis, these being in part due to gender differences in smoking. Additionally, road vehicle accidents and suicides, statistically speaking quite rare forms of death, are more likely to occur in men due to the lives which younger men lead. Prostate cancer, second only to lung cancer as a cause of cancer death in men, is of course specific to males (Department of Health, 1998).

Because of the present-day concentration of death in elderly people, it is appropriate to regard dying, for most people, as a part of the more general experience of being old. The demographic changes and associated changes to the pattern of disease that have occurred in the UK this century have had a profound effects on the physical experiences of dying, the meaning of death both individually and for society as a whole, and on the sources of help and support available for people who are ill to the point of death. I shall review each of these in turn.

Physical experiences of ageing and dying

Government social surveys investigating the prevalence of illness and disability, as well as surveys of the circumstances of people in the last year of life, are useful in describing the physical problems of elderly and dying people, as well as estimating trends over time in these, as the population has aged. Broadly speaking, the prevalence of disability reflects the aging of the population over time, as well as gender and class divisions. Since the General Household Survey (GHS) began in 1972, the proportion of adults reporting a longstanding illness that limited daily activities rose from 15 per cent of people living in private households to 22 per cent in 1996. Women at each time point are somewhat more likely to report this than men, and the prevalence of limiting longstanding illness, unsurprisingly, shows a sharp rise with age, so that amongst people aged 75 and over, 52 per cent report such illness. The GHS also shows an association of this measure with social class, with lower levels reported for people from professional and managerial occupations (ONS, 1998c). The 1991 census included a similar question, making it possible to include people resident in institutions who, as one would expect, were far more likely than people living in private households to report the presence of such disabling conditions (Grundy, 1996).

The perception that increased life expectancy may bring with it a greater burden of disability towards the end of life led some researchers to calculate a new statistic of 'healthy life expectancy' to modify the traditional life expectancy statistic. This showed that between 1976 and 1994, when life expectancy rose by over four years for males and more than three years for females, healthy life expectancy showed almost no change (ONS, 1998a). As a result of this increased level of disability, 30 per cent of people aged 85 or more surveyed in the 1996 GHS needed help at home in climbing the stairs; 24 per cent needed help with bathing or showering; 8 per cent with dressing and undressing, as well as smaller proportions needing assistance with other self-care activities (ONS, 1998c).

Table 5.1 Symptoms experienced in the last year of life, 1990

	Cancer %	Heart disease %	Stroke %
Pain	88	77	66
Breathlessness	54	60	37
Nausea and vomiting	59	32	23
Difficulty swallowing	41	16	23
Constipation	63	38	45
Mental confusion	41	32	50
Pressure sores	28	11	20
Urinary incontinence	40	30	56
Bowel incontinence	32	17	37
N=	2063	683	229

Source: Addington-Hall, 1996

The symptoms and restrictions experienced by people in the last year of life have been recorded in three UK surveys, describing people dying in 1969, 1987 and 1990, by means of interviews with surviving relatives and others who knew the deceased. The first two of these (Cartwright et al., 1973; Seale and Cartwright, 1994) were from nationally representative samples, permitting a comparison over time. On both occasions respondents were asked to say which of a number of areas of restriction had been experienced by the people who died. These included such activities as getting in and out of the bath, dressing and undressing and washing. The major changes concerned the length of time that such restrictions were experienced. In 1969, 30 per cent had needed help with at least one of these for a year or more. By 1987 this had risen to 52 per cent. In this respect the figures support those from the GHS.

Respondents were also asked, on both occasions, to report whether certain symptoms were experienced at all during the last 12 months of life and, for symptoms reported at this stage, how long they had been experienced by the person who died. The major changes since 1969 again concerned the duration of some of the symptoms: mental confusion, depression and incontinence were all experienced over a longer time period by people in the later study. Controlling for age showed that these increases were all related to the greater proportion of people aged 75 or more in the 1987 study.

Recalling that cancer, heart disease and stroke have become increasingly prevalent as causes of death as infectious diseases have declined in importance, the analyses conducted for these separate groups in the 1990 survey (Addington-Hall, 1996) are of interest. This survey, the Regional Study of Care for the Dying (RSCD) (Addington-Hall and McCarthy, 1995), was not nationally representative, but its large size permits comparison of these different leading causes of death. This is shown in Table 5.1. Pain, nausea and vomiting, difficulty swallowing, constipation and pressure sores are more prevalent amongst people dying from cancer. Breathlessness is a particular problem for people with heart disease; mental confusion and incontinence affect a high proportion of people dying from strokes. Overall, cancer caused, on average, a larger number of symptoms and a larger proportion of these were considered by respondents to have been 'very distressing' for the dying person. However, the duration of symptoms in cancer was less than for other conditions (Addington-Hall et al., 1998). This pattern was also found in the earlier study of deaths in 1986 (Seale and Cartwright, 1994), which suggested that an experience of longer term disability was more typical in people not dying from cancer, who also tended to be a little older, on average, than those dying from cancer (see also Table 5.2 for this in the 1990 study).

Living circumstances and sources of care for people who die

In 1996–1997 15 per cent of households in the UK consisted of a single person above pensionable age living alone; in 1961 this figure had been only 7 per cent (ONS, 1998a). At the more recent date, approximately four times as many elderly women as men lived alone, for reasons that should by now be clear. The 1996 GHS showed 87 per cent of people aged 65 and over living either alone or with only a spouse (ONS, 1998c), a figure that has also been steadily increasing over time (Grundy, 1996). Grundy (1996) also reports surveys showing reductions since 1962 in the proportion of elderly parents with at least one child living within 10–15 minutes travelling distance.

The consequences of these changes for the sources of informal help and care that people could draw upon as they approached death were charted in the 1987 survey of the last year of life (Seale and Cartwright, 1994). People living alone in the 1987 sample were in a particularly unfortunate situation for potential sources of help. They were the least likely to have any children or siblings alive and were most likely to be widowed or divorced and old. They were also the group most likely to progress to institutional care.

Those living with others, but without a spouse, were the next oldest group, although this type of household was about half as common as those living alone. They were also quite likely to be elderly widows and to be single people, but, perhaps because they were somewhat more likely than those living alone to have children or siblings alive, they could live with them when they started becoming restricted. In fact this group reported the highest proportion of long-term restriction, a condition which, if they had been living alone, would have meant a larger proportion entering institutional care.

Those living with their spouse only were the next most elderly group, as well as this being the most common type of household. With an average level of restriction, and being more likely than average to have children alive, their prospects, both in terms of need for help and for sources on which they could draw, were better than the previous two groups. Such

Table 5.2   *Circumstances by cause of death in the last year of life,*
1990

	Cancer %	Heart disease %	Stroke %
Age at death			
<65	26	9	7
65–74	28	27	14
75–84	33	40	40
85+	13	23	39
Lived alone	31	38	44
Marital status			
married	51	41	26
widowed	35	47	59
other	14	12	16
Place of death			
own home	29	29	9
hospital	50	55	67
hospice	14	0	0
residential/nursing home	7	12	24
other place	0	4	0
N=	2063	683	229

Source: Addington-Hall, 1996

people were more likely to be men, and this was even more likely to be true with the youngest group: those living with their spouse and others. This last group was the smallest, but all had children alive and less than a fifth experienced long-term restriction. Both of these last two household groups contained high proportions of people dying from cancer, suggesting that cancer patients were more likely to have access to sources of informal care than sufferers from other terminal conditions.

Patterns of care reported in this survey reflected these underlying variations. Where restrictions were reported, respondents were asked who had helped, and who had borne the brunt of care. Analysis of the replies showed the average number of relatives and friends helping in 1987 (2.0) was significantly lower than for 1969, when the figure was 3. However, this varied a great deal across the different types of households, with people living alone having an average of 1.7 such helpers, and people living with their spouses and others having 3.1. Women were most likely to bear the brunt of caring: 43 per cent were wives or daughters of the deceased, only 21 per cent husbands or sons.

These patterns were also reflected in the 1990 RSCD survey, as is shown in Table 5.2, which indicates the way in which the cause of death varies across these dimensions. The relatively younger age of people dying from cancer shows associations with a reduced likelihood of living alone or of being widowed, compared with heart disease and stroke. The patterns for place of death reflect the provision of specialist hospice services for dying cancer patients, whereas people dying from strokes, being older, more likely to be widowed and living alone than the other two groups, are much less likely to die in their own homes. For these people, death in a hospital or residential or nursing home is more likely, since the availability of informal care to enable death to occur at home is less likely than for other conditions.

Controlling death

Clearly, demographic change exercises a profound influence on the experience of the last year of life. What is less often recognized is the influence of this upon more general practices and beliefs about appropriate ways to approach death in a society showing the patterns of mortality thus far outlined. There are of course other more purely cultural factors to consider here, most notably increasing secularization and a rise in individualism, which exert independent influences, but it is worth considering how these combine to produce some rather prominent trends in attitudes towards dying.

Two of the most notable trends in public and professional attitudes have been the advocacy of the benefits of an open acknowledgment of the presence of terminal disease, and of euthanasia as a solution to the problems of suffering towards the end of life. On the first of these, it has been shown conclusively that people who die of cancer are considerably more likely to have acknowledged that they are dying than used to be the case 30 years ago. Additionally, situations of 'closed awareness' where all but the dying person share the knowledge that a condition is terminal in a conspiracy of silence, is rarer, whether deaths are from cancer or not (Seale et al., 1997). This is in part due to changed disclosure practices on the part of doctors (Seale and Cartwright, 1994). On the second point, Donnison and Bryson (1995), reviewing the trend towards rising public support for the legalization of euthanasia, report that 82 per cent of a random, representative sample of the UK public agreed that doctors should be 'allowed by law to end the patient's life' if someone with a 'painful incurable disease' makes such a request, compared with 75 per cent 10 years earlier. This rising trend has been documented in several other developed countries (Seale, 1997).

These two trends stem from the same source: a desire to control the timing and manner of death in a climate where lack of such control is felt to lead to unbearable and pointless suffering. People who acknowledge an open awareness of dying are more likely to plan for their deaths, and to achieve what they want, in terms of a home death, or a death with close relatives present. They are also more likely to enter hospices and to express an interest in euthanasia as an alternative means of control over their deaths

(Seale et al., 1997). This active orientation to death is a typical feature of the approach people in modern societies take to a number of matters which in pre-modern societies were felt to be beyond human influence. They are enhanced where there is a system of medical knowledge that is often able to predict the manner and timing of death, and to offer some realistic hope that physical suffering can be alleviated by technical measures.

Yet these trends also arise from the simple fact that death has increasingly become concentrated amongst elderly people in such societies. As well as physical suffering, dependency is feared, and such dependency is particularly associated with becoming old. Control over one's fate at this time of life then appears particularly desirable, by planning for death in various ways, just as one might plan other aspects of life in old age. In societies where death appears to be more capricious, occurring at all ages and for reasons that are beyond human control, dying is less readily perceived as a matter for personal management strategies. Additionally, the perception that useful life has finished is a more widespread experience when more survive to great old age, particularly in a society which has developed routinized methods for separating older people from the family, social and economic activities of younger groups. We therefore see these trends in public opinion and professional and lay practices with all the personal advantages and dangers that they represent.

Conclusion

Trends in life expectancy and disease patterns have had profound consequences for the structure of the UK population, and for the experience of dying, which has become increasingly concentrated in old age. Gender differences exert a greater influence than class differences in determining living circumstances towards the end of life, which increasingly reflect a pattern of living alone in the context of higher levels of disability, but lower availability of informal care than in previous times. The illness conditions suffered towards the end of life also affect the experience of dying, particularly when dying from cancer is compared with death from other conditions. Underlying demographic factors interact with cultural factors, namely increases in secularization and individualism, to promote people's interest in the active management of their dying, through such means as becoming aware of any terminal illness, and through consideration of euthanasia as an option.

References

Addington-Hall, J. (1996) 'Heart disease and stroke: lessons from cancer care', in G. Ford and I. Lewin (eds), *Managing Terminal Illness*. London: Royal College of Physicians of London. pp. 25–32.

Addington-Hall, J., Altmann, D. and McCarthy, M. (1998) 'Variations by age in symptoms and dependency levels experienced by people in the last year of life, as reported by surviving family, friends and officials', *Age and Ageing*, 27: 129–36.
Addington-Hall, J. and McCarthy, M. (1995) 'Dying from cancer: results of a national population-based investigation', *Palliative Medicine*, 9: 295–305.
Cartwright, A., Hockey, L. and Anderson, J.L. (1973) *Life before Death*. London: Routledge and Kegan Paul.
Craig, J. (1995) 'Males and females: some vital differences', *Population Trends*, 80: 26–30.
Department of Health (1998) *Health and Personal Social Services Statistics for England*. London: The Stationery Office.
Donnison, D. and Bryson, C. (1995) 'Matters of life and death: attitudes to euthanasia', in R. Jowell, J. Curtice, A. Park, L. Brook and K. Thomson (eds), *British Social Attitudes: The 13th Report*. Aldershot: Dartmouth Pub. Co. pp. 161–84.
Drever, F. and Whitehead, M. (eds) (1997) *Health Inequalities*. London: The Stationery Office.
Grundy, E. (1996) 'Population review: (5) the population aged 60 and over', *Population Trends*, 84: 14–20.
Office for National Statistics (1998a) *Social Trends 28*. London: The Stationery Office.
Office for National Statistics (1998b) *1996 Mortality Statistics: General Series DH1, No. 28*. London: The Stationery Office.
Office for National Statistics (1998c) *Living in Britain: Results from the 1996 General Household Survey*. London: The Stationery Office.
Office for National Statistics (1999) *Annual Abstract of Statistics 1999*. London: The Stationery Office.
Seale, C.F. (1997) 'Social and ethical aspects of euthanasia: a review', *Progress in Palliative Care*, 5: 141–6.
Seale, C.F. and Cartwright, A. (1994) *The Year before Death*. Aldershot: Avebury.
Seale, C.F., Addington-Hall, J. and McCarthy, M. (1997) 'Awareness of dying: prevalence, causes and consequences', *Social Science and Medicine*, 45: 477–84.
Wilkinson, R. (1996) *Unhealthy Societies: The Afflictions of Inequality*. London: Routledge.
World Health Organization (1998) *The World Health Report 1988*. Geneva: World Health Organization.
Wrigley, E. and Schofield, R. (1989) *The Population of England 1541–1871: A Reconstruction*. Cambridge: Cambridge University Press.

6

Health policy and services for dying people and their carers

Christina R. Victor

In this article the current pattern of mortality in England and Wales is outlined and the configuration of service provision for dying people and their carers is described. Following this the patterns of service organization and the broad social and policy contexts which determine the provision of care to this group are set out.

Patterns of mortality

In order to understand the service needs of dying people and their carers it is important to be aware of the patterns of mortality within society, the main demographic characteristics of those who die and the principal causes of death.

Death in Britain is a highly medicalized event. Under the 1836 Births and Deaths Registration Act a doctor is required to certify both death and the immediate and underlying cause of death. Collation of information from these death certificates provides information about the pattern of deaths or mortality in Britain. Such data form a useful background to identifying the service needs of dying people and their carers.

In 1997 there were 555,281 certified deaths in England and Wales, the majority of which, 492,029 (83 per cent) were of people aged 65 and over (Table 6.1). Despite all the attention focused upon them, premature deaths (those before the age of 65 years) represent only a minority of all deaths. For example, in the 45 to 54 age range there were 22,500 deaths in England and Wales compared with 159,997 in the over 85 years age group. It is only for a few very specific causes of death (accidents, suicide and liver diseases) that the mean age of death is under 60 (Table 6.2). However, in order to better to understand the patterns of mortality within the area it is necessary to relate this to the population size within each age group. One useful indicator expresses the total number of deaths per 1,000 total population in that age group. Table 6.3 demonstrates that the pattern of deaths within England and Wales shows a J-shaped curve. Mortality is relatively high in the first year of life and then decreases during childhood. From the age of 15 years mortality then steadily increases with age, although at all ages women illustrate lower mortality rates than men. This differential is at its

Table 6.1 *Total deaths by age and sex: England and Wales 1997*

	Male	Female	Total
<1	2,137	1,663	3,800
1–4	412	297	709
5–14	592	386	798
15–24	2,389	916	3,305
25–34	3,440	1,718	5,158
35–44	6,207	3,714	9,921
45–54	13,484	9,016	22,500
55–64	28,907	17,974	46,881
65–74	68,024	48,293	116,317
75–84	90,207	95,508	185,715
85+	49,066	110,931	159,997
Total	264,865	290,416	555,281

Source: ONS (1998) Table 3

Table 6.2 *Mean age at death from selected causes by sex: England and Wales 1996*

	Mean age at death	
Cause	M	F
All	71.9	78.2
Stomach cancer	71.9	76.6
Colon cancer	71.5	75.7
Lung cancer	71.1	71.5
Skin cancer	62.0	66.4
Female breast cancer	–	68.9
Cervix cancer	–	62.5
Prostate cancer	77.6	–
Leukaemia	67.0	69.9
Diabetes	72.9	77.8
Ischemic heart disease	73.2	80.1
Stroke	76.9	82.0
Bronchitis, emphysema and asthma	73.1	74.6
Liver disease	56.9	60.9
Injury and poisoning	46.5	63.9
Car accidents	38.8	49.1
Suicide/self inflicted	43.9	50.1

Source: ONS (1997) Table 25

greatest for the 15–34 age group where mortality rates are 2.5 times higher for males as compared with females.

As well as the general pattern of mortality, the cause of death is also an important issue when considering the service needs of dying people. The main causes of death in England and Wales in 1987 are shown in Table 6.4. Overall the most important are diseases of the circulatory system, such as heart attacks and strokes, which account for 41 per cent of male and female deaths. Deaths from cancer, which have been the focus of most of the

Table 6.3 *Death rates by age and sex: England and Wales 1997*

	Rate per 1,000,000		
	Male	**Female**	**M:F ratio**
<1	6,494	5,313	1.22
1–4	305	232	1.31
5–14	171	117	1.46
15–24	735	297	2.47
25–34	928	425	2.18
35–44	1,543	1,031	1.49
45–54	3,940	2,630	1.49
55–64	11,453	6,942	1.64
65–74	33,221	20,189	1.64
75–84	82,489	54,572	1.51
85+	190,327	151,749	1.25
Total all ages	10,529	9,787	1.07

Source: ONS (1998) Table 4

literature concerned with death and dying, account for 27 per cent of all deaths and 22 per cent of deaths of those aged under 65 years.

The pattern of mortality is not, however, constant across the different age and sex groups. At different ages there are variations in the importance of the different causes of death. Accidents and violence are most common amongst causes of death in the younger age groups. In the 15–44 age group injury and poisoning accounts for 43 per cent of male deaths and 20 per cent of female deaths whilst cancers account for 15 per cent and 37 per cent respectively. These groups will, therefore, present quite a different set of service requirements from the older age groups where circulatory diseases, cancers and respiratory disease are important sources of death.

Patterns of mortality are not static but are, in fact, constantly changing. Table 6.5, using standardized mortality ratios, illustrates that overall mortality rates have decreased by approximately 20 per cent over the last two decades. For most major causes of death these improvements, resulting from improved treatment and diagnosis are evident. However some causes of death, notably skin cancer, prostate cancer, diabetes, lung cancer (women), bronchitis (women) and chronic liver disease, have not benefited from this improvement.

The analysis of the current patterns of mortality in England and Wales illustrate several important points which have to be taken into account when considering the issue of services for dying people and their carers. First, death is most common amongst the older age groups. Consequently many of the issues surrounding the provision of care to dying people are those which apply to the general area of the care of older people. Secondly, death from cancers, which have been the focus of much of the literature in this subject area, represent only a minority of deaths at any age. Thirdly, and following on from this, many deaths are, therefore, 'unexpected' particularly amongst

Table 6.4 Deaths by underlying cause by age and sex: England and Wales 1997*

	<1		1–14		15–44		45–64		65+		Total	
	M	F	M	F	M	F	M	F	M	F	M	F
Infectious disease	68	58	53	51	381	194	382	221	908	1,179	1,792	1,703
Neoplasms	12	12	169	147	1,790	2,361	14,986	13,387	54,295	49,959	71,252	66,366
Endocrine	17	14	38	24	185	151	626	404	2,544	3,370	3,410	3,973
Blood disorders	3	5	16	8	44	26	108	60	546	992	917	1,091
Mental disorders	–	–	2	2	564	131	260	131	2,599	6,035	3,425	6,300
Nervous system	52	48	135	94	516	337	748	629	3,197	4,016	4,648	5,124
Circulatory	35	17	61	35	1,803	800	16,958	6,539	90,589	111,609	109,446	119,000
Respiratory	75	72	82	57	510	358	3,179	2,133	37,669	48,342	41,515	51,002
Digestive	10	3	19	17	674	380	2,258	1,459	5,935	9,652	8,896	11,511
Genitourinary	3	1	7	4	55	44	255	196	2,727	3,465	3,047	3,710
Pregnancy/childbirth	–	–	–	–	–	35	–	–	–	–	–	35
Skin	–	–	–	–	8	3	16	33	251	714	275	750
Musculo-skeletal	–	–	1	5	21	42	90	181	742	2,477	854	2,705
Congenital	133	118	114	82	162	122	118	114	132	188	659	624
Perinatal	72	41	9	8	–	1	–	–	–	–	81	50
Ill-defined	226	129	20	12	196	56	189	54	2,277	9,133	2,908	9,384
Injury/poisoning	33	25	278	137	5,127	1,320	2,218	924	2,686	3,563	10,342	5,969
Total	739	543	1,004	683	12,036	6,348	42,391	26,990	207,297	254,732	264,865	290,416

* Excludes deaths under 28 days

Source: ONS (1998) Table 8

Table 6.5 *Standardize mortality ratios for selected causes by sex: England and Wales 1971–1996*

Cause	Male			Female		
	1971	**1981**	**1996**	**1971**	**1981**	**1996**
All	111	100	74	110	100	81
Stomach cancer	131	100	74	110	100	81
Colon cancer	106	100	86	110	100	74
Lung cancer	106	100	86	110	100	74
Skin cancer	63	100	154	79	100	132
Breast cancer				94	100	132
Cervix cancer				119	100	57
Prostate cancer	92	100	128			
Leukaemia	101	100	89	100	100	97
Diabetes	102	100	114	132	100	102
Ischemic heart disease	104	100	63	106	100	70
Stroke	135	100	62	133	100	65
Bronchitis, emphysema	143	100	68	125	100	141
Asthma	79	100	75	83	100	97
Liver disease	72	100	194	75	100	153
Chronic renal failure	120	100	39	97	100	36
Car accidents	141	100	63	162	100	55
Suicide/self inflicted	85	100	95	104	100	54

Standard rate = 1980–82 = 100
Source: ONS (1998) Table 5

younger age groups, where a large percentage of deaths are the result of accidents. The issue of providing appropriate care and services for dying people therefore ranges across the entire spectrum of health care provision from paediatrics to geriatrics.

Care of the dying: patterns of care

Data about patterns of mortality within England and Wales provide a crude indication of the needs of dying people and their carers. The focus upon the event of death does not provide us with any information about the circumstances of the individual before their death and the actual experience of death. Such data are not collected routinely upon a national basis. However, Cartwright et al. have undertaken two surveys in 1969 and 1987 (1973: 1990) which attempted to look at the care received and circumstances of a random sample of adults who had died, by collecting information about the last year of life from relatives, friends and others who knew the deceased.

The vast majority of deaths in Britain, about 60 per cent, now take place in hospital and only 25 per cent die at home and 3.5 per cent in hospices. In urban areas it is probable that this percentage is very much higher. However, this overall percentage of deaths at home, about 25 per cent, is a higher percentage than in some Scandinavian countries where the majority of deaths are not at home. This trend for deaths to take place in hospitals represents a marked change with the situation before 1945 when most deaths took place at home.

However, although deaths may take place in hospital, Cartwright and Seale (1990) have indicated that most of the care of the dying patient takes place at home or in other social settings such as nursing homes. In their 1987 sample of adult deaths in England, 12 per cent of those who died had spent some time in an old people's home or nursing home. The variety of agencies involved in the care of the dying are, therefore, highly diverse and include public and voluntary agencies.

The pattern of household circumstances of dying people affects their needs for care. Given that the majority of those who die are elderly, their household circumstances reflect those of the population of older people. Cartwright and Seale's survey reported that 32 per cent of those who died lived alone, and 38 per cent lived with only their spouse. Women were more likely to live alone than men were – this reflects the general pattern in the elderly population. Compared with the survey conducted in 1969, the number of those people dying who lived alone had more than doubled from 15 per cent to 32 per cent whilst the percentage living with others (not their spouse) decreased from 53 per cent to 30 per cent. The percentage living and dying in institutional care increased from 3 per cent to 10 per cent. These changes in the household circumstances of dying people represent two important social changes: the trend for the establishment and maintenance of independent households by both young adults and those in the post-retirement age groups.

The needs of dying people and their carers are very diverse given the variety of different causes of death, which were described earlier. Seale (1990) has described the types of problems reported by people in their last year of life. Common symptoms included mental confusion, pain and incontinence as well as problems with 'activities of daily living' such as self-care like bathing, shaving and cutting toenails. Overall, 59 per cent reported health restrictions in the year prior to death and 65 per cent needed help with the activities of daily living: 52 per cent had required help with these activities for one year or longer. It is probably important from a policy perspective to distinguish between deaths preceded by a period of disability and those where the mortal event has no such antecedent.

Who provides care to those people who die following a period of disability or restricted activity? Overall 16 per cent of care to dying people was provided from official sources such as district nursing or general practitioner services. The pattern of care provision varies with the age and household circumstances of the dying person. The most vulnerable group are those who live alone and who are supported by a network of relatives. We might expect that such people would be well supported with help from official sources. However Seale (1990) reports that even for those living alone only a minority 38 per cent received care from official sources. The bulk of care to dying people is therefore provided from non-formal sources and reflects the general pattern of care provision to older people, with spouses and daughters being the prime source of such care (Green, 1988).

Almost one-half of main carers reported that they could have done with more help in caring for the dying person whilst 45 per cent reported that their own health problems made caring difficult (Seale, 1990). These data indicate that there is a vast well of unmet need amongst those who are caring for dying people which also mirrors the general pattern of care provision in the community for older people.

Resources and service provision

Perhaps the key assumption upon which the National Health Service (NHS) had been planned was the notion that there was a 'fixed' amount of illness in the community which the NHS would gradually diminish. Consequently it was assumed that expenditure on the NHS would eventually decline and level off, once existing diseases had been eliminated. It soon became evident that this was a false premise and expenditure on the NHS had increased steadily. Ham (1985) indicates that at 1949 prices, expenditure per capita on health care increased from £437 in 1949 to £1,490 in 1984. In 1949 total expenditure on the NHS was £437 million; by 1984 this had risen to £16,695 (Ham, 1985). The cost of the services has increased threefold in real terms and it now represents 6.2 per cent of Gross National Product as compared with 3.9 per cent in 1948. These expenditure increases prompted the following comment from the Royal Commission on the NHS: 'the demand for health care is always likely to outstrip supply . . . the capacity of health services to absorb resources is almost unlimited' (HMSO, 1979: 51).

A key factor in determining the current pattern of services to dying people is the way that the health care budget is distributed. We may consider the distribution of the health care budget in four main ways: between geographical regions; between different sectors of the service (e.g. hospital versus community); between varying client groups; and between differing age groups. Acute hospital in-patient care accounts for one-third of all NHS expenditure. Despite numerous attempts to redress the balance, hospital medicine because of its greater 'prestige' had managed to maintain a stranglehold on the allocation of NHS resources. The result of this dominance of acute hospital medicine is that community forms of provision are constantly under-funded. For dying people this may be manifest in the insufficient provision of community nursing, hospices and nursing home provision.

Within the local authority sector there is also competition for finite resources both between social services and other departments and within social services between client groups. How decisions are made between competing services with social service departments remains difficult to articulate empirically. However, statutory duties of the local authority towards children mean that these services often take priority over the needs of other client groups. Typically the local authority provides domestic and meals services. However it is questionable as to how appropriate some of the typical social services are in meeting the needs of dying people and their carers. The implementation of the community care reforms that stress the provision of services which meet the needs of clients rather than fitting clients to services may improve the situation.

Co-ordination of care

To meet the diverse needs of dying people appropriately a variety of different agencies are required. However, in meeting these needs a number of problems arise, including differences in the geographical areas served by the varying agencies and lack of clarity about the boundaries of responsibility between agencies and professions. The geographical areas served by these different agencies are not necessarily coterminous. Such problems of overlapping boundaries are most acute in inner-city districts and may well result in a less than optimal service being provided to those who are dying, especially if they require help at home before the mortal event.

In organizing the care of dying people and their carers there are a variety of agencies involved. As well as overlapping administrative boundaries in many circumstances there are no clear professional boundaries between the responsibilities of those organizing and providing care to older people in both hospital and community settings. The system of providing care is characterized by fragmentation of responsibility and a multiplicity of agencies and professionals involved. For example, home nursing is the province of the District Health Authority, whilst home caring is provided by the local authority social services department. Co-ordinating care under such circumstances is, therefore, problematic and largely the result of historical events which have vested responsibilities for social and health care provision between varying agencies which have not developed in a co-ordinated and coherent fashion.

There is another layer of provision, that of the voluntary sector. Voluntary agencies are involved in the provision of a wide range of services to dying people and their carers. Indeed may of the innovations in service provision such as hospice care and bereavement counselling originated in this sector. Within a local area voluntary agencies may be specific to that locality or be branches of national organizations such as the Crossroads Care Attendant Schemes. The hallmark of the voluntary sector is that it is very dependent upon local activists and enthusiasm. We may distinguish between agencies providing care to people who may die, such as the Crossroads Care Scheme for the very disabled, and those specifically aimed at those with a terminal illness, such as the hospice movement. A particularly fertile and innovative part of the voluntary sector has been the development of services for people with AIDS. Agencies such as the Terrance Higgins Trust, London Lighthouse and the Mildmay Mission have developed a plethora of services for those in the terminal phases of AIDS.

We may speculate as to why the voluntary sector has been the source of much innovation. The enterprise and enthusiasm of the voluntary sector have much to commend them. However, from a wider perspective, there are problems with the development of services by this sector. First, the patchy availability of such schemes adds to the current pattern of geographical inequality in care provision observed within the formal sector. Secondly, such services many be adopted by the formal sector without proper evaluation and study, which means that services may be adopted by the statutory sector for emotive reasons without proper evaluation.

Community care

An important policy context is that of the trend towards community care. Across the range of Western industrial societies there is a trend towards decreased institutional provision and a greater emphasis upon the care and maintenance of those with long-term care needs in their own homes for as long as possible. To achieve this, priority is being given to the development of domiciliary provision and the encouragement of measures designed to prevent or postpone the need for long-term care in hospital or residential homes. Thus, it is argued, care of the dying is a responsibility that should be shared by all and not one which solely involves statutory services. In this manifestation community care is seen as the responsibility of the family, with state services only playing a rather residual role. The receipt of services by only a minority of the dying is the manifestation of this policy. Despite current policy taking too little account of changes in family and household formation, policy is not stressing the need to mobilize the resources of the informal sector, notwithstanding evidence that care is supplied mainly by family and friends rather than the wider community.

Conclusion

The provision of care to dying people and their carers illustrates most of the key issues confronting the health and social welfare system in Britain. First it is important to take into account the epidemiology of death and dying. Most people who die are elderly and they die from a variety of diseases, not just cancers that have dominated the debate about services for the dying. Such a broad perspective makes it difficult to generalize about this group. The dying are not a homogeneous social category and in developing services and policy the diversity of the group must be recognized. The pattern of service provision to this group reflects the fragmentation of responsibility between agencies resulting from a variety of historical circumstances that have proved difficult to change. The power of the medical profession and the dominance of the hospital sector result in the concentration of death in hospital, where the ethos of acute care may be inappropriate for those who are in the 'terminal' phases of their illness. The separation of primary, secondary and home care services and the lack of coterminosity of the areas served results in problems in the co-ordination of services. Overcoming these difficulties requires a fundamental overhaul of the way that services are provided.

References

Cartwright, A., Hockey, L. and Anderson, J.I. (1973) *Life Before Death*. London and Boston, MA: Routledge & Kegan Paul.

Cartwright, A. and Seale, C.F. (1990) *The Natural History of a Survey: an Account of the Methodological Issues Encountered in a Study of Life before Death*. London: King's Fund.

Green, H. (1988) 'General Household Survey (GHS)', *Informal Carers*. London: OPCS, HMSO.

HMSO (1979) *Royal Commission on the National Health Service*. London: HMSO.

Ham, C. (1985) *Health Policy in Britain*, 2nd edn. London: Macmillan. p. 38.

ONS (1997) *Mortality Statistics: England & Wales 1996, General*. London: Stationery Office.

ONS (1998) *Mortality Statistics: England & Wales 1997, Cause*. London: Stationery Office.

Seale, C. (1990) 'Caring for people who die', *Ageing and Society*, 10: 413–28.

7

Sudden death from suicide

Stella Ridley

The concept of illness in our society carries with it the possibility of treatment, and the hope of the relief of suffering. Death following illness is one possible outcome of a progression of events which fall into a sequence and become meaningful in retrospect, according to the kind of illness and the settings in which it occurs.

It is far harder to find or create meaning in sudden death from suicide or self-inflicted injury. For the individual who chooses to commit suicide it would seem that life has become a struggle with no meaning, or a terror from which death is the only escape. The one factor common to suicide or self-inflicted injury is the intention to harm the self; the question common to those left behind is 'Why?' About a third of those who take their own lives give little or no warning and leave no clue as to the reasons behind their feelings of despair; often their family and friends are no wiser. Others talk of suicide and death for a period beforehand, and then take their lives; this is reflected in the tripled rate of suicide for hospital inpatients compared with the general population (Ritter, 1989: 99). A further group attempt suicide and survive, but with perhaps a higher risk of completing the act on a subsequent attempt.

In 1997 the deaths of 5,993 people in the United Kingdom were officially attributed to suicide or self-inflicted injury; to put this in perspective it is almost double the toll from road traffic accidents (Office for National Statistics, *DVS3.H Mortality Statistics – 1997 Boundaries (Registrations)*. Figures for Scotland are from the Registrar General for Scotland, *Annual Report 1997*, and those for Northern Ireland come from the General Register Office for Northern Ireland, Belfast). Suicide statistics are of doubtful accuracy and this can be taken to be the minimum. Coroners are often reluctant to deliver a suicide verdict and this tends to be determined by the means of death; for example, hanging or death from fumes from a motor vehicle exhaust pipe leading into a car are normally seen as valid indicators, while road traffic accidents are rarely interpreted as showing suicidal intent. It is thought that in excess of 140,000 people attempt suicide each year.

If one-third of those who take their lives give no warning of their intention, there are many others among those who are contemplating suicide who do offer signs. In 1953 Chad Varah formed the Samaritans organization, in response to the suicide of a young girl, with the aim of being there for those who were suicidal or in despair, to listen to what they had to say, and to offer emotional support or befriending in times of crisis. The organization is now divided into 204 local branches throughout the UK and Ireland (with others world-wide), staffed by 20,900 trained and selected volunteers from a wide cross-section of society, who answered 4.2 million contacts in 1996 – one every eight seconds. The callers range in age from children to the elderly, through all socio-economic groups. A fundamental tenet is that every caller has a need to be listened to, in confidence, and to have his or her feelings acknowledged and respected. This includes a respect for the caller's right to choose to end his or her life.

The question of choice is of paramount importance. Alvarez (1971) describes suicide as an act of choice, when life is not worth living. Listening to individuals who are profoundly suicidal, often it would seem to them that there is no choice open, and that suicide is the only way out. This constitutes not so much a choice as a forced choice, where there is no alternative but to die.

In 'A Letter from Jill' (from Foster and Smith, 1987: 53–4) reproduced as the appendix to this article, Jill says at the end of her suicide note, 'I can't not kill myself after writing this'. This lack of choice is echoed by descriptions given by others:

> It was as if I'd already gone over, somehow – the problem was not how to die but would have been how to stay alive. (After an incompleted suicide)

Tolstoy, in 'Death and the meaning of life', says:

> The truth was that life was meaningless. It was as though I had just been living and walking along, and had come to an abyss, where I saw clearly that there was nothing ahead but perdition. And it was impossible to stop and go back, impossible to shut my eyes, in order that I might not see that there was nothing ahead but suffering and imminent death, – complete annihilation. (Tolstoy, 1899; see p. 83 in this Reader)

How can someone be empowered to make an open choice between life and death instead of this forced choice? The Samaritans say that they are concerned with 'the affirmation of life and its quality'. On a practical level this entails recognizing suicidal feelings, and encouraging the caller to talk of his or her fears and expectations, to acknowledge plans he or she may have for ending life, and to talk of the feelings that have led up to the present day. Acceptance rather than denial of distress, a belief in what the caller says rather than 'Oh you can't really mean that', are ways in which the caller may learn that he or she is really being heard. There is no formula, each Samaritan volunteer finds his or her own way to facilitate the kind of real human contact that can open a route back into life for someone who has become isolated and without hope. However, it can be a precarious path; depression often inhibits action. As it begins to lift there can sometimes be a critical period when suicidal ideation still exists and increasing energy at last allows for an active suicide attempt.

Do the activities of the Samaritans help to prevent suicide? When 500 Samaritans were asked 'Have you ever contemplated taking your own life?' two-thirds said yes. When asked 'Have you ever attempted to take your own life?' one-sixth said yes (The Samaritans, 1998). This implies that many of the volunteers themselves recognize the need for and the value of the service from their own personal experience.

Are certain groups of people more vulnerable to suicide? Sadly, yes. Suicide is a major cause of death, second only to road accidents, in the 16–24 age group. A high number of older people also take their lives, but suicide accounts for a much smaller proportion of deaths in this age range. Certain occupational groups run a higher risk too, health care professionals and farmers among them. A high proportion of those attempting suicide have suffered major changes or life events in the preceding year. This can be illustrated by the detail that another group vulnerable to suicide is the prison population, where in 1997 the rate was ten times that of the general population. The most frequent prison suicide is on remand – 63 per cent of those in prison who took their lives were on remand, and, of these, 36 per cent were under 25 years old. Recognizing this, the Samaritans have worked hard to make their services increasingly available to prisoners over recent years.

Throughout the general population twice as many males as females take their lives, and the method varies. Male deaths are more likely to be of a violent nature, such as hanging, while the most common method for women is by overdose. Violent methods carry a greater risk of completion (Ritter, 1989); the higher rate of non-fatal deliberate self-harm among girls and women may be related to this. The chosen method does have considerable significance, and varies widely across different cultures.

Many who read this will know from first-hand experience what it feels like to be suicidal, or will have known someone who has died in this way. Feelings of loneliness and despair are difficult to share, and friends and family may seem to turn a blind eye to distress because it touches too deeply on hidden fear and pain of their own. Finding the words to describe these feelings, and someone who will listen to and accept them, may be one step towards discovering meaning where, for a time, there threatened to be none.

References

Alvarez, A. (1971) *The Savage God*. London: Weidenfeld & Nicholson.

Foster, S. and Smith, P. (1987) *Brief Lives*. London: Arlington Books.

Ritter, S. (1989) *Bethlem Royal and Maudsley Hospital Manual of Clinical Psychiatric Nursing Principles and Procedures*. London: Harper Collins Nursing.

The Samaritans (1998) Report 'Defining Suicide'. Samaritans Symposium, November, 1998.

Tolstoy, Leo (1899) 'Death and the meaning of life', in *A Confession*, trans. Leo Wiener. New York: Thomas Y. Crowell & Co. (Abridged version reproduced on pp. 82–5 of this Reader.)

Appendix: A letter from Jill

On 28 December 1984, Jill died, aged 15 years, on the Liverpool to Manchester railway line. She told her parents she was taking the dog for a walk, tied him in a safe place and threw herself under a train. She left a letter.

Dear Mummy,

Please don't waste too much effort on a large funeral after all the heartache I have caused you, it is hardly worth it. I am sorry it happened at Christmas. I killed myself because I had made a mess of so many things.

I know you feel that that isn't true, but it was. It was never your fault, mind. I love you and Daddy very dearly, always remember that. I could just not get the act together, that's all. My future didn't seem very attractive. I think I was just one hell of a cracked-up person. I have always felt inferior. I could never talk to anyone and know they had respected what I have said. Maybe I didn't let it show before because then I was younger and adulthood seemed a long way away and I thought as I got older my thoughts would change. Sadly they didn't.

Always remember me as you thought I was, not as a stupid person, which is how I feel about myself.

I can't not kill myself after writing this. (Sorry)

Love, Jill xxxx

Your disobedient daughter

8

The dream

T.R.S.

LITTLE BOYS AND GIRLS, THIS IS FOR YOU

'OH, what a sweet dream! – oh, what a lovely dream! Oh, mamma, you don't know what a charming sight these eyes saw but a short time ago!' These simple words were from the lips of a dying child to her mother. The child was ill in a little cot in the bedroom of her mother, who was anxiously watching her child with all the love of a parent's heart; and delighted once more to hear the voice of her dear little one, she replied, 'What, my dear child – what sight has my Lucy seen?' 'Oh, mamma – mamma!' said the charmed girl, 'Such a sight! I thought I was in heaven, and on my head was such a lovely crown of sweet flowers; a golden harp was in my hand, and when I just touched one of its chords, such sweet sounds came, like most delightful music; and I sang to it with all my power. There was dear little Reuben – yes, darling brother Reuben, that used to be so kind and make me little boats to sail on the water; and he looked so happy: he didn't cry, mamma, like he did before he died and was buried in the cemetery. There was dear little baby, too – poor Mary, that was so pretty, with white hair, and such beautiful blue eyes. But, oh, mother, I can't tell you about it, it was so wonderful! Don't cry, mamma; for doesn't the Bible say, if you're good, both you, papa, and brother William, shall go? I shall soon go to help them to sing; and you'll stop to comfort them, mamma, when they cry because I'm gone, won't you, mamma? Dry your tears; for then all of us will be together, so happily, in heaven.'

The beautiful simplicity of her innocent child deeply impressed the parent. Alas! soon Lucy died; but her mamma had a great comfort. She knew Lucy was with baby and Reuben, in heaven!

From *The Child's Own Magazine for 1856*, London: The Sunday School Union.

9

The good death?

Mary Bradbury

What do we mean when we say a death was 'good'? Peoples across the world engage in discussions as to whether a death was 'good' or 'bad' and it is useful to look to non-Western societies before discussing contemporary representations of the good death in Britain.

It has been argued that in non-Western societies 'good' deaths are those that demonstrate some kind of control over events (Bloch and Parry, 1982). Such good deaths can be seen to represent a victory over nature. For the Lugbara of Uganda, the 'good' death, described below, is one in which the dying predict that their demise is imminent and prepare for it. It is easy to identify with the account that follows:

> A man should die in his hut, lying on his bed, with his brothers and sons round him to hear his last words; he should die with his mind still alert and should be able to speak clearly even if only softly; he should die peacefully and with dignity, without bodily discomfort or disturbance; he should die loved and respected by his family. (Middleton, 1982: 142)

Mortuary rituals serve to deny the finality of the good death by claiming that this death actually represents a kind of rebirth. Discussions of such good deaths serve to reassure the survivors that the deceased has indeed gone on to a new life. In a fascinating study of themes of regeneration in mortuary rituals in non-industrial societies, Bloch and Parry (1982) argue that a belief in the 'good' death may be harnessed to reassert the power of the group. They note that 'good' deaths may be seen to increase the productiveness of the group, in terms of crops, successful hunting or human fertility.

In contrast, bad deaths are uncontrolled; they happen at the wrong place at the wrong time. 'Bad' deaths preclude the chance of regeneration, both for the individual and the group. Suicide is often viewed as the ultimate 'bad' death. While suicide may be seen by an individual as the only way to assert control over their destiny, the survivors are likely to be left feeling helpless. To them, a suicide can appear to be a selfish act of personal frustration or despair. In contrast, 'selfless' self-sacrifice is often positively sanctioned by society (Durkheim, 1952). In reality, however, this is something of a grey area and, as Bloch and Parry point out, there can be disagreement as to whether a death was a 'bad' suicide or an example of 'good' self-sacrifice; one only needs to think of the gaoled hunger striker to appreciate the subjective nature of such labels.

Contemporary representations of death in a segment of British society

Anthropologists such as Bloch and Parry have noted that one would not expect to find beliefs in the afterlife and the good death so strongly emphasized in contemporary Western cultures where the forces of individualism, secularism and the dominance of the natural and medical sciences have worked together to undermine religious and spiritual belief systems (see Houlbrooke, 1989). Changes in demography have also led to the death rate being concentrated in the elderly, who are often undervalued in this culture. The deaths of the very old and infirm do not always excite much comment. It is therefore interesting to examine the character of British good deaths.

A qualitative study in London looked at current representations of death among medical staff, deathwork professionals (such as the funeral director, the coroner and the registrar) and bereaved women (Bradbury, 1999). The findings from this study suggest that social representations of good or bad death continue to be used, although these representations are rather different from those found in a non-Western context. I came across several contrasting descriptions of good and bad deaths. These can be loosely grouped into three ideal types: the traditional sacred 'good' death; the medicalized 'good' death; and the 'natural' good death. As one would expect these representations are rarely presented in pristine form, yet it is still useful to consider these broad categories.

Sacred good deaths

For those with faith, the sorrow and pain of loss caused by the death of a loved one can be tempered by a sense of celebration or even joy. For such people the afterlife is a reality. The religious or sacred death is one in which great emphasis is placed upon the way in which the deceased lived their life and the manner of their death. While the details vary from religion to religion, being prepared and conscious are often key features of such deaths. Such accounts may appear to be very traditional and may seem at first glance to be similar to those described in non-Western cultures (see Bloch and Parry, 1982) or in pre-industrial Britain (see Ariès, 1987), but closer analysis reveals them to be quite different. I found that they were invariably married to descriptions of medical interventions and of the medical good death, outlined below.

Medicalized good deaths

The majority of deaths take place in a medical context of some kind, whether in a hospital, hospice or at home, under the supervision of a GP. In this context, it is not surprising that we have embraced those medical techniques which allow us to control death to some extent, for example, by prolonging life or easing pain. In my study I found that the majority of deathworkers subscribed to a representation of the medical good death in which the dying patient was unconscious, and free of pain. In this struggle against death the locus of control had shifted from the dying person to those who care for him or her.

Natural good death

I came across two different types of natural good death. In both instances, the essential ingredient of control of the death has been reinterpreted. The first type of natural good death is quite straightforward. In this instance, people take control of their own expected deaths by becoming active agents in the illness. They become involved in decisions regarding their care and treatments, often rejecting what are increasingly seen as unnecessary medical interventions. In many ways these 'natural' deaths really represent 'less-medicalized' deaths. Yet, the theme of nature may continue into the post-mortem period. The dying person may plan their own alternative funeral, in which they choose, say, a shroud rather than an ecologically wasteful coffin, or have a tree planted to mark their burial spot, instead of erecting a headstone.

The second type of natural good death is slightly more unusual. In these instances the deceased is seen to have died a natural good death simply because it was sudden and unexpected. Often the person dies in some kind of 'natural' setting, such as at sea, or as a result of illness which struck during a leisure pursuit, such as trekking. Somewhat to my surprise, I found that my respondents felt that these sudden, unexpected deaths were both natural and good. These were deaths in which the deceased was spared the stress and pain of a lengthy dying trajectory, something that many of us fear in times in which the dying process has become prolonged. It is of note that the concept of 'natural' death which is also good is a modern, secular, development (see Beier, 1989).

Medical practitioners and deathwork professionals

Medical practitioners and deathwork professionals may cherish personal representations of 'good' and 'bad' death which affect the way they treat the dying, the dead and the next of kin. They may be unaware that others do not necessarily share their worldview. Indeed, sometimes there are conflicts between the representations of 'good' death held by the bereaved and those of the professionals.

If you bring them in and they are obviously dead, you will wait ten minutes so the relatives think you have done something. (Casualty doctor, 1991)

The representation of the medical good death, which is characterized by active interventions by medically qualified personnel, appears to have informed this team's decision to stand around a corpse for the benefit of the waiting next of kin. While the erroneous belief that the death followed a frantic fight for life may have been a comfort to the relatives, this team had no way of knowing that their assumptions about them were correct.

> I once spent eight hours embalming a person, I had to suture an arm back on – the relatives didn't know. (Funeral director, 1991)

During the post-mortem period representations of death continue to have an impact on our speech and behaviour. I found that funeral directors made a great deal of effort to hide any evidence of violent, or bad, deaths. When preparing the corpse for viewing, staff tried to create the illusion that the deceased had died a good death, be it in sacred, medical or natural terms. Trying to make the body look reposeful is therefore not so much a symptom of our denial of death, but our denial of 'bad' death through the attempt to make all deaths appear as if they had been good.

> I am against personal visual identification, unless [the body appears to] lie there serenely asleep. But, if the body is disfigured, then it's probably unwise to let somebody [view] who is not, as it were, used to it. (Coroner, 1991)

Getting access to the remains of a severely damaged body can be difficult for relatives, especially if the next of kin are female (women are often not viewed as being strong enough to cope with the sight of broken bodies). Our representation of the bad death lies at the heart of such prohibitions.

Summary

To summarize, we currently have multiple representations of what makes a death 'good' or 'bad'. These representations are formed by our cultural heritage, our biographies, our psychological states and the context of the death under consideration. Given the wide range of social representations currently in use, it seems particularly important that medical practitioners and deathwork professionals realize that bereaved people may not share their representation of what makes a death good.

References

Ariès, P. (1987) *The Hour of our Death*. Harmondsworth: Penguin.
Beier, L. (1989) 'The Good Death in Seventeeth Century Britain', in R. Houlbrooke (ed.), *Death, Ritual and Bereavement*. London: Routledge.
Bloch, M. and Parry, J. (eds) (1982) *Death and the Regeneration of Life*. Cambridge: Cambridge University Press.

Bradbury, M.A.I. (1999) *Representations of Death: A Social Psychological Perspective.* London: Routledge.

Durkheim, E. (1952) *Suicide: A Study in Sociology.* London: Routledge & Kegan Paul.

Houlbrooke, R. (ed.) (1989) *Death, Ritual and Bereavement.* London: Routledge.

Middleton, J. (1982) 'Lugbara Death', in M. Bloch and J. Parry (eds), *Death and the Regeneration of Life.* Cambridge: Cambridge University Press.

10

Little Henry; or, God will take care of me

H.M. Benson

Did you ever, dear children, think of a time coming when your dear father or mother might be taken from you? Oh, no, you are ready to say, I never thought of such a dreadful thing. I am sure I should break my heart if my own dear mother or father were to die. Well, so little Henry once thought, and so he said, but alas! he did lose his kind father, and although he was only seven years of age, he knew what sorrow was then. It was a mournful day for Henry, when he walked by the side of his poor weeping mother, and with her followed the remains of his father to the grave. 'I shall never see him any more' he thought within himself. 'He will never again call me his own little Henry', and then his tears flowed fast, and he held his mother's hand tighter, as if he were fearful of losing her also.

Poor child! when he returned home the house seemed so desolate, and he went sorrowfully up to his little bedroom, and kneeling down quite alone, he sobbed as if his heart would break; shortly, however, he brushed off the tears and began to pray. 'Lord, look upon me now,' he said, 'and be my Father. Help me to love my mother and do every thing I can for her.'

He then rose, more comforted, and on going down stairs was met by his mother, and in a moment was in her arms. She did not speak, but Henry felt the big tears on her cheek, and knew *why* she wept; so he looked up into her face and said, 'Mother dear, you have *me* still. Father is gone to heaven. He is happy there. God is *my* father now. He will take care of me. I am your own little Harry, and I will *try* to be good. I shall soon grow up to be a man, and then, mother dear, nobody shall hurt you.'

'You are indeed my own good little boy,' replied his mothers, 'and I bless God that you are left to me; so we will try to dry up our tears, knowing that God *will* take care of us.'

And now, dear children, you will wish to know how poor little Henry got on. On the Sunday following his father's funeral, he went as usual to the Sabbath school, but he could hardly hold up his head, his heart was so sad. His kind teacher was deeply grieved, and, drawing him towards her, while she gently took his hand, said, 'My poor child, look up. Your heavenly father will never leave nor forsake you. You must now try to comfort your mother all in your power. Remember, dear, God is a "father to the fatherless".'

From *The Child's Own Magazine for 1856*, London: The Sunday School Union, pp. 156–9.

Many other tender and encouraging words his teacher added, so that little Henry was cheered; and when school was over, he hastened home to tell all the things his teacher had been saying. It was a lovely Sabbath morning. The air was so fresh, the little birds were singing, and the sun shone so sweetly, making every thing in nature look gay. Henry, however, did not observe the general gladness of creation, he hurried down the lane leading to his home, and, running in, exclaimed, 'Oh, mother dear, I am sure now that God will make us happy again. Teacher says God will never leave nor forsake us, and I am sure God would not say so if He did not mean it. Mother, God is a father to the fatherless, so do not weep any more, for I am sure I believe God, and I want *you* to believe just as I do.'

The mother raised her little boy on her knees, and while she kissed him, silently praised God who had given her such a comforter in her child, at the same time resolving that however poor and desolate she might be, her hope and trust should ever be in God.

Well, time went on, and Henry grew fast. When he was fourteen years of age, he had to go far away from his mother, but still God was with him, taking care of him, and preserving him from evil. When he became a man, God prospered him in the world, and then, like a dutiful son, he did not forget his mother, who had during his early days been obliged to work hard in order to maintain him. Every year he sent her home a sum of money which enabled her to have many comforts in her declining days; and what was better, there always came with it a sweet pious letter, making the widow's heart to sing for joy.

Now, dear children, this is a true story, and I want you to remember it, because the same God that took care of little Henry can and will take care of you. But remember, that Henry asked God in prayer to do so, and God heard and answered him, because he asked in faith, that is, he *believed* God was able to do it. And then he asked in the name of Jesus Christ, through whom alone little children must expect to be heard. Henry too was in *earnest* when he prayed. Children are often thinking of other things when they kneel down to pray. Now this is nothing else than mocking God, because He *looks* into children's hearts, and knows whether they really mean what they are saying or not. You must, dear children, be in earnest about every thing, *especially* in prayer; and then, if it should please God to remove from you by death, your dear parents or friends, you will be able, like little Henry, to go and ask *earnestly* that you may be taken care of by your Father who is in heaven, who has promised never to leave, never to forsake you. And now, in bidding you farewell, I will leave with you a sweet text, which you can learn for the next Sabbath school lesson. You will find it in St. John's Gospel, 16th chapter, 23rd verse: 'Whatsoever ye shall ask the Father in my name, he will give it you.'

11

Death be not proud

John Donne

Death be not proud, though some have called thee
Mighty and dreadfull, for, thou art not soe,
For, those, whom thou think'st, thou dost overthrow,
Die not, poore death, nor yet canst thou kill mee;
From rest and sleepe, which but thy pictures bee,
Much pleasure, then from thee, much more must flow,
And soonest our best men with thee doe goe,
Rest of their bones, and soules deliverie.
Thou art slave to Fate, chance, kings, and desperate men,
And dost with poyson, warre, and sicknesse dwell,
And poppie, or charmes can make us sleepe as well,
And better than thy stroake; why swell'st thou then?
One short sleepe past, wee wake eternally,
And death shall be no more, Death thou shalt die.

From *Complete Poetry and Selected Prose of John Donne*, ed. J. Hayward, London: Nonesuch Press, 1978.

12

Aubade

Philip Larkin

I work all day, and get half-drunk at night.
Waking at four to soundless dark, I stare.
In time the curtain-edges will grow light.
Till then I see what's really always there:
Unresting death, a whole day nearer now,
Making all thought impossible but how
And where and when I shall myself die.
Arid interrogation: yet the dread
Of dying, and being dead,
Flashes afresh to hold and horrify.

The mind blanks at the glare. Not in remorse
– The good not done, the love not given, time
Torn off unused – nor wretchedly because
An only life can take so long to climb
Clear of its wrong beginnings, and may never;
But at the total emptiness for ever,
The sure extinction that we travel to
And shall be lost in always. Not to be here,
Not to be anywhere,
And soon; nothing more terrible, nothing more true.

This is a special way of being afraid
No trick dispels. Religion used to try,
That vast moth-eaten musical brocade
Created to pretend we never die,
And specious stuff that says *No rational being
Can fear a thing it will not feel*, not seeing
That this is what we fear – no sight, no sound,
No touch or taste or smell, nothing to think with,
Nothing to love or link with,
The anaesthetic from which none come round.

From *Times Literary Supplement*, 29 November 1977.

And so it stays just on the edge of vision,
A small unfocused blur, a standing chill
That slows each impulse down to indecision.
Most things may never happen: this one will,
And realization of it rages out
In furnace-fear when we are caught without
People or drink. Courage is no good:
It means not scaring others. Being brave
Lets no one off the grave.
Death is no different whined at than withstood.

Slowly light strengthens, and the room takes shape.
It stands plain as a wardrobe, what we know,
Have always known, know that we can't escape,
Yet can't accept. One side will have to go.
Meanwhile telephones crouch, getting ready to ring
In locked-up officers, and all the uncaring
Intricate rented world begins to rouse.
The sky is white as clay, with no sun.
Work has to be done.
Postmen like doctors go from house to house.

13

Do not go gentle into that good night

Dylan Thomas

Do not go gentle into that good night,
Old age should burn and rave at close of day;
Rage, rage against the dying of the light.

Though wise men at their end know dark is right,
Because their words had forked no lightning they
Do not go gentle into that good night.

Good men, the last wave by, crying how bright
Their frail deeds might have danced in a green bay,
Rage, rage against the dying of the light.

Wild men who caught and sang the sun in flight,
And learn, too late, they grieved it on its way,
Do not go gentle into that good night.

Grave men, near death, who see with blinding sight
Blind eyes could blaze like meteors and be gay,
Rage, rage against the dying of the light.

And you, my father, there on the sad height,
Curse, bless, me now with your fierce tears, I pray.
Do not go gentle into that good nigh.
Rage, rage against the dying of the light.

From *The Collected Poems*, New York: New Directions Publishing Corporation.

14

The Prophet

Kahlil Gibran

Then Almitra spoke, saying, We would ask now of Death.
And he said:

You would know the secret of death.

But how shall you find it unless you seek it in the heart of life?

The owl whose night-bound eyes are blind unto the day cannot unveil the mystery of light.

If you would indeed behold the spirit of death, open your heart wide unto the body of life.

For life and death are one, even as the river and the sea are one.

In the depth of your hopes and desires lies your silent knowledge of the beyond;

And like seeds dreaming beneath the snow your heart dreams of spring.

Trust the dreams, for in them is hidden the gate to eternity.

Your fear of death is but the trembling of the shepherd when he stands before the king whose hand is to be laid upon him in honour.

Is the shepherd not joyful beneath his trembling, that he shall wear the mark of the king?

Yet is he not more mindful of his trembling?

For what is it to die but to stand naked in the wind and to melt in the sun?

And what is it to cease breathing but to free the breath from its restless tides, that it may rise and expand and seek God unencumbered?

Only when you drink from the river of silence shall you indeed sing.

And when you have reached the mountain top, then you shall begin to climb.

And when the earth shall claim your limbs, then shall you truly dance.

Extract from *The Prophet*, London: Heinemann, 1979. pp. 93–4.

15

Doctor's mask on pain

Jane Martin

On 1 August 1988, with eagerness and some trepidation, I began my first 'house job' as a junior doctor, at a district general hospital in the north of England. On 12 September, in a similar hospital some 250 miles to the south, my father died.

I was on call the day I heard he had been admitted with extensive secondary cancer and was not expected to live much longer. It was a busy night: at one point four patients with acute myocardial infarction (heart attack) arrived almost simultaneously on the geriatric ward where I was working. We were all up all night. At around 4 a.m. I grabbed a cup of coffee in the ward kitchen with the husband of one of my patients. He mentioned that his daughter had begun travelling through the night from her home on the south coast: she had set aside her own life and its commitments to be with her parents in their time of crisis. I nodded reassuringly through the haze of exhaustion, and wondered why the world had gone suddenly mad.

I left the following day, after twenty-four hours' continuous duty and some hastily snatched sleep and arrived in time to be with my mother and father during the last three days of his life. He was a gaunt skeleton: my mother had hidden from me the true extent of his illness, in order not to impose further stress on me during my first few weeks as a doctor, in order to allow me to care for others while others cared for my dad.

We kept vigil day and night. My mother was alone with him at the moment of his death, which was right and good. I have seen how easy it is to die but for her it was the first encounter, and she was startled and relieved; how much harder was all the suffering than the leaving of it.

Afterwards I stayed with my mother for nearly two weeks, arranging my father's affairs, the funeral, trying to help her through those first bewildering days. She is 72 and has known no other husband or lover.

When I returned to work, I was informed that part of my 'compassionate leave' would be deducted from my annual holiday entitlement. It was difficult to comprehend the mentality that could conceive of the nightmare through which I had just lived as being interchangeable with a *holiday*. With this dawned the realization that nobody at work was going to acknowledge my desperate need for time to reflect, to grieve for my father in a way which had not been possible when my role had, of necessity, been that of supporting my mother.

From *The Guardian*, 'First Person', 5 April 1989.

In re-donning the white coat, it seemed, I had covered up my claim to be a human being with the capacity to be hurt and the right to crawl away and lick my wounds. I felt confused by all the role-swapping and began to re-evaluate my behaviour as a doctor.

The care my father was given by nursing staff had been superb, and their attitude to the grieving relatives almost as unblemished, except for the unbelievable crassness of one or two individuals. My identity was challenged one night by a new nurse. Suddenly realizing, she laughed: 'Oh, you're with the man dying in room seven. That's all right then.' When the strain was really beginning to tell, I had turned in anguish to a student nurse and whispered: 'It's all the waiting that's so terrible.' 'Yes,' she said, 'it must get really boring.'

Could *I* ever be as unthinkingly cruel to a patient or their relatives? Surely not. Really? Not after a weekend on call, fifty-six hours of continuous duty when I'm so tired I can scarcely remember my own name?

The stereotype of the doctor must be called into question if we are not to be dehumanized by the job. Doctors cannot pretend to stand back in scientific detachment from human suffering. Most of us work with people, not test-tubes, and under our white coats we suffer too. I may grieve for my father, but only in my own time, what precious little there is of that. For my patients, I must not grieve, although, were I a nurse, a few tears would be permissible.

It would benefit both our own emotional health and that of our patients if doctors could refashion this outmoded macho image of invulnerability. I need the space to work through my grief and put it behind me. How wonderful it would be to be able to speak of death with colleagues in terms other than those of 'turning up the toes' or any of the other euphemisms medics use to shield themselves from the reality. Instead I work my horrendous hours, storing up the pain until it erupts in a flood of exhausted irritability when I come off duty.

Last week I was called to see a patient who had begun to deteriorate rapidly. It had already been decided that nothing more could be done to save him. I confirmed that he was, indeed, dying and the staff nurse hurried away to telephone his wife, adding: 'It's all right. We'll stay with him.' My role as the doctor was now superfluous.

Instead of going off to fill in forms and order investigations, I chose to sit with the man for the half-hour it took him to die. His wife arrived an hour later and I broke the sad news. Her first words were: 'Oh! He couldn't even wait for me!' But I was then able to describe to her exactly how he had died: peacefully, in no pain, holding my hand. It seemed to bring her comfort and some solace.

But it wasn't really doing my job.

16

Spiritual care of dying people

Alyson Peberdy

Current approaches to caring for dying people acknowledge the need to pay attention to the person as a whole, not just the physical symptoms. An English Nursing Board Course, for example, ambitiously speaks of aiming to produce a 'competent practitioner in all aspects of care, one who recognizes the total needs of the dying patient and the family' (END 931, Sir Michael Sobell House, Churchill Hospital, Oxford). It goes on to describe these needs as physical, psychological, social and spiritual. Whilst most of us have a clear picture of what is meant by the first three terms, there is generally much less certainty about the meaning of the word 'spiritual' and of how it relates to others. During recent years a very wide-ranging understanding of spiritual care has become prominent in nursing theory, if not always in practice, and this chapter explores some aspects of this development.

It is sometimes assumed that spiritual care is simply the province of religion in general and the clergy in particular. In this view the role of carers is primarily one of contacting the appropriate religious representative, such as a priest or imam, or ensuring that family and friends are enabled to perform the necessary rituals before and immediately after death. Carers who are themselves believers may perhaps want to offer more direct support, though some clergy want to be entirely in control of religious care. One hospice chaplain, for instance, takes the view that it is inappropriate 'for a nurse to assess and attempt to meet effectively the spiritual/religious needs of a patient or family' (Hoy, 1983: 173). Others, however, work with a much broader understanding of spirituality and of whose role it is to respond to spiritual concerns. Len Lunn, chaplain at St Christopher's Hospice, argues strongly for an inter-disciplinary and personal approach.

> We all know the big 'why' questions are unanswerable in terms of definitive answers but our combined inter-disciplinary response can, and often does, bring meaning into inexplicable suffering . . . Whatever disciplines we represent it is 'me, this person' that is the vital answer and the authentic response while our words are only secondary. (Lunn, 1990: 87, 91)

The search for meaning, love, self-worth and hope

In our society the terms spiritual and religious are not necessarily synonymous. This becomes obvious when we consider how for many people religion either has negative associations or feels irrelevant. Yet few have an entirely materialistic view of themselves and others. People commonly say 'I am not religious', they do not say 'I am not spiritual' (Working Party . . ., 1991: 152). Without giving it formal religious expression there is a spiritual dimension to their living and dying. In the face of death questions about the meaning and purpose of life may surface with considerable intensity especially in people who have not considered such questions before

Perhaps it may help to see spirituality as a search for meaning, and religion as a particular expression of that (one that usually involves God-language). Along these lines Peter Speck suggests that spirituality may be understood as '[a] search for *existential* meaning within a life experience, with reference to a power other than the self, which may not necessarily be called "God"' (Speck, 1998: 22). The concept of spirituality is then much broader than religion since both the atheist and the religious person are concerned with describing the world we experience and the purpose of life (Berggren-Thomas and Griggs, 1995).

Much nursing or hospice literature that discusses spirituality focuses on the concept of a search for meaning. An American community liaison nurse, for instance, writes that spiritual care 'entails a putting together of the broken pieces, the meaningless pieces. It involves a mending, a healing and a search for new meaning and purpose that has always been the challenge of what it means to be human' (Granstom, 1985: 39). 'Spiritual distress', writes Burnard, 'is the result of total inability to invest life with meaning' (1987: 377).

Sometimes this search for meaning is expressed in the form of questions about the cause or purpose of the suffering the dying person is experiencing, especially when death seems premature. 'What have I done to deserve this?' 'Why now?' The question of whether there is an existence beyond death may also be put into words. 'What happens after death?' 'Will I meet loved ones again?' For people from religious traditions involving harsh ideas of judgement after death considerable anxiety may underlie their thoughts about the possibility of an afterlife.

Although the search for meaning forms a major element in the way in which spiritual need tends to be understood in the literature, also included is the need for identity and relatedness, which is sometimes expressed in terms of the need to feel loved or accepted, and of having a sense of self-worth. This longing for a sense of being connected with and affirmed by others is understood by many to be a core spiritual need (Dombeck, 1998). Questions like 'what have I done to deserve this?' or 'am I being punished for something?' may be the questions of people wanting help with knowing themselves to be accepted (Lunn, 1990). Even amongst people with no formal religious beliefs there may arise a need for reassurance about their acceptability to God.

A further facet of the need for identity and relatedness may be seen in people facing death in a country other than the one that has shaped their sense of who they are. Expressions of a profound longing for reconnection with 'home' clearly have a spiritual dimension as the following extract from an interview with an African-Caribbean man with lung cancer demon-strates:

> And I wouldn't like to die over here. No. And I told my wife if I dead over 'ere she must try her best to get some 'elp and send me 'ome . . . I would be 'appy. My spirit would be free . . . If I die over 'ere my spirit wouldn't be free. That's what I wish for and pray to God not to let me die 'ere. I want to go 'ome and bury in our land, and me spirit free . . . can get up and fly like a bird and see the Mango tree, the 'happle' tree, the rivers, the sea. I've got nothing to see over 'ere. (Y. Gunaratnam, n.d.)

McCavery identifies four spiritual needs in acute illness: meaning, love, self-worth and hope (1985: 131). It is important to clarify the meaning of the word hope in this context. In clinical usage it tends to be used in the narrow sense of survival or recovery, but has a much wider use in everyday language. It is the second and wider meaning which is crucial to spiritual care. In the face of death the desire for life that fuelled a person's hope for recovery *may* become transformed into a wider sense of hope which con-tinues to discover and affirm creative possibilities despite the prospect of death. According to Bruce Rumbold (1986) this happens when a person: (a) has a realistic knowledge of the situation; (b) focuses attention on the quality of life and is able to look beyond their immediate situation; (c) is able to live in the moment; and (d) affirms the value of life even in the face of their own death.

Providing spiritual care

In practice what does it mean to recognize and try to meet the spiritual needs of a dying person? This question seems easiest to answer where a person definitely identifies with a faith community within which there will be a body of knowledge and experience to draw upon. For example, within the Christian tradition the story of the crucifixion and resurrection of Jesus may help give a dying believer a sense of purpose and future, and rites of confession and absolution may help restore a sense of right relationship. Amongst Hindus the same sense of right relationship may be arrived at through the presence of the wider family carrying out the rituals that precede and surround death. Similar resources are to be found throughout the various religious traditions. But what of people who have found the tradition they know best unhelpful, harshly judgemental or plain irrelevant in their lives? And what of those who have never had any real connection with a religion? What might spiritual care mean in relation to them?

Nursing literature in the United States has attempted to provide guide-lines to help carers gain some understanding of the perspective and needs of those dying people with whom they are not already familiar. So, for example, nurses have been advised to develop a spiritual history of their patients which involves asking four main questions (Stoll, 1979: 1574 7).

What is the person's concept of God or duty? What is the person's source of hope or strength? What is the significance of religious practice or rituals to this person? What is the person's perceived relationship between spiritual beliefs and his/her state of health? The aim here is to identify areas of spiritual need and to plan appropriate support.

Whilst questioning may well be a good idea, an insensitive approach could do more harm than good. Any idea that spiritual needs can be identified, classified, recorded and responded to in much the same way as bowel dysfunction is obviously highly problematic and rejected by most people. Yet the notion that spiritual care can be delivered from active carer to passive patient tends to be present even in more nuanced and softer versions of what might be called an interventionist model of spiritual care. A British nurse researching the area of spiritual care argues that the extent to which patients are able to find, experience or anticipate meaning is dependant on what she calls the skills of knowing, hoping and trusting, and that these can be *taught* by nurses as a central part of spiritual care (Simsen, 1988: 41–2). But if we look at our own experience of life we find that hope and trust are not so much skills that can be taught as qualities that emerge out of, and are fostered by, certain kinds of relationship in which we have been valued, where life has felt trustworthy and reality can be faced.

The process by which hope may emerge in the face of the prospect of one's own death is complex but not random. Extending a model put forward by Avery Weisman, a psychiatrist interested in the defences used by dying people to protect themselves from the knowledge of their imminent death, Bruce Rumbold suggests that there is a recognizable shape or pattern to the development of hope. People who are ill normally entertain the hope for recovery. This is usually shared by patient, carers and family who together tend to want to maintain this hope by limiting information that might challenge it. But if the possibility of dying cannot be faced and explored a hope which goes beyond insistence upon recovery cannot emerge.

When the possibility of death is acknowledged a person becomes free to choose to hope for death rather than life at any price, to hope for a certain kind of death and for certain circumstances to prevail. Often family and hospital staff fail to allow these hopes to be articulated or may hear them as expressions of despair, themselves insisting on an unrealistic hope for recovery. But it is only through acknowledging the imminence of death that it becomes possible for a person to look back over his or her life to affirm its value, take a wider perspective and allow a wider sense of hope and integration to emerge. The content of such hope may or may not be linked to an established system of belief (Rumbold, 1986: 64–6).

This understanding of the way in which hope develops suggests that spiritual care is the concern of all carers and it is perhaps as a force for integration that spiritual care may best be understood. 'The spiritual dimension transcends and holds together the physical, psychological and social dimensions. The spiritual integrates the other three dimensions into an "I"' (Working Party . . ., 1991: 152). Such integration will not be fostered where spiritual care is considered as simply another aspect of care alongside physical, social and psychological care. Attempts to classify, clarify, evaluate and categorize spiritual need and create interventionist spiritual care plans which are separate from and parallel to other care plans are likely to increase rather than reverse the disintegrating impact of suffering.

Hospital chaplain Janet Mayer concluded an extensive review of the nursing literature with the suggestion that spiritual care can best be seen as a quality pervading care as a whole. It is something we all give when we are fully attentive to another; something we all receive when someone gives us that same full attention. A nurse who expertly dresses a patient's wound while engaged in conversation with a colleague about her holidays is caring for the wound but not the person. The manner in which the nurse carries out her nursing tasks and relates to both dying people and other members of staff provides a vital basis to the spirituality of the dying person's experience. A nurse whose touch is gentle and whose observations are perceptive not only reduces physical pain but also provides evidence of a sensitivity on which a trusting relationship can be formed (Mayer, 1989).

Conversely, a nurse who is too busy to sit with a lonely or anxious patient will further reduce that's person's self-esteem. When asked what he most looked for in those caring for him, a patient replied 'or someone to look as if they are trying to understand me'. He did not ask for success, but only that someone should care enough to try.

In an interview conducted for the Death and Dying Course, Edith Campbell, a lay chaplain, describes this kind of active listening as being like a tour guide accompanying the person who is going through the journey (of dying), travelling in unknown territory along the road together. The fact that the professional is walking with the person gives them the courage to explore further to see what they'll find.

> What the person needs from the person accompanying is not to be told what to look at and having things explained to them, but rather someone who will clear the way so that the person on the journey is able to tell them what they see; is able to point out to them the fullness and the strangeness and the beauty of the territory they are going through. It takes mutual co-operation to allow that to happen. You need a relationship of trust and shared humanity. At the bottom line that's what's needed. The understanding that this person is here as a full human being with me in my full humanity and we are struggling in the midst of this to make sense of what we are going through.

The ability to listen and encourage is clearly important, but are there any guidelines to help nurses and carers know what they are listening out for? Dombeck suggests that whilst information about a patient's religious resources and concerns may be gathered mainly by direct questioning, information about a patient's spiritual framework is best obtained by listening carefully to their stories and encouraging them to articulate their concerns. In listening to these stories the listener is listening for information about the person's beliefs and values, and their connections with other humans, with a creator or with other cosmic realities . . . What does this person believe in? Is what he or she values helping or crippling him or her? What gives strength, comfort or hope? . . . Assessing the spiritual connections involves understanding what is central to a person's life . . . The sense of spiritual connectedness describes the deepest and most central experiences of persons. (Dombeck, 1998: 370–1)

In such listening sensitivity to both depth and metaphor is crucial. 'The vocabulary of the spirit belongs to a language of depth, and meaning unfolds in the context of relationship, rather than presenting itself for dispassionate analysis' (Stanworth, 1997: 20). The importance of symbolism is also stressed by Jane Millard, a chaplain in a hospice for people with HIV and AIDS.

> I work very strongly on symbols, bearing in mind that a lot of people who come within my care are not Christian, but everyone . . . is a spirtual being . . . some gay men who have had no children they have a great sorrow, they've got nothing to leave, and so we talk about planting seeds, growing things, painting, making music, being creative, and even something like reminding them of a good time you've had with them, or a good time they've had with their friends. These things are never lost. They stay on. They live on. (from a recorded interview)

But the question has to be asked, how far do nurses have the confidence, ability and freedom to listen and respond with this kind of sensitivity and depth? A large-scale survey of staff nurses and charge nurses working in 12 Health Boards in Scotland of perceptions of spiritual need and spiritual care showed that whilst almost 94 per cent of nurses in the sample considered it a shared responsibility to respond to patients' spiritual needs, over half preferred to refer them to others. In-depth interviews offer some clues as to why this might be. Factors include difficulties in communication and nurses' insensitivity to patients' cues as well as structural factors such as shortage of time and staffing levels (Ross, 1997). In addition it seems likely that a nurse or carer's spiritual maturity will directly affect their willingness and ability to engage with the spiritual needs of others (Olsen, 1997).

Ross suggests that nurses are best able to respond to patients' spiritual needs when they themselves have:

- an awareness of the spiritual dimension of their own lives
- a personal search for meaning
- a personal experience of crisis
- a perception of spiritual care as part of their role
- a sensitive/perceptive nature. (Ross, 1997: 41)

Assessment and audit of spiritual care

If spiritual care is as wide-ranging as has here been argued is it open to evaluation and assessment? Is it possible to identify some basic standards of care and develop appropriate audit tools without, at the same time, adopting a managerial mentality concerned to tidy away the awfulness and tragedy of death? Some commentators suspect it is not (for instance Bradshaw, 1996; Walter, 1997).

During the 1990s a small group of hospice chaplains and a medical director were invited by the Trent Hospice Audit Group to design a questionnaire which could be used to assess spiritual well-being. The stated aim of their work was to provide a means of assessment that would be applicable to patients of any or no faith and that would produce the same results whether performed by a person of any or no faith. The definition of spirituality they gave to both patients and nursing staff was broad: 'the lived experience that gives meaning to life and death'. Patients found this definition easy to understand (though nursing staff tended to restrict their interpretation to religious aspects).

Their assessment tool was concerned to allow sequential comparison that would indicate whether there had been any change in spiritual well-being. It sought to identify both spiritual well-being and spiritual distress and involved the following five categories:

A   Spiritual matters are the most important thing in life and give immense support
B   I am interested in the meaning of life and spiritual matters and take comfort from this
C   I am comfortable with my own philosophy and meaning of life, and spiritual matters do not affect me one way or another
D   Spiritual considerations considerably interfere with my life
E   I feel so troubled by spiritual matters that they are totally taking over my life

The group conclude

> [we] have some doubts regarding the usefulness of the scale purporting to indicate progressive improvement or otherwise in a patient's spiritual status . . . The meaning of the improvement may be very different to that in the assessment of other symptoms . . . [but] it would be wrong to infer that spiritual assessment . . . is of no value or unduly difficult. (Catterall et al., 1998: 168)

The group went on to develop a statement of standards of spiritual care explicitly rooted in the view that 'The spiritual part of life is part of a person's development, a journey rather then something you have more or less of' (1998: 166). They also developed a related patient/carer questionnaire as an audit tool. Such an attempt to marry a very broad definition of spirituality with the culture of audit and cost-effectiveness is not unique (see, for instance, Keighly, 1997).

The future

How far nursing approaches will in practice be able to accommodate and work with the journeying concept of spiritual care is an open question. The answer will depend in part on structural and organizational factors. Indeed it will be crucial to remember that spiritual care is not just a matter of relationships between individuals: the spirituality of institutions also needs to be considered. This involves thinking about a hospital or hospice's general atmosphere, rules and even furnishings and asking what impact they may have on a dying person. Even the fact of having china cups rather than disposable mugs may well influence people's ability to discover meaning and value in their lives and in the world in general. So too will the morale of carers. In this respect the employment conditions of nurses and carers and the amount of support and recognition given to informal carers are matters of profound spiritual significance.

References

Berggren-Thomas, P. and Griggs, M.J. (1995) 'Spirituality in ageing: spiritual need or spiritual journey?', *Journal of Gerentolical Nursing*, 21 (3): 5–10.

Burnard, P. (1987) 'Spiritual distress and the nursing response: theoretical considerations and counselling skills', *Journal of Advanced Nursing*, 12: 377–82.

Bradshaw, A. (1996) 'The Spiritual Dimension of Hospice: the secularization of an ideal', *Social Science & Medicine*, 43 (3): 409–19.

Catterall, R.A., Cox, M., Greet, B., Sankey, J. and Griffiths, G. (1998) 'The Assessment and Audit of Spiritual Care', *International Journal of Palliative Nursing*, 4 (4): 162–8.

Dombeck, M. (1998) 'Spiritual and pastoral dimensions of care', *Journal of Interprofessional Care*, 12 (4): 361–72.

Granstom, S. (1985) 'Spiritual care for oncology patients', *Topics in Clinical Nursing*, April: 39–45.

Gunaratnam, Y. (n.d.) From written communication to the Death and Dying Course Team.

Hoy, T. (1983) 'Hospice chaplaincy in the caregiving team', in C. Corr and D. Corr (eds), *Hospice Care Principles and Practice*. London: Faber & Faber. pp. 177–96.

Keighly, T. (1997) 'Organisational structures and personal spiritual beliefs', *International Journal of Palliative Nursing*, 3 (1): 47–51.

Lunn, L. (1990) 'Having no answer', in C. Saunders (ed.), *Hospice and Palliative Care*. London: Edward Arnold. Chap. 11.

McCavery, R. (1985) 'Spiritual care in acute illness', in F. McGilloway and P. Myco (eds), *Nursing and Spiritual Care*. New York: Harper & Row. pp. 129–42.

Mayer, J. (1989) 'Wholly responsible for a part or partly responsible for a whole? An evaluation of the nursing concept of spiritual care'. Unpublished paper.

Olsen, J. (1997) *Healing the Dying*. New York: Delmar.

Ross, L. (1997) 'The nurse's role in assessing and responding to patients' spiritual needs', *International Journal of Palliative Nursing*, 3 (1): 37–42.

Rumbold, B. (1986) *Helplessness and Hope*. London: Routledge.

Simsen, B. (1988) 'The spiritual dimension', *Nursing Times*, 26 November: 41–2.

Speck, P. (1998) 'The meaning of spirituality in illness', in M. Cobb and V. Renshaw (eds), *The Spiritual Challenge of Health Care*. Edinburgh: Churchill Livingstone. pp. 21–33.

Stanworth, R. (1997) 'Spirituality, language and depth of reality', *International Journal of Palliative Nursing*, 3 (1): 19–22.

Stoll, R. (1979) 'Guidelines for spiritual assessment', *American Journal of Nursing*, September: 1574–5.

Walter, T. (1997) 'The ideology and organization of spiritual care; three approaches', *Palliative Medicine*, 11: 21–30.

Working Party on the Impact of Hospice Experience in the Church's Ministry of Healing (1991) *Mud and Stars*. Oxford: Sobell Publications.

17

Death and the meaning of life

Leo Tolstoy

In my writings I advocated, what to me was the only truth, that it was necessary to live in such a way as to derive the greatest comfort for oneself and one's family.

Thus I proceeded to live, but five years ago something very strange began to happen to me: I was overcome by minutes at first of perplexity and then of an arrest of life, as though I did not know how to live or what to do, and I lost myself and was dejected. But that passed, and I continued to live as before. Then those minutes of perplexity were repeated oftener and oftener, and always in one and the same form. These arrests of life found their expression in ever the same questions: 'Why? Well, and then?' [. . .]

The questions seemed to be so foolish, simple, and childish. But the moment I touched them and tried to solve them, I became convinced, in the first place, that they were not childish and foolish, but very important and profound questions in life, and, in the second, that, no matter how much I might try, I should not be able to answer them. Before attending to my Samára estate, to my son's education, or to the writing of a book, I ought to know why I should do that. So long as I did not know why, I could not do anything, I could not live. Amidst my thoughts of farming, which interested me very much during that time, there would suddenly pass through my head a question like this: 'All right, you are going to have six thousand desyatínas of land in the Government of Samára, and three hundred horses, – and then?' And I completely lost my senses and did not know what to think farther. Or, when I thought of the education of my children, I said to myself: 'Why?' Or, reflecting on the manner in which the masses might obtain their welfare, I suddenly said to myself: 'What is that to me?' Or, thinking of the fame which my works would get me, I said to myself: 'All right, you will be more famous than Gógol, Púshkin, Shakespeare, Molière, and all the writers in the world, – what of it?' And I was absolutely unable to make any reply. The questions were not waiting, and I had to answer them at once; if I did not answer them, I could not live.

I felt that what I was standing on had given way, that I had no foundation to stand on, that that which I lived by no longer existed, and that I had nothing to live by.

From *A Confession*, trans. Leo Wiener, New York: Thomas Y. Crowell & Co., 1899 (abridged).

My life came to a standstill. I could breathe, eat, drink and sleep, and could not help breathing, eating, drinking and sleeping; but there was no life, because there were no desires the gratification of which I might find reasonable. If I wished for anything, I knew in advance that, whether I gratified my desire or not, nothing would come of it. If a fairy had come and had offered to carry out my wish, I should not have known what to say. If in moments of intoxication I had, not wishes, but habits of former desires, I knew in sober moments that that was a deception, that there was nothing to wish for. I could not even wish to find out the truth, because I guessed what it consisted in. The truth was that life was meaningless. It was as though I had just been living and walking along, and had come to an abyss, where I saw clearly that there was nothing ahead but perdition. And it was impossible to stop and go back, and impossible to shut my eyes, in order that I might not see that there was nothing ahead but suffering and imminent death, – complete annihilation.

What happened to me was that I, a healthy, happy man, felt that I could not go on living, – an insurmountable force drew me on to find release from life. I cannot say that I *wanted* to kill myself.

The force which drew me away from life was stronger, fuller, more general than wishing. It was a force like the former striving after life, only in an inverse sense. I tended with all my strength away from life. The thought of suicide came as naturally to me as had come before the ideas of improving life. That thought was so seductive that I had to use cunning against myself, lest I should rashly execute it. I did not want to be in a hurry, because I wanted to use every effort to disentangle myself: if I should not succeed in disentangling myself, there would always be time for that. And at such times I, a happy man, hid a rope from myself so that I should not hang myself on a cross-beam between two safes in my room, where I was by myself in the evening, while taking off my clothes, and did not go out hunting with a gun, in order not to be tempted by any easy way of doing away with myself. I did not know myself what it was I wanted: I was afraid of life, strove to get away from it, and, at the same time, expected something from it.

All that happened with me when I was on every side surrounded by what is considered to be complete happiness. I had a good, loving and beloved wife, good children and a large estate, which grew and increased without any labour on my part. I was respected by my neighbours and friends, more than ever before, was praised by strangers, and, without any self-deception, could consider my name famous. With all that, I was not deranged or mentally unsound, – on the contrary, I was in full command of my mental and physical powers, such as I had rarely met with in people of my age: physically I could work in a field, mowing, without falling behind a peasant; mentally I could work from eight to ten hours in succession, without experiencing any consequences from the strain. And while in such condition I arrived at the conclusion that I could not live, and, fearing death, I had to use cunning against myself, in order that I might not take my life. [. . .]

The former deception of the pleasures of life [. . .] no longer deceives me. No matter how much one should say to me, 'You cannot understand the meaning of life, do not think, live!' I am unable to do so, because I have been doing it too long before. Now I cannot help seeing day and night, which run and lead me up to death. I see that alone, because that alone is the truth. Everything else is a lie. [. . .]

'My family – ' I said to myself, 'but my family, my wife and children, they are also human beings. They are in precisely the same condition that I am in: they must either live in the lie or see the terrible truth. Why should they live? Why should I love them, why guard, raise and watch them? Is it for the same despair which is in me, or for dullness of perception? Since I love them, I cannot conceal the truth from them, – every step of cognition leads them up to this truth. And the truth is death.'

'Art, poetry?' For a long time, under the influence of the success of human praise, I tried to persuade myself that that was a thing which could be done, even though death should come and destroy everything, my deeds, as well as my memory of them; but soon I came to see that that, too, was a deception. It was clear to me that art was an adornment of life, a decoy of life. But life lost all its attractiveness for me. How, then, could I entrap others? So long as I did not live my own life, and a strange life bore me on its waves; so long as I believed that life had some sense, although I was not able to express it, – the reflections of life of every description in poetry and in the arts afforded me pleasure, and I was delighted to look at life through this little mirror of art; but when I began to look for the meaning of life, when I experienced the necessity of living myself, that little mirror became either useless, superfluous and ridiculous, or painful to me. [. . .]

'Well, I know', I said to myself, 'all which science wants so persistently to know, but there is no answer to the question about the meaning of my life.' But in the speculative sphere I saw that, in spite of the fact that the aim of the knowledge was directed straight to the answer of my question, or because of that fact, there could be no other answer than what I was giving to myself: 'What is the meaning of my life?' – 'None.' Or, 'What will come of my life?' – 'Nothing.' Or, 'Why does everything which exists exist, and why do I exist?' – 'Because it exists.' [. . .]

Rational knowledge in the person of the learned and the wise denied the meaning of life, but the enormous masses of men, all humanity, recognized this meaning in an irrational knowledge. This irrational knowledge was faith, the same that I could not help but reject. That was God as one and three, the creation in six days, devils and angels, and all that which I could not accept so long as I had not lost my senses.

My situation was a terrible one. I knew that I should not find anything on the path of rational knowledge but the negation of life, and there, in faith, nothing but the negation of reason, which was still more impossible than the negation of life. From the rational knowledge it followed that life was an evil and men knew it, – it depended on men whether they should cease living, and yet they lived and continued to live, and I myself lived, though I had known long ago that life was meaningless and an evil. From faith it followed that, in order to understand life, I must renounce reason, for which alone a meaning was needed.

PART 2

CARING FOR DYING PEOPLE

Introduction

Palliative medicine or palliative care are the labels given to the modern package of skills, procedures and practices that have been sponsored and refined mainly within the hospice movement. Its application is not – and should not be – restricted to people who are dying. In practice, however, its combination of pain relief and the reduction of fear and distress tends to be reserved for those at the terminal stage of illness. Much attention is given to the physical treatments which enable physicians to control pain and disturbing symptoms. But these are only a small, if vitally important, element of the growing repertoire of actions which can aid people to contemplate and cope positively with their imminent death. This section begins with an article written by two social scientists who have focused their research on caring for dying people in a variety of settings. Field and Addington-Hall explore the concept of specialist palliative care and consider why and how these principles might be appropriate for people dying from a variety of other illnesses. Sidell, Katz and Komaromy, look at alternative ways in which older people might be cared for, exploring the palliative care needs of dying older people. Like Field and Addington-Hall they too focus on whether certain aspects of palliative care may be appropriate for those dying of other conditions, and in this case in residential and nursing home settings.

Good palliative care is based on assessing what works in terms of relief for the individual person. For many people complementary therapies provide both physical relief and mental comfort. Dr Patrick Pietroni is well known as the founder of the Marylebone Centre Trust which combines traditional allopathic medicine with a wide range of complementary therapies. In his article he describes a number of approaches to the relief of pain and anxiety, ranging from breathing exercises and meditation to massage, aromatherapy and acupuncture. These are presented not as new in themselves, for many of them have long histories, but so as to lodge them firmly in the palliative care toolbox. We include the piece to ensure that readers are aware of these therapies, whilst recognizing that there are others which also deserve attention.

We now move on to a number of personal accounts, starting with the experience of carers and then moving on to the experience of dying people. The first first-person account is that of 'Sarah Palmer', who expresses her frustrations about the quality of care her grandmother received. Then Susan Leifer in a graphic and honest way reports what it felt like to care for her mother and in her postscript she contrasts the availability of support for those dying at home with cancer and those with other illnesses.

Three dying people then describe what they experience as physical handicaps. First Richard Were, who himself suffers from MS, lucidly illustrates some of the difficulties that he faces in looking after himself and how he has come to terms with a rather limited range of physical activities. John Diamond in the first of two *Saturday Times* columns expresses in writing what he cannot in words – what is it like not to be able to speak. Bauby, like Diamond also a journalist, not only cannot speak but cannot write, nor move at all. 'The Alphabet' graphically illustrates Bauby's determination to communicate with the outside world and like Diamond he pushes his journalistic talent to the edge despite tremendous odds.

Having looked now at what physical difficulties may hamper communication from the point of view of the dying person we consider what hampers professional health carers from interacting helpfully with dying people and their 'families of carers'. By far the greatest part of the range of measures which comprise palliative care is good and sensitive communication. So, whilst treatments and procedures have a proper place in this volume, the focus is now on how human beings relate to each other. As we saw in the first part of the book, the historical legacy of ways of dealing with the end of life and the diseases which hasten people to it has heightened guilt, fear and anguish. The iconography of death depicts constant images of the grim reaper and souls in torment on the one hand and poetic representations of the afterlife on the other. The timeless elusiveness of death and the dismaying notion of mortality have driven human interpreters over the ages to the creation of metaphysical and religious explanations which comfort some but terrify many. Against the background of this cultural heritage, most contemporary societies have developed defences which make talking openly about death when it is close at hand difficult for all concerned. Here we offer a selection of articles and accounts which provide both scientifically tested and experiential accounts of the therapeutic power of good communication.

Robert Buckman addresses communication with dying people at all stages of the illness. This extensive piece follows on many publications on this topic addressing different audiences, lay, part-professional as well as Buckman's own profession, the physicians. Although extremely long in comparison with other articles in this book, this is a condensed version of a chapter which was published in the *Oxford Textbook of Palliative Medicine*. He speaks directly to doctors, but much of what he has to say applies to all health and social care professions as well as to informal carers. He identifies a range of problems which hinder communication, those which are fostered by society, those which relate to professional socialization, and those which may be seen as individual. Arising from these characteristics he observes deep-seated fears – including emotional inadequacy, of acknowledging not knowing the answers, of the dying person's reaction and of personal inability to copy with the frailty of life. The analysis is a thoughtful melding of professional and personal experience and the bulk of the chapter is devoted to explaining strategies for improving communication with not only the dying person, but with their families as well as professional colleagues.

In another column published in the *Saturday Times*, John Diamond describes how he was told that his cancer had not been cured. He provides a sensitive rendition of the reactions of his consultant and describes his own need to harness his emotional resources for his wife and children. Communicating unwelcome information to adults is difficult enough, but engaging with dying children is a challenge with extra dimensions. Dorothy Judd integrates practitioner experience with the psychological literature on cognitive processes in children. Her writing is hallmarked with a deep personal concern for a better understanding of how to relate to terminally ill young people. Like Buckman, she provides clear guidelines for adults, both professional and lay.

Human beings, whether adult or child, are not part of an undifferentiated mass. One of the significant differences, at the macro-level, is the set of religious and cultural rules which surround the individual. These dimensions are reflected throughout the book, but in this section we examine Jewish perspectives. In her article Jeanne Samson Katz seeks to inform readers about the requirements and practices of Judaism, rather than to advocate any particular approach. In doing so she makes two distinct contributions. The first is a clear exposition of law and custom, mapping out the ways in which the separation of the sexes applies even in death. Jewish law dictates that it is forbidden for Jews to be cremated but convention dictates how the rules of mourning are interpreted. In differentiating the core elements, she provides a case study which illuminates the ways non-Jews should approach dying Jewish people – and a paradigm for working with anyone from a non-indigenous culture or religion.

This is followed by an extract from an American bestseller, *Tuesdays with Morrie*, which chronicles how Mitch Albom made sense of the dying trajectory of his beloved former professor, and particularly Morrie's strength which enabled his loved ones to rally round him. This moving account is set against ground-breaking research undertaken in the 1960s. In his book *Anguish*, Anselm Strauss describes the 'dying trajectory' of a single case study – Mrs Abel. The study carries further the celebrated research he did with Barney Glaser, which produced the concept of 'awareness contexts' in ward situations and established an empirical description of how patients continually negotiate with nurses over information about their condition. The short extract here explores what Strauss calls the temporal aspects of dying which influence the shape of the pathway (the dying trajectory) to death. It provides sociological research evidence about how staff, their expectations and regimes, prefigure the way their patients proceed towards death.

The final contributions are further first-person accounts, first from the carers, and finally from a dying person, herself a doctor. The first is from an anonymous old woman who speaks through Elizabeth Dean, a nurse in an old people's home. Its matter-of-fact description of the routines of Sunnyside Lodge tells a story of finitude in an unimaginative care situation. Simone de Beauvoir's emotionally loaded recollection is the last chapter of her book about her mother's death. In *A Very Easy Death* the reader follows Maman's last months after a fall, and all the evocative biographical reflection it generated in this distinguished writer. The last contribution is from a dying mother, Clare Vaughan, a poignant piece written once she realized that she would be denied seeing her children grow up.

18

Extending specialist palliative care to all?

David Field and Julia Addington-Hall

Introduction

Palliative care has its origin in the modern hospice movement and is concerned with the physical, psychosocial and spiritual care of patients with life threatening disease and their families, focusing on both the quality of the remaining life of the patient and on the support of the family and those close to the patient (Saunders, 1996). Initially, it focused on the care of dying cancer patients, but has more recently extended its remit to include cancer patients at an earlier stage of the disease trajectory (Ahmedzai, 1996). Nearly one-fifth (17.5%) of cancer patients in the UK now die in a hospice or specialist palliative care unit, and a further 39% die whilst in the care of a palliative home-care team or Macmillan community nurse[1] (Eve et al., 1997). The proportion of dying cancer patients who receive some care from specialist palliative care services is likely to be higher than these figures suggest as some receive care from hospital palliative care teams or attend a hospice day unit but die elsewhere. Palliative care for cancer patients has therefore extended rapidly since the inception of modern hospice care 30 years ago with the opening of St Christopher's Hospice, London, UK.

To date, palliative care has been focused almost entirely on cancer patients: in 1995 in the UK 3.3% of new referrals to inpatient services in hospices and specialist palliative care units had a non-cancer diagnosis, as did 3.7% of new referrals to home-care services (Eve et al., 1997). Since their inception, some hospices have provided care for patients with neurological conditions, particularly motor neurone disease and multiple sclerosis and more recently for patients with AIDS/HIV, initially in freestanding hospices and more recently in non-specialized units. Very few patients receiving palliative care fall outside these disease groups. However, it has been recognized since the beginning of modern hospice care that its principles may benefit patients dying from other causes (Saunders, 1978; Saunders and Baines, 1983) and the extension of palliative care beyond cancer has been advocated since at least 1980 (Wilkes, 1980). In 1992 the joint report of the Standing Medical Advisory Committee and Standing Nursing and Midwifery Advisory Committees on the principles and provision of palliative care recommended that 'all patients needing them should have access

From *Social Science and Medicine*, 1999, 48: 1271–80.

to palliative care services. Although often referred to as equating with terminal cancer care, it is important to recognize that similar services are appropriate and should be developed for patients dying from other diseases' (Standing Medical Advisory Committee and Standing Nursing and Midwifery Advisory Committee, 1992). This message has been reinforced by the 1996 NHS Executive letter on palliative care (NHS Executive, 1996). In contemporary Britain palliative care has been promoted as a right for everyone who is dying. Before attempting to assess the feasibility of this, it is first necessary to be clear about what is being suggested, as palliative care is not necessarily well understood and definitions of it vary. In the UK, the National Council for Hospices and Specialist Palliative Care Services (NCHSPCS) distinguishes between the palliative care approach and the specialist palliative care services (NCHSPCS, 1995). The palliative care approach 'aims to promote both physical and psychosocial well being. It is a vital and integral part of all clinical practice, whatever the illness or its stage, informed by knowledge and practice of palliative care principles and supported by specialist palliative care'. In contrast *specialist palliative care services* are those services with 'palliative care as their core speciality'. These 'are needed by a significant minority of people who deaths are anticipated'. Specialist palliative care services in the UK take a variety and changing range of forms, including inpatient and day hospices, Macmillan community nurses, hospice home-care teams, hospital support teams and hospice-at-home services. It is specialist palliative care services, rather than a palliative care approach, which are the focus of this article.

In this article the case for extending specialist palliative care to non-cancer patients is presented and critiqued. The article will first consider the arguments to support the case for extending specialist palliative care services beyond patients with cancer. These mainly revolve around establishing that there is indeed an unmet need for specialist palliative care services among patients with chronic, non-malignant conditions. Five potential barriers to extending specialist palliative care to these patients are then reviewed: the skill base of current specialists in palliative care, difficulties in identifying candidates for specialist palliative care, the views of potential users of these services, resource implications and vested interests in present health service arrangements.

Arguments for extending specialist palliative care services to non-cancer patients

The case of extending specialist palliative care services to chronic conditions other than cancer can be made in terms of equity and in terms of need.

Equity

Concerns about equity underpin the pressure from the British government, local health commissioners and others for specialist palliative care services to be made available to non-cancer patients (George and Sykes, 1997). However, in themselves, such concerns are likely to be insufficient grounds for effective action. For example, concerns about equity were one of the factors leading to the establishment of the British NHS in 1948 yet, despite continuing concern, inequalities in health have persisted throughout its history regardless of the political party in government. With the transformation of British society during the 1980s the 'collectivist' values upon which the NHS and the post-World War II British welfare state was based have become less central. One consequence is that arguments based upon equity are now as likely to be couched in terms of the rights and choices of individuals as they are in terms of groups or categories. Thus, the increasing emphasis upon the rights of individuals to exercise choice and control over their own dying may now have as much, or greater, persuasive power as concerns about equitable access between different groups or categories of patients. Palliative care is premised upon the aware individual exercising choice and control and upon the right, even the responsibility, of the individual to know their fate. In this view modern dying, like the rest of modern life, is about control and choice. Extending specialist palliative care services beyond cancer patients would extend such choice and control.

Need

Any discussion of whether non-cancer patients have unmet needs for specialist palliative care should first establish what problems and issues lie within their remit. The hospice movement began with a clear focus on alleviating the physical, psychological and spiritual distress associated with dying from cancer, on enabling cancer patients to continue living full lives until they died (Saunders, 1984). More recently, as indicated above, the focus has broadened to include the symptom control, psychological and (to a lesser extent) spiritual needs of cancer patients at an earlier stage of the disease trajectory, even, in some models, from diagnosis (Ahmedzai, 1996). The change in name from 'terminal' to 'palliative care' is, in part, a reflection of this shift in emphasis, which has been (and continues to be) the subject of controversy and debate within palliative care (Ahmedzai, 1993; Biswas, 1993; Field, 1994; Corner and Dunlop, 1997). Considering the question of whether specialist palliative care should be provided for non-cancer patients brings into sharp focus the question of what is palliative care and for which patients it is appropriate.

It is essential to differentiate between the earlier hospice focus on people who are dying and the more recent broader focus on holistic care throughout the disease progress proposed by WHO and others (Higginson, 1993) and to clarify which focus is being used. Patients who die suddenly from, for example, acute illness do not fall within the remit of either approach to palliative care. If what differentiates specialist palliative care from other branches of health care is simply its emphasis on and expertise in care for those who are dying then the question becomes whether patients dying from other chronic conditions, such as chronic heart failure, rheumatoid arthritis, end-stage renal disease, have unmet needs for physical, psychosocial and spiritual care. If, however, specialist palliative care has the remit of meeting the symptom control, psychological and spiritual needs of patients at *any* stage of their disease then it is less clear what might be seen as indicative of the need for specialist palliative care services. Within this broad remit, one possible model is that specialist palliative care services are seen as addressing the holistic needs of patients whilst other disciplines attend to patients' physical needs. As discussed below, such a view could cause conflict with health professionals currently providing care for non-cancer patients, not least because many of them, particularly in health care of the elderly and primary care, also aim to address patients' holistic needs.

Turning to the question of whether patients who die from non-malignant diseases have unmet needs within the remit of specialist palliative care, the available evidence is limited as the focus on cancer care has applied to research in palliative care as well as to service delivery. Nevertheless, it suggests that there is a case to be made. Several key studies which had been used to demonstrate deficiencies in terminal cancer care actually included both cancer and non-cancer patients in their sample (Hinton, 1963; Wilkes, 1984; Hockley et al., 1988; Mills et al., 1994). Other studies have demonstrated a considerable unmet need for symptom control and psychosocial support among patients who die from non-malignant disease. For example, the US SUPPORT study found that in the last three days of life two-fifths of patients across the 10 categories included (of which 3 were malignant diseases) had severe pain at least half the time, and at least a quarter had moderate or severe dysponea (Lynn et al., 1997). Two-thirds were reported by family members to have found it difficult to tolerate physical and emotional problems. Other studies have looked specifically at the needs of people dying from dementia (Volicer et al., 1994; Lloyd Williams, 1996), stroke (Addington-Hall et al., 1995, 1997), chronic obstructive airways disease (Skilbeck et al., 1997), heart disease (McCarthy et al., 1996), motor neurone disease (O'Brien et al., 1992; Barby and Leigh, 1995) and kidney failure (Cohen et al., 1995). They demonstrate considerable symptom burden, psychological distress and family anxiety.

Evidence from the Regional Study of Care for the Dying (RSCD), the largest UK study of the last year of life to date (Addington-Hall and McCarthy, 1995), demonstrates that many patients who die from heart disease or stoke need better symptom control, more psychological support and more open communication with health care professionals (Addington-Hall, 1996). Although cancer patients were more likely to be reported to have had pain in the last year of life, there was no difference in the proportion of cancer patients and patients with heart disease who had pain in the last week of life and in both heart disease and stroke, patients are more likely to have had pain for six months or more. Non-cancer patients were less likely to have died at home or (not surprisingly) in a hospice than cancer patients and were more likely to have died in a hospital or in a residential/nursing home.

The evidence that patients dying from non-malignant diseases need better care and that their needs lie within the remit of specialist palliative care, is, therefore, convincing. The evidence that patients living with progressive life-threatening non-malignant disease have unmet needs requiring specialist palliative care is less so. There is a substantial body of literature which has investigated the experiences of patients and families living with chronic diseases, both those which are life threatening and those with a more stable course (Anderson and Bury, 1988). Together with the growing literature on quality of life in these patients, this research shows that many patients and their families need, for example, better psychological support, improved communication with health professionals and more attention to the needs of informal carers. To take this as evidence that these patients require specialist palliative care would, however, ignore the fact that many are already in contact with health professionals with considerable expertise in their care, many of whom (as indicated above) already aim to adopt a holistic approach to patient care. The question of whether specialist palliative care services have anything further to bring to their care remains to be answered. The remainder of this paper is thus focused on issues involved in the expansion of specialist palliative care services to patients who die from non-malignant diseases (although, as will be demonstrated, the differentiation between patients living with and dying from these diseases is less clear than this discussion implies).

Although there is convincing evidence for unmet need for symptom control, psychological support, family care and better communication with health professionals amongst patients dying from non-malignant diseases, this does not in itself demonstrate a need for *specialist* palliative care services; the adoption of the palliative care approach to their care by existing primary health care and hospital services may be sufficient. There is currently a lack of specificity about what distinguishes patients who require specialist palliative care services from patients requiring a palliative care approach. As indicated above, the definition from the National Council of Hospices and Specialist Palliative Care Services talks about 'patients with particular severe needs', a definition which is hard to operationalize (NCHSPCS, 1995).

As a first step towards identifying which non-cancer patients may require specialist palliative care, data from the RSCD were used to match non-cancer patients with the top third of cancer patients receiving specialist palliative care services in terms of their symptom severity (Addington-Hall et al., 1998). Results showed that 17% of non-cancer patients had a pattern of symptom severity which was comparable to that of the cancer patients receiving specialist palliative care. The actual proportion of non-cancer patients who have levels of need comparable to that of cancer patients who receive specialist palliative care may well be higher as the RSCD did not include good measures of psychosocial or family need, which are known to be important indicators of need for specialist palliative care. The limited available evidence therefore strongly suggests that about a fifth of people who die from non-malignant disease have unmet needs for symptom control, psychological support, family care and open communication with health professionals, which are comparable to (although not identical to) those of cancer patients who currently receive specialist palliative care services.

However, confirming that there is a case for extending specialist palliative care services to people who die from chronic non-malignant diseases does not guarantee that this will happen. Barriers to the extension of these services to patients dying from non-malignant disease are discussed below.

Barriers to extending specialist palliative care service to non-cancer patients

There are at least five potential barriers to achieving such an extension:

- The potential lack of skills amongst specialist palliative care experts in the care of non-cancer patients.
- The difficulties of identifying candidates for specialist palliative care services.
- The lack of information on the acceptability of these services to non-cancer patients.
- The resource implications of extending specialist palliative care services.
- Vested interests in present arrangements.

Skills

It should not be presumed that having expertise in the care of dying cancer patients equips hospices or specialist palliative care teams to care equally effectively for patients dying from other chronic diseases. Many of the principles of palliative care (such as open communication, careful attention to symptoms, the recognition of the psychological and spiritual components of distress, the aim to treat patients and families as the joint unit of care) may seem to be unquestionably 'good things' which can only benefit patients. Even if this is so, it does not mean that specialist palliative care will necessarily provide any additional benefits over and above the adoption of the palliative care approach by those health professionals who are already familiar with the management of these conditions.

In addition, the potential for the widespread uncritical adoption of these principles to cause harm needs to be recognized. For example, attention to symptom control in the absence of good knowledge of underlying disease pathology could lead to patients receiving palliative care for symptoms which were indicative of an underlying, curable, pathology. An over-emphasis on avoiding 'futile' treatments in a condition with which the clinician has had little experience could mean patients not receiving treatments which could have substantially improved the quality, and even the quantity, of their lives. For instance, those palliative care specialists who hold the view that artificial hydration should be avoided in care for the dying might decide not to start it for a patient left unconscious by a stroke who, to the best of their knowledge is unlikely to recover. A stroke specialist, skilled in ordering and interpreting appropriate tests and with extensive clinical experience with these patients, may be reasonably certain that this patient will recover well, provided they do not become dehydrated. A referral to a hospital palliative care team for this patient rather than to a stroke unit could lead to them dying peacefully rather than recovering to enjoy a reasonable quality of life. This is an extreme example, easily preventable given good communication between clinicians. It is not, however, impossible, particularly perhaps given the perceived need in some quarters to reduce 'unnecessary' treatments in people who go on to die (Bayer et al., 1983; Emanuel and Emanuel, 1994) and on resource allocation arguments which value the young over the old (Grimley Evans, 1997; Williams, 1997).

The lack of expertise in non-cancer patient care is inevitable given the predominance of cancer patients within specialist palliative care services and the fact that many doctors and nurses within specialist palliative care come from an oncology background. It is neither an insurmountable nor permanent barrier; as specialist palliative care extends its remit, knowledge and expertise in the care of other conditions will grow. In the meantime it is important that palliative care specialists recognize the limits of their knowledge, question and investigate the ways in which knowledge acquired in cancer care applies to other patients and develop good working relationships with clinicians with existing expertise in the care of these patients (although, as discussed below, this may be difficult given the vested interests involved).

Identifying candidates

It seems difficult for community and hospital doctors to identify candidates for specialist palliative care among patients with chronic conditions. For example, GPs interviewed by Field (1998) identified two important differences between patients with cancer and those with non-malignant conditions. First, differences in disease progression mean there is a continuing benefit from curative/restorative interventions and treatments for the latter category. Second, there was greater uncertainty about the fact and likely time of death with non-cancer patients. The latter appears to be the key 'blockage' to extending specialist palliative care services to non-cancer patients because they will not be seen as suitable candidates for palliative care until they have been defined as 'terminal'. Whether or not there are 'intrinsic' differences in disease progression or not is open to debate. What is not in doubt is that these doctors were less likely to see such patients as 'terminally ill' and in need of palliative care. Evidence from elsewhere shows, for instance, that the annual mortality of patients with advanced heart failure may exceed 60% (Dargie and McMurray, 1994). They are, however, much less likely to be referred to specialist palliative care services than cancer patients with a similarly poor prognosis (Eve et al., 1997).

Evidence from the SUPPORT study demonstrates that it is more difficult to predict the life expectancy of hospitalized non-cancer patients with advanced disease than it is for cancer patients, with 43% of patients with end-stage heart failure estimated by physicians to have less than a 20% chance of surviving for 2 months doing so, compared with 14% of lung-cancer patients given this prognosis (Lynn et al., 1996). If doctors require the same degree of certainty about the timing of death in non-cancer patients as in cancer patients few are likely to be referred to specialist palliative care services, or are likely to be referred very close to death. Current research into ways of improving prognostication in non-cancer patients may improve this situation.

The risk to specialist palliative care services of encouraging referring physicians to adopt a less stringent criteria for timing of death (but not for the certainty of death) for non-cancer patients is that hospice beds become blocked and team workloads dominated by non-cancer patients who have lived longer than expected. However, the issue of prognosis becomes less of a problem for specialist palliative care services if they have clear goals for their intervention and if they are willing to discharge patients once these goals are reached (a controversial idea for some within palliative care). Recent moves towards shorter admissions for cancer patients and (in some services) towards discharging patients once problems within the remit of specialist palliative care have been resolved indicates a way forward (Eve et al., 1997). This does not, however, overcome the reluctance of doctors to refer to specialist palliative care services until they are certain that the patient will die in the foreseeable future. This remains a barrier to providing specialist palliative care to all who need it.

Client expectations and wishes

The current drive to extend specialist palliative care services to all has been very much based upon professionally defined need and the question of what the proposed new clients of these services might want seems to have been largely ignored. It seems ironic that a movement committed to including its patients and their families in their treatment and the continuing delivery of care and to representing and soliciting their wishes should ignore this aspect. There appears to be an assumption that patients dying from non-malignant conditions want care from specialist palliative care services; this is demonstrated by, for example, the anxiety expressed by some specialist palliative care providers that their services will be swamped by referrals from non-cancer patients (Jones, 1995). However, the extent to which these patients would access specialist palliative care services if available is not known.

Cancer is still a strong taboo in our society and patients with non-malignant disease may be unwilling to access services traditionally associated with cancer. They may also be unwilling to use services strongly associated with dying, particularly as they are much less likely to have their prognosis discussed with them than cancer patients. The effects on non-cancer patients of witnessing a succession of deaths on hospice wards or amongst fellow patients in day care units is also unknown. Although there is some evidence to suggest that cancer patients find witnessing deaths of fellow patients helpful (Honeybun et al., 1992; Payne et al., 1996), anecdotal evidence suggests that at least some non-cancer patients find it extremely distressing. It cannot, therefore, be presumed that patients dying from non-malignant disease will want to access specialist palliative care services. On the other hand, some patients and families have expressed bewilderment that hospices restrict their care to cancer patients (Jayes, 1996) and there are powerful accounts contrasting one family member's death from cancer in a hospice to the less well-resourced, poorly managed death of another family member in a nursing home or hospital. Further research is therefore needed to investigate attitudes of patients with progressive non-malignant diseases to specialist palliative care services, the barriers to them accessing this care and the incentives for them to seek it out (which may well include the greater degree of physical comfort and more attractive surroundings apparent in many hospices compared to NHS hospitals).

Resources

The resource implications of any extension to current specialist palliative care services and how these might be met are crucial (Addington-Hall, 1998). At the local level, health authority commissioners are likely to welcome the extension of specialist palliative care services in terms of equity, effectiveness and better integration of services. It might also give them better power and control as commissioners. At the national level, however, the implications of resourcing such an extension to current services may be crucial. The question at this level is whether extended hospice-based specialist palliative care services will continue to be subsidized so heavily by private and voluntary sector contributions, or whether it would lead to a greater demand on the state's 'health pound'.

Looking at the three main causes of death in our society suggests that a simple extension of specialist palliative care services to patients who die from circulatory diseases and respiratory diseases could at least double the cost of resources needed (Table 18.1). Based upon the finding (reported above) that 17% of non-cancer patients in the RSCD had symptoms of severity comparable to the top third of cancer patients receiving specialist palliative care services it was estimated that over 71,000 people per year in England and Wales might require specialist palliative care services, compared with 91,000 cancer patients who received this care in 1994/1995

Table 18.1   Selected causes of death, England and Wales, 1993

Neoplasms	142,446	(25%)
Circulatory diseases	258,156	(45%)
Respiratory diseases	90,870	(16%)
Accidents[a]	16,843	(3%)
Suicide and self-inflicted harm	3,952	(<1%)
Infectious diseases[b]	3,781	(<1%)
All causes	578,170	(100%)

Source: Central Statistical Office, Annual Abstract of Statistics, 1996[a]
1992[b] includes HIV/AIDS deaths

(Addington-Hall et al., 1998). This was estimated to require an increase of 79% in specialist palliative care provision to meet the needs of non-cancer patients. This might be an under-estimation as the non-cancer patients were matched to only one-third of the cancer patients who had received care from specialist palliative care services. Indeed, the actual number could be three times as high at 215, 322, representing half of all non-cancer deaths in England and Wales. Thus, extending specialist palliative care services to non-cancer patients might therefore require an expansion in resources from those needed to care for half of all cancer deaths, as at present, to those needed to care for half of *all* deaths.

The source of funding for such an expansion is unclear. Further, this potential increase in the demand for specialist palliative care services comes at a time when the implementation of the recommendations of the Calman-Hine report, with its increased emphasis upon palliative care for cancer patients, is likely to lead to further demands on hospices and other specialist palliative care services (Department of Health, 1995).

It is certainly a moot point whether hospice services can be extended very much further from the present level without substantial additional resources. The resources of existing hospices are already stretched to cope with terminally ill cancer patients and the small number of mainly neurological patients they admit. One can see this in a variety of ways:

* The reduction in the length of stay of hospice inpatient admissions.
* The shift towards symptom management and away from long-term terminal care.
* The greater use of day care for clinical tasks.

It is doubtful whether hospice services could be extended to include other terminal conditions without the exclusion of some cancer patients who currently receive their services. Although this might be seen by health planners and possibly by some health providers as a more effective and efficient use of a scarce resource, it may not be acceptable to hospice volunteers and to those who make charitable donations to support their local hospice. If the nature of hospice care changes too much it may lose its support in the community, with potentially severe financial consequences.

Approximately half the costs of current hospice services in Britain are met through voluntary contributions and volunteers make a substantial contribution to hospice functioning and the quality of hospice care (Field et al., 1997). Although there is no evidence to date that extending hospice-based specialist palliative care services to include non-cancer patients will adversely affect fundraising and voluntary support in this way, this possibility should be considered carefully.

One solution might be for those who are concerned to provide specialist palliative care services for people dying from non-malignant conditions to follow the hospice example and raise their own money to provide equivalent services. Since the beginning of modern hospice care, Dame Cicely Saunders amongst others, have seen this as the way forward for patients with non-malignant disease (Saunders, 1996). The precedence has already been established with children's hospices, which often accept children with all terminal conditions and HIV/AIDS (although increasing numbers of generalist hospices now take these patients). However, this would create further competition within an increasingly tight competitive fundraising environment and does not address the cost implications of substantially extending other specialist palliative care services, such as hospital support teams.

Charitable giving accounts for much of the funding of hospices and specialist palliative care services in the UK. It is questionable whether voluntary contributions would be forthcoming to fund an expansion of specialist palliative care on this scale. Indeed, there are concerns that expanding to non-cancer patients would actually lead to reduction in voluntary contributions, especially if it were perceived that care for non-cancer patients was being provided at the expense of cancer patients. Many existing services report being fully stretched simply trying to meet the needs of local cancer patients. Thus, the wide availability of specialist palliative care services would probably require more state funding. Despite the apparent recognition by government of the need to extend specialist palliative care services to non-cancer patients the increased cost of these could be a formidable barrier to their extension. If part of the attraction of extending such services to non-cancer patients is that the services are heavily subsidized by voluntary contributions it is at least possible that the enthusiasm of government and health commissioners might diminish sharply if it became apparent that a high level of state funding was required.

Relationships with other health providers

Constraints upon extending specialist palliative care services beyond cancer are not simply a matter of how to find the additional funding and other resources to do so. The consequences for other sectors and groups in the health services elsewhere have also to be considered.

A crucial question concerns whether, or to what extent, specialist palliative care is intended to replace or to supplement existing services. Although inpatient hospices take over patient care, most other specialist palliative care services are based on models of supplementing and complementing existing services rather than taking over patient care. In some areas this undoubtedly works well but in other areas, and with some disciplines, there are already concerns that palliative care services takeover care, leading potentially to the 'de-skilling' of, for example, community nurses. One possible model for the extension of specialist palliative care services to non-cancer patients is that patients move towards palliative care as their disease progresses, with specialist palliative care services taking responsibility for the majority of people who die. However, in addition to the difficulties of identifying non-cancer patients who are dying and the possible lack of skills in care of non-cancer patients discussed above, the complexity of existing service arrangements, the likelihood of severe disruption to services during the transitional period and the vested interest already entrenched in the health service would make this very difficult to introduce. This is not, therefore, contemplated as a viable option (NCHSPCS, 1997).

In the community, working effectively with current generalist health providers will be a pre-requisite of any successful expansion of specialist services. While the present cancer-based specialist palliative care services are broadly welcomed by GPs and community nurses there are also some strains between specialist and generalist providers in the community (Field, 1998). These might well become worse with the extension of specialist palliative care services to patients with chronic diseases, i.e. to the patients who provide the bulk of the work for GPs and community nurses. Patients with chronic respiratory and circulatory conditions comprise a significant volume of their work; those who are dying from cancer do not. The relationship of extended specialist palliative care services to Social Services would also need to be considered. It is likely that similar (but more widespread) problems would be met to those already existing between 'health' and 'social service' agencies in negotiating and deciding responsibility for and funding of the community care of people who are dying. Further, although not a barrier to extending specialist palliative care, it is perhaps worth considering the argument that in the long run this may lead to the 'de-skilling' of GPs and community nurses in their care of people who are dying. This might have long-term negative consequences for the care of these dying people by GPs and community nurses.

Existing specialist palliative care services in British hospitals vary both in terms of what they offer and in their range of patient coverage. However, there appears to be a trend towards increasing the range of patient conditions which are covered. As these teams have an advisory role the scope and success of present services relies very much on the personal skills of the palliative care specialists (usually nurses), the attitudes of consultants and the success of negotiations between palliative care specialists and consultants. Further extension of such services to provide a comprehensive coverage of non-cancer patients will depend upon convincing non-cancer consultants that palliative care has appropriate skills to offer to their patients.

There is also the question of existing tensions within specialist palliative care. Within the current provision of community specialist palliative care services there is already some competition and rivalry between existing hospices and other specialist palliative care services which are causing strains and local difficulties. Although not widely publicized, examples are well known amongst those working in palliative care. These would be exacerbated if existing specialist palliative care services were competing for 'new' categories of patients and for funding for these, especially if funding continues to 'follow the patient'. It is also unclear what the effect of extending community specialist palliative care beyond cancer patients might be on their relationships to services such as hospices and other organizations which are restricted to cancer patients, such as the Macmillan Cancer Relief Fund.

To summarize, whatever the model, extending specialist palliative care services beyond cancer would require greater integration of these and other 'mainstream' health services. This would threaten vested interests in the present pattern of service delivery, both those in the mainstream health services and also those within specialist palliative care. Even if specialist palliative services are simply intended to supplement existing services, they will at least be partly replacing them. This would have significant consequences for staffing levels, prestige and influence of existing services.

Concluding comments

There is a growing body of opinion and evidence that specialist palliative care services should be extended to non-cancer patients. Although there have been almost no evaluations of specialist palliative care provision for patients who die from causes other than cancer, there is now convincing evidence that conventional care alone is not meeting the needs of such patients. Thus, what is not in doubt is that the status quo is unacceptable (Addington-Hall, 1998). This must be recognized by the health professionals currently providing care for these patients, as well as by specialists in palliative care. However, as this paper has argued, there is at present insufficient clarity about what this might entail. In particular, three areas should be clarified: the patients (and patient problems) which lie within the remit of palliative care; the relationship between specialist palliative care services and other specialist and generalist services already providing care for these patients; and the scope and resourcing of such extended palliative care provision.

Whether the expansion of the existing pattern of *specialist* palliative care services is the best solution is unproven. Although the concern to extend specialist palliative care services towards non-cancer care is motivated by hospice/palliative care ideals, it should be recognized that the move to expand such services may be driven at least in part by an organizational 'imperative'. Continued expansion is a means of increasing the power and influence of specialist palliative care providers at local and national levels. Within the context of a capitalist society it would be unrealistic to imagine that specialist palliative care services are immune to the dynamics of organizational expansion or to the equation that success is measured by expansion. During the 1990s hospice and palliative care organizations and their representatives have become influential at local and national levels in the UK. At the national level this is perhaps best exemplified by the increased influence of the National Council for Hospice and Specialist Palliative Care Services. The National Council was established in 1991 to provide a forum for the various parties providing palliative care, to co-ordinate and develop joint position papers promoting good practice in palliative care, and to act as a lobbying force for palliative care (Gaffin, 1996). Subsequently it has extended its remit to include activities such as data collection and, potentially, standard setting. At the local level, pro-viders have become involved in policy and decision making about palliative care with Local Health Authorities.

Both institutional and personal rewards follow on from exercising power and influence at local and national levels. As the particular interests of hospice and other palliative care organizations and professions become linked to continuing expansion, more jobs within specialist palliative care services sustains the increasing specialization and professionalization of specialist palliative care services workers and enhances their possibilities for career progression. There is a danger that continued expansion is being seen as unquestionably good for patients and their relatives because it is good for professionals. Organizational analysis warns that, even with the best of motives, continuing growth and expansion may lead to 'goal displacement' as initial goals and activities become challenged and replaced by new goals and activities. The challenge is to find imaginative and innovative solutions to the undoubted problems experienced by people dying from causes other than cancer which are evidence-based, collaborative with other health pro-fessionals and which genuinely put the needs of patients and families first.

References

Addington-Hall, J.M. (1996) 'Heart disease and stroke: lessons from cancer care', in G. Ford (ed.), *Interfaces in Medicine: Managing Terminal Illness*. Royal College of Physicians, London.

Addington-Hall, J.M, (1998) *Reaching Out: Specialist Palliative Care for Adults with Non-malignant Disease*. National Council for Hospices and Specialist Palliative Care Services, London.

Addington-Hall, J.M., Fakhoury, W. and McCarthy, M. (1998) 'Specialist palliative care in non-malignant disease', *Palliative Medicine*, 12: 417–27.

Addington-Hall, J.M., Lay, M., Altmann, D. and McCarthy, M. (1995) 'Symptom control, communication with health professionals and hospital care of stroke patients in the last year of life, as reported by surviving family, friends and carers', *Stroke*, 26: 1248–2242.

Addington-Hall, J.M., Lay, M., Altmann, D. and McCarthy, M. (1997) 'Community care for stroke patients in the last year of life: results of a national retrospective survey of surviving family, friends and officials', *Health Soc. Care Community*, 6: 112–19.

Addington-Hall, J.M. and McCarthy, M. (1995) 'Regional study of care for the dying: methods and sample characteristics', *Palliative Medicine*, 9: 27–35.

Ahmedzai, S. (1993) 'The medicalization of dying: a doctor's view', in D. Clark (ed.), *The Future for Palliative Care: Issues of Policy and Practice*. Open University, Buckingham. pp. 140–7.

Ahmedzai, S. (1996) 'Making a success out of life's failures', *Prog. Palliative Care*, 4: 1–3.

Anderson, R. and Bury, M. (eds) (1988) *Living with Chronic Illness: the Experience of Patients and their Families*. Unwin Hyman, London.

Barby, T. and Leigh, P.N. (1995) 'Palliative care in motor neurone disease', *International Journal Palliative Nursing*, 1: 183–8.

Bayer, R., Callahan, D., Fletcher, J., Hodgson, T., Jenning, B., Monsees, D., Sieverts, S. and Veatch, R. (1983) 'The care of the terminally ill: morality and economics', *New England Journal Medicine*, 309: 1490.

Biswas, B. (1993) 'The medicalization of dying: a nurse's view', in D. Clark (ed.), *The Future for Palliative Care: Issues of Policy and Practice*. Open University, Buckingham. pp. 132–9.

Cohen, L.M., McCue, J.D., Germain, M. and Kjellstrand, C.M. (1995) 'Dialysis discontinuation. A "good" death?', *Arch. International Medicine*, 155: 42–7.

Copp, G. (1994) 'Palliative care nursing education: a review of research findings', *Journal of Advanced Nursing*, 19: 552–7.

Corner, J. and Dunlop, R. (1997) 'New approaches to care', in D. Clark, S. Ahmedzai and J.M. Hockley (eds), *New Themes in Palliative Care*. Open University, Buckingham. pp. 288–302.

Dargie, H.J. and McMurray, J.J. (1994) 'Diagnosis and management of heart failure', *British Medical Journal*, 308: 321–8.

Department of Health (1995) *A Policy Framework for Commissioning Cancer Services. A Report by the Expert Advisory Group on Cancer to the Chief Medical Officers of England and Wales*. Department of Health and Welsh Office, London.

Emanuel, E.J. and Emanuel, L.L. (1994) 'The economics of dying. The illusion of cost savings at the end of life', *New England Journal of Medicine*, 330: 540–4.

Eve, A., Smith, A.M. and Tebbit, P. (1997) 'Hospice and palliative care in the UK 1994–1995, including a summary of trends 1990–1995', *Palliative Medicine*, 11: 31–43.

Field, D. (1994) 'Palliative medicine and the medicalization of death', *European Journal of Cancer Care*, 3: 58–62.

Field, D. (1995) 'Education for palliative care: formal education about death, dying and bereavement in UK medical schools in 1983 and 1994', *Medical Education*, 29: 414–19.

Field, D. (1998) 'Special not different: General practitioners' accounts of their care of dying people', *Social Science and Medicine*, 46: 1111–20.

Field, D., Ingleton, C. and Clark, D. (1997) 'The costs of unpaid labour: the management and use of voluntary staff in the King's Mill Hospice', *Health Soc. Care Commun.*, 5: 198–208.

Gaffin, J. (1996) 'Achievements and intentions: the work of the National Council for Cancer and Specialist Palliative Care Services', *European Journal of Palliative Care*, 3: 100–4.

George, R. and Sykes, J. (1997) 'Beyond cancer?', in D. Clark, S. Ahmedzai and J.M. Hockley (eds), *New Themes in Palliative Care*. Open University, Buckingham. pp. 239–54.

Grimley Evans, J. (1997) 'Rationing health care by age: the case against', *British Medical Journal*, 314: 820–5.

Higginson, I. (1993) 'Palliative care: a review of past changes and future trends', *Journal Public Health Medicine*, 15: 308.

Hinton, J. (1963) 'The physical and mental distress of the dying', *Q. J. Med.*, 125: 1–20.

Hockley, J.M., Dunlop, R. and Davies, R.J. (1988) 'Survey of distressing symptoms in dying patients and their families in hospital and the response to a symptom control team', *British Medical Journal*, 296: 1715–17.

Honeybun, J., Johnston, M. and Tookman, A. (1992) 'The impact of a death on fellow hospice patients', *British Journal Med. Psychology*, 65: 67–72.

Jayes, A.M. (1996) 'Open letter from a carer', *British Medical Journal*, 313: 369.

Jones, S. (1995) 'Palliative care in terminal cardiac failure', *British Medical Journal*, 310: 805.

Lloyd Williams, M. (1996) 'An audit of palliative care in dementia', *European Journal of Cancer Care in England*, 5: 53–5.

Lynn, J., Harrell, F.E., Cohen, F., Hamel, M.B., Dawson, N. and Wu, A.W. (1996) 'Defining the "terminally ill": insights from SUPPORT', *Duquesne Law Rev.*, 35: 311–36.

Lynn, J., Teno, J.M., Phillips, R.S., Wu, A.W., Desbiens, N., Harrold, J., Claessens, M.T., Wenger, N., Kreling, N. and Connors, A.F., Jr. (1997) 'Perceptions by family members of the dying experience of older and seriously ill patients', SUPPORT Investigators. Study to understand prognoses and preferences for outcomes and risks of treatments. *Ann. Intern. Med.*, 126: 97–106.

McCarthy, M., Lay, M. and Addington-Hall, J.M. (1996) 'Dying from heart disease', *J. R. Coll. Phys.*, London, 30: 325–8.

Mills, M., Davies, T.O. and Macrae, W.A. (1994) 'Care of dying patients in hospital', *British Medical Journal*, 309: 583–6.

NCHSPCS (1995) 'Specialist palliative care: a statement of definitions', *Occasional Paper 8*. National Council for Hospice and Specialist Palliative Care Services.

NCHSPCS (1996) 'Education in palliative care', *Occasional Paper 9*. National Council for Hospice and Specialist Palliative Care Services.

NCHSPCS (1997) 'Dilemmas and directions: The future of specialist palliative care', *Occasional Paper 11*. National Council for Hospice and Specialist Palliative Care Services.

NHS Executive (1996) EL(96)85 'A policy framework for commissioning cancer services', *Palliative Care Services*.

O'Brien, T., Kelly, M. and Saunders, C. (1992) 'Motor neurone disease: a hospice perspective', *British Medical Journal*, 304: 471–3.

Payne, S., Hillier, R., Langley-Evans, A. and Roberts, T. (1996) 'Impact of witnessing death on hospice patients', *Social Science and Medicine*, 43: 1785–94.

Saunders, C. (1978) *The Management of Terminal Disease*. Edward Arnold, London.

Saunders, C. (1984) 'On dying well', *Cambridge Rev.*, Feb 27: 49–52.

Saunders, C. (1996) 'Hospice', *Mortality*, 1: 317–22.

Saunders, C. and Baines, M. (1983) *Living with Dying: the Management of Terminal Disease*. Oxford University Press, Oxford.

Skilbeck, J., Mott, L., Smith, D., Page, H. and Clark, D. (1997) 'Nursing care for people dying from chronic obstructive airways disease', *International Journal of Palliative Nursing*, 3 (2): 100–6.

Standing Medical Advisory Committee and Standing Nursing and Midwifery Advisory Committee (1992) *The Principles and Practice of Palliative Care*. Standing Medical Advisory Committee and Standing Nursing and Midwifery Advisory Committee, London.

Volicer, L., Collard, A., Hurley, A., Bishop, C., Kern, D. and Karon, S. (1994) 'Impact of special care unit for patients with advanced Alzheimer's disease on patients' discomfort and costs', *Journal Am. Geriatr. Soc.*, 42: 597–603.

Williams, A. (1997) 'Rationing health care by age: the case for', *British Medical Journal*, 314: 820–5.

Wilkes, E. (1980) *Terminal Care: Report of a Working Party*. Standing Medical Advisory Committee, HMSO, London.

Wilkes, E. (1984) 'Dying now', *Lancet*, I: 950–2.

19

The case for palliative care in residential and nursing homes

Moyra Sidell, Jeanne Samson Katz and Carol Komaromy

Introduction

Most deaths in Western societies occur in old age and increasingly in extreme old age. Deaths occur predominantly in hospital or at home, but a sizeable proportion of older people die in *residential* or *nursing* homes because they either require long term specialist nursing care or because they have no source of social support. During the last two decades the hospice movement has advanced our knowledge of the diverse needs of dying people and pioneered improvements in pain relief and symptom control now known as palliative care. At the same time a great deal of attention has been paid to the quality of life in residential homes for older people but the quality of dying has received rather less attention.

The research reported here has sought to investigate the degree to which hospice philosophy has permeated the ethos of *residential* and *nursing* homes for older people and more specifically to assess the potential for applying the principles and practice of palliative care to these settings. We use the World Health Organization definition of palliative care, which suggests that palliative care:

- affirms life and regards dying as a normal process and neither hastens nor postpones death
- provides relief from pain and other distressing symptoms
- integrates the psychological and spiritual aspects of patient care
- offers a support system to help dying people live as actively as possible until death
- offers a support system to help the family cope during the patient's illness and their own bereavement.

This was a three stage study. Stages 2 and 3 were funded by the Department of Health and Stage 1 was funded by the Open University.

In Stage 1 we surveyed 1,000 *residential, nursing* homes and *dual registered* homes in three geographical areas of England, the North West (including Merseyside and Lancashire), the West Midlands (Warwickshire

This article will be published in *Ageing and Society*, 2001.

and the Black Country) and the South East (divided into South London and the South Coast stretching from Hastings to Brighton).

A postal questionnaire was sent to the heads of the sampled homes. This collected data on home size, number of residents, numbers of staff, demographic details of the residents, number and times of deaths and transfers to and from other institutions. In addition they were asked to comment on training issues of staff relating to caring for dying residents. Four hundred and twelve homes returned the questionnaires – a response rate of 41%.

Stage 2 was based on the returns to the postal questionnaire. One hundred homes were sampled (for home type, size and geographical area) to take part in Stage 2 of the study. This entailed an interview with the head of home on site. The interviews were tape recorded and included structured and semi-structured elements. The interviews covered staffing arrangements and training issues. The interviewees explained their philosophy of care for dying residents and the management of death and dying in their home through a detailed exploration of the care of the last three residents to die in the home. This discussion focused on the period that they identified as the terminal stage, their reasons for transferring residents to hospital (if relevant) and their relationship with other carers and the relatives of the deceased. Their knowledge and views about the appropriateness of palliative care were also sought.

In Stage 3 we drew a purposive sample of 12 homes for detailed case study observation in order to assess first hand the care that was given to dying residents and their family and friends. Where possible we interviewed a range of other professionals who were involved in the home, in particular, community nurses, GPs, Macmillan nurses and palliative care specialists. We also held informal discussions with care staff and other residents in the home and we interviewed relatives of residents who died during the study period.

Living with dying

About 32,000 old people die in residential care in England and Wales annually. This may be a conservative estimate because many deaths in 'homes' are registered in mortality statistics as 'at home'. There is some evidence that the care given to dying people in residential homes and the management of death and dying is cause for concern (Hanvey, 1989; Hockey, 1990). The evidence, however, is sparse and based on very small samples. Two studies highlight some of the issues which this research seeks to explore further. A small qualitative study by Shemmings (1996) involved interviews with 20 care staff working in local authority homes for older people and revealed that staff were unprepared to meet the emotional and physical demands of caring for dying residents. Likewise the small study by Counsel and Care (1995) contrasts the willingness of staff to provide good care with the lack of support and training they receive.

Despite studies like these which focus on the views of small numbers of staff, little attention is paid in the literature to issues of death and dying in residential homes, whereas great emphasis is placed on matters of maintaining active life in them. For example, the Wagner Review of Residential Care (Wagner, 1988) makes little reference to death and dying except in relation to alerting relatives when a resident is close to death. The Centre for Policy on Ageing in *A Better Home Life: The Code of Practice for Residential Care* (1996) makes 13 out of a total of nearly 100 specific recommendations to the management of death and dying, which represents a slight increase in the focus on this area from their previous report of 1984.

Although there is some evidence of increased awareness of the management of dying, there are good reasons for the continued focus on the quality of living in residential care. Most efforts to improve the quality of life in residential homes have concentrated on rehabilitation in an effort to counter what Booth calls the 'induced dependency hypothesis' (Booth, 1985). Researchers of residential care have focused attention on integrating homes into the local community and on promoting a more positive environment (Clough, 1981; Willcocks et al., 1982). The emphasis has been on striving to compensate for the loss of home and the effort to counter induced dependency, a task made more difficult by demographic changes and increasing numbers of older people living beyond the age of 85 (Phillipson and Walker, 1986). This philosophy of care may no longer be appropriate to the care of older and frailer people who now inhabit residential and nursing homes.

The community care policy of maintaining older people in their own homes for as long as possible has escalated the changes in the profile of residents entering care; residents tend to be from the very old and frailer population who lack other forms of support (Sinclair, 1988). One of the reasons for this increased frailty is that as people get older they tend to suffer more from highly symptomatic chronic illness and disability, such as arthiritis, cardiac and pulmonary conditions, blindness and deafness (Sidell, 1995). The combination of an ageing population already in care becoming increasingly frail and older people entering care at a stage when they need intense care has changed the character of a lot of homes.

Since the early 1960s when Townsend published *The Last Refuge* (1962) and Goffman *Asylums* (1961) attention has focused on keeping older people out of residential care. But despite attempts to maintain people in their preferred setting, at home, admissions to residential care have increased from 219,100 in 1975 to 499,400 in 1994 in the UK (Laing's Review of Private Health Care, 1995).

More recently Peace et al. (1997) have explored why, particularly since the 1990 Community Care Act, increasing numbers of older people continue to live in residential homes. They consider both the choices which people make as well as the ability of homes to provide clinical support to frail and increasingly dependent residents. The authors point out that since the numbers of NHS long stay hospital beds have declined there has been a subsequent increase in nursing home provision, dramatically reducing the ratio between nursing and residential beds.

In the 1980s, encouraged by government subsidies, there was a sharp rise in the provision of private homes for older people and the overall number of people entering residential homes has increased steadily (Peace et al., 1997). The shift from public to private means that whereas in 1975 there were 128,300 places in Local Authority homes and only 25,800 in private residential homes plus a small voluntary sector, today there are 95,500 public sector places, 50,700 voluntary and 167,500 private places (Laing's Review of Private Health Care, 1995). The number of people in private nursing homes has increased to 178,800 with 16,000 in the voluntary nursing sector; in 1975 there were 24,000 private and voluntary places altogether.

Within the nursing and residential home sector there are eight types of registered homes. The three residential categories are: local authority, private and voluntary provision, all of which receive community nurse support. Nursing homes are also in three types of provision which are NHS (of which there are very few), private and voluntary (in which there may be registered NHS beds). These homes are all expected to have continuous registered nurse cover. Some nursing homes also have beds which are registered as terminal care beds and to qualify for this status the home must have a nurse with a recognized palliative care qualification. Dual registered homes, either private or voluntary provision, combine residential and nursing beds. Residents are categorized according to their assessed social or nursing needs. These homes must also provide registered nurse cover but the nursing needs within the residential part of the home are met by community nurses. In theory residential homes provide social care, while nursing homes provide nursing care and this is how registration, allocation and nursing support are organized.

With the diversity of types of homes and the increasing lack of distinction between social and nursing care it is not surprising that the management of death and dying is a complex issue. Decisions affecting where residents die are difficult and not totally dependent upon the homes' resources and willingness to manage dying residents. Field (1996) discusses the lack of certainty about 'long-term conditions' both in relation to whether the death will occur and when, especially in the absence of a significant event to mark the terminal stage of illness. An American study of decision making in nursing homes goes further in suggesting that, 'Medical decision making is often an emotionally laden, multi-faceted, difficult process, especially when the illness is grave, the outcome is uncertain, death is or may be imminent, and the family rather than the patient must make the decision' (Kayser-Jones, 1995: 339). Nevertheless, it is estimated that a quarter of all people over the age of 85 live in a residential home setting and with such a greatly increased population of older people deaths are frequent occurrences – between a quarter and a third of all residents are likely to die each year (Clough, 1981).

Hockey (1990) in her ethnographic account *Experiences of Death* goes so far as to claim that residential homes are primarily dying spaces concerned with the slow process of deterioration (1990: 92). She maintains that the attempt to create a 'homely here and now' atmosphere demands that the categories 'life' and 'death' be kept separate lest one should intrude upon the other. The job of 'keeping them going' is the overt preoccupation of the staff. The task of supervising the process of dying and the event of death becomes more covert and is carried out in the sickbay and mortuary, separated from the 'living' spaces (1990: 116). Discussion of ageing and dying is discouraged in this environment. This runs directly counter to the philosophy of terminal care developed by the hospice movement which hopes to re-integrate the two categories of experience, 'life' and 'death', thereby highlighting the processual rather than the oppositional nature of their relationship (1990: 155).

The modern hospice movement claims to have re-introduced the 'natural' process of living with dying which existed in previous centuries. This can be viewed as in conflict with both the 'rehabilitation' philosophy of residential care for older people and also the prevailing medical model which sees death as a failure of modern medicine. We would envisage that the use of palliative type medication would be motivated by the intention to improve the quality of remaining life rather than trying to extend it (i.e. adding life to years, rather than years to life – Department of Health, 1991).

The speciality of palliative medicine emerged out of the hospice movement of the 1960s. This strove to involve medical practitioners more in the process of dying and its implications for the dying person and his/her significant others. Palliative care as a multi-disciplinary field also developed adapting many principles of the inpatient hospice practice, spearheaded by Dame Cecily Saunders, to outpatient and community care of dying people.

Palliative care has many distinctive features such as assessing the dying person's emotional and social support needs, integration of relatives, friends and volunteers in caring roles. Indeed the boundaries between health care and social care are necessarily blurred and interdependent with the focus on the centrality of the dying person and his or her carers. Communication between dying people and their carers about the life-threatening illness and the probability of a truncated life is a hallmark of the psycho-social component of palliative care and has received a good deal of attention (Buckman, 1988; Maguire and Faulkner, 1988a, 1988b).

Palliative care emphasizes pain relief and symptom control. Pain is widely conceptualized as encompassing physical, emotional, social and spiritual components. Symptoms are similarly broadly defined, including weakness, anorexia, constipation and depression. Methods of addressing pain and symptoms include elements from any disciplines which, although drawing primarily upon developments in modern medicine also draw upon skills and expertise from paramedical professionals, the counselling and psycho-analytic disciplines and complementary therapies. The dying person and his/her intimates are central to decision making – the palliative care team, rather than one specialist or a GP, provide the care based on multi-disciplinary principles.

Contained within the hospice movement are the generic roots of making palliative care available to everyone who is dying. Sadly, in practice the hospice movement has not permeated very far beyond the care of people with terminal cancer and more recently AIDS, making more credible the assertion made by Douglas (1992, cited in George and Sykes, 1997) that the hospice movement is too good to be true and too small to be useful. If palliative care is to be expanded to meet the needs of older people, the form which it needs to take may differ from the current traditional practice.

We recognize that palliative care can be provided at different levels from the basic premise of treating dying people and their relatives and friends with respect and dignity, to the advanced technological interventions of symptom control in its widest sense.

The case for adopting palliative care in homes for older people

We asked heads of homes for their views on the appropriateness of adopting the principles and practices of palliative care in their settings. One of the most striking features of their responses was a lack of familiarity with the principles and practice of palliative care. Those who are familiar with it do not perceive this type of care as appropriate to any conditions other than cancer. This view was echoed by the GPs interviewed. They rarely had any training in palliative care and they equated it with symptom control mostly in relation to cancer, and tended to believe that it was best left to the hospice. However Macmillan nurses and specialist palliative care nurses do not subscribe to these views. They saw their role as advising on the care of dying people whatever the cause of their dying, as one reflected:

> Just because a patient hasn't got cancer and maybe has had a stroke or may be at the end stage of another disease does not mean that they should be treated any differently from somebody with cancer.

In spite of this lack of awareness of the potential of palliative care for their own settings, when asked what they considered to be a well managed death many heads of homes mentioned that it should be pain free, the resident should be as comfortable as possible, their physical, emotional and spiritual needs should be taken care of and their relatives and friends should be supported. Clearly they aspired to much that fits into the palliative care remit. But because they are not aware of what palliative care could achieve nor have they the resources to put it into practice many older people in these settings do not receive the quality of care that might be achieved.

In order to assess the feasibility of adopting the principles and practices of palliative care in residential and nursing homes, we have used the Trent Palliative Care Core Standards (Trent Hospice Audit Group, 1992) as a framework for analysing the care which is currently available in these settings. Although the Trent Standards are also written for use as audit measures for hospices, with detailed outcome and process measures suited to those settings, the six core statements, which make up the Trent Standards, address more general palliative care approaches and attitudes which we believe are achievable in non-specialist palliative care settings.

Standard No 1: collaboration with other agencies

Standard statement: *There is effective collaboration with other agencies, professional and voluntary, providing continuity of care and support for patients, and their carers.*

The ability to care for dying people in residential and nursing homes rather than transferring them to hospital was heavily dependent on the help received from external sources. Their relationship with the GP is of utmost importance and this varied a great deal. Staff found some GPs very helpful and co-operative whilst others were less helpful and some downright obstructive. Where GPs had a large number of residents in one home they were more likely to have a better relationship with the home because they would visit frequently and get to know the staff well.

Community nurses were extremely important to residential care homes. They frequently provided advice and planned the actual nursing care. However the degree of their intervention was often dependent on the relationship they had with the head of home and the degree to which the home staff would try to cope without help. Community nurses expressed a preference for being called in early rather than in a crisis. They liked to be involved in drawing up care plans and saw themselves as having an educational as well as caring role. They have the potential to play a pivotal role in caring for dying residents, acting as a liaison person for the different professionals who might be involved.

Community nurses are not usually involved in nursing homes because these types of homes are staffed by their own qualified nurses. However, many community nurses feel that they could offer a lot to nursing homes, especially in the care of their dying residents. They felt that because they were obliged regularly to update their training they might be in a position to offer a better service than the staff, many of whom had qualified many years ago and had not updated their skills. However, there exists a potential threat to the professional autonomy of qualified nursing home staff who may feel threatened by external professionals.

Macmillan and other specialist palliative care nurses provide another line of support which is generally underused mainly because they are associated almost exclusively with cancer care. This is a freely available service which remains largely untapped but which could greatly improve the quality of care for dying people in these settings. The same situation holds with the use of specialist palliative care teams who again are mainly associated with the care of cancer patients. Their expertise in symptom control could be invaluable to residential and nursing homes. This issue is addressed under Standard 2.

Very few representatives from other agencies seem to be called upon by the homes. In a minority of homes dieticians had been consulted on how best to provide nutrition to a dying resident and only very occasionally the services of a complementary therapist had been used. Complementary therapy is increasingly used in hospices and many of these therapies such as massage and aromatherapy are particularly useful for relieving the pain of musculoskeletal conditions which afflict many residents in the homes. There does seem to be a lack of imaginative use of agencies other than the purely medical. Religious and spiritual leaders could also provide a good deal of support to dying residents and their family and friends but often they are only called in to perform last rites. They then become the harbinger of death rather than a source of comfort and solace. This situation however did not hold in the overtly religious homes where religious leaders were integral to the day-to-day running of the home.

In terms of this standard there appears to be much missed opportunity to collaborate with other professionals or voluntary agencies. There is often a sense of isolation and struggling on alone rather than bothering other agencies. This is compounded by a feeling that because they are very familiar with the residents then they know best how to care for them. A combination of anxiety over perceived cost implications and professional autonomy are possible explanations for this isolation.

Standard No 2: symptom control

Standard statement: *All patients have their symptoms controlled to a degree that is acceptable to them, and achievable by multidisciplinary team intervention within current palliative care knowledge.*

In residential and nursing homes achieving this standard is very much dependent on achievements in relation to Standard 1. The need for adequate pain relief for their dying residents was acknowledged by most heads of homes whether residential or nursing. They were all in one way or another dependent on the co-operation of the GP to prescribe appropriate analgesia. Many GPs were reluctant to prescribe strong analgesia, especially opiates, because they felt that this was inappropriate medication for older people. General practitioners varied a great deal in their knowledge and understanding of pain relief. Some were aware of this and would call in expert help from a palliative care specialist but this was rare. Residential homes were also dependent on community nurses to administer pain relief especially if this entailed using specialist equipment such as syringe drivers.

Macmillan nurses can be a great help in assessing the level of pain that a resident is experiencing and in persuading a GP to prescribe adequate medication. The few Macmillan nurses we interviewed who had been called in to advise on pain control expressed the view that although the homes were keen to provide adequate pain relief they were not very good at recognizing when someone was actually in pain. They found residents who were said to be pain free who were tense and difficult to move and they also found that staff did not recognize different sorts of pain, particularly emotional pain. There was little recognition by heads of homes or the GPs of pain relief as a preventative measure. Such pain relief that was available was always administered after breakthrough pain had occurred. We also found that staff did not recognize different sorts of pain, particularly emotional pain. Symptom relief was, in the views of most heads of homes synonymous with pain relief. Other symptoms such as nausea, constipation, breathlessness or general weakness were not really addressed. However a good deal of attention was focused on keeping pressure sores at bay. This was something about which most heads of homes were particularly vigilant.

On the whole good terminal care was not couched in terms of symptom control but rather in keeping people comfortable. But it is precisely the definition of 'comfortable' to an untrained eye which is open to question. A more acute awareness of what needs to be done and what can be done is necessary in most homes, both residential and nursing, if this standard of palliative care is to be achieved.

Standard No 3: patient/carer information

Standard statement: *The patient and his or her carers have the information they seek, relating to the diagnosis and progress of the disease, care options, and allied support services available to enable them to make informed choices.*

Residential and nursing homes have in the past engendered a great deal of passivity in their residents. Because of physical and or mental frailty this user group is not the most vociferous in terms of stating their own needs. Things are beginning to change. Private space is now an acceptable part of a resident's rights and they are not invariably cajoled into communal eating and living. The range of choices open to residents is increasing and some more progressive homes have residents' committees and a regular residents meeting to discuss a whole range of issues from the menus to the social calendar. This notion of the resident having more control over their lives than used to be allowed could in theory be translated into their care when dying. In this study we found that there is a general view held by most heads of homes and GPs that dying older people are not wholly aware of what is happening to them, that they are accepting of death and only too happy to leave their care in the hands of the experts. Decisions about whether to transfer them to hospital tend to be made for them, as is the aggressive use of medication. The decision whether or not to treat pneumonia, say, is not normally taken with the resident's full consent. This position is not entirely untenable. Residents are old and frail and when they are actually dying many are not fully conscious. There is a sense of weariness and an understandable readiness to let others take responsibility for their care. However the danger lies in assuming that this is invariably the case. There is a noticeable tendency to see residents as a totally homogenous group and to underestimate their diversity and needs.

Questions about whether the residents wished to be buried or cremated and other religious or cultural preferences in relation to their care in death and dying were dealt with in a rather ad hoc way. Some included these questions in their admission procedures, others asked the relatives. Another way was to leave what were considered difficult questions until the resident had settled in and then try to ascertain their wishes subtly in the course of conversations. Sometimes relatives were required to sort out these issues after the resident had died.

This Standard is also applicable to those residents who have relatives and friends who are concerned about their care. In our interviews with relatives of residents who had recently died we found some evidence that relatives felt that they were not kept informed and would like to have been more proactive in the care of their loved one but felt unsure and inhibited about asserting themselves. They needed more information on the process of death and dying and some idea of what to expect so that they could respond in appropriate ways.

The degree to which they are involved in the decision making about the care of a dying resident is a complex matter and much depends on the relationship that the home staff have with the particular relatives and friends. Many who have been involved in the actual care of the dying person, feeding, washing and providing emotional support, tend to have a good relationship with the home and will be in close touch with the formal carers and thus involved in the decision-making process. Some relatives were actually viewed with suspicion. They are typically those who do not visit regularly and are thought by the home to put their own interests before those of the resident. Tensions can exist between them, the home staff feel protective towards the resident and resentful of any 'interference' on the part of such relatives.

Overall this Standard requires constant vigilance on the part of home staff to make sure that, when appropriate, dying residents and their friends and family are consulted and have as much choice and control over their circumstances as is possible.

Standard No 4: emotional support

Standard statement: *The patient and his or her carers have access, in confidence, to expertise in counselling, psychological and spiritual care, to provide emotional support.*

Heads of homes talked of the importance of giving emotional support to their dying residents. Nevertheless there is a widespread notion, that we all tend to operate with, of 'timely' and 'untimely' deaths, where death in someone well past their 'span' is less tragic than the death of someone of a younger age (Sidell, 1995). This can lead to an assumption that older people are accepting of death and therefore are less fearful and less emotionally traumatized than younger people. This assumption may be valid for some older people. Others may be no more reconciled to their own death than they were in their youth. The fear of death is not necessarily something which fades with its increasing proximity. Indeed it could be argued that it becomes more acute as death becomes a reality.

In this study we found that heads of homes perceived a need for people not to die alone. Indeed one of the upsetting aspects of sudden deaths for home staff was that the person died without the comfort of another human being. Good practice in terminal care was thought by most heads of homes to include having someone to sit with the dying person so that they did not die alone. Mechanisms such as two-hourly attention to pressure areas were aimed at keeping a regular – if not constant – vigil and many homes managed to spare a member of staff for long periods. This was very much dependent on the staffing ratios in the home and could be a problem at night when staffing levels are particularly low. Family and friends were a much-appreciated resource in maintaining that vigil. The view that people might prefer to die alone was not one to which many subscribed.

Many expressed the view that a residential home afforded the support that was sometimes lacking when older people lived alone, often in isolated circumstances, and that the comfort and security of being part of a community was one of the benefits of entering residential care. Religious homes provided overt spiritual support and some homes used the services of ministers of religion. But, as noted earlier, this is a source which could be tapped more frequently for those who hold religious beliefs.

Standard No 5: bereavement care and support

Standard statement: *The carers of the dying person have access to bereavement counselling, information, and support services, including external agencies.*

A death in a residential or nursing home affects the whole of the home and therefore this standard relates not only to formal and informal carers but to the other residents in the home.

Many heads of homes recognized that relatives and friends needed help as they watched their loved ones die and they took on this role. Older spouses were recognized as in particular need of such support. This was much more likely to occur where they had a long-standing relationship with the relatives.

It was also recognized that care staff in the home could be very vulnerable when caring for a dying resident. It was not uncommon in the homes for care staff to grow close to a particular resident. This was especially the case where residents had no relatives or friends living locally who could visit and staff felt that they replaced the function of the family. Particular care was taken with young care assistants who had not previously experienced death.

Care staff were mostly encouraged to express their emotions when a resident died and some homes were very sensitive about the way they told off-duty staff of a death that had occurred while they were away. These homes would ring the key carer at home to let them know, or they would ensure that they intercepted the carer as they entered the home so that they would not simply learn about the death in a casual manner.

We found very different views and practices in supporting other residents when one of their number has died. Some heads of homes were sensitive to the impact that the death of a fellow resident might have on the other residents and aware of the grief that they might experience. Typically they would tell each one individually and pay special attention to residents who had been particularly close to the deceased. Other practices included telling small groups of residents in unit sitting-rooms at the same time or making a collective announcement at meal times. Most tried not to make such announcements at bedtime when residents were more likely to be alone for a longish period. A small minority of heads of homes did not actually tell anyone about a death but let the information filter out. The least sensitive practices were invariably accompanied by the view that the other residents showed little concern for their fellows and that death did not have much impact on them anyway, either because they had 'come to terms with it' or were too mentally frail to understand what was going on.

The immediate procedures which follow a death can have an impact on the experience of bereavement, especially for relatives. Best practice was to seek the relatives' wishes beforehand about being kept informed and about the likely time of death so that they could be present if they so wished. Some wanted to be called in the night, others preferred to leave it till the next morning. Relatives were usually allowed to stay with their loved one for as long as they wished to make their farewells and would be plied with cups of tea as a gesture of solace. Apart from those relatives who were considered to be 'undeserving', every effort was made to help them cope with their grief. They were made to feel welcome as visitors to the home after the death but this was taken up in only a small number of cases.

Funerals are an important part of bereavement care. We had some examples in our study of homes which hosted funerals and held wakes and memorial services in the home. This was relatively unusual but most homes encouraged care staff to attend funerals for their own sakes and for the sake of the relatives who indeed did appreciate their presence. Some heads of homes said that they invited other residents to attend funerals but they rarely took up this offer.

In general the need for bereavement care was recognized by most heads of homes and this was something that they attempted to do well. It was also something which they acknowledged as a training need.

Standard No 6: specialist education for staff

Standard statement: *Specialist knowledge gained through courses, work experience and seminars, exists, is kept up-to-date within the multidisciplinary team, and disseminated to other professionals.*

In many ways this standard is the key to achieving the other standards. Heads of all nursing and dual registered homes were qualified nurses and many heads of private residential homes also had a nursing qualification. However, most of these nursing qualifications had been gained many years previously. Some nursing home staff were regularly updated, others were not. Staff with actual qualifications in palliative care were rare. Our study revealed very little training either in-house or by attendance on courses which were specifically about the care of dying and bereaved people. Many homes say they are involved in NVQ training but we had little evidence of staff completing courses. Some homes talk about informal training when they discuss issues of death and dying as and when they arise. But compared to training in lifting, or management of pressure sores, death and dying is conspicuous by its absence.

When asked about what training they thought ought to be available, we met with quite different reactions. There were those who saw this as a great gap in their education and those at the other end of the spectrum who felt that care of dying people was down to common sense and goodwill. Staff training has great financial implications and some, particularly the private homes, were worried that their investment in training would be wasted if staff moved on.

Conclusion

Achieving any of these palliative care core standards in residential and nursing homes is dependent on three elements, all of which we believe are attainable. The degree and quality of external support, the training available for staff and the resources, especially adequate staffing levels, available in the home provide an environment where the best quality of care for dying people can flourish.

George and Sykes believe 'that palliative care for all is the only moral, intellectual and practical way forward' (1997: 252). Nevertheless they usefully discuss some of the difficulties in translating practices developed mainly in relation to cancer into feasible practices for older people, dying from a much more diverse and multisystem pathology. They highlight the problem of communicating with older people who may be confused or have impaired hearing or vision. We would argue that this is a training issue as it represents a challenge for carers who need to be aware that pain and other symptoms may not be easily articulated.

George and Sykes also acknowledge that 'emphasis on family involvement and support may be less appropriate than in cancer' (1997: 247). It is certainly the case that many residents in homes have outlived their family and friends or are geographically so distant that they lack that support. Home staff frequently take on the role of family resulting in a much greater and more intense involvement. This serves only to emphasize the need for bereavement support for both formal and informal carers which is the essence of good practice in palliative care.

The dying trajectory in homes is very different from those dying in hospices. It is usually interpreted very narrowly by heads of homes as a few days or maybe one or two weeks before death. This is based on a retrospective assessment, but when asked about the cause of deaths in the homes most talked of general deterioration and for many residents this will have been a long and slow process. The period of dying is so narrowly defined by heads of homes, sometimes to just a few days, that it makes it very hard to engage with other professionals and set in motion good palliative care practices. Making artificial distinctions between living and dying is the way the homes cope with a situation which they see as otherwise too depressing for themselves and the other residents. But palliative care in its broadest sense is about relieving distress and discomfort and would be an appropriate approach to helping all residents who suffer from debilitating chronic illnesses.

References

Booth, T. (1985) *Home Truth: Old People's Homes and the Outcomes of Care*. Aldershot: Gower.

Buckman, R. (1988) *I Don't Know What to Say*. London: Macmillan.

Centre for Policy on Ageing (1984) *Home Life: A Code of Practice for Residential Care*. London: Centre for Policy on Ageing.

Centre for Policy on Ageing (1996) *A Better Home Life: The Code of Practice for Residential Care*. London: Centre for Policy on Ageing.

Clough, R. (1981) *Old Age Homes*. London: Allen and Unwin.

Counsel and Care (1995) *Last Rights*. London: Counsel and Care.

Department of Health (1991) *The Health of the Nation: A Consultative Document for Health in England*. London: HMSO.

Douglas, C. (1992) 'For all the Saints', *British Medical Journal*, 304: 579.

Field, D. (1996) *Awareness and Modern Dying*. Paper delivered at the BSA Medical Sociology Conference, September 20–22.

George, R. and Sykes, J. (1997) 'Beyond cancer?', in S. Ahmedzai, D. Clark and J. Hockley (eds), *New Themes in Palliative Care*. Buckingham: Open University Press. pp. 239–54.

Goffman, Erving (1961) *Asylums: Essays on the Social Situation of Mental Patients and Other Inmates*. London: Penguin Books.

Hanvey, C. (1989) 'Death in residence', in T. Philpot (ed.), *Last Things*. London: Reed Publishing/Community Care.

Hockey, J. (1990) *Experiences of Death*. Edinburgh: Edinburgh University Press.

Kayser-Jones, J. (1995) 'Decision making in the treatment of acute illness in nursing homes: framing the decision problem, treatment plan, and outcome', *Medical Anthropology Quarterly*, 9 (2): 236–56.

Laing's Review of Private Health Care 1995: and Directory of Independent Hospitals, Nursing and Residential Homes and Related Services. London: Laing and Buisson.

Maguire, P. and Faulkner, A. (1988a) 'Improve the counselling skills of doctors and nurses in cancer care', *British Medical Journal*, 297 (2): 847–9.

Maguire, P. and Faulkner, A. (1988b) 'Communicating with cancer patients: (1) handling bad news and difficult questions', *British Medical Journal*, 297 (2): 907–9.

Peace, S., Kellaher, L. and Willcocks, D. (1997) *Re-evaluating Residential Care*. Buckingham: Open University Press.

Phillipson, C. and Walker, A. (eds) (1986) *Ageing and Social Policy – A Critical Assessment*. Aldershot: Gower.

Shemmings, Y. (1996) *Death, Dying and Residential Care*. Aldershot: Avebury.

Sidell, M. (1995) *Health in Old Age, Myth, Mystery and Management*. Buckingham: Open University Press.

Sinclair, I. (1988) 'The elderly', in I. Sinclair (ed.), *Residential Care: The Research Reviewed*. London: NISW.

Townsend, P. (1962) *The Last Refuge – a Survey of Residential Institutions and Homes for the Aged in England and Wales*. London: Routledge and Kegan Paul.

Trent Hospice Audit Group (1992) *Palliative Care Core Standards: A Multi-disciplinary Approach*. Nottingham: Trent Hospice Audit.

Wagner, G. (1988) *Residential Care: A Positive Choice*. Report of the Independent Review of Residential Care. London: HMSO.

Willcocks, D., Kellaher, L. and Peace, S. with Ring, J. (1982) *Residential Lives of Old People*. Research Report, No. 12, Survey Research Unit, Polytechnic of North London.

20

Complementary medicine – its place in the care of dying people

Patrick C. Pietroni

Probably there is no greater factor which determines the nature of our health care system than our attitude towards death, and indeed whether we believe in life after death. Different cultures have different concepts of death in the same way as there are different attitudes towards courtship, marriage and birth. Medical practice that is linked to these 'rites of passage' is influenced profoundly by the cultural attitudes and beliefs associated with these life events. In the nineteenth century, with the increasing influence of science in medicine, the use of powerful drugs and anaesthesia, we begin to see a separation between natural death and abnormal death.

Natural death was seen to come without previous sickness or obvious cause. It is very rare to find a picture of a doctor or nurse at a deathbed scene before the nineteenth century. After the First World War, pictures depict doctors fighting valiantly against death, tearing a young woman from the arms of a skeleton – locking a skeleton in the cupboard. And as our own modern culture has developed we have become adept not only at denying the possibility of death but at seeking ways to delay the ageing process. The consequence of this cultural shift is that our own Health Service has assumed a role more akin to a 'death prevention service'. Medical practice in most Western cultures developed an impressive array of drugs, surgical procedures, heroic interventions, to ward off and delay the time of death. Many of these initiatives are now considered to be good medical practice, but have in the last 30 years been influenced by the pioneers of palliative care, including Elisabeth Kübler-Ross and Cicely Saunders.

Complementary medicine is a 'pot-pourri' of approaches to health care that are not, as yet, taught in Western undergraduate medical schools. Some of these approaches, for example osteopathy, require four to five years' rigorous training and draw upon a Western framework of illness and disease. Others, such as spiritual healing, have no formal training and operate from a belief system that has no place in Western medicine and is rejected by most scientific doctors. Many, if not all, of those therapies that have found a place in the care of dying patients have arisen from non-Western cultures whose attitudes and approaches to death are at variance with the traditional views we are familiar with, that is, death is to be denied, death is to be feared, death is to be delayed and death is the end.

Although Socrates felt that philosophy – the love of wisdom – was 'simply and solely the practice of dying – the practice of death', this view has not taken root firmly in Western civilizations. However, it is found to form the basis of much Eastern philosophy from which many health care practices in complementary medicine are derived. In the *Tibetan Book of the Dead*, which is a treatise on how to die, it is considered that it is not possible to judge the value of a person's life until one has witnessed his or her manner of dying. Shavasana – the corpse posture – is one of the first postures taught in Yoga as a preparation for death. The aspirant Yogi is then taught Udana Prana – the control of breath during the last few hours of life – and Yoga Nidra – dreamless sleep – which is a practice to help students experience the 'state of death'. These exercises would be unacceptable to the majority of Western patients if expressed in the language and belief systems of Yoga. However, these have been adapted by many practitioners and are now finding favour in many hospitals, including hospice centres.

Breathing exercises and progressive muscular relaxation

The vicious cycle of anxiety, muscle tension, pain is not uncommon in patients dying with terminal cancer. Even when the terminal phase of someone's life does not involve physical pain, the fear and mental anguish often linked to dying may ensure that the last few days or hours are made far worse for both the dying person and his or her family. Breathing and relaxation exercises which can be taught and learnt before the event can provide great solace for all concerned. In the same way as a pregnant woman can learn to moderate and modulate the pain of childbirth through breathing exercises, many patients can learn to reduce the level of distress following surgery and during painful procedures.

Most of us develop a pattern of *chest breathing* during anxiety-laden situations. Breathing tends to be shallow and fast with an emphasis on inhalation and increased muscle tension. This pattern of breathing can be prolonged after the frightening or painful event is over and become the regular and 'normal' breathing pattern. *Diaphragmatic breathing*, which does not involve the movement of the chest muscles, leads to a deeper, more prolonged breathing pattern with an emphasis on exhalation and is the pattern observed in people who are relaxed and whose metabolism is in a restful state. Teaching individuals how to shift from chest to diaphragmatic breathing in classes or through the use of cassette tapes when they can practice at home is both simple and easy. It provides for a self-help 'tool' to be used in difficult and stressful situations as well as a health-promoting exercise to enhance well-being.

This simple skill is often taught alongside a muscular relaxation exercise which can help to undo physical tension present in the face, back of the neck, hands or other muscle groupings. There are several techniques described, from a systematic and progressive muscular 'tensing and releasing' exercise through to one where each muscle group in turn is encouraged to relax using a count of one to five: 'On the count of one, allow your arm to feel heavier and relaxed. On the count of two . . . etc.' Once individuals have mastered these simple skills which allow them to obtain some mastery and control over their bodies, it is possible to introduce more complex skills which allow them to have some control over their thoughts, feelings and imaginative processes.

Meditation

This 'skill' of calming the mind is associated with many Eastern spiritual traditions. It received a boost in the 1960s when the Beatles were photographed sitting at the feet of Maharishi Mahesh Yogi. The practice of meditation is, however, well-founded in Christian mystical texts as well: for example, the spiritual exercises of Ignatius Loyola. In the last 40 years it has achieved scientific respectability after many research studies identified the effect it had on blood pressure, heart rate, brain-wave patterns, anxiety levels and performance under stressful conditions. It has now been used as a 'complementary therapy' in such diverse conditions as high blood pressure, migraine, asthma, breast cancer and coronary prevention. There are several different techniques used in meditation, some focusing the mind on an object (picture, flame) or sound (mantra), others which encourage the mind to 'open up' and transcend normal human consciousness. The aim of all such processes is to achieve a state of mental calmness where troubled thoughts, worries and anxieties no longer intrude and the individual is freed for a while from painful, emotional experiences.

Individuals who meditate regularly find there is a 'carry-over' effect, that is, the state of calmness persists during the remaining 24-hour period and not only whilst the individual is meditating. Learning to meditate may require a few lessons from a teacher, although some people can learn from a cassette tape. Some individuals find learning in a group much easier, although others can be too self-conscious to join a group. Learning the basics of diaphragmatic breathing and muscular relaxation is an important first step as the distractions that come from a physical body that is in pain or uncomfortable can make the meditative state difficult to obtain.

Meditation is most often taught sitting upright in a chair, although there is no reason why someone who is bedridden cannot be taught it. It is important to explain to 'students' that meditation taught within a caring or medical context need not carry any spiritual connotations, whether Christian, Buddhist, agnostic or atheist. That some people who meditate regularly find a re-awakening of their own spirituality may be a by-product which, for some, will be welcome. Many dying patients have found the peace and inner calmness that regular meditation brings of particular help in their last few weeks of life. Unfortunately, many patients in the West will only learn how to meditate when they know they are approaching death. If they are in physical pain as well, this may make it impossible for them to achieve the state of 'physiological non-arousal' (the scientific term for the meditative state). The inability to learn how to meditate in such circumstances is unfortunately all too common and enthusiasts and teachers of meditation must guard against this and caution patients whose distress is too great from attempting to learn. All too often the wholesale application of self-help techniques to vulnerable individuals who are unable to make use of these techniques only helps to increase their burden and, at times, their guilt – 'It's my fault I can't meditate. . . .'

Visualization

Visualization, or guided imagery, like meditation, is a self-help and therapeutic technique that is well described in Eastern spiritual and medical texts and has become increasingly popular in the West, although, as yet, it is not well integrated with more orthodox approaches. The technique involves the imagining of 'mental pictures', 'a calm sea' or a 'beautiful garden rose', for a period of time whilst in a state of deep relaxation. In the same way that imagining cutting a lemon will produce physiological changes (salivation), it is believed that visualizing peaceful and calm scenes will decrease the level of stress hormone and effect cellular changes in the immune system that play a part in warding off infection and destroying cancer cells.

It is in the treatment of cancer that visualization has made most public impact. In the Simonton technique, the patient is encouraged to imagine his/her white blood cells eating/destroying the cancer cells in his/her body. In the initial study, the Simontons claimed that those patients who were able to visualize in this way were able to make their cancers regress and thereby live longer. Subsequent studies have failed to support this initial claim, although it has been shown that less aggressive images (a peaceful scene) can significantly affect the mood of patients with cancer and reduce their level of depression. Visualization is more difficult to learn than meditation, and if attempted as a 'last resort' can be of little or no value.

It is interesting to observe how techniques which arose out of an Eastern cultural attitude to death, that is, 'expect and accept', when used by many Western therapists and patients become altered and are used as a way to prolong life and avoid death. The *positive health* movement that has taken over many of these therapies is, at times, responsible for deluding not only itself but many vulnerable and distressed patients that these techniques are another form of the 'magic bullet'. That they can help to reduce unnecessary suffering and pain and ease the process of dying there is no doubt, but they must not be sold as some form of do-it-yourself radiotherapy which can dissolve away all cancerous and diseased tissue.

Massage and aromatherapy

So far we have discussed 'self-help' techniques. Massage and aromatherapy (the use of essential oils) are particularly good examples of complementary therapy in the care of dying patients. Massage is one of the oldest healing interventions. It was written about in 3000 BC and Hippocrates himself wrote: 'The way to health is to have a scented bath and an oiled massage each day.' Until the nineteenth century, massage was commonly referred to in medical textbooks, but with the advent of drug therapy it lost its appeal and it is only fairly recently that it has regained a respectability within the medical and nursing professions. There is nothing more natural or human than the use of touch to relieve pain and distress, whether it is a hug, a hand on the shoulder or a mother rubbing around the injured knee of her young child.

Massage is a form of 'structured touch' or 'therapeutic touch' which has been and can be used systematically to relieve muscle pain and tension, bring about a sense of relaxation, and for those isolated and lonely, re-affirm their humanity with contact from another human being. In the care of the dying, it can be most powerfully used to help with the sense of hopelessness and despair that surrounds the deathbed. Many relatives who sit helplessly round the hospital bed can be taught to massage the foot or hand of their wife, husband, father or mother, which will reduce the anxiety and bring pleasure to both the giver and the recipient. For unlike many other therapies, massage can be used as a form of communication between therapist and patient as well as a specific intervention for the relief of pain and muscle tension. Apart from simple common-sense caveats of avoiding open wounds, vein thromboses and areas of extreme sensitivity, massage for the dying patient is of particular use.

Most modern Western massage techniques are derived from the work of Per Henrik Ling, who devised what is now called Swedish massage, which involves one of four main techniques: percussion – short, sharp, fast rhythmic movements; effleurage – slow, rhythmic strokes usually performed with the hands close together; petrissage – involving grasping and squeezing sections of the skin such as those close to the waist or stomach; and friction – a series of small circular movements made by one or more fingers, the heel of the hand or the pads of the thumbs. Many weekend courses teaching massage now exist and it is not uncommon to find massage therapists attached to hospital wards, working in hospices or linked to a general practice.

The use of oils in massage is important to avoid unnecessary pain and friction and aromatherapy takes this practice further by using aromatic, highly concentrated essential oils during massage. This is not always necessary and inhalation and scented baths are additional ways of obtaining the benefit of these oils. The oils are produced by the tiny glands in the petals, leaves, stems, bark and wood of many plants and trees. They are extracted through a process of distillation and concentration. Their modern use was pioneered by a French chemist, Professor Renie Gattefosse, who accidentally discovered the power of lavender essence when he plunged his hand into it after receiving a bad burn. Qualified aromatherapists will use different oils for different conditions: for example, cedarwood, because of its sedative effect, will be used for anxiety and for troublesome coughs, and rosemary, which has an invigorating and refreshing effect, will be used for someone who is depressed, tired or has lost his or her memory.

Acupuncture

The placing of sterile needles in the skin forms one element of traditional Chinese medicine (TCM). It has received much interest recently in the care of the dying because of its ability to reduce pain, enhance muscular relaxation and induce anaesthesia. TCM, like many approaches to healing derived from Eastern traditions, is based on the concept of 'Chi' or life force. Chinese practitioners believe that in addition to a circulatory and nervous system in the body there is an equivalent energetic system. Illness, disease, well-being and ultimately death are dependent on the harmonious and balanced flow of energy through the channels known as meridians.

Acupuncture needles are placed along points in this energetic system to help unblock and release the flow of 'Chi', thus restoring health. This model of understanding traditional Chinese medicine and acupuncture was disregarded by Western-trained doctors. In the last 20 years, as a result of a number of serious studies, it has become evident that not only can acupuncture help in pain relief but that its mode of action can be easily understood in Western terms. Several studies have demonstrated that during acupuncture, the body releases endorphines, a class of chemicals known to relieve pain and decrease muscle arousal. In clinical settings, acupuncture is now frequently used for pain relief and in the care of the dying patient this can be of particular benefit, especially when the use of oral or parenteral [not absorbed through the digestive tract] analgesia produces sedation. This specialized use of acupuncture requires a skilled practitioner.

Spiritual healing

By far the most common complementary therapy sought for and used by dying patients is spiritual healing, according to the most recent survey of complementary therapists in the UK. The laying on of hands and blessings have always formed part of spiritual practice and derive their authority from the Scriptures. European royalty, who claimed to rule by Divine Right, took on this power – 'The King's Touch' – but by 1600 itinerant healers were common all over England. Modern science, notwithstanding some rather elegant research studies, dismisses this approach as a 'placebo effect', and regards the 'miraculous' cures occasionally reported as examples of spontaneous remission only. Whether or not healing works does not belie the fact that many dying patients receive enormous comfort and hope after being visited by a healer. Healing is generally considered to be a two-way process. The first thing a healer will do is to talk soothingly and generally calm the patient. A state of deep relaxation is then encouraged and the healer will then focus on his or her powers and allow them to flow through his/her hands to the patient. The patient may also be instructed to visualize projections of white or coloured light which are thought to aid the healing process. Sessions are usually undertaken once a week and many healers will visit patients in their own homes – a decided advantage. Indeed, many healers will not charge for their services. A register of practitioners willing to visit patients in hospital as well as in their home is available from the Confederation of Healing Organizations (CHO). Several Christian Churches now hold regular healing services where the 'laying on of hands' and anointment with oils is carried out within the context of receiving the sacrament. But in orthodox medicine, doctors are justifiably concerned that false hopes may be raised and that patients may not seek orthodox treatments for complaints because they are seeking a spiritual healer.

Conclusion

A range of complementary therapies are now in widespread use in European countries and in North America, both through independent practitioners and within established health systems. They are most notably present in the care of dying people and have been welcomed more in hospices and within the developing specialism of palliative care than within mainstream curative medicine.

21

Speaking out

*Sarah Palmer**

My grandmother, aged 98, was admitted to hospital following a rectal bleed shortly after losing her daughter (my mother) and her closest sister.

Perhaps understandably she was initially put on a surgical ward, although she had a history of diverticulitis that explained the bleeding, and meeting her basic needs of nutrition, fluids, pressure area care and mobilization was the priority for her quality of life at that time.

My grandmother was grieving and felt very isolated. I live and work in another part of the country. The journey to see her at weekends took five and a half hours each way.

I requested an assessment of care in the hope that a nursing home placement could be found. I did not feel she was fit to return to residential care. The hospital made it clear that they wanted her bed. My request for a referral to the physician specializing in the care of the elderly was rejected out of hand.

Meanwhile, many of my grandmother's needs were neglected. She was neither helped to feed, nor hydrated nor mobilized, yet she was subjected to clinical investigations that were pointless. Even had an operable cause for the bleeding been found, it would have been inappropriate to operate at her age.

I was horrified to see the deterioration in her, and I continually appealed to nursing staff to attend to her needs. There was little interest and no compassion. I was repeatedly told that my grandmother was not a surgical priority. I had the feeling that conversations were the result of a meticulous briefing. The ward sister was adamant that my grandmother's condition was unchanged, even though she was visibly failing fast.

Where was the consultant in this? He refused to see me at any time when I could get there and would not speak to me on the telephone. Nurses seemed to take no initiative without him yet I could not gain access to the unseen omnipotent.

My heart breaks to recall my grandmother's distress about her wasting skin and unquenched thirst. Now I wish I had dropped everything to stay near her throughout the hospital stay. But I had my mother's home to sort out, a job and a mortgage.

---

*Sarah Palmer is a pen name.

From the *Nursing Times*, 30 September 1998, 94(39): 15.

In moments of rashness I thought of discharging her and caring for her myself, but there was nowhere that I could take her. She would never have survived the journey to my home and her own rented home was gone.

As I did the round trip each weekend, and telephoned each day, I allowed myself to believe that if I appealed long and often enough, some shadow of the sensitivity that must surely have been present when these people had first entered the 'caring professions' would break through and respond to my grandmother's needs and my own. Sadly, I was wrong.

My persistence was to no avail. My grandmother suffered unnecessarily before dying. I have lost her and my faith in nurses, the NHS and human nature.

22

Caring for mother

Susan Leifer

The incident – the diagnosis

In August 1989 my mother, aged 64, suffered a severe and damaging stroke. The fact that I was on a small Greek island with my two young children, didn't get the news for two days and then had to travel back without a ticket, in mid-season, via Athens airport represents graphically the disruption and distress that ensued and continues.

Prior to this occurrence, she had experienced 20 years of sad widowhood, had a propensity to become very 'worked-up' very fast, and had suffered small strokes of a mildly disabling nature leaving her with an unpleasant residue called 'thalamic syndrome' – intractable pain caused by a lesion in the brain.

She was discovered on the floor by a neighbour who called an ambulance and she was admitted to the Royal Free Hospital where she remained until November. I was told by the Consultant Geriatrician that she would never walk again and that the prognosis, although uncertain, was very poor. She was doubly incontinent, could not speak properly, was aware of her circumstances enough to be depressed and distressed. Her vision was affected and her quality of life was nil. In this state, I was her only representative towards the rest of the world, and her only child.

She and I had not been the best of friends since my adolescence. She was an elegant, houseproud, traditional middle-class lady. She didn't like my hair (unruly and wild), my clothes, my bad language, pseudo-intellectualism, lack of respect for the establishment, etc. In turn I was disappointed that she didn't help me with my children like a grandma should – play with them, read to them, have them for weekends. She couldn't. She was too ill, even before the stroke, because she was stroke-bound, but this was hard to accept.

The options after discharge from the hospital

(i) My home with a nurse

I would have wanted to do this if I knew it had a foreseeable end. I would have enjoyed trying to get closer to her and making her comfortable for 'the end', if this was the end. But it might not be. It could be months – years.

Maybe this would have been a possibility if the relationship had been better, but I couldn't do it.

(ii) Residential care

Fortunately my mother's finances, quite unbeknown to me before, were sufficient to cover the indefinite cost of a nice residential home. Local to me, pretty curtains, constant Philippino ladies to care, but totally out of the question. My mother didn't even enjoy the company of the refined, educated lady in the next bed – let alone a house full of people.

(iii) Home to her flat with a nurse

I told myself that this is what she would want. I tried to talk to her to elicit a real response, but basically I put all I knew about her, gathered in 40 years, together and pretended she'd decided. She is a very private, home-loving person; not sociable and hating strangers, strange places, strange routines, etc.

I advertised in the local paper and contacted agencies and hired a cheerful, resourceful New Zealander with great references and an air of confidence. My mother started eating again – she was informed of all the plans and met Karen *before* she was hired. I pretended she had helped to make the decisions.

Some spontaneous recovery occurred and Karen trained her (a) to be continent in the day and (b) to walk with two hands held in front. This took six months.

We had to find a *sub-structure of carers* to relieve Karen – who needed time off. I am not great as an employer so I found this an enormous strain.

At first, my mother attended the day centre twice a week. After a couple of months of the day centre there was *an incident*. My mother flung her tea at a care assistant. The member of staff flung it back. The former got evicted from the day centre; the latter got disciplined. I cried. We needed the day centre. Too bad, my mother was now a known risk to other attenders.

Daily routines and the effect on our life

From the beginning, I felt I had to visit every day. Her flat is only five minutes' drive away and, in spite of our history, I am the only person she is pleased to see. I punctuate her day. Also, the carer – no longer Karen, who left after eight months, but Belinda, from Australia – needs support. It is an isolated and depressing job.

This is a considerable burden and usually means I'm not helping with homework, or making the supper when I should be. Sometimes I get there earlier in the day and then it is 'done'.

Every Sunday since her return from hospital, my mother has come to lunch. This seems 'the right thing to do' and helps the Sunday relief carer who is a medical student.

Some of the problems

I want to show *my children* that you must care for your loved ones with respect and affection and make them comfortable and happy. I suspect they pick up that there is a good deal of resentment, bitterness and anger.

Why should I pull down her knickers, do everything for her, pull them up again and again and again, when she never looked after my children and didn't like my hair?

When she says, 'I want to go home', when she *is* at home, how can I help her feel at home, when her home inevitably feels like the annexe of an Antipodean party?

Her friends

She actually has some very nice friends, whom she was good to when she was well. She had many friends. They have deserted her to a man. And yet, when she dies and I ring and tell them, they will all come to the funeral. I am very upset about this and I do not want them to come. It will be too late.

My relationship with her

The animosity of my rather extended teenage years is gone. I now feel great pity. She was an upright, moral person, why should she suffer so much now? She is like my child, she often calls me 'Mummy' – but she is a huge burden which will not lighten.

I wish she would die

The consultant, who gave her such a poor prognosis, told me at the last check-up that I had kept her alive. Terrific. To whom was I doing any favours? Her quality of life is still nil. The best things that happen to her are a bath, a nice meal, seeing me (with the hair) singing along with *Neighbours*. I think *she'd* rather be dead. I think; I don't know.

POSTSCRIPT
written in 1998, almost six years after her death

Exactly two years after her massive stroke, my mother, aged almost 66, gradually stopped taking nourishment. As a lay person, I believe that this was partly due to the deterioration in her swallowing reflex, and partly due to her diminishing desire to fight for her life. We had our third Antipodean carer, who had more medical, as opposed to social caring, qualifications, which was fortunate.

The NHS consultant, who had originally and incorrectly told me that my mother would never walk again, would not provide any domiciliary care, and urged me to admit my mother to the geriatric ward, although it was unlikely that they could help her. I knew that she was dying. She was not going to die in any geriatric ward. I said 'thank you' and inevitably 'good-bye' to the hospital service. We were now really alone with what looked like a terminal situation and this was neurology and not cancer, so Macmillan and Marie Curie were not on offer.

Fortunately, funds permitted us to bring in a private GP. He immediately fixed up a drip to my mother's neck. I found this a very upsetting procedure, and decided to call my aunt, her sister, in Boston, who got on the next flight. My mother, with her eyes open, and a meaningful expression on her face, pulled the drip out of her neck three times. The GP took my aunt and me to one side and asked us if we wanted him to keep inserting the drip, or do something else (I can't remember what, but it was a serious and invasive medical procedure), otherwise he would give her Valium and allow nature to take its course. This decision was way beyond me, but my aunt was quite clear that her sister should not be forced to endure further suffering.

After that, my mother slipped away over a period of about two days. The night before she died, I gave the nurse/carer the night off, as she had been under great stress. We had one of the medically unqualified previous carers there instead, and had to call out the GP in the night to administer intravenous Valium. I felt I had mismanaged the almost end. She died at lunchtime: I had left the room and was in the kitchen preparing my children's lunch. I think that she needed to die alone.

Two important things that have happened since

1. A year after my mother's death, my mother-in-law, aged 85, was diagnosed as having cancer of the lung. She was a very frail old lady who had lost her husband two years previously and was living in a home for the elderly. The prognosis was very poor. I had no hesitation in saying that she

must come to die in our home: we would get a nurse. I collected her almost immediately and managed, after 'phoning New Zealand, to locate Karen, the same first carer that we had engaged for my mother three years earlier.

Because this was cancer, the Marie Curie/Macmillan system was available to us: skilled and charming people, who came in the night when necessary, letting themselves in with a key, to successfully administer pain relief.

My mother-in-law was a pleasure to care for, she enjoyed the interest and bustle of the children's company. Friends and relations came to visit and she died within three weeks. It was a positive experience for all of us. She also died when we slipped out of the room. But after this 'good end', I felt absolutely dreadful that this hospitality and care had not been offered to my own mother. Rationally, the difference was that the cancer had a definable end and a structured support system for us as carers; whereas my mother's stroke could have gone on indefinitely and there was no relief for her anguish or system to help us.

2. There has not been one day in the last six years that I have not thought of and missed my mother. We had a difficult, and sometimes furious relationship, but I would do anything to have her back at my table for Sunday lunch, and do the toilet duty and hear her criticisms of me just to have her there. Also, I wish I had held her more, touched her and cuddled her, for who else was there but me to show physical affection?

No one's wealth, looks or husband ever incites jealousy in me, but I am envious of people of my generation with parents. I hate being a 47-year-old orphan.

23

Living with MS

Richard Were

Richard Were is 52 years old and married to Ann with three children: John, 23; Anna, 17; and Joseph, 8. He was diagnosed with Multiple Sclerosis in 1992 and last worked in May 1993 as a computer consultant project manager. Apart from brief holidays, he has lived at home for the last six years. Today, he spends most of his leisure time at art classes, at the cinema, with friends, swimming, watching rugby or trying to make his fortune on the stock market.

When I was asked to write about living with MS I was pleased. It's always nice to think that you might have something interesting to say. I thought it would be easy. After all, I have MS and I am living. Just write down a few thoughts, wrap it up, send it off and sit back feeling smug. Well, it's not turning out like that at all. It's more like opening Pandora's box. Facing up to things I'd rather not face up to. Weeping into the keyboard. I'm going to write about my life as if it is happening as I write, so that you may imagine what it is like to be me, so here goes.

I got up twice during the night for a leak. It's a nuisance and it doesn't seem to matter much what I drink the previous day. Getting to the bathroom is a bit of a struggle. I can stand and walk a few steps using two sticks. I flip the duvet off me onto the middle of the bed, or sometimes onto Ann, my wife, which annoys her, then I get my legs over the side of the bed and sit up. My legs often become straight and rigid during the night, with the muscle spasms. My legs also stay locked together and won't stay apart. Often my feet cross over. This has the curious and destabilizing effect that I sometimes place one foot on top of the other when I walk, or even one leg behind the other! There are drugs to help with this spasticity but I don't take anything. I did try some once but it made me sleepy during the day, which I didn't like, so I prefer the spasms.

First, I use my hands to move my legs over the edge of the bed then I push myself up into a sitting position. Next I stand up, using one stick and keeping the other hand on the bed. Once I'm steady enough, I pick up the other stick and straighten up slowly. This is a dangerous moment as my balance is very poor. Now I walk forward to the bathroom door, six or eight feet away. Usually my legs feel as if they are fixed to the floor and I drag my feet a few inches at a time. After a time I reach the bathroom door and then I can hold on to the door frame, the walls and the wash basin until I reach the toilet. I sit down with a bit of a crash and get comfortable by levering on the nearby surfaces. Made it!

Now for the leak. Usually the quantity is disappointing and doesn't seem worth the effort. It takes several minutes before I feel ready to make the return trip to bed. This is similar to the outward journey except that I am heading back into the bedroom, which is darker, and I am even less stable. It is a relief to get back to the bed. I sit midway along the side and roll backwards, lifting one leg with my hand. Usually the other leg comes with it and I get into bed, flip the duvet back over me and snuggle down. The whole adventure may take as much as 15 minutes!

I don't usually sleep very well, turning over most of the night to try to get comfortable. My back aches particularly and I'm glad when morning comes. Ann goes downstairs to make the tea and brings it back upstairs. We have tea in bed every day. I used to make the tea on Sundays when I was working, until I fell up the stairs carrying it one day, years ago now. Afterwards I wash, get dressed and go downstairs. Everything takes a long time. I am pleased to reach the relative safety of my wheelchair.

One day I expect to fall downstairs and break something. I imagine life will become difficult then. Ann has told me that she does not intend to look after me if I become incapable. I will have to get a carer. I wondered if a new wife might be preferable. Since my MS was diagnosed seven years ago, Ann has been quite down to earth and practical, leaving me to get on with my life as independently as possible. She has not been sentimentally sympathetic, helping out when it was not necessary. From time to time, especially in the early days, I resented this attitude but I have come to realize that it has been a significant strengthening influence on us all.

I am not sorry I have MS. I do not feel hard done by and resentful. I am not looking for a cure. My life has changed completely over the last few years, mostly for the better. MS means I do some things painfully slowly and awkwardly and some things I cannot do at all. This is frustrating sometimes, but generally it's just the way things are. A French friend of mine with MS, who also uses a wheelchair, summed it up by taking hold of his leg in both hands and pretending to throw it away over his shoulder, following the gesture with a Gallic curse and a shrug of contempt.

About the time I was diagnosed with MS I had an old Volvo automatic car and my wife drove a car with manual gears. Gradually, over many months, I began to feel more and more uneasy driving, as it took me too long to move my foot from one pedal to the other. I had to anticipate stopping in good time and I knew I'd never be able to make an emergency stop. As my car was very old, I decided not to fit hand controls and I just gave up driving. My wife, friends and acquaintances took me where I needed to go, which was never far, and I enjoyed getting to know people better. Every cloud has a silver lining they say. However, in August 1996, after about 18 months of not driving, we bought a caravan and needed a bigger car to tow it. This gave me the opportunity to buy a newer car with automatic gears, power steering and power braking and have hand controls fitted. The hand controls are just marvellous. There is an unobtrusive lever by the steering wheel which operates both pedals, with a switch on top for the indicators. There is a knob for steering. It's a very simple, well made and robust system which gives me great confidence in driving. The car may also be driven normally using the original controls. The car has been instrumental in extending my day-to-day freedom and independence. A major result has been to allow me to take up art classes and to make new friends, one of whom I give a lift to. When we get there she gets someone to help me in my wheelchair from the car across the deeply luxurious and quite impassable gravel in front of the village hall.

MS has humbled my view of myself. Before MS set in, I used to think I was the bees knees. I was extremely clever, arrogantly superior and quite unbearable, even though the results I achieved were often mediocre. I *knew* I could have got a first at university, if I'd tried. I *knew* I could do the job better than anyone else at work. I *knew* that as a Catholic I was a member of the true religion and had a good chance of going to Heaven, instead of the other poor mugs. I must have been awful! MS has changed my attitude quite dramatically, although it has not been swept away completely.

There are some concrete benefits to MS. I am quite well off financially, thanks to a permanent health insurance policy which I had the good fortune to take out despite thinking at the time that it was too expensive and I'd never need it anyway. In fact, my wife persuaded me to take it, so all thanks to her. Currently, in 1999, MS is incurable, which means that the disability benefits that I receive from the insurance company and from the state continue week by week, month by month and year by year without undue fuss.

There are no unpleasant drugs or painful treatments which apply to people with MS, unlike with cancer for example, so there is nothing to take and no stress and worry that the treatment may not succeed. On the positive side, there are some attractive drugs which may apply to people with MS and may become available on the NHS, particularly cannabis and Viagra. I am looking forward to trying both in due course.

MS has expanded my world by giving me new interests, especially art and music, and the opportunity to meet new and interesting people. I now value friends much more and try to keep in touch with them even after the situation where we met has changed and we have parted company. Previously, I had rarely, if ever, retained friends from one phase of life to another. School friends, university friends, work friends, leisure friends – all were forgotten when my situation changed. Now, my friends are a very important part of my life.

In September 1996 when I started a watercolour class, I made several close friends and we meet regularly to do some art together, or that may be just an excuse. I have enjoyed the art classes and I feel that I am on the fringes of a completely different world to the one I knew when I was working. Last October, in 1998, I started going to a life drawing class which was another change. I found I like life drawing very much and in the last few months two further life classes have started up near home. Now, there are some weeks when I go to three or four art classes, as well as spending an evening with friends. I feel that art has become a significant part of my life.

I usually go swimming twice a week with a friend I met via the local Catholic Helpline and we both enjoy swimming and each other's company.

For quite a lot of the rest of the time, I follow the stock market and try and make my fortune. This has not happened so far but I have every confidence that it will, given enough time. About two years ago, I joined an investment club to pursue this interest and also to meet new people. Last year I was elected Treasurer of the club, which I found flattering, and I enjoyed my duties over the year. However, I have now left the club because I found the lack of positive decision making frustrating. Or, in terms of my earlier character confessions, I left because they wouldn't always do as I said!

My son Joseph, started playing under-eight mini-rugby this season on Sunday mornings at Newbury Rugby Football Club. He is the star player and won the Player's Player trophy recently – the team voted for him unanimously. I bask in his reflected glory. Taking him and watching him play has opened up another new world of friends and acquaintances associated with rugby. We often go to watch the first team play home matches on Saturday afternoons as well.

As a practising Catholic, the church used to be a friendly place and I grew to know many people over the years. Recently, and with some regret, I have stopped going to church and I miss the friendly familiarity of the Sunday morning service. I stopped going because I found it hard to believe the articles of faith.

I joined the Newbury & District Branch of the MS Society several years ago and I am a committee member responsible for communications with the press and for taking bookings for the Branch's holiday chalet on the south coast. The Branch is very active with a strong and enthusiastic chairman, a keen committee and about 140 members in total, 80 or so having MS. During the last year, a new Welfare Secretary has been appointed and he has made it a priority to visit as many members with MS as possible to understand their situation and discover their needs. The overwhelming result from these visits is that the majority of people with MS are badly off in many ways. They need more money and better care to achieve a basic level of comfort but, most of all, they lack friendly company and are very lonely. Many members are unable to go out and do things without help and they depend on their partner or carer. I am so fortunate in comparison to many fellow members. I joined the MS Society several years after being diagnosed with MS and it may be interesting to explore why I was so reluctant.

The diagnosis of my MS was a lengthy process, taking several years from feeling that something was wrong, to the conclusion that I had MS. In the latter stages my neurologist gathered information from a variety of tests undertaken at hospitals in the region. The tests caused me some anxiety because I did not understand what they were testing for. When I arrived at the MRI scanner unit I was expecting that the scan would be of my lower back, which I hurt years before. I remember my consternation when they told me it was to be a brain scan. What! Was there something wrong with my brain! There must be some mistake! I was so anxious, I asked them to check with my neurologist before going ahead.

I also had a lumbar puncture, where some fluid is extracted from the spine for analysis, MRI brain scans, where the patient lies inside a huge magnetic scanner which produces an image of the brain, or other parts of the body, and nerve transmission time or reaction time tests where electrodes were taped to my skull and lights were flashed in my eyes. I was frightened by the tests themselves, particularly the lumbar puncture test, when I was terrified. Since then, my admiration for women, who routinely and stoically endure the unknown processes of childbirth with epidural pain relief is limitless.

None of these tests produced a conclusive result by itself, but the overall conclusion was that I had MS.

My neurologist delivered the final verdict in a brisk and matter of fact way, suggesting that I must have suspected that I had MS. I left his surgery in a daze, not really understanding what was wrong with me or what the future might hold. It was a long time, probably several years, before I could see my position more calmly and clearly.

Because of the length of time the diagnosis took, and because none of the tests produced a definite and incontrovertible conclusion, I preferred, rather irrationally and emotionally, to believe that there was room for a mistake and that I might not have MS after all. This reluctance to accept the verdict may explain why I was reluctant to join the MS Society initially. It would have been admitting that I really did have MS and I wasn't ready for that acceptance.

During the long transition period, from believing I was 'normal' to believing I was 'disabled by an incurable disease' there were many little incidents which stick in my mind. For example, I remember my boss at the time who joked that I would lose the use of my legs when he spotted me taking the lift to go up one floor. Most people who saw me stumbling about assumed I was drunk. One day, at home and feeling good, I decided to walk to the Post, about 400 metres away. I got there without much trouble but on the way home I walked slower and slower, stopping frequently for a rest. Finally, 50 metres from home, I sat in a ditch to try to recover some strength. A group of young mothers returning from school with their children passed by me sitting there, and they all laughed.

The transition has been hard for my two elder children, who knew me when I was in good health and could walk and run and play with them. My daughter, Anna, who was about 10 at the time things started to go wrong, was rather ashamed of me. I think I was an embarrassment to her in front of her friends. During her teens she was very aggressive and rude to me and it is only in the last year or two that we have resumed a more loving relationship. My eldest son, John, was old enough to cope better. At 16, he was already more independent and living his own life. I don't feel that my

MS had such a negative influence on him. My youngest son, Joseph, who at 8 has not known me any other way, is generally pretty good, even though I can't play games with him. When we are with friends he naturally plays with them instead of me, making me rather jealous! The transition must also have been hard for my wife, Ann, but she has coped remarkably well and treats me as if I didn't have MS.

In conclusion, I currently enjoy my life with MS. I have made new friends and I do lots of interesting things. But what about the future? This is more difficult. I know lots of people with MS who are very ill. Some can hardly move at all and need everything done for them. Will I be like that soon? Will I be able to cope? Who can tell? I suspect that I might not cope very well.

24

Saturday Times column 3.10.98

John Diamond

Fuelled by the morphine, which turns dreaming's scatter-gun impressionism into neat and formal narrative, I must have had the *Miraculously, His Voice Returns!* dream half a dozen times over the past fortnight. It comes in various versions linking various parts of my life – voice returns in the staff room of the school I used to teach in, voice returns at the magazine I worked for 15 years ago, voice returns at a party the summer before last – which makes it, I suppose, rather like drowning incredibly slowly and your life running before your eyes in stop-frame motion.

Normally I wake up just as I break the news to a happily weeping family but a recent version went on to the end: the sudden rediscovery of my vocal powers, the slight and not unattractive lisp which is all that remains of the surgery and the return in triumph to the microphone.

Which is odd, because knowing, as I now know, that I won't broadcast again is the least of it. I was only ever a print journalist talking his writing into the mike or the camera, and it is only as a fatherly story-teller, husbandly joke-maker, chatterer to friends, scorner of enemies that I miss the voice. Or miss its prospect, at least, for as things stand I'm not sure what it might be that I will have instead of a voice in six months' or a year's time. Last time I was here I know I said that there was a chance that the operation would actually improve my voice, but that turned out to be as probable as Shergar coming back to win the next Grand National.

You will know that I have an almost childish belief in the power of modern medicine, and therefore when I speak of its failings it's not because I'm one of those modern cynics trying to find some reason in the randomness of physical nastiness by forever giving the latest smug statistic of the amount the medical profession *doesn't* know. But there is some part of me which feels that I've fallen foul of some medical con trick. I'm not saying that I've been tricked out of the tongue and the sundry other glottal accountrements which the surgeons have just spent some time and skill whipping away, for I'd have lost those anyway and, by the scalpels of less-skilled surgeons, more besides. Rather it was the creeping but unseen inevitability of it all, the swiftness with which black turned to white and I was through the mirror and into a new world.

Every so often since the big operation last year I would visit my surgeon who would look inside my mouth, ask me some questions and tell me how well I seemed to be doing. Without carving me up every week such a pronouncement could only ever be made on a more-or-less clinical basis but generally speaking it seemed that all those symptoms which I took along to my surgeon's rooms were signs of improvement. Those pains were nerves knitting: that food trap was a perfectly normal sinus growth. Moreover, my bruised tongue was starting to get some movement back, my voice was improving and my nights were ever more restful.

Until the other week, as I reported here, I had a full biopsy and suddenly those very same details became symptoms not of improvement but of recurrent cancer. The pains were tumour growth, the food trap was a sinus in the tumour, the lack of movement in my tongue was obviously suspicious and it was apparent that my voice wasn't improving as it might. And strangely all these pronouncements were made as if they were the logical continuation of the opposite pronouncements made the week before. The shepherd who had one night looked at the red sky and told what delights it augured looked the next morning at the same red sky and pointed out that it was that very redness which was the warning.

Either way round, here we are again: half a step forward and 20 back. The surgical word is that this time they've done for the bastard and that now all I have to do is learn to live with an unclear future. Will I ever eat again? (At the moment I suck in liquid food through a tube in my stomach.) Will I ever talk in words that anyone other than Nigella, the children and speech therapists can begin to understand?

For those readers who were looking forward, but certainly no more than was I, to the column returning to its former jollities, I'm afraid that I can offer no more than this: now read on.

25

The alphabet

Jean-Dominique Bauby

I am fond of my alphabet letters. At night, when it is a little too dark and the only sign of life is the small red spot in the centre of the television screen, vowels and consonants dance to a Charles Trenet tune: 'Dear Venice, sweet Venice. I'll always remember you . . .'. Hand in hand the letters cross the room, whirl around the bed, sweep past the window, wriggle across the wall, swoop to the door and return to being again.

E S A R I N T U L O M D P C F B V H G J Q Z Y X K W

The jumbled appearance of my chorus line stems not from chance but from cunning calculation. More than an alphabet, it is a hit parade in which each letter is placed according to the frequency of its use in the French language. That is why E dances proudly out in front whole W labours to hold on to last place. B resents being pushed back next to V, and haughty J – which begins so many sentences in French – is amazed to find itself so near the rear of the pack. Roly-poly G is annoyed to have to trade places with H, while T and U, the tender components of 'tu', rejoice that they have not been separated. All this reshuffling has a purpose: to make it easier for those who wish to communicate with me.

It is a simple enough system. You read off the alphabet (ESA version, not ABC) until with a blink of my eye I stop you at the letter to be noted. The manoeuvre is repeated for the letters that follow so that fairly soon you have a whole word, and then fragments of more or less intelligible sentences. That at least is the theory. But the truth is that some visitors fare better than others. Because of nervousness, impatience or obtuseness, performances vary in the handling of the code (which is what we call this method of transcribing my thoughts). Crossword fans and Scrabble players have a head start. Girls manage better than boys. By dint of practice, some of them know the code by heart and no longer even turn to our special notebook – the one containing the order of the letters, and in which all my words are set down like the Delphic oracle's.

Indeed, I wonder what conclusions anthropologists of the year 3000 will reach if they ever chance to leaf through these notebooks, haphazardly scribbled with remarks like 'the physiotherapist is pregnant', 'mainly on the legs', 'Arthur Rimbaud', and 'the French team played like pigs' are

Extract from *The Diving-Bell and the Butterfly*, London: Fourth Estate 1998, pp. 27–30.

interspersed with unintelligible gibberish, misspelled words, lost letters, omitted syllables.

Nervous visitors come most quickly to grief. They reel off the alphabet tonelessly, at top speed, jotting down letters almost at random: and then, seeing the meaningless result, exclaim: 'I'm an idiot!' But in the final analysis their anxiety gives me a chance to rest, for they take charge of the whole conversation, providing both questions and answers, and I am spared the task of holding up my end. Reticent people are much more difficult. If I ask them, 'How are you?' the answer 'Fine', immediately putting the ball back in my court. With some the alphabet becomes an artillery barrage, and I need to have two or three questions ready in advance in order not to be swamped. Meticulous people never go wrong: they scrupulously note down each letter and never seek to pierce the mystery of a sentence before it is complete. Nor would they dare dream of finishing a single word for you. Unwilling to chance the smallest error, they will never take it upon themselves to provide the 'room' that follows 'mush', the 'ic' that follows 'atom', or the 'nable' without which neither 'intermi' nor 'abomi' can exist. Such scrupulousness makes for laborious progress, but at least you avoid the misunderstandings in which impulsive visitors bog down when they neglect to verify their intuitions. Yet I understood the poetry of such mind games one day when, attempting to ask for my glasses (*lunettes*), I was asked what I wanted to do with the moon (*lune*).

26

Communication in palliative care
a practical guide

Robert Buckman

Introduction: objectives of this article

Effective symptom control is impossible without effective communication. The most powerful analgesics will be of little value if health care professionals do not have an accurate understanding of the patient's pain, and this can be obtained only by effective communication. [. . .]

There is very little in the general medical literature that provides detailed practical assistance for the palliative care practitioner in improving his or her communication skills. The major objective herein is to remedy that omission, and to provide an intelligible and coherent approach to communication in a palliative care setting between professionals and their patients. Much of this material may be known to experienced professionals, but very little of it has previously been published or documented. The objectives of this article are, therefore, practical and pragmatic, and its somewhat unusual structure and style reflect that emphasis.

The details of communication can be considered under three headings.

1   Basic listening skills;

2   The specific communication tasks of palliative care:
     (a) breaking bad news;
     (b) therapeutic dialogue;

3   Communicating with the family and with other professionals.

However, before considering the details of doctor–patient communication, it is worthwhile undertaking a brief survey of the major obstacles to good communication with the dying patient. It is an undeniable fact that in our society any conversation about death and dying is awkward and difficult, and even more so when it occurs between doctor and patient. Some of that awkwardness is social and has its origins in the way society currently views death, some of it originates with the individual patient, and some originates with the professional, since our own professional training, while it prepares us to treat sick people, paradoxically leads us to lose touch

Adapted from the *Oxford Textbook of Palliative Medicine*, 2nd edn, eds D. Doyle, G.W.C. Hanks and N. MacDonald, Oxford: Oxford University Press, 1998, pp. 141–158 (abridged).

with our own human skills when the medical treatment of the disease process fails.

In addition, there is no adequate working concept of the process of dying. Currently accepted systems do not provide a good working model of the transition from living to dying. Without such a conceptual framework or model to guide us, communication will always be suboptimal because we will be unable to understand or interpret what we are hearing, and will be unable to anticipate what may happen next, or to place the patient's feelings within the broader context of the dying process or of that individual's life and experience.

The first section of this article will provide an overview of these issues, starting with a summary of the main areas of difficulty in discussing death and dying, and moving on to put forward a new three-stage concept of the process of dying which, it is hoped, will be of practical value to all practitioners in palliative care.

Sources of difficulty in communication with dying patients

Whatever the experience – or lack of it – of the health-care professional, a conversation with a dying patient almost always causes some degree of discomfort or awkwardness. It is important to recognize the fact that this discomfort is universal and is not the product of any personal fault or deficiency of the health-care professional. The major causes of this sense of unease originate long before the individual patient and the individual doctor begin the conversation. Therefore, a brief overview of the causes of that discomfort may have some value in relieving the sense of awkwardness, personal inadequacy, or even guilt which so commonly hinders communication in palliative care.

The sources of difficulty can be divided into three groups: first, those related to society (the social causes), second those related to the individual patients, and third those related to the health-care professional, arising from the professional's own social background and also from the professional's training – in medical school or nursing college for example.

The social denial of death

Contemporary society is going through a phase of virtual denial of death.[1] Such attitudes are probably cynical, and we may now be seeing this denial phase beginning to fade. However, the price of the current attitude of denial or avoidance is paid by the person whose life is threatened and who has to face death, and by those who look after and support the patient – the family and the professionals. The major social roots of the contemporary fear of dying are discussed below.

Lack of experience of death in the family

Nowadays, most adults have not witnessed the death of a family member at home when they themselves were young and still forming their overall view of life. Whereas a century ago approximately 90 per cent of deaths occurred in the home, for the last few decades over 65 per cent (varying with regional demographics) occur in hospitals or institutions. This is associated with a change in family structure as the norm has changed from the extended family to the nuclear family. Thus, elderly people are less likely to be living with their grandchildren and are usually without young, fit relatives to support them at the time of their last illness. By the same token, a normal childhood and adolescence in contemporary society does not include a personal experience of death in the family occurring in the home.

Another factor in determining the place of most deaths is the rise and range of modern health services and the increase in facilities and treatments on offer. While these services undoubtedly offer advantages in medical and nursing care for the person dying in an institution, it means that there is disruption of family support for the patient as well as lack of experience and understanding of the dying process for the surviving relatives.

This is not to imply that witnessing a death at home in the past was always a serene or tranquil experience. But even if a death at home was not a pleasant event, a child growing up in such a home would be imprinted with a sense of the continuity of life, the process of ageing and the natural inevitability of death ('when you are older you look like dad, when you are much older you look like grandad, when you are very very old you die'). As the extended family has disappeared, so dying has become the province of the health-care professional and/or institution; most people have lost that sense of continuity and now regard the process of dying as intrinsically alien and divorced from the business of living.

High expectations of health and life

Advances in medical sciences are often over-reported in the media and hailed as major breakthroughs. The constant bombardment of the public with news of apparently miraculous advances in the fight against disease subconsciously raises expectations of health and even offers tantalizing hopes of immortality. It, thus, becomes even harder for an individual to face the fact that he or she will not be cured despite the many miracles seen on television or in the papers.

Materialism

It is beyond the scope of this article to assess the materialist values of the modern world, except to point out that our society routinely evaluates a person's worth in terms of material and tangible values. This is our current social system of values and is neither good nor bad. However, it is universally accepted in our society that dying means being parted from material possessions. Hence, a society that places a high and almost exclusive value on material possessions implicitly increases the penalty of dying for its members.

The changing role of religion

The role of religion has changed, and the previously near-universal view of a single exterior anthropomorphic God is now fragmented and individualized. Religion is currently much more of an individual philosophical stance than it was in the last century, and it is no longer possible to assume that everyone shares the same idea of a God or of an after-life. Whereas a Victorian physician might have said to a patient 'Your soul will be with your Maker by the ebb-tide' and may have meant it genuinely as a statement of fact and of consolation, we cannot nowadays assume that such a statement will bring relief to all, or even most, patients.

For all these reasons, then, our society is passing through a phase of development during which the process of dying is perceived as alien and fearsome, and during which the dying person is separated and divided from the living. This increases the discomfort that surrounds any conversation about dying.

Patients' fears of dying

The fear of dying is not a single emotion. It can be composed of any or all of many individual fears, and it is probably true to say that every human being will have a different and unique combination of fears and concerns in facing the prospect of dying. An illustration of some of these is shown in Table 26.1. This concept of the patient's fear of dying has important implications for communication in palliative care. First, recognizing that fear of dying is not a single monolithic emotion should prompt the professional into eliciting from the patient the particular aspects of terminal illness that are uppermost in his or her mind. Thus, a patient's statement that he or she is afraid of dying should become the beginning of a dialogue, not the end of one.[2] Second, being aware that there are so many different aspects of dying that may cause fear will help the professional recognize some triggers of the patient's feelings. This recognition and the ensuing familiarity with the causes of fear often enhances the professional's ability to empathize with the patient and thus increases the value of his or her support.

Factors originating in the health-care professional

As professionals in any health-care discipline we are subject to several sources of pressure that add to the discomfort caused by talking about dying. Some of these factors arise simply because we are human beings (albeit professionals whose behaviour has been ostensibly modified by

---

Table 26.1   *Common fears about dying*

Fears about physical illness
  e.g. physical symptoms (such as pain, nausea), disability (paralysis, loss of mobility)

Fears about psychological effects
  e.g. not coping, 'breakdown', losing mind/dementia

Fears about dying
  e.g. existential fears, religious concerns

Fears about treatment
  e.g. fear of side-effects (baldness, pain), fears of surgery (pain, mutilation), fears about altered body image (surgery, colostomy, mastectomy)

Fears about family and friends
  e.g. loss of sexual attraction or sexual function, being a burden, loss of family role

Fears about finances, social status and job
  e.g. loss of job (breadwinner), possible loss of medical insurance with job, expenses of treatment, being 'out of the mainstream'.

---

training) and are in the presence of another person, the patient, who is in distress. Other factors arise from, or are amplified by, the same professional training that purports to prepare us for the death of our patients, but which usually has not. The following is a brief survey of the factors operating on the health-care professional (fuller discussions have been published elsewhere).[3,4]

Sympathetic pain

We are likely to experience considerable discomfort simply by being in the same room as a person who is going through the distress of facing death. This sympathetic pain may seem so patently obvious that it does not need to be stated, but it is often the case that professionals feel distressed by a painful interview and markedly underestimate the intensity of feeling that has originated from the patient. Commonly, and particularly with trainees and junior staff, a consideration of the intensity of the patient's distress leads to the realization that this was indeed the major source of the professional's stress. Until this is openly acknowledged, the professional may feel personally inadequate or guilty – another factor blocking good communication.

Fear of being blamed

As professionals we have a fear of being blamed that is partly justified. There are two main components of this fear.

First, if we are bearing bad news we are likely to be blamed for the news itself ('blaming the messenger for the message'). This is probably a basic human reaction to bad news and one with which we are all familiar in daily life (for instance, blaming a traffic warden for writing out a parking ticket). We, thus, justifiably expect it when it is our role to bring bad news.

Furthermore, many of the trappings of our profession (such as uniforms, jargon, ward rounds) help support the concept that we are in control of the situation. This may be valuable when the patient's condition is improving, but the same trappings increase the likelihood that we will become targets for blame when the patient's clinical condition begins to deteriorate.

Second, there is the concept imbued into us during our training that when a patient deteriorates or dies there must be somebody at fault. This attitude is strongly reinforced by medico-legal practice in which monetary sums are attached to deteriorations in health. For physicians, training in medical school inadvertently reinforces this feeling. Medical school education prepares doctors (appropriately) to deal with the myriad of reversible or treatable conditions (whether they are common or rare). However, there is usually little or no teaching on the subject of what to do when the disease cannot be reversed. Most medical schools do not teach palliative medicine in the undergraduate curriculum and as a result most medical students evolve into physicians who are keen to treat the curable conditions and who have little training in what to do with chronic, irreversible diseases. This omission makes it even more difficult for the physician to deal with his or her own sense of therapeutic failure when communicating with the dying patient.[5]

Fear of the untaught

We also fear talking to a dying patient if we do not know how to do it properly. In all professional training, trainees are rewarded for doing a particular task 'properly'. In essence this means 'by following conventional procedures' and avoiding deviations from standard practice. While this is the accepted and justifiable norm for any procedure for which there are established guidelines, if it happens that there are no guidelines – as is the case with communicating with the dying – then the professional will naturally feel ill at ease and will show a tendency to avoid the area entirely.[6]

Fear of eliciting a reaction

In the same way in which, as professionals, we dislike doing tasks for which we have not been trained, we also avoid the side-effects or reactions caused by any intervention unless we have been taught how to cope with them.[7] It is an axiom of medical practice that we 'don't do anything unless you know what to do if it goes wrong'. If there has been no effective training in this form of interview,[8] there will also have been no training in dealing with complications or side-effects of these interviews (such as the patient becoming angry or bursting into tears). Not knowing how to cope with these reactions to the interview will further increase the aversion of an untrained person to communicating with a dying patient.[9]

Furthermore, interviews in which patients show emotional reactions may earn discouraging responses from other professionals. Although it is now less common than a few years ago, there are still senior physicians and senior nurses who think it is a bad thing to 'get the patient all upset'. It should be an obvious fact (but it is often ignored) that if you have had an interview about a patient's grave prognosis and if the patient, for example, bursts into tears, it is not the interview that has caused the tears but the medical situation.

Fear of saying 'I don't know'

No matter what discipline we are trained in, health-care professionals are never rewarded for saying 'I don't know'. In all training, and particularly in examinations, we expect our standing to be diminished if we confess that we do not know all the answers. In everyday clinical practice, by contrast, any honesty shown by the professional strengthens the relationship, increases trust, and encourages honesty from the patient in return. Conversely, attempts to 'flannel' or 'snow' the patient, or attempts to disguise ignorance or to pretend greater knowledge or experience weaken the bond between the patient and the doctor or nurse and discourage honest dialogue. Thus, our fears of displaying our ignorance – appropriate in examinations but not in clinical practice – make communication increasingly difficult when the answers are unknown and, often, unknowable.

Fear of expressing emotions

We are also encouraged and trained to hide and suppress our own emotions (more true of medical students than of nursing students or trainees in other disciplines). It is, of course, essential for truly professional behaviour that we do not show such emotions as irritation or panic (or that we try not to show them). However, while we are being trained not to show panic or rage, inadvertently we are being encouraged to envisage the ideal doctor as one who never shows any emotions and is consistently calm and brave. While that is not necessarily a bad paradigm for a doctor dealing with emergencies or reversible crises, it is unhelpful in the palliative care setting. When a patient is facing death, a professional who expresses no emotions is likely to be perceived as cold or insensitive. [. . .]

Own fears of illness/death

Most of us have some degree of fear about our own deaths – perhaps more so than the general population.[10] In fact, some psychologists would suggest that the desire to deny one's own mortality and vulnerability to illness is a component of every health-care professional's desire to be a doctor or nurse. This is sometimes called counter-phobic behaviour, and means in real terms that each time we go into an encounter with a sick person and emerge from the encounter unharmed we are reinforcing our own illusions of immortality and invulnerability. If this is indeed a major constituent of the desire to be a health-care professional, then it might lead to avoidance of those situations in which those illusions are challenged.[11] Hence the professional's own fear of dying will lead to avoidance or block of any communication with the dying patient.

Fear of the medical hierarchy

Finally, there is the discomforting fact that not all professionals think of these issues as important, perhaps because of their own fears of illness and death, or fears of the untaught and so on. A junior member of a medical team may, thus, be under pressure from a senior staff member when trying to hold conversations with patients about dying. In more old-fashioned hierarchical systems (in the United Kingdom in the 1960s for instance) it was quite possible for a senior physician to state 'no patient of mine is ever to be told that they have cancer'. Nowadays that stance is less tenable for ethical and legal reasons, but there are still occasional instances of this attitude which then make it difficult to respond to the patient's desire for information and support. (Fortunately, this problem has a solution since in any circumstances, however adverse, the health-care professional can always perform advocacy and transmit the patient's questions and reactions and knowledge or suspicions upwards to the senior person concerned.) [. . .]

A practical guide to communication in palliative care

[. . .] First there is a summary of general listening skills which are essential for all professional–patient interviews, not just those in palliative care. Next, the two most common tasks of palliative care – breaking bad news and therapeutic (or supportive) dialogue – are discussed. The criteria by which the patient's response can be assessed, together with some suggestions for resolving conflict, are considered. Finally some guidelines for improving communication between health-care professionals and family, and between different health-care disciplines, are offered.

Basic listening skills for palliative care

All medical interviews, and particularly those with a dying patient, contain the potential for going wrong. Often the seeds of failure are sown in the first few minutes. [. . .] Under the pressure of a difficult interview it is often the simplest omissions that cause the biggest problems.[12] Furthermore, patients are more likely to disclose their understanding of their medical situation to those staff who demonstrate that they are prepared to listen and discuss.[13]

The basic listening skills that are most crucial in palliative care may be considered under the headings of physical context, facilitation techniques, and the empathic response. [. . .]

Physical context

The physical context of an interview sends important signals to the patient even before verbal communication begins.[14] It is, therefore, extremely important to observe with particular care the usual rules of good interviewing. A few seconds spent establishing the physical context may save many minutes of frustration (for both the professional and the patient). The rules are not complex but are often omitted in the heat of the moment.[15] Although privacy is difficult to obtain in institutions, consider the patient's dignity and ensure that trenchant conversations of great import are carried out in a private setting if at all possible.

Introductions

Ensure that the patient knows who you are and what you do. Many practitioners, including the author, make a point of shaking the patient's hand but this is a matter of personal preference. Often the handshake tells you something about the family dynamics as well as about the patient. Frequently the patient's spouse will also extend his (or her) hand. It is worthwhile making sure that you shake the patient's hand before that of the spouse (even if the spouse is nearer) in order to demonstrate that the patient comes first, and the spouse (although an important member of the team) comes second.

Sit down

This is an almost inviolable rule. It is virtually impossible to assure a patient that she or he has your undivided attention and that you intend to listen seriously if you remain standing up. Only if it is absolutely impossible to sit should you try and hold a medical interview while standing. Occasionally, in hospitals or hospices, the only available seat is a commode. If so, it is worth asking permission to sit and then saying that you are aware of what you are sitting on to reduce embarrassment. Whatever you sit on, the result will be better than if you remain standing.

Clinical impressions (B. Mount, personal communication) suggest that when the doctor sits down, the patient perceives the period of time spent at the bedside as longer than if the doctor remains standing. Thus, not only does the act of sitting down indicate to the patient that he or she has control and that you are there to listen, but it also saves time and increases efficiency.

Next, get the patient organized if necessary. If you have just finished examining the patient, allow or help him or her to dress and to restore the sense of personal modesty.

Then, get any physical objects out of the way. Move any bedside tables, trays, or other impedimenta out of the line between you and the patient. Ask for any televisions or radios to be turned off for a few minutes. If you are in an office or room, move your chair so that you are adjacent to the patient not across the desk. If you find the action embarrassing, state what you doing ('It may be easier for us to talk if I move the table/if you turn the television off for a moment').

Your body language

It is important to be seated at a comfortable distance from the patient. This distance (sometimes called the 'body buffer zone') seems to vary from culture to culture, but a distance of 50 cm to 90 cm will usually serve the purpose for intimate and personal conversation.[16] This is another reason why the doctor who remains standing at the end of the bed ('six feet away and three feet up', known colloquially as 'the British position') seems remote and aloof.

The height at which you sit can also be important: normally your eyes should be approximately level with the patient's. If the patient is already upset or angry, a useful technique is to sit so that you are below the patient, with your eyes at a lower level. This often decreases the anger. It is best to try and look relaxed, particularly if that is not the way you feel. To achieve an air of relaxation, sit down comfortably with both you feet flat on the floor. Let your shoulders relax and drop. Undo your coat or jacket if you are wearing one, and rest your hands on your knees.

Touching the patient

Most of us have not been taught specific details of clinical touch at any time in our training.[17] We are, therefore, likely to be ill at ease with touching as an interview technique until we have had some practice. Nevertheless there is considerable evidence (although the data are somewhat 'soft') that touching the patient (particularly above the patient's waist to avoid mis-interpretation) is of benefit during a medical interview, even though patients may not expect to be touched the first time that they meet the physician.[18] It seems likely that touching is a significant action in the context of palliative care and should be encouraged, with the proviso that the professional should be very sensitive to the patient's reaction. If the patient is comforted by the contact, continue; if the patient is uncomfortable, stop. Touch can be misinterpreted (as lasciviousness, aggression, or dominance for example) so be aware that touching is an interviewing skill that requires extra self-regulation.

Facilitation techniques

As dialogue begins, the professional should show that she or he is in 'listening mode'. This is the fundamental interviewing skill known as facilitating. The most important guidelines to good facilitation are listed below.

Let the patient speak

If the patient is speaking, don't talk over him or her. Wait for the patient to stop speaking before you start your next sentence. This, the simplest rule of all, is that most often ignored, and is most likely to give the patient the impression that the doctor is not listening.[19]

Encourage the patient to talk

You can use any of all of the following gestures: nodding, pauses, smiling, saying 'Yes', 'Mmm hmm', 'Tell me more', or anything similar. Maintain eye contact for most of the time while the patient is talking (sometimes if things are very intense it may be helpful to the patient for you to look away briefly).

Tolerate short silences

Silences are important and revealing.[20] Usually, a patient will fall silent when he or she has feelings that are too intense to express in words. A silence, therefore, means that the patient is thinking or feeling something important, not that he or she has stopped thinking. If you can tolerate a pause or silence, the patient may well express the thought in words a moment later. If you have to break the silence, the ideal way to do so is to say 'What were you thinking about just then?' or 'What is it that's making you pause?', or something to that effect.[21]

Having encouraged the patient to speak, it is necessary to prove that you are hearing what is being said. The following techniques enhance your ability to demonstrate this.

Repetition and reiteration

Repetition is probably the single most important technique of all interviewing skills (apart from sitting down). To show that you are really hearing what the patient is saying, use one or two key words from the patient's last sentence in your own first one. Reiteration means repeating what the patient has told you but in your words, not hers or his. If the patient says 'Since I started those new tablets, I've been feeling sleepy' a response such as 'You seem to be getting some drowsiness from the tablets' is reiterative (using the word 'drowsiness' where the patient said 'sleepy') and confirms to the patient that she or he has been heard.

Reflection

Reflection, the restating of the patient's statement in terms of what it means to the listener, takes the act of listening one step further, and shows that you have heard and have interpreted what the patient said. (For example 'If I understand you correctly, you're telling me that you lose control of your waking and sleeping when you're on these tablets . . .'.)

The empathic response

The empathic response is an extremely useful technique in an emotionally charged interview, and yet is frequently misunderstood by students and trainees. There are three essential components of the empathic response.

(a) identifying the emotion that the patient is experiencing;
(b) identifying the original and root cause of that emotion;
(c) responding in a way that tells the patient that you have made the connection between (a) and (b).

Often the most effective empathic responses follow the format of 'You seem to be . . .' or 'It must be . . .'; for example 'It must be very distressing for you to know that all that therapy didn't give you a long remission'. The objective of the empathic response is to demonstrate that you have identified and acknowledged the emotion that the patient is experiencing, and by doing so you are giving it legitimacy as an item on the patient's agenda. In fact, if the patient is experiencing a strong emotion (rage or crying, for example) you must acknowledge the existence of that emotion or all further attempts at communication will fail. If strong emotions are not acknowledged in some way, you will be perceived as insensitive and this will render the rest of the interaction useless.

In making an empathic response, however, you do not necessarily have to feel the emotion yourself – you do not have to 'cry and bleed for every patient'. In fact, if you experience the same emotion as the patient, your feelings are termed sympathetic rather than empathic (see under 'sympathetic pain' above). It is therefore possible to formulate an empathic response for all your patients, provided that you identify and acknowledge the feelings that they are describing.

Two specific tasks of communication in palliative care

Communication in palliative care is important from the moment that the patient first meets a palliative care professional until the last moment of life. Most significant conversations in palliative care comprise two major elements: one in which medical information is transmitted to the patient ('bearing the news'), and the other in which the dialogue centres around the patient's feelings and emotions and in which the dialogue itself is a therapeutic action ('therapeutic or supportive dialogue'). In practice most conversations are a mixture of the two, although commonly there is more medical information transmitted in the early conversations shortly after starting palliative care, and there is usually a greater need for therapeutic dialogue in the later stages.

For the purposes of clarity, the two components will be considered separately.

Table 26.2   *Six-step protocol for breaking bad news*

1. Getting the physical context right
2. Finding out how much the patient knows
3. Finding out how much the patient wants to know
4. Sharing information (aligning and educating)
5. Responding to the patient's feelings
6. Planning and following through

Breaking bad news

In palliative care, there are many occasions when new medical information needs to be discussed. This is almost universal when the patient is first assessed in palliative care, and is quite common later on. Hence it is essential to have a logical and systematic approach to the sharing of medical information.[22] The following protocol has been detailed at greater length elsewhere.[4] In practice, it has been found to be useful in all interviews concerning bad news, whether the patient and the professional know each other well or not. However, formal studies of this protocol (or any other) have not been carried out, and even the design of such investigations pose major difficulties.[23] It consists of six steps or phases, which are summarized in Table 26.2.

Physical context

The physical context of the interview has already been reviewed. It is of even greater importance for the interview in which bad news is shared than for any other.

Finding out how much the patient knows or suspects

It is always important to obtain directly from the patient an impression of what he or she already knows about the seriousness of the medical condition and about its effect on the future before providing further information. In fact, sharing information may be awkward, superfluous, or even impossible without first knowing what the patient already knows.[24] In all cases, you should be trying to establish what the patient knows about the impact of the illness on his or her future, not about the fine details of basic pathology or nomenclature of the diagnosis. There are many ways in which this information can be gathered. Some of the phrases that may be useful include:

'What have you made of the illness so far?'

'What did the previous doctors tell you about the illness/operation etc?'

'Have you been worried about yourself?'

'When you first had symptom X, what did you think it might be?'

'What did Dr X tell you when he sent you here?'

'Did you think something serious was going on when . . .?'

As the patient replies, analyse the response. Important information can be obtained from three major features of the reply.

The factual content of the patient's statements

It must be established how much the patient has understood, and how close to the medical reality is the impression. Some patients may at this point say that they have been told nothing at all. This may or may not be true, but even if you know it to be false, accept the patient's statement as a symptom of denial and do not confront it immediately. First, the patient may be about to request information from you, and may, in part deliberately, deny previous information to see if you tell the same story. Second, if the patient has previously been given information, you are unlikely to appear support-ive to a patient in denial by immediate confrontation.

In fact, a patient denying previous information quite often precipitates anger or resentment on the professional's part ('My goodness, doesn't Dr Smythe tell his patients what he found at the operation?'). If you find yourself feeling this, pause and think. You may be seeing a patient in denial and this may be causing you to suffer from the professional syndrome known as the 'nobody-ever-tells-their-patients-anything-until-I-do' syndrome. It is very common when patients are sick and the emotional atmosphere is highly charged.

The style of the patient's statements

Much can be gleaned about the patient's emotional state, educational level, and articulational ability by the manner in which she or he is speaking. Listen to the vocabulary, the kind of words being said, and the kind of words being avoided. Note the style so that when you come to speak, you can start at the right level.

You should, however, ignore the patient's profession in making this assessment, particularly if he or she happens to be a member of a health-care profession. Far too often you will find yourself making assumptions. Even physicians when they are patients may not be experts in their own disease and may not understand something like 'It's only a Stage II but I don't like the mitotic index' when they hear it as a patient.

Emotional content of the patient's statements

There are two major sources of these – verbal and non-verbal. Both may yield information about the patient's state, and discordance between the two (for instance, apparent calm in the speech, but major anxiety in the body language) may give valuable signals regarding state and motivation.

Finding out how much the patient wants to know

This is the single most crucial step in any information-giving discussion. It is far easier to proceed with giving the news if there is a clear invitation

from the patient to do so. Conversely, although it is universally acknowledged that in contemporary society patients have a right to truth and
information,[25,26] it is often impossible to predict which patients will not
want to hear the truth[27] (for fuller reviews see Billings and Reiser[28,29]). The
exact proportion of patients who do want full disclosure varies from study
to study, but current figures range from 50 to 98.5 per cent depending on
patient demographics and the diagnosis suspected[27,30–33] (for a detailed
review see McIntosh[34]). Since no characteristics predict whether a patient
desires disclosure,[30] it seems logical simply to ask him or her.[35] The way in
which this important and sensitive question is phrased is largely a matter of
personal style. Some examples are given below.

> 'Are you the kind of person who likes to know exactly what's going on?'

> 'Would you like me to tell you the full details of the diagnosis?'

> 'Are you the kind of person who likes the full details of what's wrong – or would
> you prefer just to hear about the treatment plan?'

> 'Do you like to know exactly what's going on or would you prefer me to give you
> the outline only?'

> 'Would you like me to tell the full details of your condition – or is there
> somebody else that you'd like me to talk to?'

Note that in all of these, if the patient does not want to hear about the
full details you have not cut off all lines of communication. You are saying
overtly that you will maintain contact and communication (for example
about the treatment plan) but not about the details of the disease. If the
patient does not want to hear the information, you should add that if, at
any time in the future, the patient changes her or his mind and wants
further information you will provide it. The phrase '. . . the sort of person
who' is particularly valuable because it suggests to the patient that there are
many patients like him or her, and that if he or she prefers not to discuss
the information, this is neither unique, nor a sign of extraordinary feeble-
ness or lack of courage.

Sharing medical information

The process by which medical information is transmitted can be thought of
as consisting of two crucial steps.

Aligning

At this point in the interview, you have already heard how much the patient
knows about the situation, and something of the vocabulary used to express
it. This is the staring point for sharing the information. Reinforce those
parts which are correct (using the patient's words if possible) and proceed
from there. It gives the patient a great deal of confidence in himself or
herself (as well as in you) to realize that his or her view of the situation has

been listened to and is being taken seriously (even if it is being modified or corrected).

This process has been called 'aligning',[22,36] a useful term to describe the process by which you line up the information you wish to impart on the baseline of the patient's current knowledge. (Maynard uses the word 'aligning' to describe one particular style of doctor–patient communication.[36] The meaning has been extended in this schema to describe the first part of the information-sharing process.)

Educating

In the next phase of the interview, having started from the patient's starting point (i.e. having aligned your information on the patient's original position) you now have to bring his or her perception of the situation closer to the medical facts as you know them.

There is no word in current usage that fully describes this part of the interview, but perhaps 'educating' is the closest. The process of sharing information should be a gradual one in which the patient's perception is steadily shifted until it is in close approximation to the medical reality. This part of the interview can usefully be compared to steering an oil tanker. You cannot make sudden lurches and expect the patient's perception to change instantly. You have to apply a slow and steady guidance over the direction of the interview, observing the responses as you do so. In the process, you build upon those responses from the patient that are bringing him or her closer to the facts, and emphasize the relevant medical information if it becomes apparent that the patient is moving away from an accurate perception of the situation. The key ingredients are steady observation and continued gentle guidance of the direction of the interview rather than sudden lurches.

Give information in small amounts: the warning shot

Medical information is hard for patients to digest and more so if it concerns a grave prognosis or threat of death. Recall of information is poor at the best of times and likely to be very poor if medical facts are grim ('The moment you said "cancer", doctor, . . . I couldn't remember a thing from that moment on . . .'). The rule is, therefore, give the information in small amounts.

One of the most useful principles is the idea of 'the warning shot'. If there is clearly a large gap between the patient's expectations and the reality of the situation, you can facilitate understanding by giving a warning that things are more serious than they appear ('well, the situation was more serious than that . . .') and then grading the information, gradually introducing the more serious prognostic points, waiting for the patient to respond at each stage.[37,38]

Use English

Technical jargon ('medspeak') is an efficient language for transmitting codified information in a short time. Since it takes many years to learn, it is also comforting to the professional. However, the patients have not learned to speak it and cannot express their emotions in it; hence it reinforces the barrier between patient and professional, and is most likely to make the former feel angry, belittled, and isolated. We should avoid jargon if we are trying to support the patient at a difficult time.

Check reception frequently

Check that your message is being received – and check frequently.[39] You can use any phrase that feels comfortable – anything to break the monologue. Examples are:

'Am I making sense?'

'Do you follow what I'm saying?'

'Does this all seem sensible to you?'

'This must be a bit bewildering, but do you follow roughly what I'm saying?'

'Do you see what I mean?'

These interjections serve several important functions: (a) they demonstrate that it matters to you if the patient doesn't understand what you are saying; (b) they allow the patient to speak (many patients feel so bewildered or shocked that their voices seem to seize up, and they need encouragement and prompting to speak); (c) they allow the patient to feel an element of control over the interview; (d) they validate the patient's feelings and make them legitimate subjects for discussion between you.

You should also check that you are transmitting the information at the same intellectual level as the patient is receiving it, by ensuring that your vocabulary and that of the patient are similar.

Reinforce the information frequently

There are several ways in which you can reinforce what you are telling the patient.

1. Get the patient to repeat the general drift of what you have been saying.
2. Repeat important points yourself: because it is difficult to retain information, particularly if the news is serious, and even more so if denial is operating, you may have to repeat crucial points several times. Accept this as a fact of life when looking after seriously ill patients (you can cover this with a phrase such as 'I know it's difficult to remember all this stuff at one go . . .').

3.   Use diagrams and written messages. A few simple scribbles on the back of an envelope or a scrap of paper may serve as a useful *aide-memoire*.

Blend your agenda with that of the patient

While transmitting information to the patient, it is important to elicit his or her agenda or 'shopping list' of concerns and anxieties, so that further information can be tailored to answer major problems. The following are useful guidelines.

Elicit the 'shopping list'   Quite often the patient's major concerns are not the same as those of the professional. For instance, patients may be more worried about severe pain or loss of mental functioning than about the primary disease itself (see above). You do not necessarily have to deal with the items at that particular moment, but you should indicate that you understand what the patient is talking about and will return to it in a moment. ('I know you're very worried about drowsiness, and I'll come to that in a moment, but can I first cover the reasons that we recommend increasing the painkillers in the first place?')

Listen for the buried question   Deep personal worries may not emerge easily. Sometimes the patient asks questions while you are talking. These questions ('buried questions') are often highly significant to the patient. When the patient does this, finish your own sentence and then ask the patient what he or she was saying. Be prepared to follow that train of thought from the patient – it is quite likely to be important.

Be prepared to be led   Quite often you may draw an interview to a close and then find that the patient wants to start part of it again. This is not simply contrary behaviour. It often stems from fear and insecurity; by restarting the interview the patient is exerting some measure of control.

Responding to the patient's feelings

In many respects the patient's reactions to his or her medical condition, and the professional's response to those reactions, define their relationship and determine whether or not it offers support for the patient. Hence, the professional's ability to understand and respond sensitively to the emotions expressed by the patient are central to all communication in palliative care. In essence, this part of the communication becomes therapeutic (or supportive) dialogue.

In the short space of this article it is not possible to illustrate the wide range of patients' reactions to dying or to bad news in general. However, a detailed analysis has been published elsewhere,[4] together with several options available to the professional in each situation. The central components of the professional's response are (a) assessment of the response and (b) empathic responses from the professional. For the sake of convenience, these two topics are discussed under the heading of therapeutic dialogue below.

Organizing and planning

The sixth and final step in the breaking bad news protocol is the stage at which the professional summarizes the situation and makes an operational plan and a contract for the future. This process is of great importance to the patient, and is a process that should conclude every interview with a palliative care patient, not just an interview in which bad news is discussed. [. . .]

At this point in the interview, it is important to try to put together what is known of the patient's agenda, the medical scenario, the plan of management, and a contract for the future. This process can be logically divided into six tasks.

Demonstrate an understanding of the patient's problem list

If the interview has been effective so far, this is what you have been achieving since the beginning. From the outset, you have been demonstrating that you have been hearing what bothers the patient most, and a brief 'headline' reference to the major concerns of the patient reinforces the fact that you have been listening.

Indicate that you can distinguish the 'fixable' from the 'unfixable'

With both medical problems and psychosocial problems, some are 'fixable' and some are not. We shall be discussing this further in relation to the patient's responses in the next section on therapeutic dialogue, but it is a pragmatic step without which your support will appear to be less effective. If the interview gets stuck or bogged down as the patient explores her or his problems, it is often helpful to try to enumerate the problems as a list, getting the patient to arrange them in order of priority. You can then begin to set your own agenda – stating the problems you are going to try and tackle first. This leads logically to the next step.

Make a plan or strategy and explain it

When making a plan for the future, it is quite permissible for that plan to include many uncertainties, 'don't knows', and choices ('if the dizziness doesn't get better, then we'll . . .'), acknowledging that uncertainty is often a painful and difficult state to cope with.[40] What you are actually doing is presenting a decision-tree or algorithm. Patients need to know that you have some plan in mind – even if it consists of little more than 'we'll deal with each problem as it arises' – which, at least, implies that you will not abandon the patient. The act of making a plan and explaining it to the patient is part of what the patient sees as support – it defines the immediate future of your relationship with this particular patient and reinforces the individuality of this person and what you are going to do for him or her.

Identify coping strategies of the patient and reinforce them

There is a lot of emphasis in our training on what we do to patients or for patients. [. . .] However, this attitude of 'we will do it all for you' may influence the professional's approach to all patients in every situation, particularly if the patient is feeling overwhelmed and helpless in the face of bad news. This may be bad for the patient, and also bad for us as we may later become overwhelmed by the sense of our responsibilities. At this point in the interview, then, it is important to look at the resources available to the patient, both internally and externally.[41] We cannot, and should not, live the patient's life for him or her. Hence, as the problem list and the plan begin to take shape the professional should begin helping the patient to evaluate what he or she can do for himself or herself. This part of the process involves helping the patient to identify his or her own coping strategies and is a continuous process, not usually completed in one interview. It also leads logically on to the next component.

Identify other sources of support for the patient and incorporate them

Not only do we tend to forget that the patient has capabilities of his or her own, we also tend to forget that there is anyone outside the professional–patient relationship who can assist. Most people have at least one or two friends and relatives who are close in some way and can add support. For those patients who have no social supports of their own, it will be necessary to enrol and co-ordinate the other services available.

Summary and conclusion

The final part of the interview is the summary and contract for the future. The summary [. . .] should show the patient that you have been listening and that you have picked up the main concerns and issues. [. . .] It need not be a long statement, and often consists of no more than one or two sentences.

Having summarized the main points, you should then ask 'Are there any (other) questions that you'd like to ask me now?'. Sometimes the patient has been bottling up concerns over some issue that simply has not arisen, or one aspect of the treatment or the disease that you have merely touched on. This part is as important as the question period after a lecture – it is the time when any unresolved issues can be discussed.

Finally, you should make a contract for the future. Even though this may be very simple ('I'll see you at the next visit in two weeks' or 'We'll try the new anti-sickness medicine and I'll see you tomorrow on the ward-round'), patients may otherwise be left at the conclusion of the interview with the feeling that there is no future and may be glad to hear that there is one.

Therapeutic (or supportive) dialogue

[. . .]

Supportive dialogue, during any stage of palliative care, is an exceptionally valuable resource and may be the most important (and sometimes the only) ingredient in a patient's care. The central principle of effective therapeutic dialogue is that the patient should perceive that his or her emotions have been heard by the professional and acknowledged. It may then become apparent that there are problems that can be solved, emotions that can be resolved, and needs that can be met, but even if there are no solutions, the simple act of supportive dialogue can reduce distress. [. . .]

The empathic response is one of the most reliable methods of demonstrating effective listening. In addition to responding in this way, the professional should also attempt to assess the nature and value of the patient's responses in coping with the situation, to disentangle the emotions that have been raised by the discussion, and to try to resolve any conflicts that may have arisen.

Assessment of the patient's responses

[. . .] There are three criteria by which patients' responses may be assessed.

Acceptability

First, a patient's reactions must meet the broadest definitions of socially acceptable behaviour. These definitions vary from culture to culture (and some of the gravest misunderstandings arise from misinterpretation – behaviour that is normal in one culture being seen as aberrant in another). In the context of palliative care, however, interpretation of 'socially acceptable' should be very wide. The professional should err on the side of generosity and only if extreme behaviour is a genuine danger to the patient, staff, other patients or family members should assistance be called in. For all but these very rare cases, you should accept the behaviour even if you do not like it, and assess it on the other two criteria – does it help the patient, and (if it does not) can it be improved by intervention?

Distinguishing the adaptive from the maladaptive

Second, facing the end of life usually induces major stress and distress: an individual's response to that distress may either help the person to reduce it (an adaptive response) or may increase it (a maladaptive response). Frequently, it is difficult to distinguish one from the other at the first interview and it may require several interviews over a longer period to decide whether a patient is adapting to the medical circumstances.

It is not easy to be dogmatic about which responses are always maladaptive but some guidelines are shown in Table 26.3. There seems to be a consensus opinion that, for example, a feeling of guilt is always maladaptive

Table 26.3 *Some adaptive and maladaptive responses*

Adaptive	Maladaptive
Humour	Guilt
Denial	Pathological denial
Abstract anger	
Anger against disease	Anger against helpers
Crying	Collapse
Fear	Anxiety
Fulfilling an ambition	The impossible 'quest'
Realistic hope	Unrealistic hope
Sexual drive	Despair
Bargaining	Manipulation

and cannot help a patient. It may be somewhat more controversial, but still helpful, to regard denial in the early stages as an adaptive response, allowing the patient to adjust to the situation in small 'bites' when otherwise the threat would be overwhelming. It is also important to note that some responses will buy the patient an immediate short-term decrease in distress, but will accumulate trouble later on. For instance, denial that is prolonged and that prevents a patient from making decisions with which he or she is comfortable ('We won't even think about that . . .') may later increase distress. Only the professional's clinical experience and the passage of time can define the situation in some cases.

Distinguishing the 'fixable' from the 'unfixable'

The third criterion by which responses may be assessed is what might be termed 'fixability'. If there is a problem that is increasing the patient's distress or obstructing adaptation, can it be remedied? [. . .][42] Two points, however, are worth stressing. First, the chance of damage is higher when the professional feels that he or she can fix a problem, and then perseveres without seeking help, than when a professional knows his or her own limitations. Second, it is even more important that, if there appears to be a problem that is not 'fixable', a second opinion is sought – preferably from a psychologist or psychiatrist. In problems that appear to the medical team to be 'unfixable', some improvement can be achieved by psychologists in up to two-thirds of cases.[43]

Distinguish your emotions from those of the patient

[. . .] We should try to be aware of our own emotions in dealing with an individual person who is dying. We may experience strong emotions because of our own previous experience (counter-transference) or we may be moved, attracted, or irritated and intolerant as a result of the patient's behaviour patterns. In any event, whenever emotions arise it is essential to try to take a step back and ask yourself what you are feeling and where that feeling comes from. If the professional can recognize a strong emotion in

Table 26.4 *In the event of conflict*

1. Try to take a step back
2. Identify your own emotions and try to describe them, not display them
3. Try to define the area of conflict that is unresolved
4. Try to obtain agreement on that area of difference, even it it cannot be resolved
5. Find a colleague and talk about it

himself or herself, the recognition itself partly negates the effect of the emotion on judgement and communication. If the emotion goes unrecognized, it is far more likely to produce damage.

Dealing with conflict

We all want to do our best for the patient, but we all have our limits. Sometimes we simply cannot ease a patient's distress, sometimes the patients do not wish to be relieved, and sometimes they appear to have a need for antagonism or conflict in order to give themselves definition or some other gain.

Despite pretences to the contrary, all of us at some time feel exhausted, frustrated, and intolerant. This is unavoidable. There are, however, a few guidelines that may reduce the impact of those feelings in our professional life.[44] The most useful are shown in Table 26.4.

In summary, the single most useful tool of therapeutic dialogue is the empathic response which indicates to the patient that the emotional content of his or her reaction is being heard and is legitimized. In addition, the professional should attempt to assess the patient's response, disentangle his or her emotions from those of the patient, and try to resolve conflict.

These, then, are some of the most important aspects of communicating with the dying patient. However, there are almost always other parties involved, and in the next section we shall deal with communication issues concerning the family and those that may arise between health-care disciplines.

Communication with other people

All efforts in palliative care are directed to ameliorating the situation of the patient. However, there are other parties to be considered who may assist or hinder efforts at effective communication (for a major review of communication issues with cancer patients, their families, and professionals see Northouse and Northouse[45]). Only a few broad guidelines can be offered in this limited space, but attention to even these simple issues can improve quality of care noticeably.

Communication with friends and family

The responses of friends and family to the imminent death of the patient may be as varied as those of the patient himself or herself. Similarly, they may assist the patient and be of support, or they may be counter-productive and form part of the patient's problem rather than part of the solution. They may be similar in nature to the patient's responses or they may be qualitatively different. Even when they are the same as those of the patient, they may be asynchronous with the patient's responses; for example the patient may have resolved his or her anger and may have come to accept his or her death, while the family are still angry or in denial. In the same way, therefore, as the patient's responses may be considered adaptive or mal-adaptive, so the family's responses may also serve to decrease or increase the patient's distress and increase or decrease support.

When a patient's treatment is palliative, some effort should always be made to identify leading members of his or her support systems (friends and family). However, in communicating with the family, there are two prin-ciples which may at first seem mutually exclusive.

The patient has primacy

A mentally competent patient has the right (ethical and legal) to determine who shall be informed about his or her medical condition. All rights of friends or family are subsidiary to this. If a patient decides not to share information with anyone else, although that may be an aggressive and vengeful action, it cannot be countermanded by the professional at the family's request. Similarly, however well intentioned, a relative stating that 'the patient is not to be told' does not have primacy over the patient's wishes if the patient wishes for full disclosure.

The family's feelings have validity

Despite the secondary rank of the family's feelings, those feelings have validity and must be acknowledged even if their wishes or instructions cannot be acceded to. Often a family's wishes arise from a desire to show that they are good and caring sons or daughters (rationalizing their own feelings as 'If I cannot stop mother becoming ill, I can at least stop her finding out too much about it'). It is important for the professional to identify the family's emotions and to acknowledge them; for this purpose, the empathic response is of great value.

Communication between physicians

Doctors are notoriously bad at communicating with each other. We do not do it frequently enough, and more importantly, when we do communicate with each other, we are often disorganized and unfocused in our communi-cation. Perhaps the most dangerous gaps in doctor–doctor communication occur when a patient moves from one care setting to another – for example into a palliative care unit or from a hospital to home.

It is difficult to give useful guidelines about something as ill-defined as interspeciality communication, but perhaps the key principles are that all communication should be task-orientated and should clearly define frontiers of responsibility. This means that communications should be related to those aspects of the patient's situation that may have an impact on the care. Much of what is discussed between doctors is found to be, on analysis, simply opinion or conjecture. Although there is nothing wrong with this in itself, it often gives us the feeling that we have thoroughly discussed the care, when in fact vital management issues have not been discussed at all.

The five-point checklist that follows may be of some value when considering a letter or telephone call to another physician about a palliative care patient.

1.   Am I addressing the right person? (For instance, does the patient know the family practitioner well? Have I asked the patient whom he or she wished me to contact?)
2.   What do I know about this patient that the other person should know? (and/or what do I want to know from the other person?)
3.   What does this mean for the patient's future care?
4.   Who is going to do what? Who is now 'the doctor' for this patient?
5.   How shall we communicate again if things are not going well?

Even if communications are limited to these five points, they will be more effective than many of the current communications between doctors – not because we are negligent or malevolent, but because we are often too polite and too afraid of stepping on each other's toes in making suggestions for the patient's benefit.

Communication between physicians and nurses

By definition, professionals belong to different teams because they have special expertise and training that identifies them with that discipline. This is essential for good patient care. However, there is a side-effect – namely that we each speak a different language and we all tend to believe that our particular language is the only one truly relevant to the patient's care. As a result, different aspects of the patient's problem are often poorly integrated and there are often large gaps in communication between the teams. The most common gaps – because of the way the jobs inter-relate occur between doctors and nurses.

One of the greatest paradoxes (and perhaps one of the greatest losses) in the recent evolution of the nursing profession has been the diminishing of the ward-round as the standard method for exchanging information between patient, doctor and nurse. Although this idea that the ward-round is essential in patient care is a controversial one, it is a view that is now receiving increasing support from all disciplines and from patients and families. The days of the three-hour ward-round during which four patients are reviewed are over – nursing time is at a premium and nursing tasks have increased greatly in number and complexity. However, without the 'trinity' of patient-doctor-nurse present in the same place at the same time, in-patient care is rendered unnecessarily complex and incomplete. In hospitals or hospices where time is limited, it is often possible to agree on time-limits (for example an average of 10 minutes per patient can accomplish almost all of the necessary exchanges).

In our own unit, we ensure that the three following points are addressed during the minimum 10-minute period allotted to each patient for discussion.

1. The medical game-plan: what is known about the patient's medical status, what measures are planned or being considered? What is the prognosis?
2. Nursing concerns: what are the main difficulties in the day-to-day care of the patient?
3. What does the patient know and what are the patient's major concerns? For instance, does the patient have strong views about the type of therapy or where she or he would like to be looked after?

It is surprising how efficient communication can be if all concerned are aware that time is limited and that these three main areas must be covered in the discussion.

Conclusion

In palliative care, everything starts with the patient – including every aspect of symptom relief and every aspect of communication. There is no doubt that we all want to do our best, but often the major challenges in palliative care arise because we do not know how to approach the problem. Nowhere is this more true than in communication – a professional who feels ill-equipped and inept at communication will become part of the problem instead of part of the solution. The act of following relatively straight-forward guidelines, however simplistic they may appear, will at least give us a feeling of competence and enhance our ability to learn as we practise.

An expert in palliative care is not a person who gets it right all the time: an expert is someone who gets it wrong less often – and is better at concealing or coping with his or her fluster and embarrassment. We are, after all, only human beings.

References

1 Becker, E. *The Denial of Death*. New York: Free Press, 1973.
2 Saunders, C.M. and Baines, M. *Living with Dying*. Oxford: University Press, 1983; 10.

3 Buckman, R. Breaking bad news: why is it still so difficult? *British Medical Journal*, 1984; 288: 1597–9.

4 Buckman, R. *How to Break Bad News – a Guide for Healthcare Professionals*. London: Macmillan Medical, 1993.

5 Seravalli, E.P. The dying patient, the physician and the fear of death. *New England Journal of Medicine*, 1988; 319: 1728–30.

6 Maguire, P. and Faulkner, A. How to do it: improve the counselling skills of doctors and nurses in cancer care. *British Medical Journal*, 1988; 297: 847–9.

7 Gorlin, R. and Zucker, H.D. Physicians' reactions to patients. *New England Journal of Medicine*, 1983, 308: 1059–63.

8 Perez, E.L., Gosselin, J.Y. and Gagnon, A. Education on death and dying: a survey of Canadian medical schools. *Journal of Medical Education*, 1980; 55: 788–9.

9 Michaels, E. Deliver bad news tactfully. *Canadian Medical Association Journal*, 1983; 129: 1307–8.

10 Streim, J.E. and Marshall, F. The dying elderly patient. *American Family Practitioner*, 1988, 38: 175–83.

11 Radovsky, S.S. Bearing the news. *New England Journal of Medicine*, 1985; 513: 586–8.

12 DiMatteo, M.R., Prince, L.M. and Taranta, A.J. Patients' perceptions of physicians' behaviour: determinants of patient commitment to the therapeutic relationship. *Community Health*, 1979; 4: 280–90.

13 Hinton, J. Whom do dying patients tell? *British Medical Journal*, 1980; 281: 1328–30.

14 DiMatteo, M.R., Taranta, A., Friedman, H.S. and Prince, L M. Predicting patient satisfaction from physicians' non-verbal communication skills. *Medical Care*, 1980; 18: 376–87.

15 Maguire, P. Communication skills. In: *Patient Care Health Care and Human Behaviour*. London: Academic Press, 1984: 153–73.

16 Hall, E.T. *The Silent Language*. New York: Doubleday, 1959 (reprinted Anchor, 1981).

17 Older, J. Teaching touch at medical school. *Journal of the American Medical Association*, 1984; 252: 931–3.

18 Larsen, K.M. and Smith, C.K. Assessment of nonverbal communication in the patient–physician interview. *Journal of Family Practice*, 1981; 12: 481–8.

19 Blau, N. Time to let the patient speak. *British Medical Journal*, 1989; 298: 39.

20 Frankel, R.M. and Beckman, H.B. The pause that refreshes. *Hospital Practice*, 1988; Sept 30: 64–7.

21 Bendix, T. *The Anxious Patient*. London: Livingstone, 1982.

22 Maynard, D. On clinicians co-implicating recipients' perspectives in the delivery of diagnostic news. In: Drew P., Heritage J., eds. *Talk at Work: Social Interaction in Institutional Settings*. Cambridge: University Press, 1990.

23 Waitzin, H. and Stoeckle, J.D. The communication of information about illness. *Advances in Psychosomatic Medicine*, 1987; 8: 180–215.

24 Maynard, D. Notes on the delivery and reception of diagnostic news regarding mental disabilities. In: Helm D.T., Anderson W.T., Meehan A.J., eds. *The Interactional Order: New Directions in the Study of Social Order*. New York: Irvington Publishers, 1989: 54–67.

25 Lichter, I. Rights of the individual patient. In: Stoll B.A., ed. *Ethical Dilemmas in Cancer Care*. London: Macmillan, 1989: 7–16.

26 Goldie, L. The ethics of telling the patient. *Journal of Medical Ethics*, 1982; 8: 128–33.

27 Jones, J.S. Telling the right patient. *British Medical Journal*, 1981; 283: 291–2.

28 Billings, A. Sharing bad news. In: Billings A. *Out-patient Management of Advanced Malignancy*. Philadelphia: Lippincott, 1985: 236–59.

29 Reiser, S.J. Words as scalpels: transmitting evidence in the clinical dialogue. *Annals of Internal Medicine*, 1980; 92: 837–42.

30 Cassileth, B.R., Zupkis, R.V., Sutton-Smith, M.S. and March, V. Information and participation preferences among cancer patients. *Annals of Internal Medicine*, 1980; 92: 832–6.

31 Henriques, B., Stadil, F. and Baden, H. Patient information about cancer. *Acta Chirurgia Scandinavica*, 1980; 146: 309–11.

32 McIntosh, J. Patients' awareness and desire for information about diagnosed but undisclosed malignant disease. *Lancet*, 1976; ii: 300–3.

33 Kelly, W.D. and Friesen, S.R. Do cancer patients want to be told? *Surgery*, 1950; 27: 822–6.

34 McIntosh, J. Processes of communication, information seeking and control associated with cancer: a selective review of the literature. *Social Science and Medicine*, 1974; 8: 167–87.

35 Reynolds, P.M., Sanson-Fisher, R.W., Poole, A.D., Harker, J. and Byrne, M. Cancer and communication: information giving in an oncology clinic. *British Medical Journal*, 1981; 282: 1449–51.

36 Maynard, D. Breaking bad news in clinical settings. In: Dervin B., ed. *Progress in Communication Sciences*, Norwood NJ: Ablex Publishing Co, 1989: 161–3.

37 Maguire, P. and Faulkner, A. How to do it: communicate with cancer patients. 1 Handling bad news and difficult questions. *British Medical Journal*, 1988; 297: 907–9.

38 Premi, J. Communicating bad news to patients. *Canadian Family Physician*, 1981; 27: 837–41.

39 Rando, T.A. Caring for the dying patient. In: *Grief, Dying and Death* Chicago: Research Press Company, 1984: 278–83.

40 Maguire, P. and Faulkner, A. How to do it: communicate with cancer patients. 2 Handling uncertainty, collusion and denial. *British Medical Journal*, 1988; 297: 972–4.

41 Manuel, G.M., Roth, S., Keefe, F.J. and Brantley, B.A. Coping with cancer. *Journal of Human Stress*, 1987: 149–58.

42 Skinner, J.B., Erskine, A., Pearce, S., Rubenstein, I., Taylor, M. and Foster, C. The evaluation of a cognitive behavioural treatment programme in outpatients with chronic pain. *Journal of Psychosomatic Research*, 1990; 34: 13–19.

43 Buckman, R. and Doan, B. Enhancing communication with the cancer patient: referrals to the psychologist – who and when? In: Ginsburg D., Laidlaw J., eds. *Cancer in Ontario 1991.* Toronto: Ontario Cancer Treatment and Research Foundation, 1991: 78–86.

44 Lazare, A., Eisenthal, S. and Frank, A. In: Lazare A., ed. *Outpatient Psychiatry: Diagnosis and Treatment.* 2nd edn. Baltimore: Williams and Wilkins, 1989: 157–71.

45 Northouse, P.G. and Northouse, L.L. Communication and cancer: issues confronting patients, health professionals and family members. *Journal of Psychosocial Oncology*, 1987; 5: 17–45.

Further reading

Becker, E. *The Denial of Death.* New York: Free Press, 1973.

Rando, T.A. *Grief, Dying and Death.* Chicago: Research Press Company, 1984.

Buckman, R. *How to Break Bad News – a Guide for Healthcare Professionals.* London: Macmillan Medical, 1993.

27

Saturday Times column 23.1.99

John Diamond

I know what I said last week and that I wasn't meant to be here today: as we speak I should be back on the ward with the surgeons chasing the cancer further down my neck. But as soon as we arrived at the outpatients' clinic we knew it was all up. Normally, and despite BUPA's hefty chequebook, we conduct our clinical meetings in an ordinary white cubicle in the general outpatients' clinic; this time the receptionist gave us a tight smile and said Mr Rhys-Evans had asked for us to be shown over to one of the chain-hotel designed consulting rooms in the Marsden's private wing. You do not ask for your patients to be taken to the comfy chairs if you're about to tell them that after all the shadow on the scan was a packet of Woodbines left on the machine by one of the cleaners.

When Rhys-Evans arrived it was with the unspoken hint of worse news still. The list of clinical possibilities thus far have all been either surgical or radiological, and I've known for some time that if a medical doctor ever turned up to a consultation then we were no longer talking about cure but about remission.

Accompanying my surgeon were two men I'd not met before: a consultant medical oncologist and his registrar. Standing behind them, looking embarrassed, was a tallish man in hood and gown with a scythe over his shoulder.

Statistics tell us that anyone whose job is treating those diagnosed as having cancer will, in around 60 per cent of cases, eventually have to dole out the worst possible news, and you'd suppose that after some years of doing it most doctors would find a way somewhere between the mawkish and the unnecessarily brusque which would serve them comfortably in the majority of cases. I suppose it's testimony to Peter Rhys-Evans that he gave us the news white-faced, nervous, with eyes downcast, much as he must have given the news the first time he ever had to, as if it were something both unsayable and already said.

And the news is this:
The cancer is in too many places around my throat and neck to warrant any more surgery. I could ask for a second opinion, I suppose, but quite honestly it's bad enough having one expert telling you how soon you're going to die without bringing in a second to rub it in. If I leave the cancer to take its natural course I have about six months left. If I have

chemotherapy, and assuming the chemotherapy works in my case and that it is not so arduous as to be unbearable, then I might double or treble that time and there is a small but significant chance of my doing even better than that given that the cancers are tiny and I feel healthier than I ever have.

I'll take the chemotherapy, of course. Why would I not?

I'd imagined that I'd feel terrified when I got the news, but what I felt most of all was sad. Sad for Nigella, for the children, for my parents. As if, of course, sad were a word up to this particular job. I realized that the reason I don't seem to be going through the standard denial/anger/bargaining with God/acceptance shtick is because that's what I've been doing for the past 20 months or so. As soon as I heard the first diagnosis I heard a death sentence being passed, and I suppose I never thought of the various operations and procedures as much more than temporary reprieves. Living with cancer must always mean living with the threat of death even, I imagine, if you manage to increase the distance between you and the diagnosis to the five years which counts as a cure.

Meanwhile, I have some affairs to get in what passes for order. We haven't told the children yet and won't for a while at least, and so if you come across them – and some of you, I know, do – please don't say anything. I'll carry on working for as long as I can and, given that one of the side-effects of the chemotherapy is fatigue, I'm sure you'll understand if I don't answer all your mail individually from now on. And we're planning a big party for March to celebrate Nigella and my ten years of being together. It's strange, isn't it, how in the middle of all this madness there are some things worth celebrating?

28

Communicating with dying children

Dorothy Judd

> Look, the dying, –
> surely they must suspect how full of pretext
> is all that we accomplish here, where nothing
> is what it really is.

> (Rilke, Fourth 'Duino Elegy')

Children with a life-threatening illness sense that it is serious, and that they might die or are dying, even if not explicitly told. Recent research has challenged the 'protective' approach in relation to whether to talk to the child about his or her impending death. It seems from the weight of evidence that children need to be given the opportunity to speak 'about their concerns so that they can receive support in their struggles' (Spinetta, 1982).

Background

Before we can approach how, when and why we might talk to dying children about their situation, we need to think about children's understanding of the concept of death. This varies according to age, intelligence, life experience, environment, the seriousness of their illness, and their 'inner world' of fantasies and dreams.

Kane (1979) gives a useful summary of children's concepts of death. She writes that children from approximately 6 years of age have a more-or-less mature grasp of the concept of death, including its irrevocability and universality, whereas younger children do not generally understand these and other more subtle qualities, such as that dead people or creatures cannot *feel*. The most clear and feared implication for younger children is of the implied separation from those who are loved and needed, as well as that dead people/creatures cannot move. Generally it is not until the age of 12 that children grasp all the complex implications of death: for example, that the dead person may, or may not, look as though he were alive.

These cognitive findings, although useful as broad categories, do not adequately reflect the vicissitudes of the child's inner world and unconscious fantasies which colour and inform the perceptions of the outer world, including thoughts about death. In other words, we cannot simply look at a child's intellectual grasp of a concept without paying adequate attention to the fantasies and emotions which abound.

The developing child's response to separation and death reflects the extent of his or her ability to have an inner representation, idea or memory of the mother/main care-taker in a way which is hopeful, sustaining and promises its return. This capacity develops as a result of the mother's or main carer's repeated sensitive management of the infant's anxieties, in conjunction with the infant's ability to 'take in' and hold onto the image of a good mother.

Rochlin (1959, 1967) has focused on the influence of emotional states on children's attitudes to death. He writes that children clearly know about death as the extinction of all life at a very early age, but that they then utilize a range of defences in order to avoid the full implications of this awareness. As Orbach (1988) so clearly summarizes, children 'reflect the duality of knowing and denying the existence of death'. The child's use of denial, omnipotence, magical thinking and actual independence all influence the extent of his/her fear or acceptance of the subject. Of course all this is set against the influential background of adults' oscillation between acceptance and denial of death. Adults' protective concern for children over issues around death clearly reflect their own fears and use of denial in a society where the taboo may be lifting in a widespread social and intellectual sense, but not necessarily in a personal or private sense (Judd, 1995: 3–16).

If children have had to negotiate the concept of death through the actual death of someone close, or of a pet, their understanding may well be enhanced. However, if the death is too overwhelming, the child may regress to an earlier stage of 'not knowing'. Similarly, if they are fatally ill, they are more aware of their own mortality, but may hide defensively behind denial. This has been shown in studies where the fatally ill child's level of anxiety is markedly higher than that of the chronically ill, even if undergoing the same number and duration of hospital treatments (Spinetta et al., 1973). This anxiety, as well as a sense of isolation, persists when they are not in hospital, and even during remission in the case of leukaemic children (Spinetta, 1975).

The hospitalized dying child's awareness of death is more sharply focused when another child dies on the ward. If the child has the same illness, of course the link between that event and the dying child's imminent death is made more immediate. Fortunately nowadays there is a more open and truthful attitude on children's wards in most hospitals, where the event is often discussed openly in response to parents' questions, and sometimes with children, depending on the ethos of the unit. This is not always the case, however. Some hospitals have not altered much since this account by a consultant paediatrician of the approach to the death of a child on the ward, over 30 years ago:

> Our present method of dealing with the solemn situation that arises when a child dies in a children's ward is both ugly and obscene. There is a whispering and a scuffling behind the screens, a furtive moving of white-covered trolleys out of the

ward, usually during the night. Nurses and doctors are preoccupied and don't answer questions and are unduly irritable. Above all, there is a stupid pretence that nothing at all unusual is happening. . . . But do we really think that the 'secret' is not known to every child on the ward? (Yudkin, 1967: 40)

This account is a useful reflection not only of ways of handling actual deaths, but of the days or weeks or months of illness preceding a death, when the 'pretence that nothing at all unusual is happening' is adopted by some parents and some professionals. Yudkin writes that this furtive behaviour was an affront to children's intelligence. Instead of helping them to regard death as a 'very sad but solemn and dignified event', it characterized death as something fearful and secretive, depriving the child of the opportunity to talk about his or her fears.

Richard Lansdown (personal communication, 1987) of the Hospital for Sick Children, London, has usefully summarized the stages that a dying child goes through of understanding their own death:

I am very sick
I have an illness that can kill people
I have an illness that can kill children
I may not get better
I am dying

However, as stated earlier, the child's age, anxiety level, cognitive development, inner world and environment would all influence the course of that understanding. For a child under 3 years of age, the 'I am dying' concept would probably not embody a real understanding of dying, with its irreversibility, but may be a feeling of not understanding what is happening to his body and an anxiety that this unpleasant state of being unwell separates him from his parents.

Communicating with the dying child

It is clear that dying children need to be given an age- and development-appropriate opportunity to share and explore their fears and concerns. This does not mean imposing a discussion, but involves attempting to be open to the child's willingness – or otherwise – to talk. For example, 9-year-old Helena (recently diagnosed with a very large osteosarcoma – bone tumour – below her knee) said she was 'fine' when first meeting the hospital child psychotherapist, whilst lifting her long skirt to reveal the conspicuous tumour. The psychotherapist took up the non-verbal cue, saying, 'Well, you're letting me know that you're not altogether "fine"'. Helena then talked openly about her cancer: about her worries that it had been caused by falling over and about whether her mum was 'sick with worry'.

Laura, a 10-year-old, also with a bone tumour in her leg, carefully drew the branch of a tree, delineating each leaf and their veins, during a session with the child psychotherapist. Laura had previously readily shared her feelings about having cancer being 'scary'. Now, in this drawing, she abruptly drew the branch as not being attached to a tree, but appearing cut off. The psychotherapist asked, 'What happens if a branch is no longer joined to the tree?' Laura replied, 'It dies', glancing up into the therapist's eyes meaningfully. This was an opportunity to begin to explore Laura's fears of dying and of being cut off from her mother to whom she was very close. On later occasions, she discussed her not unrealistic fears of amputation of her leg being like the branch of a tree being cut off. However, all these developments towards a sharing of her anxieties required the right moment and an appropriate setting of reasonable privacy and calm.

Laura's mother had given permission for her child to be seen by the psychotherapist. Although the mother felt unable to talk to her daughter about the possibility of dying, she was willing for someone else to 'hear' her daughter's concerns. Without this permission, the professionals or other adults involved need to try to explain their reasons for believing in the helpfulness of open communication. If the parents have a first hand experience of *their* fears being listened to, they may gain the confidence to explore the child's fears, or to allow someone else to begin the process. With adolescents, where their understanding is usually more mature and close to that of adults, it is usually easier for the professionals to explain to the parents that they cannot lie about the situation and will aim to foster the patient's trust by answering questions truthfully and letting them know the situation.

Adolescents tackling death have specific problems. Unlike younger children, adolescents are caught in a more polarized struggle: they are often powerfully attempting to stake out their independence and identity and to *live* life fully, all of which greatly conflicts with having a terminal illness. Therefore, in this most difficult task, there is often an impressive determination to continue to live their life despite the limitations and constraints brought by the illness. The alternative to this attitude could be to regress to an earlier more infantile state of dependence on nurses or parents. Therefore, in communicating with a dying adolescent we need to respect the denial – or as it may be viewed, the living for a future, albeit a limited one, and the struggle for a sense of identity and control.

The idea of 'stages' of understanding is useful to have at the back of one's mind when talking to children who are dying, but should not be the main guide. Receptivity to the young person's willingness or need to talk is paramount, as well as to *their* level of understanding. These discussions need repeated opportunities for the information to be digested, as well as for further exploration. The adult may simply spend a few meaningful minutes with a child or young person, but may end by saying, 'I will come back tomorrow and we can talk some more if you want'. The child may well then save up some thoughts to share the next day. A useful introductory approach may be, 'Would you like to talk about anything that's bothering you?' and, in a follow-up discussion, 'I wonder what thoughts you've had about our last discussion?' Of course the child's age is very relevant to the type of verbal exchange, and with younger children the communication may well be symbolic, through their play with toys, or plasticine, or drawing with the provision of coloured crayons. A set of hospital play dolls can be useful, but again the toys are the child's vehicle for communication, and the adult's ability to observe, listen and not pre-empt is important. However, there are times when the child has used a symbolic communication and may feel uncomfortable, or interrogated, with the externalization of the unconscious into words. In this case the drawings or play-sequence may have to be 'received' unconditionally. The child may need to cling to the unspoken conspiracy of mutual protectiveness between child and parents, especially if the parents are very repressed in their expression of pain. With symbolic, non-verbal communication the adult might simply describe what the child seems to be 'saying', thus acknowledging the child's fantasies and, possibly, fears. A child will usually say if the response is wrong, and usually gives several opportunities to get the message before finally giving up trying to communicate.

Usually hopelessness in the face of impending death is interspersed with hopefulness. Indeed, it seems there is always some hope, even if not for cure, then for some last wish or achievement to be fulfilled, or for a comfortable last phase, or for a death that is peaceful. Children may need to overcome a fear of being buried before they can express their own wishes about how they would like to die: where, with whom, and even about the content of the funeral service. Where the family has strong religious or spiritual beliefs the child may be helped by optimistic images of an afterlife. This, however, does not usually remove the pain of loss and separation from those he or she loves.

What can seem like unrealistic hopefulness on the part of the dying child needs sensitive responses on the part of the adults. The dying child's fluctuating awareness of his or her reality deserves a flexible response which encourages a dialogue, rather than alienating the patient with a reminder of a reality which may be intolerable for the time being. If the child seems to be more hopeless than hopeful, and withdraws into a state of depression, or of psychic closing off, they may be helped by someone close simply acknowledging this very process: 'It seems you're giving up . . . you don't want to live whatever time is left . . . this must be very hard for you . . .'. If the child seems to be 'somewhere else' emotionally, but not depressed, this may be a very understandable separating from the world around. It is important for the child's choice, or decision, to withdraw to be tolerated – difficult though that may be for those involved – rather than pressurizing the child to be jolly, or to 'hang on' for others. This may in part be the one area of control the child has: to choose to withdraw, in the face of so much he or she cannot control.

Ultimately, the dying child *is* alone. We can accompany the child some of the way on that journey, and physically be with the child hopefully until death and after cessation of bodily functions, but emotionally, and, some would say, spiritually, we can never really fully accompany the child. This truth is part of the painfulness for the parents and others who love the child: the pain of loss and separation often begins some time before death. For many it begins at diagnosis, and then re-occurs repeatedly in frequent bursts. The parents and others may like to share with the child some of their happy memories of when the child was well, just as the child may like to do the same, or look at photographs. Thus the shared past and shared joys can have a strengthening effect: an understanding that the many memories live on in those who survive, and that the child, the whole child, includes the pre-illness state.

Where parents and the dying child have time to face the impending death gradually, and the child's condition does not cause unmanageable pain, all involved can feel that the time which is available is precious and a privilege. Alongside this awareness there may be anger at the child's life being cut short, at the death of a child being unnatural and unacceptable. Just as hopefulness and despair oscillate, so an appreciation of the time left oscillates with anger at how little of it there is. These polarities seem to exemplify the extremes of life and death itself: without one we could not have the other, and by attempting to embrace this polarity we are more able to receive the fluctuating feelings and awareness of the dying child.

References

Judd, D. (1995) *Give Sorrow Words – Working with a Dying Child*, 2nd edn. London: Whurr.
Kane, B. (1979) 'Children's concepts of death', *Journal of Genetic Psychology*, 134: 141–53.
Lansdown, R. (1987) Personal Communication.
Orbach, I. (1988) *Children who Don't Want to Live*. San Francisco, CA: Jossey-Bass.
Rilke, M.R. (1915) *Duino Elegies*. Translated by J. Leishman and S. Spender. London: Chatto and Windus, 1963.
Rochlin, G. (1959) 'The loss complex: a contribution to the etiology of depression', *Journal of the American Psychoanalytical Association*, 7: 299–316.
Rochlin, G. (1967) 'How younger children view death and themselves', in E. Grollman (ed.), *Explaining Death to Children*. Boston, MA: Beacon.
Spinetta, J.J. (1975) 'Death anxiety in the outpatient leukaemic child', *Paediatrics*, 56 (6): 1034–7.
Spinetta, J.J. (1982) 'Behavioural and psychological research in childhood cancer: an overview', *Cancer*, 50: 1939–43.
Spinetta, J.J., Rigler, D. and Karon, M. (1973) 'Anxiety in the dying child', *Paediatrics*, 52 (6): 841–5.
Yudkin, S. (1967) 'Children and death', *The Lancet*, 1: 37–40.

Recommended reading

Dyregrov, A. (1990) *Grief in Children – A Handbook for Adults*. London: Jessica Kingsley.
Judd, D. (1994) 'Life threatening illness as psychic trauma: psychotherapy with adolescent patients', in A. Erskine and D. Judd (eds), *The Imaginative Body – Psychodynamic Therapy in Health Care*. London: Whurr.

Smith, S. and Pennells, M. (eds) (1995) *Interventions with Bereaved Children*. London: Jessica Kingsley.

Some suggested books for dying children

Varley, S. (1984) *Badger's Parting Gift*. Picture Lions.
Meltonie, B. and Ingpen, R. (1983) *Beginnings and Endings with Lifetimes in Between*. Surrey: Paper Tiger, Dragon's World Ltd.

29

Jewish perspectives on death, dying and bereavement

Jeanne Samson Katz

Many theological, philosophical and practical texts have described Jewish practices regarding death and bereavement (Lamm, 1969; Rabinowicz, 1989; Goldberg, 1991; Weiss, 1991; Green and Green, 1992). These practices are based on the Old Testament texts, rabbinic literature and other precedents. This article will present those aspects which may be of help when caring for dying Jewish people who may vary in the degree of their religious observance. Although Jewish law specifies regulations and requirements with regard to death and dying, not all Jewish people will want to observe all or some of these. Jews in the UK and Europe are either of Western (Ashkenazi) or Middle Eastern (Sephardi) origin and there are considerable differences in liturgy and practices. Those British Jews who practice Judaism belong to synagogues which are affiliated to the Orthodox (amongst which there are several groups as well as independent communities), Reform, Sephardi, Conservative, Progressive and Liberal movements. Traditions vary amongst these movements and even amongst members of each community. Even observant Jews may choose not to observe all the rules, and may not be familiar with the intricacies of specific Jewish laws, such as the variations dictated by the calendar when festivals occur shortly after death or during the mourning period.

The obligation to visit the sick

'Where there is life, there is hope', is central to Jewish teachings and visiting the sick is a religious duty (*mitzvah*). This is to prevent the alienation and isolation of the sick as well as to pray for their complete recovery (*refuah shlaymah*). According to Maimonides, the medieval rabbinic codifier, one should refrain from visiting the sick only if the illness is a source of embarrassment to the sick person.

The concept of *retention of hope* applies even to dying people, for whom all avenues towards recovery should be explored (Schindler, 1982). These include several religious acts such as giving charitable donations, changing

I should like to thank Rabbi Dr Louis Jacobs for helpful comments and discussion on an earlier draft.

one's actions and adding a new name to the sick person (so that the Angel of Death will not recognize the person). Prayers for the sick person's recovery are offered. However, some commentators hold that it is permissible and even laudatory to pray that a dying person in great pain should be granted a merciful release (Jacobs, personal communication).

Jewish beliefs about life and death

Jewish practices centre on the seasons of the year. Death itself is also seen as the inevitable consequence of life: 'To everything there is a season: a time to be born, and a time to die'.

Teachings emphasize the sanctity of human life, which cannot be judged on the basis of length or quality. From this principle numerous obligations are derived, including the duty to heal the sick and the instruction to preserve human life even if this conflicts with other religious obligations, such as the observance of the Sabbath.

Traditional Jewish teachings oppose any measures which could be interpreted as hastening death, preferring life-extending measures, as long as these measures do not prolong the act of dying. The code of Jewish law (the Shulchan Aruch) states: 'A patient on his death bed is considered a living person in every respect . . . and it is forbidden to cause him to die quickly' (*Yoreh De'ah*, a compendium of law, 339: 1).

Any act which might precipitate death is forbidden by Jewish law, including shutting eyes, removing the pillow or oiling the body (Goldberg, 1991). Steps should be taken to make the dying person (*goses*) comfortable, for example, by giving water and reducing levels of noise.

The concept of 'preparing for death' therefore is alien to the Jewish tradition (Jakobovits and Philipp in Byrne et al., 1991: 190–1). Psalm 71 emphasizes retention of hope: 'cast me not off in my old age when my strength faileth, forsake me not. . . . But as for me, I will hope continually'. Hence many sources suggest that it is not in the dying person's interest to disclose the nearness of death.

When death is imminent

When approaching death, many Jewish people would like to see a rabbi. Members of a specific congregation might welcome a visit from their own rabbi. Where this is not feasible, many institutions have an associated Jewish chaplain who is willing to visit. The dying person may then be helped to recite certain psalms and prayers and, if sufficiently conscious, the 'confessional prayer on the deathbed'. In Judaism the concept of confession through an intermediary does not exist, it is solely between the individual and God. This prayer enables the dying person to participate in his/her own future. It is usually recited in Hebrew and is translated as follows:

Confession on a Deathbed

I acknowledge before You, O Lord my God and God of my fathers, that my cure and my death are in Your hands. May it be Your will to send me a perfect healing. Yet if my death is fully determined by You, I will in love accept it at Your hand. May my death be an atonement for all sins, iniquities and transgressions which I have committed before You. Grant me of the great happiness that is stored up for the righteous. Make known to me the path of life; in Your presence is fullness of joy; at Your right hand bliss for evermore.

O father of the fatherless and defender of the widow, protect my dear family, with whose soul my own soul is bound. Into Your hand I commend my spirit; You will redeem me, O Lord, God of truth. Amen and Amen. (*Singer's Daily Prayer Book*, 1990: 812)

The commentary that accompanies this confession indicates the importance of maintaining the morale of the dying person:

If a sick person is near death, Heaven forbid, someone should recite the confession with him. However, it is required that this be done in such a way that his morale not be broken because this may even hasten death. He should be told, 'Many have confessed and did not die and many who did not confess died anyway. In reward for having confessed, may you live, but everyone who confesses has a share in the World to come.' If the patient cannot speak, he should confess in his heart. One who is unsophisticated should not be asked to confess because it may break his spirit and cause him to weep. (Art scroll commentary to confession on deathbed)

Rabbinic commentators were concerned how the relatives of the dying person might react to these prayers and suggested that they not be said in front of children in case they became upset and consequently distressed the dying person (Schindler, 1982). If the dying person is unable to recite these prayers they can be said on his or her behalf.

Where possible, relatives or friends should maintain a presence at the deathbed. This reassures the dying person and ensures that he or she is not alone when the soul departs (Goldberg, 1991). As death approaches relatives should recite Psalms 90, 121 and 130 very quietly and when death occurs recite the *Sh'ma* (the basic prayer of Judaism). In some communities it is customary to open the windows when the soul departs (Goldberg, 1991). Water that is standing near the body or in jugs in the home where death has taken place should be discarded.

The body

The treatment of the Jewish body is seen as a religious act and strict rules must be observed. Weiss (1991: 27) suggests that: 'In keeping with the life-affirming nature of Judaism, the human body becomes the chief source of ritual impurity when it is bereft of life'. The body should not be moved until death has been established, when the eyes should be closed, all tubes removed and the body covered with a white sheet, the arms and legs straightened with the feet pointed towards the door (Abeles, 1991). The body should be handled as little as possible (Green and Green, 1992) and not left alone. Where possible, relatives or fellow Jews should guard (*wacht*) the body until the burial society (*Chevra Kaddisha*) come to collect it (Katz, 1996). Volunteers from the *Chevra Kaddisha* will take the body to their own premises where trained persons of the same sex as the dead person will perform *tahara*, the ritual cleansing of the body. Although embalming is generally forbidden in Judaism, to conform with international health regulations certain forms of embalming are permitted to enable bodies to be transported across international boundaries. Rabbinic advice should be sought to establish which forms of embalming are permitted.

Autopsies (post-mortems)

The Jewish view is that although the human body is no longer usable it was once a person and should not be violated. The body is compared with the Torah scroll (the Pentateuch handwritten on parchment and used in synagogue services). Both the body and the scroll should be allowed to decompose naturally and not be burnt. Deuteronomy 21: 22–3 forbids the desecration of the body, encouraging speedy burial. Post-mortems and any disfigurement of the corpse are thus forbidden in Jewish law except where civil law requires it (Green and Green, 1992) or it is viewed that the autopsy might save the life of another, when it may be permitted; in any event all the organs should be returned and buried with the corpse.

The funeral

Burial should take place as quickly as possible after death and not more than three days later. Funerals do not take place on the Sabbath nor on major Jewish festivals, and may also be delayed to enable principal mourners to attend. Some secular, Reform, Liberal and Progressive Jews opt for cremation and these communities have recently evolved a range of services to be used at crematoria. Jewish law, however, *strictly forbids cremation* for the reasons cited above. Consequently there are no traditional Jewish mourning rites following cremation.

Jews are buried in simple, undecorated, wooden coffins to comply with the 'dust unto dust' principle. No differentiation may be made between rich and poor. Jews are buried in designated burial grounds which are separated from other cemeteries and rarely surround synagogue buildings. Where cemeteries are some distance from the residential areas, parts of the funeral ceremony may take place in halls or in the home of the deceased.

The 'mourners' are delineated by Jewish law. These are sons and daughters (who have the most extensive obligations), mother, father, brothers, sisters and spouse of the deceased. Before the service begins (sometimes at the deathbed) the mourners tear an outer garment (usually a cardigan or tie) which they wear for the 'week' of mourning (*shiva*, meaning seven). This outward symbol of grief permits 'the mourner to give vent to pent-up anguish by means of a controlled, religiously sanctioned act of destruction' (Lamm, 1969: 38).

In the UK and Europe, where cemeteries are fairly accessible, the funeral service usually begins in the chapel at the gates to the cemetery. The chapel is not decorated, but stark and simple. Flowers are not customary at Jewish funerals; a more appropriate token of esteem is a donation in the name of the deceased to a worthy charity.

In keeping with the separation of the sexes in all Jewish services, men and women stand apart at the funeral service. This is conducted in a mixture of biblical Hebrew and Aramaic and is a sombre, 'but emotionally meaning-ful, farewell to the deceased' (Lamm, 1969: 36). The service is usually divided into four parts, but this may vary according to local custom. This includes a collage of various psalms, the memorial prayer and a eulogy recited in the local tongue, and in some communities a recitation from the Book of Psalms (usually Psalm 23).

> The twenty-third Psalm is the quintessential expression of faith: 'Yea, though I walk through the valley of the shadow of death, I shall fear not evil, for Thou art with me. Thy rod and staff, they comfort me.' It brings consolation, comfort and serene reassurance to the broken-hearted bereaved. The collage has been aptly titled: 'What is Man?' Its purpose is to remind the mourners of the essential brevity of life, so that they may resolve to fill their days with meaningful activity. (Weiss, 1991: 74)

The memorial prayer asks God to embrace the soul of the deceased and grant him/her spiritual reward. The eulogy (*hesped*) has two aims, to arouse the emotions of the listeners, and to focus on the worthy charac-teristics and attainments of the deceased. The eulogy should be truthful, but not hurtful – in Dr Johnson's words, 'in Lapidary inscriptions a man is not upon oath'! Eulogies are not recited on occasions such as minor festivals when expressions of sadness are not appropriate.

After the service in the chapel the coffin is wheeled or carried to the grave in a ritual procession which includes several stops during which Psalm 91 is recited. The coffin is lowered into the grave with the body facing upwards and the feet facing the gate of the cemetery and 'may he (or she) come to his (her) place in peace' is said. In some communities the male mourners (the women are present throughout the service) then recite the Burial Kaddish (others wait till they return to the chapel). This praises the Almighty:

> May His great name be magnified and sanctified in the world that is to be created anew, where He will revive the dead and raise them up unto life eternal.

The men attending the funeral fill the grave with soil, covering it com-pletely. The shovel should not be passed from hand to hand, but replaced in the soil in order to express the view that death is not contagious (Weiss, 1991). The participants return to the chapel, ritually washing their hands on leaving the burial grounds and reciting the verse from Isaiah 25: 8: 'He hath swallowed up death forever, and the Lord hath wiped tears from all the faces'. On re-entering the chapel the focus shifts from the deceased to the bereaved and the traditional consolation is recited: 'May the Lord comfort you among all the other mourners of Zion'. All the participants greet the mourners individually. The mourners then return to where they have elected to spend the week of *shiva* (usually the home of the deceased) and mourning rituals start immediately with a special meal of 'recovery' which must be prepared by non-mourners (often neighbours). The custom includes eating food which is round, for example hard-boiled eggs and round cakes, which symbolize the circular nature of life – death comes to all.

Laws and customs in the house of mourning

A candle is lit for the benefit of the deceased, preferably in the room in which death took place. If this is not possible, a candle is lit in the place where the mourners will remain for the week of *shiva*. Twenty-six-hour candles (or one-week candles) are lit and relit ensuring continuous light for the week. Mirrors are covered in the house of mourning because (a) they cause joy and the mourner is forbidden to rejoice, and (b) it is forbidden to pray in front of mirrors and prayers are recited in the house of mourning (Goldberg, 1991). In some communities, it is customary to cover all pictures.

The consolation of mourners is a scriptural precept, cited in Genesis 25: 11: 'After the death of Abraham, God blessed Isaac' (Goldberg, 1991). Jews are expected to make condolence calls and help the bereaved: for example, by taking food to the house of mourning (Levine, 1994). Mourners usually do not leave the house, except to attend services if they cannot arrange this at home, and to go to the synagogue on Sabbath, where they are greeted formally by the community.

Adult (over 13) male mourners recite the Mourner's Kaddish three times a day (morning, afternoon and evening prayers) for eleven months for children of the deceased and a month for other mourners. Wherever it is said, the Mourner's Kaddish must be recited in the presence of at least ten men (*minyan*) to ensure that the mourner is not isolated (Goldberg, 1991). This prayer is an ancient hymn of worship to God, does not refer to death, yet is said for the benefit of the soul of the deceased. As the Mourner's Kaddish developed in medieval Germany where women rarely attended synagogue services, it is not customary for women to recite this. However, it is not forbidden and some women mourners choose to attend thrice-daily services to recite the Kaddish.

The Jewish rites of mourning are believed to be of therapeutic effect, enabling expression rather than repression of grief (Lamm, 1969; Goldberg,

1991; Weiss, 1991). Mourners move through graduated stages of obligations until they are fully resocialized into society. Relatives and friends are central to this process, ensuring that mourners are cared for and not isolated and that enough men are present at the daily prayers to enable the mourner to say Kaddish. The mourner's sense of community solidarity is reinforced by daily attendance at services where other mourners are likely to be present.

Judaism has five graduated periods of mourning, each with its own laws governing the expression of grief and the process of return to the normal affairs of society. The first stage of mourning (*aninut*), is between death and burial. The mourner's despair is recognized and he (or she) is relieved of all religious obligations. Immediately after burial, the period of real mourning (*avelut*) begins, with its attendant obligations. In the *shiva* week mourners remain in the house of mourning, sit on low chairs, wear slippers rather than shoes, wear the torn clothing and receive condolence calls. Where possible the thrice-daily prayers are recited in the house of mourning with at least ten men attending to enable the mourner to recite Kaddish. Men do not shave during this time. For the first three days the mourner is expected to be distressed and not return greetings. For the rest of *shiva* mourners move from the state of intense grief to the point of talking about the deceased with those offering condolences. Depending on the origins of the mourners there are different customs marking the end of *shiva* (Levine, 1994).

The next stage is the *shloshim* (30 days from burial), during which the mourner returns to work. Many men continue not to shave nor have their hair cut, but are permitted to do so should this cause them embarrassment. Except where parents have died, the mourning period ends at 30 days. The obligation to mourn is terminated by the beginning of any major Jewish festival during this period. Mourning for parents continues to be observed for 12 lunar calendar months, although Kaddish is only recited for 11.

From the time of burial till the end of the mourning period (30 days or a year) mourners do not attend festive functions or public places, especially if music is played. This restriction aims at limiting pleasure (Goldberg, 1991). If the mourner is a professional who subsists on providing entertainment, taking photographs at functions, etc., this restriction is lifted.

A memorial stone is erected on the grave to honour the deceased usually between 30 days and a year after burial. The biblical precedent for this is the tomb Jacob placed on Rachel's grave (Genesis 35: 20). The stone should be unostentatious; if one wants to commemorate over and above that, charitable donations are encouraged. The timing of the tombstone unveiling (sometimes called consecration) varies in different communities; the UK custom is after 11 months. On the stone are engraved the name of the deceased, his (or her) dates of birth and death as well as a Hebrew abbreviation for 'May his/her soul be bound up in the Bond of Life'. The consecration of the stone is a short service either at the graveside or in the chapel. A further eulogy might be said. Thereafter mourners mark the Hebrew date annually by lighting the 26-hour candle, attending services three times that day to recite the Mourner's Kaddish, and avoiding 'pleasurable' outings. One continues to commemorate this date (the *Yarzheit*) for the rest of one's life. Memorial prayers are also said on certain holy days.

Life after death

Little mention was made of life after death in the Old Testament (Riemer, 1995), which emphasizes the value of life on earth and the here and now (Steinsaltz, 1999). However, during the Rabbinic period the two concepts, that of the immortality of the soul and the resurrection of the dead, became combined so that 'when a man dies his soul lives on in Heaven until the time of the resurrection when soul and body are reunited' (Jacobs, 1973: 158). These concepts have continued to be accepted belief and were reinforced by the reference to life after death in Maimonides' 13 principles of faith, which may be regarded as the essence of Judaism. The practical details of life after death are not specified in Jewish teachings:

> The doctrine of the immortality of the soul is affirmed not only by Judaism and other religions but by many secular philosophers as well. Judaism, however, also believes in the eventual resurrection of the body, which will be reunited with the soul at a later time. . . . The human form of the righteous men of all ages, buried and long since decomposed, will be resurrected at God's will. (Lamm, 1969: 228)

Judaism delineates bodily death as a consequence of life:

> Death is defined as the irreversible separation of body and soul. No longer required by the soul, the body degenerates and decays. The soul, however, continues to exist in a non-physical dimension which we call 'heaven'. Free of the limitations of the body, but enriched by its earthly experiences, it is conscious of its attainments and earthly associations. Death is merely one's passage into a higher, more meaningful, more spiritual, more satisfying realm of existence. (Weiss, 1991: 14)

Judaism must be viewed as both this-worldly and other-worldly (Jacobs, 1973). Jacobs quotes the second-century Rabbi Jacob who illustrates this paradox:

> Better is one hour of repentance and good deeds in this world than the whole life of the world to come; yet better is one hour of blissfulness of spirit in the world to come than the whole life of this world. (*Pirkei Avot* 4: 17, quoted in Jacobs, 1973: 164)

Thus Jewish customs emphasize behaviour on earth, value the human body even after death and consider that the expression of grief is a normal human response to bereavement.

References

Abeles, Margaret (1991) 'Features of Judaism for carers when looking after Jewish patients', *Palliative Medicine*, 5: 201–5.

Byrne, P., Dunstan, J.R., Jakobovits, Lord I., Jayaweera, R.L.A., Marshall, J., Philipp, E., Saunders, Dame C. and Seller, M.J. (1991) 'Hospice care: Jewish reservations considered in a comparative ethical study', *Palliative Medicine*, 5: 187–200.

Goldberg, Chaim B. (1991) *Mourning in Halachah*. New York: Mesorah Publications.

Green, M. and Green, J. (1992) *Dealing with Death*. London: Chapman & Hall.

Jacobs, Louis (1973) *What Does Judaism Say About?* Jerusalem: Keter.

Katz, J.S. (1996) 'Caring for dying Jewish people in a multicultural/religious society', *International Journal of Palliative Nursing*, 2 (1): 43–7.

Lamm, Maurice (1969) *The Jewish Way in Death and Mourning*. New York: Jonathan David.

Levine, A. (1994) *To Comfort the Bereaved*. London: Jason Aronson.

Rabinowicz, Tzvi (1989) *A Guide to Life: Jewish Laws and Customs of Mourning*. London: Jason Aronson.

Riemer, J. (ed.) (1995) *Jewish Insights on Death and Mourning*. New York: Schocken Books.

Schindler, Ruben (1982) 'Confronting terminal illness and death in religious Jewish society', *Advances in Thanatology*, 5: 2.

Singer, S. (1990) *The Authorised Daily Prayer Book of the United Hebrew Congregations of the Commonwealth*. Cambridge: Press Syndicate of the University of Cambridge.

Steinsaltz, A. (1999) *Simple Words: Thinking About what Really Matters in Life*. New York: Simon and Schuster.

Weiss, Abner (1991) *Death and Bereavement: A Halakhic Guide*. New York: Ktav Publishing House.

30

The syllabus

Mitch Albom

His death sentence came in the summer of 1994. Looking back, Morrie knew something bad was coming long before that. He knew it the day he gave up dancing.

He had always been a dancer, my old professor. The music didn't matter. Rock and roll, big band, the blues. He loved them all. He would close his eyes and with a blissful smile begin to move to his own sense of rhythm. It wasn't always pretty. But then, he didn't worry about a partner. Morrie danced by himself.

He used to go to this church in Harvard Square every Wednesday night for something called 'Dance Free'. They had flashing lights and booming speakers and Morrie would wander in among the mostly student crowd, wearing a white T-shirt and black sweatpants and a towel around his neck, and whatever music was playing, that's the music to which he danced. He'd do the lindy to Jimi Hendrix. He twisted and twirled, he waved his arms like a conductor on amphetamines, until sweat was dripping down the middle of his back. No one there knew he was a prominent doctor of sociology, with years of experience as a college professor and several well-respected books. They just thought he was some old nut.

Once, he brought a tango tape and got them to play it over the speakers. Then he commandeered the floor, shooting back and forth like some hot Latin lover. When he finished, everyone applauded. He could have stayed in that moment forever.

But then the dancing stopped.

He developed asthma in his sixties. His breathing became labored. One day he was walking along the Charles River, and a cold burst of wind left him choking for air. He was rushed to the hospital and injected with Adrenalin.

A few years later, he began to have trouble walking. At a birthday party for a friend, he stumbled inexplicably. Another night, he fell down the steps of a theater, startling a small crowd of people.

'Give him air!' someone yelled.

He was in his seventies by this point, so they whispered 'old age' and helped him to his feet. But Morrie, who was always more in touch with his insides than the rest of us, knew something else was wrong. This was more

---

Extract from *Tuesdays with Morrie*, New York: Doubleday, 1997, pp. 5–13.

than old age. He was weary all the time. He had trouble sleeping. He dreamt he was dying.

He began to see doctors. Lots of them. They tested his blood. They tested his urine. They put a scope up his rear end and looked inside his intestines. Finally, when nothing could be found, one doctor ordered a muscle biopsy, taking a small piece out of Morrie's calf. The lab report come back suggesting a neurological problem, and Morrie was brought in for yet another series of tests. In one of those tests, he sat in a special seat as they zapped him with electrical current – an electric chair, of sorts – and studied his neurological responses.

'We need to check this further', the doctors said, looking over his results.

'Why?' Morrie asked. 'What is it?'

'We're not sure. Your times are slow.'

His times were slow? What did that mean?

Finally, on a hot, humid day in August 1994, Morrie and his wife, Charlotte, went to the neurologist's office, and he asked them to sit before he broke the news: Morrie had amyotrophic lateral sclerosis (ALS), Lou Gehrig's disease, a brutal, unforgiving illness of the neurological system.

There was no known cure.

'How did I get it?' Morrie asked.

Nobody knew.

'Is it terminal?'

Yes.

'So I'm going to die?'

Yes, you are, the doctor said. I'm very sorry.

He sat with Morrie and Charlotte for nearly two hours, patiently answering their questions. When they left, the doctor gave them some information on ALS, little pamphlets, as if they were opening a bank account. Outside, the sun was shining and people were going about their business. A woman ran to put money in the parking meter. Another carried groceries. Charlotte had a million thoughts running through her mind: *How much time do we have left? How will we manage? How will we pay the bills?*

My old professor, meanwhile, was stunned by the normalcy of the day around him. *Shouldn't the world stop? Don't they know what has happened to me?*

But the world did not stop, it took no notice at all, and as Morrie pulled weakly on the car door, he felt as if he were dropping into a hole.

Now what? he thought.

As my old professor searched for answers, the disease took him over, day by day, week by week. He backed the car out of the garage one morning and could barely push the brakes. That was the end of his driving.

He kept tripping, so he purchased a cane. That was the end of his walking free.

He went for his regular swim at the YMCA, but found he could no longer undress himself. So he hired his first home care worker – a theology student named Tony – who helped him in and out of the pool, and in and out of his bathing suit. In the locker room, the other swimmers pretended not to stare. They stared anyhow. That was the end of his privacy.

In the fall of 1994, Morrie came to the hilly Brandeis campus to teach his final college course. He could have skipped this, of course. The university would have understood. Why suffer in front of so many people? Stay at home. Get your affairs in order. But the idea of quitting did not occur to Morrie.

Instead, he hobbled into the classroom, his home for more than 30 years. Because of the cane, he took a while to reach the chair. Finally, he sat down, dropped his glasses off his nose, and looked out at the young faces who stared back in silence.

'My friends, I assume you are all here for the Social Psychology class. I have been teaching this course for 20 years, and this is the first time I can say there is a risk in taking it, because I have a fatal illness. I may not live to finish the semester.

'If you feel this is a problem, I understand if you wish to drop the course.'

He smiled.

And that was the end of his secret.

ALS is like a lit candle: it melts your nerves and leaves your body a pile of wax. Often, it begins with the legs and works its way up. You lose control of your thigh muscles, so that you cannot support yourself standing. You lose control of your trunk muscles, so that you cannot sit up straight. By the end, if you are still alive, you are breathing through a tube in a hole in your throat, while your soul, perfectly awake, is imprisoned inside a limp husk, perhaps able to blink, or cluck a tongue, like something from a science fiction movie, the man frozen inside his own flesh. This takes no more than five years from the day you contract the disease.

Morrie's doctors guessed he had two years left.

Morrie knew it was less.

But my old professor had made a profound decision, one he began to construct the day he came out of the doctor's office with a sword hanging over his head. *Do I wither up and disappear, or do I make the best of my time left?* He had asked himself.

He would not wither. He would not be ashamed of dying.

Instead, he would make death his final project, the center point of his days. Since everyone was going to die, he could be of great value, right? He could be research. A human textbook. *Study me in my slow and patient demise. Watch what happens to me. Learn with me.*

Morrie would walk that final bridge between life and death, and narrate the trip.

The fall semester passed quickly. The pills increased. Therapy became a regular routine. Nurses came to his house to work with Morrie's withering legs, to keep the muscles active, bending them back and forth as if pumping water from a well. Massage specialists came by once a week to try to soothe the constant, heavy stiffness he felt. He met with meditation teachers, and closed his eyes and narrowed his thoughts until his world shrunk down to a single breath, in and out, in and out.

One day, using his cane, he stepped onto the curb and fell over into the street. The cane was exchanged for a walker. As his body weakened, the back and forth to the bathroom became too exhausting, so Morrie began to urinate into a large beaker. He had to support himself as he did this, meaning someone had to hold the beaker while Morrie filled it.

Most of us would be embarrassed by all this, especially at Morrie's age. But Morrie was not like most of us. When some of his close colleagues would visit, he would say to them, 'Listen, I have to pee. Would you mind helping? Are you okay with that?'

Often, to their own surprise, they were.

In fact, he entertained a growing stream of visitors. He had discussion groups about dying, what it really meant, how societies had always been afraid of it without necessarily understanding it. He told his friends that if they really wanted to help him, they would treat him not with sympathy but with visits, phone calls, a sharing of their problems – the way they had always shared their problems, because Morrie had always been a wonderful listener.

For all that was happening to him, his voice was strong and inviting, and his mind was vibrating with a million thoughts. He was intent on proving that the word 'dying' was not synonymous with 'useless'.

The New Year came and went. Although he never said it to anyone, Morrie knew this would be the last year of his life. He was using a wheel-chair now, and he was fighting time to say all the things he wanted to say to all the people he loved. When a colleague at Brandeis died suddenly of a heart attack, Morrie went to his funeral. He came home depressed.

'What a waste', he said. 'All those people saying all those wonderful things, and Irv never got to hear any of it'.

Morrie had a better idea. He made some calls. He chose a date. And on a cold Sunday afternoon, he was joined in his home by a small group of friends and family for a 'living funeral'. Each of them spoke and paid tribute to my old professor. Some cried. Some laughed. One woman read a poem:

My dear and loving cousin . . .
Your ageless heart
as you move through time, layer on layer,
tender sequoia . . .

Morrie cried and laughed with them. And all the heartfelt things we never get to say to those we love, Morrie said that day. His 'living funeral' was a rousing success.

Only Morrie wasn't dead yet.

In fact, the most unusual part of his life was about to unfold.

31

Dying trajectories, the organization of work and expectations of dying

Anselm Strauss

Before commencing the case history, it is important to locate Mrs Abel's own type of dying trajectory – lingering – within a general picture of types of dying trajectories as they relate to the temporal organizations of hospital work, the accountable features of terminal care and the progressive change of the staff's expectations of dying.

Temporal features of terminal care

While not entirely medical or technical, most writings about terminal care focus on the psychological or ethical aspects of behaviour toward dying persons. These emphases flow from generalized considerations of death as a philosophical problem, and the psychological and often ethical difficulties accompanying death and dying. Just as legitimately, however, the behaviour of people toward the dying may be viewed as involving 'work'. This is just as true when a person dies at home as when he [sic] dies in the hospital. Usually during the course of his dying he is unable to fulfil all his physiological and psychological needs. He may need to be fed, bathed, taken to the toilet, given drugs, brought desired objects when too feeble to get them himself, and near the end of his life, even 'cared for' totally. Whether the people who are in attendance on him enjoy or suffer these tasks, they are undeniably 'work'. Wealthier families sometimes hire private nurses to do all or some of this work. In the hospital, there is no question that terminal care, whether regarded distastefully or as satisfying, is viewed as work. Mrs Abel required considerable physiological and psychological care which became progressively distasteful to the staff.

This work has important temporal features. For instance, there are prescribed schedules governing when the patient must be fed, bathed, turned in bed, given drugs. There are periodic moments when tests must be administered. There are crucial periods when the patient must be closely observed, or even when crucial treatments must be given or actions taken to prevent immediate deterioration – even immediate death. Since there is a division of

Extract from *Anguish: the Case History of a Dying Trajectory*, San Francisco, CA: Sociology Press, 1971, pp. 5–13 (abridged).

labour, it must be temporally organized. For instance, the nurse must have the patient awake in time for the laboratory technician to administer tests, and the physician's visit must not coincide with the patient's bath or even perhaps the visiting hours of relatives. [. . .]

On Mrs Abel's ward nurses preferred to focus care and attention on recovering and less troublesome dying patients. The temporal ordering of work on given services is also related to the predominant types of death in relation to normal types of recovery. As an example, we may look at intensive care units: some patients there may be expected to die quickly, if they are to die at all; others need close attention for several days because death is a touch-and-go matter; while others are not likely to die but do need temporary round-the-clock nursing. Most who will die here are either so heavily drugged as to be temporarily comatose or are actually past self-consciousness. Consequently, there is little need for nurses or physicians to converse with those patients, as there is on lingering wards, where we find Mrs Abel. She continually wished to talk to nursing staff and her doctor no matter how pressed they were to keep working.

Each type of service tends to have a characteristic incidence of death, and speed of dying, which together affect the staff's organization of work. Thus, on emergency services, patients tend to die quickly (they are accident cases, or victims of violence, or people suddenly stricken). The staff on emergency services therefore is geared to give immediate emergency service to prevent death whenever possible. Many emergency services, especially in large cities, are also organized for frequent deaths, especially on weekends. At such times, the recovering (or non-sick) patients sometimes tend to receive scant attention, unless the service is flexibly organized for handling both types of patients. This patient competition also occurs on wards where patients die slowly. On the cancer ward, for example, when a patient nears death, sometimes he may unwittingly compete with other patients for nurses' or physicians' attention, several of whom may give care to the critically ill patient. When the emergency is over, or the patient dies, then the nurses may return to less immediately critical patients, reading their vital signs, managing treatments and carrying out other important tasks. Mrs Abel fared poorly in such competition with other patients during her long stay in the hospital, and especially during her last days.

All these temporal features of terminal care make for a complex organization of professional activity. The required organization is rendered even more complex by certain other matters involving temporality. Thus, what may be conveniently termed the 'experiential careers' of patients, families and staff members are very relevant to the action around dying patients. Some patients are very familiar with their diseases, but even then are encountering symptoms for the first time, such as Mrs Abel confronting her intense pain. What a patient knows about the course of his disease, from previous experience with it, is very relevant to what will happen as he lies dying in the hospital. The same may be said about personnel in attendance upon him. Some personnel may be well acquainted with the predominant disease patterns found on their particular wards; but some may be newcomers to these diseases, although quite possibly old hands with other illnesses. The newcomers may be quite unprepared for sudden changes of symptoms and vital signs, hence may be taken quite by surprise at crucial junctures: that is, they make bad errors in timing their actions. More experienced personnel are less likely to be caught unprepared, and are readier with appropriate care at each phase of the illness. [. . .]

Dying trajectories

The dying trajectory of each patient has at least two outstanding properties. First, it takes place over time: it has *duration*. There can be much variation in duration among specific trajectories, ranging from instant death to months, as for Mrs Abel. Second, a trajectory has *shape*: it can be graphed. It plunges straight down; it moves slowly downward (Mrs Abel); it vacillates slowly, moving slightly up and down before diving radically downward; it moves slowly down at first, then hits a long plateau, then plunges abruptly to death.

Neither duration nor shape is a purely objective psychological property. They are perceived properties; their dimensions depend on *when* the perceiver initially *defines* someone as dying and on his expectations of how that dying will proceed. Dying trajectories are, then, *perceived courses of dying*, rather than the actual courses themselves. This distinction is readily evident in the type of trajectory which involves a short reprieve from death. This reprieve represents an unexpected deferment of death. On the other hand, a lingering death may mean that bystanders expect faster dying, as in Mrs Abel's trajectory.

Since dying patients enter hospitals at varying distances from death, and are defined in terms of when and how they will die, various types of trajectories are commonly recognized by the hospital personnel. For instance, there is the trajectory that is a complete surprise: a patient who is expected to recover suddenly dies. A frequently found trajectory on emergency wards is the expected swift death. Many patients are brought in because of fatal accidents, and nothing can be done to prevent their deaths. Expected lingering while dying is another type of trajectory; it is characteristic, for example, of cancer patients like Mrs Abel. Besides the short-term reprieve, there may also be the suspended-sentence trajectory. Another commonly recognized pattern is entry–re-entry: the patient, slowly going downhill, returns home several times between stays in the hospital. All these generalized types of trajectories rest upon the perceivers' expectations of 'duration' and 'shape'.

Regardless of the particular attributes of a specific patient's trajectory, there are ordinarily certain events – we shall term them 'critical junctures' – which appear along the dying trajectory and are directly handled by the temporal organization of hospital work. These occur either in full or truncated form: (1) The patient is defined as dying; (2) Staff and family then make preparations for his death, as he may himself if he knows he is dying; (3) At some point, there seems to be 'nothing more to do' to prevent death; (4) The final descent may take weeks, or days, or merely hours, ending in (5) the 'last hours', (6) the death watch and (7) death itself. Somewhere along his course of dying, there may be announcements that the patient is dying, or that he is entering or leaving a phase of dying. After death, death itself must be legally pronounced, and then publicly announced.

When these critical junctures occur as expected, on schedule, then all participants – including the patient, sometimes – are prepared for their occurrence – the work involved is provided for and integrated by the temporal order of the hospital. For instance, the nurses are ready for a death watch when they can anticipate approximately when the patient will be very near death. When, however, critical junctures are not expected or are off schedule, staff members and family alike are caught off guard, or at least somewhat unprepared. This case will offer many examples of both anticipated and unanticipated junctures. The point we wish to emphasize here is that expectations are crucial to the way critical junctures are handled by all involved. [. . .]

32

Sitting it out

Elizabeth Dean

The writer has worked as a registered nurse in homes for the elderly. In this article, one of those for whom she has cared speaks through her about the diminishment – and hope – which old age brings.

My day begins around 5.30 when I'm woken by the night staff changing the sheets of the old men and women that have wet themselves during the night; my bed is dry, I am not at this stage yet.

I am 79 years old and of sound mind, at least I think I am. It's not my mind but my body that no longer functions reliably and I am termed 'unsafe' by my doctor, my daughter-in-law and my son, although for my son to say it causes him guilt and he somehow can't quite look me in the eye. Between them they arranged for my house to be sold and the money it provided has secured me a place here, in a 'home', where I can be well looked after. It's not so bad I suppose: beyond my window I can see a beautiful garden.

I never really expected my son and his wife to look after me, it was an unrealistic hope, they're busy with jobs and their children, I can remember what it was like to bring up a family, there's very little time for anything else. I understand now but I felt very hurt and bitter at first, knowing they couldn't look after me, but like so many other things these days I find I accept it. They visit me most weekends and bring pictures of my grand-children; I suppose it wouldn't be much fun for them coming to see their Granny in a place like this.

I miss my home; they call this place 'Sunnyside Lodge, Home for the Elderly', most people just call it 'The Home', to me it's just a place and there are many places like this one, large, old houses converted to take in old relics like me – storage houses really. They tend the garden well and have planted masses of flowers; sometimes, if my window is open, I can smell the scent on the breeze.

The nurses, or care assistants as they are called, are cheerful most of the time and do the best they can to ensure our physical well-being. They refer to us as 'residents', we are patients really but nobody uses that word, it smacks too much of hospitals and illness; it's all psychology jargon to try and kid you and it really doesn't matter, I suppose.

From *The Tablet*, 25 May 1991.

I think a lot these days and sometimes I find it hard to know if I'm saying what I'm thinking or just think I'm saying what I'm thinking and I become very confused but Louise seems to understand me, she's a nurse and she works here on Monday nights. I wish they were all like Louise, kind and comforting.

They give me pills, I lose count how many I take in a day. Some almost choke me, they're so big you see and my throat is very dry so they stick halfway down – it's frightening. It seems every part of me is drying up; skin, joints, hair, nails, I'm like an autumn leaf, all dry and brittle and about to disintegrate.

When I arrived at this place I could walk by myself, I could even help the others, like changing the channel on the TV or picking up a dropped newspaper, that sort of thing. Their helplessness made me feel better, now I'm just as helpless. I'm a prisoner trapped in a hard upright chair that I have to sit in all day long.

My best hours are between 11 o'clock and 1. The pain in my joints has eased by this time, with the help of the tablets. The nurses are busy making beds and cleaning medicine trolleys so we are left alone. I can still read the newspaper with a magnifying glass and I can read books as long as they are not too heavy to hold.

All things considered the food here isn't too bad. We are given our lunch at half past 12, if meat is served I have to ask someone to cut it up for me. Sometimes I try to do it for myself, but very often the knife slips and the food spills onto my lap and stains my clothes and then I've made more work for the nurses.

I try not to grumble, I never did like to hear people moaning but it's the frustration I find unbearable – the fact that my body is so useless and refuses to do what I want it to. If I was at home it wouldn't bother me, it wouldn't matter if I didn't wash my face one day or brush my hair another, these things seem unimportant but I can't tell the nurses that, they seem hurt if we complain, if we don't try and some of them can get quite cross. I'm too weary to resist their demands so I put up with their concern about washing me and dressing me and lifting me to rub my bottom so it doesn't become sore; and I let them put pills into my mouth to ease the pain and I put up with the side-effects they produce; the sickness, the constipation, and I suffer the indignity of the enemas to relieve the constipation and through all this I find myself saying 'Thank you' constantly and why? I should be clawing their eyes out for making me suffer in this way. There is no sense to any of it. Why can't they leave me alone? I know I shouldn't think this way, they are doing their best, it's not their fault I'm old.

After lunch we are toileted and arranged in chairs in a semi-circle in front of the television set and left for two hours; that's the average length of time it takes before we need the toilet again, or so the nurses say. We would all dearly love to go to bed but this is not allowed, 'It's not therapeutic' they say and we are denied our beds unless we are ill. So I am forced to sit in front of a blaring TV set, my hearing remains good whilst most of the others are deaf, consequently the TV has to be set at full volume. I am imprisoned in my chair, watching ludicrous programmes that I can't understand, unable to sleep because of the noise and every muscle and every bone in my body is creaking with tiredness.

My voice, much weaker now, cannot be heard above the noise when I call for help. I can see the bell by the mantlepiece but I can't reach it and the fear of falling keeps me rooted to my seat. The sight of that bell, so tantalizingly close, plays cruelly on my nerves. Knowing I am forced to sit here until someone happens to look into the room agitates me to the point that I feel I need the toilet; fear of wetting the chair and my clothes increases the desire to wee.

The night staff put us to bed around 9 o'clock. I am one of the first to be undressed and eased between the cold, stiff sheets. They scratch my tender, papery-thin skin but this no longer bothers me, all I want is to lie down and never have to get out of bed again.

It's Monday and Louise is working tonight and she sits on my bed chatting quietly. She seems to understand the suffering and fear that ageing forces us to endure. She doesn't try to cajole me or make light of the effort required to keep myself going. She has a gentle humour and somehow makes me laugh at my infirmities, laughter is a fine medicine.

'One day nearer', Louise says as she tucks me into bed and she says the words with such hope in her voice, not in a morbid way, as if she knows for sure that something better waits just ahead of me. And she makes it sound so natural, as if there is nothing to be frightened of and her words comfort me because I am frightened, but beyond the fear lies hope, beyond this dark tunnel of pain there is a wonderfully bright future and I just have to be patient.

Louise strokes my hair soothingly. 'God bless you', she says as she switches off the light. And I wonder – is that what death will be like, as if someone has switched off the light and as I lie in bed I pray that God in His infinite mercy does just that but I pray that He does it gently, tenderly . . . without pain, because I am bone weary and all that was once strong in me is crumbling and there is little left to support me. I am exhausted by this world.

33

A very easy death

Simone de Beauvoir

Why did my mother's death shake me so deeply? Since the time I left home
I had felt little in the way of emotional impulse towards her. When she lost
my father the intensity and the simplicity of her sorrow moved me, and so
did her care for others – 'Think of yourself', she said to me, supposing that
I was holding back my tears so as not to make her suffering worse. A year
later her mother's dying was a painful reminder of her husband's: on the
day of the funeral a nervous breakdown compelled her to stay in bed. I
spent the night beside her: forgetting my disgust for this marriage-bed in
which I had been born and in which my father had died, I watched her
sleeping; at fifty-five, with her eyes closed and her face calm, she was still
beautiful; I wondered that the strength of her feelings should have
overcome her will. Generally speaking I thought of her with no particular
feeling. Yet in my sleep (although my father only made very rare and then
insignificant appearances) she often played a most important part: she
blended with Sartre, and we were happy together. And then the dream
would turn into a nightmare: why was I living with her once more? How
had I come to be in her power again? So our former relationship lived on in
me in its double aspect – a subjection that I loved and hated. It revived with
all its strength when Maman's accident, her illness and her death shattered
the routine that then governed our contacts. Time vanishes behind those
who leave this world, and the older I get the more my past years draw
together. The 'Maman darling' of the days when I was ten can no longer be
told from the inimical woman who oppressed my adolescence: I wept for
them both when I wept for my old mother. I thought I had made up my
mind about our failure and accepted it; but its sadness comes back to my
heart. There are photographs of both of us, taken at about the same time: I
am eighteen, she is nearly forty. Today I could almost be her mother and
the grandmother of that sad-eyed girl. I am so sorry for them – for me
because I am so young and I understand nothing; for her because her future
is closed and she has never understood anything. But I would not know
how to advise them. It was not in my power to wipe out the unhappiness in
her childhood that condemned Maman to make me unhappy and to suffer
in her turn for having done so. For if she embittered several years of my
life, I certainly paid her back though I did not set out to do so. She was

---

Extract from *A Very Easy Death*, Harmondsworth: Penguin, 1969, pp. 89–92.

intensely anxious about my soul. As far as this world was concerned, she was pleased at my successes, but she was hurt by the scandal that I aroused among the people she knew. It was not pleasant for her to hear a cousin state, 'Simone is the family's disgrace'.

The changes in Maman during her illness made my sorrow all the greater. As I have already said, she was a woman of strong and eager temperament, and because of her renunciations she had grown confused and difficult. Confined to her bed, she decided to live for herself; and yet at the same time she retained an unvarying care for others – from her conflicts there arose a harmony. My father and his social character coincided exactly: his class and he spoke through his mouth with one identical voice. His last words, 'You began to earn your living very young, Simone: your sister cost me a great deal of money', were not of a kind to encourage tears. My mother was awkwardly laced into a spiritualistic ideology; but she had an animal passion for life which was the source of her courage and which, once she was conscious of the weight of her body, brought her towards truth. She got rid of the ready-made notions that hid her sincere and lovable side. It was then that I felt the warmth of an affection that had often been distorted by jealousy and that she expressed so badly. In her papers I have found touching evidence of it. She had put aside two letters, the one written by a Jesuit and the other by a friend; they both assured her that one day I should come back to God. She had copied out a passage from Chamson in which he says in effect, 'If, when I was twenty, I had met an older, highly-regarded man who had talked to me about Nietszche and Gide and freedom, I should have broken with home'. The file was completed by an article cut out of a paper – *Jean-Paul Sartre has saved a soul*. In this Rémy Roure said – quite untruthfully, by the way – that after *Bariona* had been acted at Stalag XII D an atheistical doctor was converted. I know very well what she wanted from these pieces – it was to be reassured about me; but she would never have felt the need if she had not been intensely anxious as to my salvation. 'Of course I should like to go to Heaven: but not all alone, not without my daughters,' she wrote to a young nun.

Sometimes, though very rarely, it happens that love, friendship or comradely feeling overcomes the loneliness of death: in spite of appearances, even when I was holding Maman's hand, I was not with her – I was lying to her. Because she had always been deceived, gulled, I found this ultimate deception revolting. I was making myself an accomplice of that fate which was so misusing her. Yet at the same time in every cell of my body I joined in her refusal, in her rebellion: and it was also because of that that her defeat overwhelmed me. Although I was not with Maman when she died, and although I had been with three people when they were actually dying, it was when I was at her bedside that I saw Death, the Death of the dance of death, with its bantering grin, the Death of fireside tales that knocks on the door, a scythe in its hand, the Death that comes from elsewhere, strange and inhuman: it had the very face of Maman when she showed her gums in a wide smile of unknowingness.

'He is certainly of an age to die'. The sadness of the old; their banishment: most of them do not think that this age has yet come for them. I too made use of this cliché, and that when I was referring to my mother. I did not understand that one might sincerely weep for a relative, a grandfather aged seventy and more. If I met a woman of fifty overcome with sadness because she had just lost her mother, I thought her neurotic: we are all mortal; at eighty you are quite old enough to be one of the dead . . .

But it is not true. You do not die from being born, nor from having lived, nor from old age. You die from *something*. The knowledge that because of her age my mother's life must soon come to an end did not lessen the horrible surprise: she had sarcoma. Cancer, thrombosis, pneumonia: it is as violent and unforeseen as an engine stopping in the middle of the sky. My mother encouraged one to be optimistic when, crippled with arthritis and dying, she asserted the infinite value of each instant; but her vain tenaciousness also ripped and tore the reassuring curtain of everyday triviality. There is no such thing as a natural death: nothing that happens to a man is ever natural, since his presence calls the world into question. All men must die: but for every man his death is an accident and, even if he knows it and consents to it, an unjustifiable violation.

34

Teach me to hear mermaids singing

Clare Vaughan

Five months ago I developed a chest infection which would not clear up. I had been overworking: four part-time jobs, three children, Christmas with its expectations, and a winter of coughs and colds. My general practitioner suggested a chest x-ray examination. I went with my 5-year-old daughter in tow. The result was extraordinary and the radiologist looked suitably impressed. My daughter turned to me, 'Mummy, has your cancer come back?' 'I am afraid it has, my love', I replied.

At first I crept into my bed and withdrew from the world and howled. How preposterous not to see my lovely children grow up. How unbearable to have had only half my life with my love. How disappointing to leave all my exciting work plans at such a vulnerable but optimistic stage.

So, four years after the first diagnosis, I have a tumour like an avocado pear in my right lung and a small crescent of functioning liver remaining. I am probably dying: the biggest adventure of all. The past five months have appalled, surprised and exhilarated me and given me insights into my life in a totally unexpected way. I would like to share some of this richness.

Breast cancer is a roller-coaster of an illness with windows of complete wellbeing, the last of which lasted two and a half years. I was more than well. I was fired with energy and vigour. I focused on my family with an intensity that sometimes bewildered them. This holiday must be the best yet; that school must offer my child the most; I must have all the good things now. It was my abiding luck to have had a partner who could love me and give me ease during this turbulent time. I decided not to get involved in medicalizing my remission. I took only a passing interest in oncology literature, had an open mind on tamoxifen, which I eventually took for 18 months, and had regular check ups.

I felt an enormous need to move my intellectual life along. I wanted to make changes to medical education and look at how we encourage young doctors to recognize that primary care offers riches as a career and a life. This work has been the most exciting time of my life and I have been privileged to spend it with an extraordinary bunch of colleagues as a lecturer in an academic department of primary care, as a vocational training scheme course organizer, as a general practice postgraduate tutor, and as a regional assistant adviser.

From *British Medical Journal*, 1996, 313: 565.

I began to formulate a vision for my illness. I decided not to have further chemotherapy. A very tough decision: it was the oncologist's best offer and best offers need to be respected. My heart told me to nurture all the wonderful bits of my life rather than to try again and, I suspect unsuccessfully, to poison the tumour. I decided to spend time thinking about core values, to clear the clutter, to be there for my friends and family, to follow up my ideas, and to write poetry and letters.

All my life I have been the doer and the fixer. Doctors have this terrible problem: they need to be needed so badly. I have been difficult to live with because of my quickness and my impatience but I have begun to learn the joy of receiving gifts, people's best offers. Everything from flowers and trinkets to a fellowship of the Royal College of General Practitioners. My education certainly taught me nothing about the grace of receiving. In addition, my anger has evaporated. The anger has always been a plague. I have always been quicker and brighter and more impatient than most other people. It energizes, shapes and delivers, but it can hurt and bewilder. I have put off dealing with it again and again. I am sure that always having a good five-month plan as well as a five-year plan helps to diffuse and defray this, and to some extent protect from disappointed dreams. But it also distracts from dealing with the internal focus where anger resides.

At the moment I have a golden window of time. The steroids control my liver pain, have given me comfort and stopped the catabolic state, which was beginning to get rather spooky, and in addition have given me an even sharper mental edge. Modern science has to much to offer and the teamwork that goes on between my palliative care nurse specialist, my general practitioners, and my hospital colleagues anchors my sense of knowing that this business of dying is oddly doable. Advanced cancer is a curious condition. I believe that we understand it very poorly. The spiritual and personal resources to work within it are enormously powerful, and there are many choices – fight it, accept it, reflect on it, and live with it. Fearing is the real trouble spot. We all need help with this.

Our openness about my illness has allowed so many channels of communication to blossom. My friends and colleagues have told me that dying isn't usually like that, more a sad and slow withdrawal from life with loss the dominant theme. In our society people get medicalized and pitied and feared and isolated when they are dying. They have so much to offer if we can just accept it as a time of specialness and privilege. One friend commented that what we really need are midwives for dying. The essential elements of particular skills of companionship, passage and journey with a prescribed endpoint mirror each other in birth and death. My Macmillan nurse is a very fine midwife.

I am having a wonderful time fixing treasures for my children. There are diaries and tapes of stories told and oral history which a friend has agreed to type up for me. The trinkets, the photos, and the lovely clutter of my nest are something I feel is one of my best offers. My man is desolate, but we are trying to prepare strategies to deal with this too. My children are developing ideas about levels of communication beyond death, which are very exciting to nurture.

My spiritual journey is rich and varied. I think that a mother's watching brief passes beyond death. My lifelines and the threads I have woven in my world are here and real and I will be a difficult person to forget. I am content and comfortable at home and my house is full of company and bright things. My death when it comes will be a journey. I am writing a book about this phase of my illness, about the dreams I have had, the dialogue I have entered into with my tumour. It is much clearer to me now what really matters and what is clutter. Unconditional love is a feature of this time, offered and received without judgement. I am sure that these energies are important for healing. I am much better than my liver function tests suggest I should be. The wellbeing is physical and spiritual.

I have no clear idea of my time path. I know that I have time to live and love and, despite my perilous illness, there is a curious sense of openness about my journey. Perhaps there is another chapter to unfold.

[Clare Vaughan died on 6 July.]

DILEMMAS AND DECISIONS AT THE END OF LIFE

Introduction

The second half of this Reader follows a chronological pattern, decisions at the end of life in Part 3 and bereavement in Part 4. This part presents the moral dilemmas encountered when facing death. Here we deal primarily with situations when the diagnosis is relatively clear but the timing of death is uncertain. In facing death, people confront not only what are sometimes called the 'existential uncertainties' – those about the very meaning of existence – but also other doubts: the extent to which they are seriously ill, how to handle relatives, friends and work colleagues, and in particular how to plan for those who survive them. There are also ethical dilemmas such as whether to consent to 'experimental' treatment, or to consider organ donation. For professional and informal carers, there are also ethical, legal and professional questions: is it ever appropriate to impose treatments in a paternalistic manner, how does one mediate disputes in the care team, for example in relation to do not resuscitate orders, and whether it is ever permitted to assist death? These uncertainties are raised throughout this part.

We start off with personal accounts of responses to AIDS; first Clare Williams in 'Learning the hard way' expresses her realism and acceptance after being diagnosed as HIV positive following rape. Her situation exemplifies aspects of social death raised in the last part by Strauss. People who admit to this condition may lose their job, their partner, may watch their friends disinfecting the cups they have drunk from ('I feel awful, but you know how it is'). But she also expresses a heightened zest for life: 'My life is fuller now – I daren't waste a second. That sort of thing sounds a cliché until it applies to you'. The uncertainty of how one's loved ones respond to HIV status is portrayed movingly in Anthony Master's article where he describes the mixed emotions Danny and his lover experience when returning to Ireland to reconnect and say goodbye to Danny's mother. How one's loved ones cope with the uncertainty of whether or not one is dying and some of the deceptions involved are also beautifully portrayed in Tolstoy's classic 'The Death of Ivan Ilyich'. The confused messages that Ivan receives from his family and friends simply heighten his insecurities in a similar way to those experienced by Danny in the previous account.

In 'Intimacy and Terminal Care' Judy Gilley raises some of the issues for professionals in relation to assessing dying people's needs for intimacy. Through case studies she identifies the support that dying people need in order to make the choices they want in relation to intimacy and in particular she emphasizes the centrality of listening to the dying person, echoing some of the points made by Robert Buckman in Part 2. Teasdale and Kent's exploration of 'The use of deception in nursing' examines how deception is used to reassure patients. This develops Buckman's plea for professionals to deal with dying people in ways which respect them as people. They also illustrate the enormous diversity of reactions from dying people to their illness. They consider whether it is ever right to override dying people's wishes 'in their best interests'. They demonstrate how deception can destroy trust and create a sense of isolation for dying people.

The next two articles concern the debate about do-not-resuscitate orders. Van Delden explores the strengths and weaknesses of resuscitation practices and policies, emphasizing the moral issues involved in cardiopulmonary resuscitation (CPR). He assumes that in most cases DNR decisions are taken in advance when one has time to evaluate the burdens and benefits. In contrast, in an article commissioned for this edition of the Reader, Basiro Davey explores the ways in which these decisions are made in a general hospital and the discrepancies between different levels of nursing and medical staff in their conceptualizations of this decision making. She graphically illustrates the moral dilemmas health care staff face when it is unclear whether someone is 'blue-spotted' or not, and also the rights of dying people and their relatives to know whether these decisions have been taken on their behalf.

These two articles bring into focus some of the difficult questions surrounding 'letting die' or terminating care. We enter the field of medical ethics by looking at the main arguments for and against the 'four principles' approach to ethics by Randall and Downie. They chronicle the development of modern medical ethics, explaining the Kantian perspective and how this was modified by Mill. William Grey too bases his arguments on Kantian and Millian philosophy in his exposition of euthanasia. He uses the case of Bob Dent in the northern territories of Australia to distinguish between the arguments of those against the *practice* of euthanasia from those against the *legalization* of euthanasia. The same case study is used as illustration by Luke Gormally who provides seven reasons for not legalizing euthanasia; like Teasdale and Kent his argument turns around the centrality of trust between doctors and dying people. Ethical considerations such as whether it is ever right to assist death sometimes cause understandable moral distress in carers and conflict within care teams. 'A student's story', an anonymous first-person account, was written for a workshop in which nurses were encouraged to share stories about such difficult moral problems. The incident described here continues, 16 years on, to cause the author grief and moral anguish. This powerful account underlines how important it is to take ethical issues and carers' moral concerns seriously, as well as those of dying people.

The euthanasia discussion naturally leads on to a discussion of advance directives. Christopher Ryan argues against living wills and advance directives on the grounds that those writing them are not informed that the decision they take at the time may not be their views when the advance directives are operationalized. This obviously does not apply to those who are not competent to make decisions.

The next group of articles in this part concerns the relationship between the practice of palliative care and ethics. In a specially commissioned article for this reader Stephen Wilkinson explains the interaction between palliative care and the doctrine of double effect. He notes the usefulness of the doctrine of double effect for distinguishing between *intentional* killings and those where death is an *unintentional* side effect. Eve Garrard notes some of the issues involved in resource allocation and palliative care, resonating with the points raised in Part 2 by Field and Addington-Hall.

Finally we present a debate about hydration and nutrition – first Gillian Craig argues that the policy of sedating dying people without hydration or nutrition is dangerous from medical, ethical and legal perspectives as well as potentially creating distress for family members and friends. In a response Dunlop et al. indicate that some dying people spontaneously refuse food and drink which does indeed cause relatives distress. However, they stress that there are a variety of factors that need to be taken into account when making decisions about these issues.

35

Learning the hard way

Clare Williams

I still have that photo of myself, taken 11 months ago. Taken moments before my life changed irrevocably. I'd been standing in the street with a friend who wanted to finish his film. There I am, dressed in jeans and a scarlet teeshirt, with my hair falling over my face.

I haven't changed. I still have that shirt, those jeans. My hair still falls over my face. But now I am fundamentally different. Minutes after that photo was taken, I walked into the clinic outside which I had been standing, where I was told that I had the HIV virus. And now things will never be the same again. Not only am I a year older – I'm 23 now – but I'm 'one of them'. The sort of people who, if they admit to their condition, may lose their job, their partner, may watch friends disinfecting the cups they have drunk from and find their best friend suddenly won't let them into the same room as her newborn baby – 'I feel awful, but you know how it is.'

Then there are the friends who make sure they phone every couple of weeks; who ask you to godmother their children; who will cuddle you for hours while you cry at the sheer unfairness of it all.

I don't know how I picked up the virus, why my life is now full of catch phrases like 'T-helper cells' or why I am now a threat to some of my oldest friends. I look the same as I did 11 months ago, I still fall in love, I still enjoy long suppers with friends over a bottle or three of wine. I'm still the same person. It is your society, my society, that sees me as different, as a threat to your cosy way of life. I'm a 23-year-old, heterosexual, non-drug-using, safe sex practitioner.

I'm a child of the AIDS age, you see. I know the dangers. I had unprotected sex once – I was raped and I didn't really get the chance to ask my attacker if he'd be so kind as to wear a condom. So henceforth my blood will test sero-positive; I have HIV.

Obviously things are no longer straightforward. I meet someone I like, we have dinner a few times, then the inevitable suggestion comes – 'Bacon and eggs or just toast for breakfast?' So do I tell him, or trust to the safety of the condom? So far, I've always been honest. In fact, the ignorance and complacency of people terrifies me. When will people realize that we are all at risk? If I can get HIV, then everyone can.

And then, of course, there is the big question: how to tell people. At first I told no one, not even my partner, and my family still have no idea, but I

From *The Guardian*, 'First Person', 29 May 1991.

want my friends to know, even though actually telling them is so difficult. I find myself sounding out their views; how much they know about AIDS, whether they would realize I am no threat to them, how discreet they will be.

Yet it isn't all bad news. My life is fuller now – I daren't waste a second. That sort of thing sounds like a cliché until it applies to you. Losing my job was a blessing; I decided to go to college. My relationships are far more intense now. I go to the theatre, the cinema, the ballet as often as I can – I've a lifetime of happiness to fit into maybe 10 years. I surround myself with the people I love and feel a new freedom to ignore those I don't. I now make the most of everything.

You don't appreciate life until you think it's going to be taken away. I feel that I've been given a second chance to live as wonderful a life as I can. In so many ways, I'm very lucky.

36

Somebody loves me

Anthony Masters

'She's known as Our Lady of the Goats.'

'Any good reason?'

'The goats.'

'She's also a recluse.'

As I drove Danny down the track, the valley was sharp, narrow and thickly wooded and the sun was sinking in a crimson ball. Danny hadn't seen his mother for five years. They had corresponded occasionally, but that was it, for Mrs Hegarty had no phone. She'd lived on the farm all her life, seeing only her husband and Danny and an elderly labourer called Rooney. But now her husband and Rooney were long dead. Danny had left home when he was 15 and gone to London; all she had left were the goats and the tumbledown house.

Danny was ill. AIDS was consuming him and he was wheelchair-bound now, his bones brittle and the chest infections never far way. But this trip to the west of Ireland had slipped from a dream to an obsession to a practicality, and we had spent the last two days idyllically, driving along the lanes and watching the ocean and spending the nights in remote guest houses. Last night we had stayed in a squat stone building high on a cliff-top. The wind had torn at the surf, bringing it crashing in plumes over the rocks: 'I wish I could die now,' he had whispered, 'it seems the right moment.'

'What about your Mum?' I had asked, holding him tight in my arms.

'She was always a harridan. She'll probably nag me to death. That's not a good way to go.' He looked down at the boiling waves and laughed his wheezy laugh.

'There's no one in.'

The yard was as empty as the house, the byre ghostly with its still redolent smell of cow.

'She'll come.'

'Not even a light.'

Danny looked at his watch. 'She'll be in bed by now.'

'It's only six.'

'She gets up at dawn.'

Extract from *Cry Love, Cry Hope: Responding to AIDS*, ed. Bill Kirkpatrick, London: Darton, Longman & Todd, 1994, pp. 29–36.

We had been delayed by the afternoon sun and a field of clover. Again I'd held him in my arms, my cheek pressed into the sweet earth that would soon absorb him. 'I'm not being burnt to a cinder,' he had told me. 'Find me a grave in a country churchyard.'

After a struggle with recalcitrant vicars, I had found one in Sussex. Danny had been pleased with its ivy-trailing desolation.

'You'll come, won't you? You'll come and stand by my grave.'

'Every day,' I had assured him ironically.

'You lying bastard,' he had replied.

I knocked again and thought I heard a movement. Then the bolts rattled and the door opened an inch. There was no light, not even the flicker of a candle.

'Yes?'

Danny said nothing, which was a pity because I was totally unprepared. Somehow I had expected him to greet her and, while I didn't think they'd fall on each other's necks, I felt there would at least be mumbled communication. But there was nothing.

'It's Danny,' I said woodenly.

'Who?'

'Danny.'

'Danny?' I couldn't see her face and her voice was rough and dry.

'Your son.'

There was a long silence. 'Yes?'

Yes what, I wondered. 'Can we come in?'

The door opened a fraction. 'That's not my son.'

If only Danny would *say* something, I thought, angrily now. Had he been stuck dumb? 'It is.'

'My son's not a cripple.'

'He's been ill.'

'What with?'

'AIDS.'

'What's that?'

'A virus.'

The door opened another crack, 'Danny?'

At last he spoke. 'Mother.'

'What are you doing here?'

'Thought I'd come.'

'Who's your friend?'

'That's Colin.'

'You'd better come in.'

The hallway smelt of the same earth as the fields and there was something else overlaying it – something animal. Was it goat? There was a scurrying, clattering movement. Were there goats in the house?

She led us down a narrow passage, Danny's wheelchair barely clearing the walls, and into a kitchen. Mrs Hegarty snapped on the light and I saw her properly for the first time. She gave me a shock because I had been expecting someone very old. Well, she *was* old but I had no means of guessing her age for her face, long and aquiline like Danny's, was completely unmarked. She had huge eyes, again like Danny's, but his face was wasted and hers was full, unwrinkled, unsagging. Around her the kitchen was bleak and desolate, with a range that threw out little heat. Curled up against the tepid warmth was a kid; its eyes stared up at us helplessly.

The kitchen was painted blue but the paint was coming off. On the dilapidated shelves were a few chipped cups and plates and in the centre of the room was a big scrubbed table with four chairs around it. There was a cupboard – it could have been a larder – but nothing else. The room frightened me with its spartan bleakness.

'I've not got much in the house.'

The kid moved and then resettled, making an anxious sigh.

'That's all right.' Danny was silent again and I looked at my watch. It was only ten past six. What were we going to do? Suddenly the evening seemed an eternity.

'I can do bacon. An egg and a bit of fried bread.'

'Ideal.' I cleared my throat, looking vengefully at Danny, willing him to share the responsibility of conversation.

She began to move around, placing each object of food on a tin draining board. Outside there was no wind, and an enormous stillness filled the room which was barely broken when Mrs Hegarty spoke.

'How did you get ill, Danny?'

'It just came.' His voice was neutral.

'Will you get better?'

'No.'

'That why you came?'

'Sort of.'

'Just dropped in?'

'Yes.'

'You'll be off in the morning?'

'Probably.'

She looked at him properly for the first time and then muttered. 'I'll outlive you all then.'

She served the meal and I suddenly realized I was ravenous, but Danny ate little. There was no conversation but gradually I realized it didn't matter. I was beginning to find an increasing peace in this almost empty space. The table, the chairs, the food, the kid, the range, the sink and the two cupboards. No more. No less. Peace.

'Mother—' He spoke for the first time in what must have been ten minutes. Maybe more.

'Danny.'

'Can I sleep in your room for the night?'

I froze, but quickly the resentment turned to acceptance. After all, we'd leave in the morning.

She laughed lightly. 'I've got another couple of kids in there.'

'Does it matter?' he asked.

'No.'

He turned to me. 'You come too, Colin.'

'Me? All of us?' It was ludicrous. Were we all to sleep in one bed?

She made tea, strong and bitter. Then, despite the early hour, she showed us to another small, almost empty room and I helped her put mattresses on the floor.

'You sleep downstairs then?' I asked.

'The top's empty now.'

'Empty?'

'I sold everything. Now I've just got the things I need.' She looked at me properly for the first time. 'I'll die soon. The dead don't need knick-knacks.' She looked at Danny and he laughed as I helped him out of the wheelchair and on to a mattress, covering him with a couple of rough blankets, which smelt of mothballs. Made a change from goat, I thought.

The kids came in, slightly larger than the one by the range in the kitchen, and they climbed on to her bed, lying on the dowdy eiderdown.

She stood there, watching us for a while. Maybe she was wondering why Danny had laughed. Then he said.

'We're cluttered out with stuff.'

'Where are you now?' she asked, yawning.

'Fulham.'

Mrs Hegarty went out of the room and came back wearing a nightgown. She got into bed and switched out the light. Later on I heard her making sleeping sounds.

'Danny.' I whispered. 'I feel at peace here. Do you?'

'Yes.' He paused and then his voice reached me through the darkness, 'She's just got space, hasn't she? My mother. She's taken everything away. Maybe when she dies she'll have nothing. Just bare rooms. That's the way they'll find her. In a bare room.'

'Were you happy?'

'When?'

'With her – as a child.'

'I think so. It was hard. I worked and went to school. Weekends were much the same. Except there was no school. Just Dad and Mum and Rooney, and the cows then, of course.'

'Didn't you have any friends?'

'No,' he said baldly, but without self-pity.

'What made you decide to get away?'

'Something in me. Something I needed. The streets.'

'That's where we'd met. On the streets. He was a rent boy and I was his client. Then the professional relationship stopped – and *we* began.

'But I knew all the time,' Danny said.

'Knew what?'

'Someone loved me.'

'Her?'

'Yes.'

'Why didn't you come back to see her – keep in contact?'

'Don't know. It was enough to know it, I s'pose.'

We lay in silence for a moment. There were no curtains to the window and the stars winked bright against a jet black sky.

'*Will* we leave tomorrow?' I asked.

'Yes.'

'Go back home?'

'Please.'

'And her?'

'I'll not see her again.'

'So why come?'

'To find out.'

'What?'

'If she loves me still.'

'And does she?'

'Yes.'

'What about me?' A sense of desolation welled up in me.

'You?'

'I love you.'

'I know you do.' His voice warmed me again. 'It's different,' he added.

'How?' I demanded.

'You love me as I am, Colin. I wanted to find out if Mum would love me as the person I've become – not what I was. Her little boy.'

'And does she?'

'I think she does.'

I slept deeply and woke in the grey dawn. When I turned to Danny's mattress I panicked because he was no longer there. Then I saw the two of them by the window. She was propping him up and he had his arms around her, his thin legs trailing behind him. Someone loves me. I felt nothing but joy for both of them as they stared out at the shadowy landscape of trees and mist and shifting substance. It was not real yet, as if the valley was being born. Mother and son watched the foetal development with concentration and awe.

She let him go, I thought, let him go to the city and the streets because she knew she couldn't clip his wings.

The kids got off the bed and nuzzled at their legs. As they did so, Danny turned and smiled at me.

'Come on,' he said: 'She can't hold me up forever.'

'You'd better take him,' said Mrs Hegarty softly. 'He's not much of a weight but I'm an old woman. I'll make tea.'

As she passed Danny to me there was something in Mrs Hegarty's eyes that moved me profoundly. It was as if she was finally giving him away.

'You were right to believe in her,' I whispered to him and kissed his cold cheek.

37

The death of Ivan Ilyich

Leo Tolstoy

The doctor said that this and that symptom indicated this and that wrong with the patient's inside, but if this diagnosis were not confirmed by analysis of so-and-so, then we must assume such-and-such. If then we assume such-and-such, then . . . and so on. To Ivan Ilyich only one question was important: was his case serious or not? But the doctor ignored this misplaced inquiry. From the doctor's point of view it was a side issue not under consideration: the real business was the assessing of probabilities to decide between a floating kidney, chronic catarrh or appendicitis. It was not a question of Ivan Ilyich's life or death but one between a floating kidney or appendicitis. And this question the doctor, in Ivan Ilyich's presence, settled most brilliantly in favour of the appendix, with the reservation that analysis of the urine might provide a new clue and then the case would have to be reconsidered. All this was to an iota precisely what Ivan Ilyich himself had done in equally brilliant fashion a thousand times over in dealing with persons on trial. The doctor summed up just as brilliantly, looking over his spectacles triumphantly, gaily even, at the accused. From the doctor's summing-up Ivan Ilyich concluded that things looked bad, but that for the doctor, and most likely for everybody else, it was a matter of indifference, though for him it was bad. And this conclusion struck him painfully, arousing in him a great feeling of pity for himself, and of bitterness towards the doctor who could be unconcerned about a matter of such importance.

But he said nothing. He rose, placed the doctor's fee on the table and remarked with a sigh, 'We sick people no doubt often put inappropriate questions. But tell me, in general, is this complaint dangerous or not?'

The doctor regarded him sternly over his spectacles with one eye, as though to say, 'Prisoner at the bar, if you will not keep to the questions put to you, I shall be obliged to have you removed from the court.'

'I have already told you what I consider necessary and proper,' said the doctor. The analysis may show something more.' And the doctor bowed.

Ivan Ilyich went out slowly, seated himself dejectedly in his sledge and drove home. All the way home he kept going over what the doctor had said, trying to translate all those involved, obscure, scientific phrases into plain language and find in them an answer to the question, 'Am I in a bad

Extract from *The Death of Ivan Ilyich*, London, Penguin, 1960, pp. 127–36 (abridged).

way – a very bad way – or is it nothing after all?' And it seemed to him that the upshot of all that the doctor had said was that he *was* in a very bad way. Everything in the streets appeared depressing to Ivan Ilyich. The sledge-drivers looked dismal, so did the houses, the passers-by and the shops. And this pain, this dull gnawing ache that never ceased for a second, seemed, when taken in conjunction with the doctor's enigmatical utterances, to have acquired a fresh and far more serious significance. With a new sense of misery Ivan Ilyich now paid constant heed to it.

He reached home and began to tell his wife about it. She listened but in the middle of his account his daughter came in with her hat on, ready to go out with her mother. Reluctantly she half sat down to listen to this tiresome story, but she could not be patient for long, and her mother did not hear him to the end.

'Well, I am very glad,' she said. 'You must be careful now and take the medicine regularly. Give me the prescription: I will send Gerassim to the chemist's.' And she went away to dress.

He had hardly paused to take breath while she was in the room, and he heaved a deep sigh when she was gone.

'Well,' he said to himself, 'perhaps it's nothing after all . . .' [. . .]

From the time of his visit to the doctor Ivan Ilyich's principal occupation became the exact observance of the doctor's prescriptions regarding hygiene and the taking of medicine, and watching the symptoms of his malady and the general functioning of his body. His chief interests came to be people's ailments and people's health. When sickness, deaths or recoveries were mentioned in his presence, especially when the illness resembled his own, he would listen, trying to conceal his agitation, ask questions and apply what he heard to his own case.

The pain did not grow less but Ivan Ilyich made great efforts to force himself to believe that he was better. And he was able to deceive himself so long as nothing happened to excite him. [. . .] His condition was rendered worse by the fact that he read medical books and consulted doctors. The progress of his disease was so gradual that, comparing one day with another, he was able to deceive himself, so slight was the difference. But when he consulted the doctors it seemed to him that he was getting worse, and very rapidly worse. Yet despite this he was continually consulting doctors.

That month he went to see another medical celebrity. The second celebrity said pretty much the same as the first, only he propounded his questions differently; and the interview with this celebrity only redoubled Ivan Ilyich's doubts and fears. Then a friend of a friend of his, a very good doctor, diagnosed his malady quite otherwise, and, though he predicted recovery, his questions and hypotheses still further confused Ivan Ilyich and increased his scepticism. A homoeopath made a different diagnosis still, and gave him a medicine which Ivan Ilyich took secretly for a week; but at the end, not feeling any relief and losing confidence both in his former drugs and this new treatment, he became more despondent than ever. [. . .] The pain in his side harassed him and seemed to grow worse and more incessant, while the taste in his mouth grew more and more peculiar. It seemed to him that his breath smelled very nasty, and his appetite and strength continually dwindled. There was no deceiving himself: something terrible, new and significant, more significant than anything that had ever happened in his life, was taking place within him of which he alone was aware. Those about him did not understand, or refused to understand, and believed that everything in the world was going on as usual. This thought tormented Ivan Ilyich more than anything. He saw that his household, especially his wife and daughter who were absorbed in a perfect whirl of visiting, had not conception at all and were annoyed with him for being so depressed and exacting, as though he were to be blamed for that. Even though they tried to disguise it he could see that he was in their way; but that his wife had taken up a definite line in regard to his illness and adhered to it, no matter what he might say or do. Her attitude was this: 'You know,' she would say to her friends, 'Ivan Ilyich can't do as other people do, and keep to the treatment prescribed for him. One day he'll take his drops and keep carefully to his diet and go to bed at the right time; but the next day, if I don't see to it, he will suddenly forget his medicine, eat sturgeon – which is forbidden him – and sit up playing cards until one in the morning.'

'Oh come, when did I do that?' Ivan Ilyich would ask in vexation. 'Only once at Piotr Ivanovich's.'

'What about yesterday with Shebek?'

'It makes no difference, I couldn't have slept for pain . . .'

'Be that as it may, but you'll never get well like that, and you make us wretched.

Praskovya Fiodorovna's attitude to Ivan Ilyich's illness, openly expressed to others and to himself, implied that the whole illness was Ivan Ilyich's own fault and just another of the annoyances he was causing his wife. Ivan Ilyich felt that this opinion escaped her involuntarily, but it was none the easier to bear for all that.

At the Law Courts, too, Ivan Ilyich noticed or fancied he noticed the same strange sort of attitude to himself. At one time it would seem to him that people were watching him inquisitively, as a man who would shortly have to give up his post. [. . .]

Friends would drop in for a game of cards. [. . .] He would look at his partner Mihail Mihailovich tapping on the table with his confident hand, and instead of snatching up the tricks pushing the cards politely and condescendingly towards Ivan Ilyich that he might have the satisfaction of gathering them up without the trouble of stretching out his hand for them. 'Does he suppose I'm so weak that I can't stretch my arm out?' thinks Ivan Ilyich, and he forgets the trumps, and trumps his partner's cards and misses the grand slam by three tricks. And the most awful thing of all is that he sees how upset Mihail Mihailovich is about it, whereas he does not care at all. And it is awful to think why he doesn't care.

They all see that he is in pain, and say to him: 'We can stop if you are tired. You go and lie down.' Lie down? No, he's not in the least tired, and they finish the rubber. They are all gloomy and silent. Ivan Ilyich feels that it is he who has cast this gloom upon them, and he cannot disperse it. They have supper, and the party breaks up, and Ivan Ilyich is left alone with the consciousness that his life is poisoned for him and that he is poisoning the lives of others, and that this poison is not losing its force but is working its way deeper and deeper into his whole being.

[. . .] And he has to live thus on the edge of the precipice alone, without a single soul to understand and feel for him.

So one month succeeded another. Just before the New Year his brother-in-law arrived in town and came to stay with them. Ivan Ilyich was at the Law Courts. Praskovya Fiodorovna had gone out shopping. Coming home and going into his study, Ivan Ilyich found his brother-in-law there, a healthy, florid man, unpacking his postmanteau himself. He raised his head on hearing Ivan Ilyich's footsteps and for a second stared up at him without a word. That look told Ivan Ilyich everything. His brother-in-law opened his mouth to utter an exclamation of dismay but checked himself. That movement confirmed everything.

'Changed, have I?'

'Yes . . . there is a change.'

And after that, try as he would to get his brother-in-law to return to the subject of his looks, the latter maintained an obstinate silence. Praskovya Fiodorovna came back, and her brother went to her room. Ivan Ilyich locked the door and began to examine himself in the glass, first full face, then in profile. He picked up a portrait of himself taken with his wife, and compared it with what he saw in the glass. The change in him was enormous. Then he bared his arms to the elbow, looked at them, pulled down his sleeves, sat down on the ottoman and felt blacker than night.

'No, no, this won't do!' he said to himself, sprang to his feet, went to the table, opened some official document and began to read, but could not go on with it. He unlocked the door and went into the drawing-room. The parlour door was shut. He approached it on tiptoe and listened.

'No, you are exaggerating,' Praskovya Fiodorovna was saying.

'Exaggerating? Why, surely you can see for yourself – he's a dead man! Look at his eyes – there's no light in them. But what is it that is wrong with him?'

'Nobody knows. Nikolayev' (that was another doctor) 'said something, but I don't know what. Leshcetitsky' (this was the celebrated specialist) 'says the opposite.'

Ivan Ilyich walked away, went to his own room, lay down and began to think: 'The kidney, a floating kidney.' He recalled all that the doctors had told him of how it had detached itself and was floating about. And by an effort of imagination he tried to catch that kidney and arrest and make it firm. So little was needed for this, it seemed to him. 'No, I must go and see

Piotr Ivanovich again.' (This was the friend who had a friend who was a doctor.) He rang, ordered the carriage and got ready to go out.

'Where are you off to, *Jean*?' asked his wife, with a peculiarly melancholy and unusually gentle expression.

This unusual gentleness infuriated him. He looked at her grimly.

'I want to see Piotr Ivanovich.'

He drove off to the friend who had a friend who was a doctor, and together they went to the doctor's. He was in, and Ivan Ilyich had a long conversation with him.

Reviewing the anatomical and physiological details of what in the doctor's opinion was going on inside him, he understood it all.

There was just one little thing – the least trifle – wrong in the intestinal appendix. It might all come right. Stimulate one sluggish organ, check the activity of another – secretion ensues, and everything would come right. He was a little late for dinner. [. . .] Ivan Ilyich, as Praskovya Fiodorovna remarked, spent the evening in better spirits than on other occasions, but he never forgot that there was that important matter of the intestinal appendix waiting to be considered. At eleven o'clock he said good-night and went to bed. He had slept alone since his illness in a little room adjoining his study. He undressed and took up a novel by Zola, but instead of reading it he fell to thinking. And in his imagination that desired improvement in the intestinal appendix took place. Secretion, evacuation were stimulated: regular action re-established. 'Yes, that's it!' he said to himself. 'One only has to assist nature, that's all.' He remembered his medicine, sat up, swallowed it and lay down on his back, watching for the medicine to have its salutary effect and stop the pain. 'All I have to do is to take it regularly and avoid harmful influences. Why, I am better already, much better.' He began to feel his side: it was not painful to the touch. 'There, I really don't feel it. It's much better already.' He put out the light and turned on his side . . . 'The appendix is righting itself, secretion is occurring.' Suddenly he felt the old familiar, dull, gnawing pain, the same obstinate, steady, serious pain. In his mouth there was the same familiar loathsome taste. His heart sank, his brain felt dazed. 'O God, O God!' he whispered. 'Here it is again! And it will never cease.' And in a flash the trouble presented itself in quite a different guise. 'Intestinal appendix! The kidney!' he said to himself. 'It's not a question of appendix or kidney but of life and . . . death. Yes, once there was life, and now it is drifting away, drifting away, and I can't stop it. Yes. Why deceive myself? Isn't it obvious to everyone but me that I am dying, and that it's only a matter of weeks, days . . . it may happen this very moment. There was light but now there is darkness. I was here but now I am going. Where?' A cold chill came over him, his breathing ceased, and he heard only the throbbing of his heart.

'I shall be no more, then what will there be? There will be nothing. Then where shall I be when I am no more? Can this be dying? No, I will not have it!' He jumped up and tried to light the candle, fumbled about with trembling hands, dropped candle and candlestick on the floor and fell back upon the pillow. 'What's the use? It makes no difference,' he said to himself, staring with wide-open eyes into the darkness. 'Death. Yes, death. And they none of them understand, or want to understand, and they feel no pity for me. They are enjoying themselves.' (He heard through the closed door the distant cadence of a song and its accompaniment.) 'They don't care, but they will die too. Fools! 'Twill be a little sooner for me and a little later for them, that's all; their turn will come. But now they are making merry. The brutes!' Anger choked him. And he was agonizingly, intolerably wretched. 'It cannot be that all men always have been doomed to suffer this awful horror!' He raised himself.

'I ought not to go on like this: I must be calm, I must think it all over from the beginning.' And here he began to reflect. 'Yes, the beginning of my illness. I knocked my side but I was still all right that day and the next. It hurt a little, then it got worse, then I went to doctors, then there followed depression, misery and more doctors; and all the time I got nearer and nearer to the abyss. My strength began to fail. Nearer and nearer! And now I have wasted away and there is no light in my eyes. Death is here, and I am thinking of an appendix! I am thinking of how to get my bowels in order, while death knocks at the door. Can it really be death?' Terror seized him again and he gasped for breath. He leant down and began feeling for the matches, pressing with his elbow on the little pedestal table beside the bed. It was in his way and hurt him, he lost his temper with it, pressed upon it still harder in his anger and overturned it. Breathless and in despair, he fell back, expecting death that instant.

Meanwhile the visitors were departing. Praskovya Fiodorovna was seeing them off. She heard something fall and came in.

'What is the matter?'

'Nothing. I accidentally knocked it over.'

She went out and returned with a candle. He lay there panting heavily, like a man who has run a mile, staring at her with fixed eyes.

'What is it, *Jean*?'

'No-othing. I up-set it.' ('Why speak of it? She won't understand,' he thought.)

And, indeed, she did not understand. She picked up the candle and lit it for him, and hurried away to say good-night to another visitor.

When she came back he was lying in the same position on his back, gazing at the ceiling.

'What is the matter? Are you feeling worse?'

'Yes.'

She shook her head and sat down.

'Do you know, *Jean*, I think we had better ask Leshchetitsky to come here.'

That meant, send for the celebrated specialist and not mind the expense. He smiled venomously and said 'No.' She sat a moment longer and then came up to him and kissed his forehead.

He hated her from the bottom of his soul while she was kissing him, and with difficulty refrained from pushing her away.

'Good-night. Please God you'll sleep.'

'Yes.'

38

Intimacy and terminal care

Judy Gilley

Introduction

A search on the literature on terminal illness shows it to be singularly lacking in references to sexuality and its implications for terminal care. In this article 'sexuality' is used in its broadest sense, that is, the capacity of the individual to link emotional needs with physical intimacy – the ability to give and receive physical intimacy at all levels, from the simplest to the most profound.

The doctor visiting a dying patient needs to be listening for the patient's expectations of that visit: Is the visit needed to show friends and relations that the situation is deteriorating and more help is needed? Is the doctor required for a limited 'clinical' function to alleviate symptoms, for example, to prescribe medication? Is this a 'crisis visit' for a new symptom or overwhelming 'panic' in the face of the unknown? Is the doctor called as a 'technician' to effect already formulated wishes (appropriately or inappropriately formulated), for example, 'We want you to get him into hospital'?

Or is this the opportunity for 'serious doctoring', for active joint exploration of a significant aspect of the management of the dying person? May this be the time to recognize the patient's spoken and covert wishes about intimacy and to translate these into relevant arrangements for terminal care? Not all of us wish to die at home with the potential for intimacy this may imply; the need of some people to die in the splendid isolation of a teaching hospital bed as a last event in a lifetime's avoidance of intimacy should be respected.

Case 1

This was a man in his early sixties, a retired jeweller, careful and fastidious. He and his wife did much charitable work. They were cautious, tidy people, and their home reflected this. There were two neatly folded, well-separated, single beds, which had been separate, one suspected, for a long time. They were childless. She described him as Mr B. to me. I felt there had long since ceased to be much warmth or physicality between them. He had been a smoker and a 'shadow' was discovered on a chest X-ray. There

From *Journal of the Royal College of General Practitioners*, 1988, 38: 121–2.

was no evidence of distant spread, no local symptoms, but Mr B. was overwhelmed by anxiety and despair. He became housebound overnight. I visited frequently. He wanted to sit for long periods, although he had no specific complaints of weakness or lethargy. There was discussion of the chair he wished to use. It was a reclining garden chair. It did not match the decor. Mrs B. was unhappy about its appearance and made this perfectly clear.

One morning the district nurse phoned in panic; Mr B. was suddenly in terrible pain. His screams could be heard in the background. I rushed from surgery, anxiously rehearsing the potential problems. Mr B. was in a state of acute fear. With talking, soothing and physical touch his screams diminished. There was no physical source of the pain. He started to talk in a precise, urgent tone. He knew he couldn't manage at home; he wanted to go into a hospice, where he wished to die quickly. I contemplated the potential difficulties of obtaining hospice care for a man without nursing needs.

At the door I talked to his wife. How many important conversations take place with one hand on the door knob; some pains seem to be unbearable in a closed room without the possibility of escape. Mrs B. implored 'You must do something, Doctor. We can pay'. A few tears, and then 'Doctor, you have no idea of the liberties that man is taking with me . . . the things he wants me to do for him . . .' There was a long silence in which I encouraged her to verbalize those 'liberties'. In those fraught moments, I was aware of what Casemont refers to as 'the creative tension of binocular vision',[1] that is, holding together knowing and not knowing; following with one eye those aspects of the patient about which one does not know and keeping the other eye on whatever one feels one does know. I suspected we were talking about physical intimacy, but did not know what these 'liberties' were for them. Finally, she spoke with a mixture of resignation and shame: 'Doctor, he asks me to brush his hair for him . . .'.

I was moved to tears for this fearful man, who was seeking some contact and knew the impossibility of achieving it. I realised there could be no comfort, no intimacy for him in dying at home. Perhaps he could find nurture in a hospice. He was admitted and died within weeks.

The cold, formal atmosphere of the house seemed to reflect the lack of intimacy in this marriage. Doctors trained in psychosexual medicine have commented on how women patients with sexual problems frequently use language about house and home as symbolic of their feelings about the vagina and their sexuality.[2] Perhaps Mrs B.'s resistance to her husband's wish for a chair which did not fit the decor, the reclining chair in which he could be at his ease, symbolized her fear of being manoeuvred into unaccustomed intimacy.

Mr B.'s screaming was potent 'communication by impact', stirring up feelings in the doctor which could not be communicated by words. His screams were for more than his dying, they were for dying without a wife able to brush his hair.

Case 2

Mr C. was 50 years old and had endured widespread carcinoma for two years, kept at bay but then suddenly recurring with a vengeance. He deteriorated rapidly. This was also a childless couple, but not by choice. Mr C. was installed in the living room, the centre of every comfort, with the television specially raised, flowers, cats on the bed, wife knitting by his bedside.

She was actively involved in his care. When I visited there was an immediate welcome, their dark approach road always carefully lit at night. Mr C. was able to accept her ministrations and she respected and cared for his fading body with the same robust love I suspect she had given it in health. Towards the end he needed a catheter. As she manoeuvred this tenderly on one occasion, there was a shared spark between them of old, happier touchings. 'Watch it, girl' he said, and they laughed together. She and I sat and talked when he was too weak to talk any longer. There was an intimacy and mutual respect in the relationship between this couple and those who were members of the 'caring team' which reflected their own intimacy.

The day he died I spent an hour sitting with her. It was a thundery day, the net curtains blew and it grew dark early. We sat largely in silence – I quote Elizabeth Kubler Ross 'At the end, those who have the strength and love to sit with a dying patient in the silence that goes beyond words will know this moment is neither frightening or painful.'[3] Sometimes it was difficult to feel if he was breathing. She washed his lips tenderly with glycerine – he died quietly. There remains an intimacy and respect between Mrs C. and myself to do with those last shared acts. If we extrapolate from the symbolism of this home we see its warmth adapted to his needs, moulded around him with love, as no doubt this women could mould herself in her lovemaking.

Case 3

Mr D. was a retired accountant, his wife a retired banker; both were 75 years old. Their home was tidy and utilitarian. A daughter lived abroad and visited infrequently. Many years previously Mrs D. had confided that she felt it a miracle that this daughter had been conceived because Mr D. was 'so disinterested in all that.' For years they had taken separate holidays, had separate living rooms, interests and bedrooms. I found Mrs D. difficult – she was dogmatic, with precise likes and dislikes about her doctors. She demanded 'special treatment' and it would take a brave soul to deny her special status. She would imperiously dismiss a partner who visited in my absence with a curt reprimand. However, she made it clear her wish to have me as doctor was not to do with any special perceived merit. A visit usually contained an element of confrontation. She had alienated many and had few friends.

Mrs D. developed an insidious malignancy, which was well spread before it was recognized. She returned home after major palliative surgery. It was unusual to be in the same room as them both. As we talked he wiped his eyes furtively. I was surprised at his tears and his protectiveness and wondered if he was able to show his feeling more, now that he was the 'strong' one – mobile and well. He learned to steam fish. She remained angry, demanding.

One day, he asked me into 'his' living room. With tears he said 'She can't cope'. He described her exhausted progress up the stairs the previous evening. He appeared overcome with embarrassment. 'It was so terrible . . . she couldn't undress herself . . . it was so humiliating for her . . . I had to help her undress. Not completely of course' he hastily assured me. Years of humiliation and defeat seemed to hang in the air. 'Please get her into hospital'.

She wanted the teaching hospital and her eminent surgeon: 'He must be a great man because all the nurses are terrified of him.' She died slowly, in splendid isolation, resented and argued over by the surgeons as she occupied space for longer then anticipated.

Case 4

This was a couple in their seventies. Mr E. worked as a consultant engineer. Their son died in infancy. The flat had a faded glamour, with much gilt and pink lampshades. Even as Mrs E. became very ill with metastic carcinoma they struggled on entertaining friends, having bridge parties. As he nursed here, supported by the district nursing team, his arthritis worsened and numerous visits were required for their physical problems. She was very uncomplaining. Her eyes always turned to him for comfort. He gave it and wept later in the kitchen. There was an intimacy in the flat, the curtains were usually closed even by day, the warm lights on in the bedroom, the nursing dressings and paraphernalia kept hidden. The outside world seemed far away.

Help was accepted from doctors and nurses who were then dispatched kindly on their way, but the real business continued within those four walls. I was called in the early hours one cold night. She was near to dying and had been incontinent in their shared bed. Exhausted, he asked me to help change the sheets. As we sorted linen, I shared with him the likelihood that she would die during the night. He knew. 'We've slept together for 50 years. I want one last night with her.' Together we made up the bed with fresh sheets. It was impossible not to think of a bridal bed being prepared. I helped him clean and tidy her. She died in the night. He called me in the morning to certify the death, observed by friends and priest.

In the same way that a good sexual relationship is the private pleasure of a couple, so must the relationship in terminal care be respected as unique to that couple and part of their intimacy.

Discussion

Winnicott talks of a 'nursing triad' whereby a new mother is emotionally 'held' by a third person while she holds her baby.[4] One aspect of this emotional holding is to help the mother believe she is capable of being a good enough mother to her baby. Without such holding, there may be disruptions of subsequent mothering, which are made worse for the mother by others taking over and seeming to be better mothers to her baby.

Perhaps something similar happens in the dying situation – a dying traid. The 'carer' needs to be emotionally held during the nurturing of a dying partner. This emotional holding will be the totality of that individual's capacity for loving and intimacy, but can be reinforced during this critical time by external factors – the doctors, nurses, family and others who become involved. But professionals must have a great sensitivity to avoid taking over and being 'better' carers than the real carer.

In conclusion, patients may express their needs for intimacy covertly in the terminal care situation. The doctor needs to listen and learn from the patient. The confessions of the carers – 'This man is taking such liberties'; 'It was so humiliating for her'; 'I want one last night with her' – will be the cues for the organization of appropriate care. The opportunity for the unique individual solution is easily missed, especially if the doctor uses insight borrowed from other cases, however 'similar'.

> Death belongs to life as birth does. The walk is in the raising of the foot as in the laying of it down. (From *Stray birds* by Rabindranath Tagore.)

References

1. Casemont, P. (1985) *Learning from the Patient*. London: Tavistock Publications.
2. Tunnadine, P. (1970) *Contraception and Sexual Life*. London: Tavistock Publications. Chapter 4.
3. Kubler-Ross, E. (1969) *On Death and Dying*. London: MacMillan.
4. Winnicott, D.W. (1965) *Maturational Processes and the Facilitating Environment*. London: Hogarth Press.

39

The use of deception in nursing

Kevin Teasdale and Gerry Kent

[. . .] It seems likely that non-disclosure is widespread in patient care. Doctors and nurses frequently see it as part of their professional responsibility to 'titrate' the amount of information they give to patients. This can be justified on empirical grounds since some patients are distressed if they receive more information than they desire (1), but the use of deception is another issue altogether. Deception is much harder to justify and certainly rarely acknowledged in public. Instead, many professionals prefer to use euphemisms such as 'information management' to describe times when they give inaccurate information or withhold accurate information in order to mislead.

It is sometimes argued that such situations should not be described as cases of deception, since the whole truth about a patient's situation can never be known or fully communicated; therefore one can never know whether or not the information which one gives is accurate or not. However, Bok (2) has pointed out that although we can never know the whole truth we still have the option of trying to convey the truth as we understand it. She argues that anything less is a form of deception, stating that: 'The moral question of whether you are lying or not is not settled by establishing the truth or falsity of what you say. In order to settle this question we must know whether you intend your statement to mislead' (3) [. . .]

Empirical studies have indicated that deception is used to promote what is perceived as better care for the patient, sometimes through reassurance (for example, maintenance of hope for the future) and sometimes because of organizational needs (for example, time considerations or concern that a patient would become difficult to manage). In a small-scale survey by Schrock (4) of the deceptions used by student nurses, 60 per cent of the deceptive situations were attributed to doctors' orders or ward policy, 20 per cent were carried out in order to promote better patient management (since the nurses feared that if patients knew the truth they would be unwilling to comply with treatment) and the remainder of deceptions were carried out in order to withhold information about patients' illnesses or drug treatments or because truthful explanations would have taken too long.

In a study of midwifery practice, Kirkham (5) observed frequent use of evasive answers to mothers' questions, amounting in many cases to deception. Mothers were allowed very little choice or autonomy during labour,

From *Journal of Medical Ethics*, 1995, 21: 77–81 (abridged).

and deceptive strategies were used to maintain medical and midwifery control over the situation. Bond (6) reported similar uses of deception in a cancer ward where the 'social order of the ward' was considered to require non-disclosure of diagnosis.

McIntosh (7), identified widespread use of deception by all members of the health care team working on a cancer ward. The team was consistent in its belief that disclosure of diagnosis would destroy patients' hopes of recovery and make their management difficult. McIntosh found that in many instances the patients themselves knew their true diagnosis, but supported the non-disclosure policy of ward staff. Glaser and Strauss (8) noted that nurses caring for patients with cancer were frequently hampered in their communication with patients by uncertainty over what patients already knew about diagnosis or treatment and by what they were allowed to disclose. Melia (9) in the UK found that student nurses faced similar problems, describing this as 'nursing in the dark'.

Although these studies indicate that deception is sometimes used in an attempt to manage situations, there are few indications of its 'success' or its effects on the professional–patient relationship. However, detection rates in real life may be high (10) and the pressures on those using deception increase when the message is an important one and when there are considerable adverse consequences of detection (11). In these circumstances, which are typical of clinical settings, social skills are more likely to break down and the likelihood of discovery to increase (12). The emotional costs of collusion in a deception may be considerable (13) and the need for teamwork in maintaining deception increases the risk of discovery (13). For all these reasons, the use of deception in health care is a relatively high-risk strategy.

The aim of the present study is to provide further empirical data on the use of deception in clinical settings. In a study on the use of reassurance in nursing (14), nurses were asked to describe situations in which they sought to alleviate patients' anxiety or distress. Those situations in which staff reported the use of deception form the database for this report. An analysis of these situations helps to develop a better understanding of the processes involved when nurses actively attempt to mislead a patient.

Methods

Subjects

Ninety-one student and 126 qualified nurses working in medical, surgical, community and psychiatric specialties were asked to complete a critical incident sheet (15) and 55 qualified nurses working in the same specialties were given a semi-structured interview. Although no personal details of the staff given the critical incident sheets were collected for reasons of anonymity, there were 12 male and 39 female nurses in the interview sample, with an average 16 years of nursing experience.

Procedures

The critical incident sheets asked the staff to describe situations when they (a) nursed a patient who was anxious, worried or distressed, (b) tried to help the patient become calmer, more secure or assured, and (c) were able to find out or observe the effects on the patient of their intervention. The semi-structured interviews with the nurses and patients covered the same areas but in more depth. Of the 272 nursing staff approached, 251 (93 per cent) agreed to describe such incidents. The two authors independently assessed the questionnaires and transcripts of interviews for the presence of deception or lying. The first author identified 13 incidents in which nurses used deception in their attempts to alleviate patients' concerns, while the second identified 12 incidents. Full agreement was found for 10 incidents, which form the database for the results described below.

Results

Descriptions of incidents

The 251 nurses indicated that they used a variety of interventions when attempting to help patients to be calmer, more rested or secure. As shown in Table 39.1, the most common was the use of prediction (in which staff provided information about what was to happen to the patients), followed by emotional support (touching, providing time to listen), giving the patient some control over events, direct action (making some change in their care procedures) and distraction. Although deception was not given a category in this analysis, most instances involving deception fell under the prediction and distraction categories.

While the study collected incidents concerning community-based nurses as well as those working in hospital settings, all the incidents involving deception arose from hospital settings. The 10 incidents of deception (4 per cent of the total sample) involved two types of patients: in six cases the patients were intellectually impaired while the remaining four cases involved patients who were fully competent but who were undergoing diagnostic tests or treatment.

(a) Patients with impaired intellectual abilities

Six patients were suffering from confusional states or were mentally handicapped. In four of these incidents the nurses used lies to calm the patients, while in the remaining two they used truthful forms of words which were nevertheless designed to distract the patients from the objective reality of their situation. The aim appeared to be to help the patients 'calm down', at least in the short term, in order to avoid disruption on the ward. One example, with the deception in italics, illustrates the difficulties the nurses were facing at the time of the deception:

Table 39.1 *Percentages of types of intervention used by nurses when attempting to reassure patients*

Prediction	41.2
Emotional support	29.1
Patient control	17.9
Direct action	7.7
Distraction	4.0

She was pacing the corridor, trying to leave the ward. She was also repeating questions in a distressed way, starting to cry and threatening to hit people with her walking stick if they came too close . . . I asked her if she would like to come and sit down and talk about the problem. She then repeated her questions about how she could get home. *I explained to her that she was in hospital and could not go home today as there was no transport on a Sunday. I also told here that her daughter and son-in-law would be coming to see her later in the day.*

In a second example, the patient had previously reacted poorly to changes in routine, so that the staff anticipated a strongly negative reaction to a planned move to another residence. Here, staff had come up with a 'devious package', in which the patient was deliberately misinformed about the likelihood that he would be required to move:

The patient in question was living in an old mental handicap hospital. A new community bungalow was due to open in a few months and this patient fulfilled the admission criteria. It was planned that the patient would move when the bungalow opened, but the nurses were reluctant to tell him too far in advance because he had a history of becoming very anxious when under stress, leading to anti-social behaviour and a refusal to eat, with rapid weight loss. The patient became suspicious about the possibility of a move [and] *the staff decided to lie to the patient, saying that he would not be going to the new bungalow.*

In these and the other examples in this category, nurses were either reacting to or anticipating distress, and taking steps to minimize or avoid it. As discussed later, such distress was seen as harmful to the patient but, perhaps more importantly, disruptive to the running of the ward.

(b) Autonomous adult patients

The remaining four situations involved adults who were competent, but whom nurses believed would suffer if they knew the truth. In such instances, the main objective was usually to reduce individual distress, rather than to minimize disruption. There were three examples of withholding information from patients suffering from cancer, in which the nurses used distraction techniques and gave evasive answers to patients' questions about diagnosis or prognosis. Either the patient's consultant had taken the decision to withhold the information about diagnosis, or the family had requested this, or a nurse had decided not to volunteer an opinion about the patient's prognosis. For example:

I had a gentleman who had been admitted with cancer of the knee who had come in for various operations to have little bits removed. But all the time we could see that he was deteriorating. There wasn't much hope of a recovery. We'd build up a good relationship and a very good friendship within that. He trusted me. *We kept getting the feeling that he wanted to know what was happening, but the consultant in particular was very evasive.* Then a friend of his who was a GP came in to see him and told him the truth.

The patient was suffering from myeloma, a form of leukaemia. As part of her treatment she needed blood transfusions which she had in the past found particularly painful. The doctors were putting off telling her about her diagnosis due to her anxiety problems and a history of cancer phobia. Cancer was something she could not cope with. *I did say that the doctors were still trying to find the cause of the anaemia but had to treat it by blood transfusions if she was to start feeling more well.*

In addition, there were two instances where information was not given to patients even though nursing staff possessed relevant knowledge:

A female patient aged 49 years had come into hospital for an operation on her hand. The anaesthetist had explained the operation to her and told her that he had prescribed paracetamol, in case she had any post-operative pain. The patient experienced a great deal of pain when she awoke from the anaesthetic and this led her to believe that the operation must have gone badly. She told me how painful her hand was and I got a doctor to prescribe a stronger pain-killer. I said: *'I didn't like to tell you this before, but I had this operation done two years ago and the pain I had for about 48 hours afterwards was awful'.*

The man's pet had gone to a friend's but they'd put it down because they couldn't handle it. And the patient was with us awaiting placement in a place where they don't take pets. And he was asking about the dog, but we really couldn't tell him that the dog was no longer with us. *We were saying 'You will get to see him sometime'. Really it didn't seem appropriate to tell him.* He had a couple of episodes where he got quite agitated and a little bit aggressive, so actually telling him the truth might have made him aggressive. I don't think anyone was against not telling him, we all thought it was for the best. And at handover we would discuss it.

Consequences of deception

Staff were also asked to outline the effects of their attempt to relieve anxiety or distress. For the intellectually impaired patients, the short-term consequences were generally positive, as for the woman pacing the corridors:

She seemed very happy about this and, after a cup of tea, settled down again, saying thank you to me for helping.

The mentally handicapped individual grew gradually accustomed to the idea of moving to the bungalow after a few 'visits'. In the case of the gentleman whose dog had been put down, he was moved to a nursing home without being told, so the consequences were unknown.

However, the nurses recognized that there could be longer-term difficulties when the patients were competent and staff had to face the consequences of their behaviour. Sometimes this was because communication patterns between staff are complex in the hospital environment and subject to misunderstandings. In such instances the consequences were not foreseen. In the case of the cancer patient who had been told of his diagnosis by his GP, for example:

> Unfortunately before I went off duty for a weekend I had indicated to one of my members of staff that the patient now knew his condition, knew his diagnosis and that people could be open with him. Because everyone else who had grown particularly attached to him was also finding it difficult that there was this sort of barrier . . . and it was almost like everybody was role-acting . . . playing a part. So I let this member of staff know that this had occurred. Unfortunately this member of staff didn't pass it on to the others. So all weekend he wanted to talk about it but they carried on being evasive. Consequently that added to the patient's distress and added to mine. I think that shattered a lot of trust.

And in the case of the woman who had an operation on her hand:

> The patient asked my who I did not warn her of [the post-operative pain] and I replied 'I didn't want to frighten you, because you thought it wasn't going to hurt very much'. The patient reported feeling shocked at this, saying that she would have preferred to have known what to expect.

Explanations of the nurses' actions

In some cases the nurses explained the reasons for their actions, but in other cases these must be inferred from the context. Sometimes nurses reported that they were using deception at the request of the patients' families and/or at the request of consultant medical staff. The difficulties of maintaining deception when patients were aware of their worsening physical condition were noted.

In most incidents the nurses explained their actions on grounds of non-maleficence. They used deception to keep the patients from becoming more anxious about their condition, their treatment, or their family. The nurses considered that they were acting positively to benefit their patients by giving them false information which they believed would relieve their anxiety. For the man whose dog had been put down and for the mentally handicapped resident, deception was used to facilitate management because the nurses feared these patients would react aggressively to the truth.

It is not possible to judge from these incidents the full extent to which the nurses engaged in ethical debate before using deception. In two cases (the patient with learning difficulties and the patient whose dog had died) the nurses reported that they discussed the various courses of action open to them before adopting deception. The nurse's reasoning behind her decision to withhold information about post-operative pain appeared unclear. When the patient reported pain, the nurse immediately contacted a doctor to have the patient written up for a stronger analgesic – yet she took no action before the operation either to alert the patient as to what to expect or to get the doctor to alter his prescription in anticipation. When the nurse admitted her deception after the event to the patient, this undermined the patient's trust in the way her care had been managed.

Conclusions

Although the database is limited, a number of tentative conclusions can be reached. First, it should be noted that on only 10 occasions was deception used in the sample of 251 incidents, even though the questionnaires were completed anonymously so that there was no 'public' disclosure of deception. While it would be unsound to draw any firm conclusions from this small number of reported incidents as to the actual frequency with which deceptive strategies are used by nurses (the sample is not representative of the nursing profession as a whole and the study itself treated deception as only one among a much wider array of strategies used to alleviate patients' worries), it appears the use of deception is rare.

Second, the data provide some indication of the reasons for the deceptions. Staff usually perceived themselves as acting under the principles of beneficence or non-maleficence. However, another possibility is that deception was used for organizational reasons, in order to ensure the smooth running of the ward. For example, the nurses who did not disclose the dog's death or the move to the bungalow were concerned about aggressive reactions as well as doing no harm. It seems harder to justify the deception in such instances, although it can be argued that the welfare of other patients was relevant. It is also important that many of the incidents involved patients without full intellectual autonomy, who were less likely than others to uncover the deception.

Third, the results bear on Jackson's (16) contention that deception can be justified in certain circumstances when it does not have an adverse effect on the relationship – especially the trust – between patient and professional. These cases illustrate that it is not always possible to foresee the consequences of deception. Even when the nurses were apparently working under the principles of beneficence and non-maleficence, the longer-term consequences were sometimes negative. It was particularly difficult to co-ordinate deception when patients were intellectually unimpaired, and eventual discovery sometimes had an adverse effect on the nurse–patient relationship. Furthermore, both deception and discovery resulted in some distress for the nurses themselves and could lead to what was termed 'playing a part'. Thus it seems unlikely that the consequences of deception can be foreseen with great accuracy. Even though the intention might be innocent, whether a deception will be discovered cannot always be predicted.

Finally, it is useful to note that nurses varied in their willingness to use deception in their dealings with patients. Some nurses in the larger sample reported that they would never seek to mislead patients and would always disclose the truth about a situation if they knew it and believed that the patient was genuinely seeking an honest answer. Other nurses disputed this, believing for example that relatives have the right to direct staff not to disclose information. [. . .]

References

(1) Miller S, Mangan C. Interacting effects of information and coping style in adapting to gynecologic stress: should the doctor tell all? *Journal of personality and social psychology* 1983; 45: 223–36.

(2) Bok S. *Lying: moral choice in public and private life.* Hassocks, Sussex: Harvester Press, 1978.

(3) See reference (2): 6.

(4) Schrock R. A question of honesty in nursing practice. *Journal of advanced nursing* 1980; 5: 135–48.

(5) Kirkham M. Labouring in the dark: limitations on the giving of information to enable patients to orientate themselves to the likely events and timescale of labour. In: Wilson-Barnet J, ed. *Nursing research: ten studies in patient care.* Chichester: Wiley, 1983: 81–100.

(6) Bond S. Nurses' communication with cancer patients. See reference (5): 57–80.

(7) McIntosh J. *Communication and awareness in a cancer ward.* London: Croom Helm, 1977.

(8) Glaser B, Strauss A. *Awareness of dying.* London: Weidenfeld and Nicolson, 1965.

(9) Melia K. *Learning and working.* London: Tavistock, 1987.

(10) Ekman P, O'Sullivan M. Who can catch a liar? *American psychologist* 1991: 465: 913–20.

(11) McCornack S, Levine T. When lies are uncovered: emotional and relational outcomes of discovered deception. *Communication monographs* 1990; 57: 119–38.

(12) DePaulo B, LeMay C, Epstein J. Effects of importance of success and expectations for success on effectiveness of deceiving. *Personality and social psychology bulletin* 1991; 17: 14–24.

(13) Maguire P, Faulkner A. Communication with cancer patients: 2. Handling uncertainty, collusion, and denial. *British medical journal* 1988; 297: 972–74.

(14) Teasdale K. Reassurance in nursing. Unpublished PhD thesis, Sheffield Hallam University, Sheffield, 1992.

(15) Flanagan J. C. The critical incident technique. *Psychological bulletin* 1954; 51: 327–58.

(16) Jackson J. On the morality of deception – does method matter? A reply to David Bakhurst. *Journal of medical ethics* 1993; 19: 183–7.

40

Do-not-resuscitate decisions

Johannes J. M. van Delden

Glossary

cardiopulmonary resuscitation: A treatment for acute failure of circulation and/or respiration, and of which at least chest compressions and/or breathing form a part, without which death is certain.

competence: A task-specific threshold concept that addresses the decision-making process. Someone is competent when she is able to appreciate the nature of the situation so as to reach a decision adequately.

do-not-resuscitate (DNR) decision: An explicit, anticipatory decision not to attempt cardiopulmonary resuscitation when a patient sustains a heart and/or breathing arrest.

do-not-resuscitate policy: A total of formalized agreements on the level of a unit or on the level of an institute concerning the resuscitation of patients.

do-not-resuscitate protocol: A written DNR policy.

futile: Describing treatment from which no positive effect may be expected or for which a consensus exists among physicians that the chances of such an effect are too small.

therapeutic privilege: An exception to the rule of informed consent, based on the judgment that to disclose the information would be potentially harmful to a patient in a way that outweighs possible benefits.

The fight against an untimely death is an element of medical science which comes to the fore especially with cardiopulmonary resuscitation. A successful cardiopulmonary resuscitation constitutes a victory over death. Hence modern resuscitation techniques are considered one of the breakthroughs which advanced medical science has offered humanity. The importance of resuscitation is reinforced by the fact that everyone eventually dies. For everyone there is the moment when heartbeat and/or respiration fails. Thus all humanity is a possible candidate for resuscitation.

However, resuscitation has its drawbacks. Resuscitation is more often than not unsuccessful, and practising it involves some technical violence. When the resuscitation attempt is not successful, then the process of dying may have been severely disturbed with no compensatory positive effects

Extract from *Encyclopedia of Applied Ethics*, ed. Ruth Chadwick, 1998, London: Academic Press. pp. 839–97 (abridged).

attributed to the intervention. Moreover, death need not be fought with all possible force for all people. In short, sometimes it is better not to resuscitate at all. When not to resuscitate is the subject of the present contribution.

One problem is the fact that the decision to start resuscitation needs to be taken quickly. Hence the question, 'should this patient be resuscitated or not?' must be answered when there is time to think it over. When this kind of decision-making process leads to the decision not to intervene, a do-not-resuscitate decision (DNR decision) has been taken. Only decisions taken before a possible arrest are looked upon as DNR decisions. A decision to stop a resuscitation attempt already in progress is not covered by this definition. This matter derives its moral importance from the fact that by making a DNR decision, one takes the responsibility that the decision may shorten a patient's life.

The objective of this contribution is to describe some morally relevant facts, to give a normative analysis of the reasons not to resuscitate, and to offer some considerations with which to formulate a DNR policy. The focus is on hospitals, because this is where DNR decisions are most often made. Some mention of nursing homes will also be made, however.

I. Morally relevant facts

A. Cardiopulmonary resuscitation

1. What it is

Cardiopulmonary resuscitation (CPR) is a treatment for the acute failure of circulation and/or respiration. Although it is often looked upon as another example of high-tech modern medicine, its roots are much older, probably as old as the human being. The present method of resuscitation, however, was developed in the 1950s, when the scientific basis for rescue breathing with the mouth-to-mouth technique and for closed chest compressions was provided. Even today the provision of an open *a*irway, the performance of rescue *b*reathing, and the restoration of *c*irculation by means of chest compressions form the ABC of the first phase of CPR, called basic life support (American Heart Association, 1992. *J. Am. Med. Assoc.* 268, 2171–295). In health care institutions, be it hospitals or nursing homes, this will often be done my the nursing staff.

The second phase of CPR is called advanced cardiac life support. In this phase adjunctive equipment and special techniques are used for establishing and maintaining effective ventilation and circulation. This includes electro-cardiographic monitoring of the cardiac rhythm, establishing an intravenous access, drug therapy, and intubation. Also, defibrillation by electro-shocks may be necessary. Advanced life support is provided by special resuscitation teams.

2. The results

The results of cardiopulmonary resuscitation in hospitals have been described in a considerable number of studies. The comparability of these studies is limited, however, for reasons of study design and definitions. With these limitations in mind, it can be calculated that on average resuscitation is initially successful – that is, heartbeat is restored – in 38 per cent of the cases. As many patients die later on, the chance of discharge from hospital is much smaller, to wit, 14 per cent on average (H. Tunstall-Pedoe et al., 1992. *Br. Med. J.* 304, 1347–51). One may expect these percentages to rise with the increasing number of do-not-resuscitate of (DNR) decisions because only patients with good chances of success are resuscitated. Factors determining the success rate include the underlying illness of the patient, the type of rhythm disorder with which the arrest began (fibrillation versus asystole), and the time between cardiac arrest and start of resuscitation.

Not all of these aspects are known at the moment a DNR decision is considered, but the patient's condition is. Roughly, it is possible to distinguish between cardiac patients (where resuscitation is relatively successful) and patients with an advanced, progressive, ultimately lethal illness (where resuscitation attempts are mostly without success). It has been shown that patients in the following situations have extremely low chances of survival (meaning almost zero per cent) to hospital discharge (D. J. Murphy and T. E. Finucane 1993. *Arch. Intern. Med.* 153, 1641–3):

- Metastatic cancer (patient bedfast)
- End-stage liver disease (advanced cirrhosis)
- HIV infection (after two or more episodes of pneumocystis carinii pneumonia)
- Coma patients, not awake after 48 hr
- Patients with multiple organ failure without improvement after 3 days in intensive care
- Unsuccessful out-of-hospital CPR

Whether age alone has predictive value has long been an unsettled matter. According to some studies it does, while others have seemed to prove that it does not. However, combination of the results of several studies shows that persons over 70 years of age do have a smaller chance of survival to discharge (relative risk 1.4). Nevertheless, old age alone does not preclude a successful resuscitation (Tunstall-Pedoe et al., 1992).

It is not only the chance of survival that influences the decision of whether or not to resuscitate – the quality of life after successful resuscitation is also a morally relevant fact. This quality is to a large extent influenced by the neurological condition of the patient. In spite of this, not many studies describe this factor. The study of Longstreth does, however. He found that one out of five patients who initially survive the resuscitation but who die before discharge from hospital regain consciousness. A number of neurologic disorders occur with one-third of the surviving patients (A. S. Jaffe and

W. M. Landau, 1993, *Neurology* 43, 2173–8; W. T. Longstreth et al., 1983. *Ann. Intern. Med.* 98. 588–92). These disorders range from memory deficits to persistent vegetative state.

The quality of life after resuscitation may also, at least temporarily, be influenced by complications due to resuscitation. Skin burns, broken ribs, and stomach injuries may result from CPR, even when properly performed. Incidences range from 21 to 65 per cent of resuscitations. Although the American Heart Association correctly observes that fear of complications should not prevent one from providing CPR (AHA, 1992), these complications are part of an analysis of the burdens and benefits of CPR.

B. Do-not-resuscitate decisions

1. Incidence

During the 1960s cardiopulmonary resuscitation developed from a 'treatment' for unexpected cardiac death to a technique which was always tried when a patient was found pulseless and/or without breathing. Soon, however, the inappropriateness of this policy was recognized. In 1974 the American Heart Association stated that the purpose of CPR was the prevention of sudden unexpected death and that CPR was not indicated in cases of terminal irreversible illness. This made it necessary to decide when to use CPR and when not to. Thus do-not-resuscitate decisions came into being. They can be defined as explicit, anticipatory decisions not to attempt cardiopulmonary resuscitation when a patient sustains a heart and/or breathing arrest.

The number of DNR decisions has been increasing since those days and continues to do so. The Netherlands probably had the first nationwide study of DNR decisions (J.J.M. van Delden et al., 1993. *J. Med. Ethics* 19, 200–5). All interviewed specialists, regardless of specialty, had at some time made a DNR decision. In most cases (96 per cent) they had done so at least once during the past year. It was estimated that 90,800 DNR decisions were made in hospitals in 1990. This amounts to 6 per cent of hospital admissions. Of all in-hospital deaths (the total being 53,500 per year) 61 per cent were preceded by a DNR decision. In acute deaths there is not time to make anticipating decisions. When these cases were ignored, 80 per cent of patients died with a DNR decision. With 90,800 DNR decisions per year and 32,000 deaths preceded by DNR, 65 per cent of DNR patients left the hospital alive.

The Dutch percentage of admissions in which a DNR decision is made (6 per cent) is higher than that given by American studies in the 1980s. Then it was usually reported that a DNR decision was made for 3–4 per cent of all hospitalized patients (B. Lo et al., 1985, *Arch. Intern. Med.* 145, 1115–17; C.J. Stolman et al., 1989. *Arch. Intern. Med.* 149, 1851–6). More recent American investigators reported incidences of 9–12 per cent. The percentage of deaths preceded by a DNR decision is reported to be 62–70 per cent in the United States (Stolman, 1989). This coincides with the Dutch figure (61 per cent). DNR decisions thus clearly form an intrinsic part of daily medical practice in hospitals on both sides of the Atlantic Ocean.

2. Different interpretations

One of the problems with DNR decisions is that doctors (and nurses) interpret them differently. In spite of the fact that the scope of the decision in almost all definitions is limited to resuscitation, a DNR decision often leads to other limitations of medical treatment. In one study DNR decisions de facto led to limitations in the use of artificial respiration, ICU admission, blood transfusions, antibiotics, and even analgesics. In another study the author found that some form of treatment was withdrawn for 28 per cent of patients for whom a DNR decision had been made (S. E. Bedell et al., 1986, *J. Am. Med. Assoc.* 256, 233–7). And yet another reported that nurses are significantly less likely to perform a variety of monitoring modalities and interventions for patients with DNR decisions.

Some comments need to be made at this point. Generally speaking, two situations have to be distinguished. On the one hand the mere fact that a DNR decision is made might lead a doctor to assume that other care needs to be limited as well. This type of reasoning endangers the efficacy of any DNR policy since other doctors, in response, might become reluctant to make DNR decisions out of fear of stigmatizing their patients.

On the other hand the circumstances that justified the DNR decision might also form the reason for other nontreatment decisions (NTD). If these NTDs are discussed with the patient or his surrogate and have a sound medical (and ethical) basis there is no need to condemn them. In short, DNR decisions are compatible with maximum medical care (short of CPR), but may also be accompanied by other NTDs. This is especially true because DNR decisions seem to mark a change in the chances attributed to a patient. When the hope for recovery lessens, a DNR decision is often the first of a series of NTDs. [. . .]

II. Ethical aspects of DNR

A. Why bother?

Why should doctors think about the appropriateness of CPR and record DNR decisions in medical charts? Why do they not 'simply' resuscitate everyone with an arrest? After all, if the patient lives, a life is saved, and if she dies, the outcome would be the same as without resuscitation. What, then, is the benefit of DNR decisions?

The purpose of thinking about whether or not to use CPR is to prevent a pointless reduction of the quality of dying. Quality of dying is defined as the quality of life at the end of life. An unsuccessful resuscitation attempt disturbs the process of dying while adding nothing. All treatments that are greatly appreciated as tools for saving a life become violent and intrusive techniques if they are used without a chance of success. The loss involved when CPR fails is not the death of the patient, but the damage to the quality of the last part of life.

Although the reason mentioned above seems to be the most important one, other reasons for thinking about CPR can be given. In some cases patients themselves will not want to fight death at all costs. Moreover, in certain circumstances CPR may not be a wise or just use of limited medical resources. In some Dutch nursing homes, for instance, the management (working with a fixed budget) preferred extra nursing staff over resuscitation facilities, arguing that the emphasis should be on care instead of a (high-tech) cure. Finally, medical and nursing staff will get demoralized by too many unsuccessful resuscitations. That is why it is sometimes better not to resuscitate at all and always good to determine the appropriateness of CPR.

B. Who decides?

1. Involvement of the patient

If DNR decisions are (sometimes) justified, then who is to make the decision? In this section the following 'candidates' are considered: the patient and the physician. In some circumstances the patient may be represented by someone else. This will be discussed in Section C.

In health care it is of supreme importance to respect patients as autonomous people. Therefore, the same requirements stand for CPR as for any other treatment: it may only be performed after obtaining informed consent from the patients. And the same goes for deciding not to resuscitate. This latter point needs more justification, because doctors normally are not required to seek consent for everything they do not do. But if they plan to withhold a treatment that a patient may reasonably expect to get, as is the case with CPR, they should discuss this, generally speaking, with the patient involved.

But let us see what actually happens. Are patients involved in the decision-making process and do they want to be? In the Netherlands the decision not to resuscitate was discussed with the patient in 14 per cent of all cases (van Delden et al., 1993). These patients constituted 32 per cent of all competent patients with DNR, which means that 68 per cent of competent patients were not involved in the DNR decision.

One study found a similar practice of infrequent discussions with patients in Sweden. This contrasts rather sharply with the United States, where a large majority (77–98 per cent) of competent patients are involved in the decision (Bedell, 1986; Lo, 1985; Stolman, 1989).

Patients themselves have been shown to want to participate in deciding about CPR in a number of studies. One of these contains the interesting observation that patients would rather be informed about their situation (e.g. prognosis) than decide themselves. It is not without value to mention at this point that the way in which the information is given is very influential. It would need a very self-assured patient to answer in the affirmative the question, Do you really want us to do all the heroics and pound on your chest and maybe break your bones?

One of the reasons for not involving a patient may be the concern of the doctor that the patient cannot cope with discussing CPR. In that case the physician invokes the therapeutic privilege. In the Dutch study this was done quite often (van Delden et al., 1993). There were 60 cases (30 per cent of total) in which the DNR decision was not discussed with a competent patient. In 35 of these the physician stated in one way or another that this discussion would be too burdensome for the patient, thus invoking the therapeutic privilege. In 10 cases of these the respondent added that for this reason it was his policy never to talk about DNR decisions with a patient.

In accordance with the views of many ethicists (e.g., T. L. Beauchamp and J. F. Childress, 1994. *Principles of Biomedical Ethics*, 4th edn. Oxford Univ. Press, New York) one should reject such a practice. It seems to be a relic of paternalistic behavior in medicine that no longer fits the present day views on the physician–patient relationship. One fears that discussing DNR is rather too burdensome for the physician instead of for the patient. One should plead, therefore, for a strict interpretation of the therapeutic privilege. Moreover, empirical evidence indicates that negative effects such an anxiety materialize less often than physicians tend to think.

At the beginning of this subsection it was stated that patients should be involved in the DNR decision. We saw that quite often they are not, and also that this happens for the wrong reasons. It seems, therefore, that medical practice, in this respect, still has to catch up with moral theory.

2. Decisions by physicians

One reason for not involving a patient may be the thought that resuscitation is futile. Often it is understood that nontreatment decisions based on the futility of treatment are the sole responsibility of the physician; this means that in those cases the patient does not have to be involved in the decision.

Hence, the 'futile' judgment does two things: first, it implies that a certain treatment should not be carried out, and second it implies that (only) the doctor decides, because she is the expert. 'Futility' has the air of the objectivity of scientific evidence. This is what provides the justification for not involving the patient: his opinion cannot change the facts. Leaving aside the philosophical question of whether such objective truths exist at all, the test for any definition of futility is the reasonableness of the combination of the two implications.

What, then is the definition of futility? For this, two aspects should be distinguished: one concerns the effectiveness of the treatment and the other the proportionality (burden/benefit ratio) of it. Applying the test just specified, one is tempted to conclude that determining the effectiveness of resuscitation is a medical judgment whereas determining the proportionality in the individual case is not, that is, not solely. However, the matter is a little bit more complicated.

Firstly, determining the effectiveness of resuscitation is not free of value judgments. Describing effectiveness, one uses certain end points; in the case of CPR these are, for instance, restoration of cardiac rhythm, 24-hr survival, survival to discharge, and long-term survival. The choice for one of these is based on values. It is common to describe success rates of CPR in terms of survival to hospital discharge, for instance. This implies that the time before discharge has less value.

Secondly, if only treatments with 0 per cent chance of success were considered futile, there would hardly be any futile treatments in medicine. Mostly, one uses a cutoff point below which one considers the treatment futile. The choice of this cutoff point is precisely that, a choice. Still, as long as these choices are shared among peers and as long as they are made on a population level, determining effectiveness should be left to the physician(s!).

The assessment of the burden/benefit ratio on the individual level, however, is incomplete without the patient's perception of both the burdens and the benefits. Determining the proportionality of CPR in the individual case is therefore a matter for discussion between doctor and patient.

This is not to say that doctors are not entitled to opinions. It is only that opinions should not be 'medicalized'. Doctors are good judges of what a patient may be advised to choose, but it must be advice only, not a decision the patient is not even aware of. This is of course supported by the nowdays common adherence to the principle of autonomy. However, one should warn against an atomistic view on autonomy. It is only by shared decision making, not by leaving patients alone with the decision, that the mutual trust between patient and physician is strengthened.

C. Deciding in the case of incompetent patients

In spite of DNR policies seeking an early discussion with the patient, it is inevitable that sometimes a physician has to decide about resuscitating an incompetent patient. It is beyond the scope of this contribution to discuss at length the rules of decision making in these circumstances, but the main lines may be described.

In accordance with what was previously said, a physician may unilaterally make a DNR decision if resuscitation is futile. The patient's opinion is not decisive in these circumstances, and the fact that the opinion is unknowable, due to the state of incompetence, does not influence the decision-making process.

However, when disproportionality forms the basis for a DNR decision, the opinion of the incompetent patient is deeply missed. There are several ways to compensate for this; none of them, however, are completely satisfactory. These compensatory strategies all aim at constructing an autonomous wish of the now incompetent patient.

The most important strategy is to look for written evidence of the patient's opinion. If she, before becoming incompetent, made up an advance directive, one usually accepts this as a substitute for the actual wish. In spite of the apparent strength of this substitute (no need to guess, it is all written down!), there are at least two problems with advance directives.

Because of the fact that the patient at the time of writing the directive does not know what is to come, she will use broad terms to cover different situations. Thus the specificity decreases and one will be able to ask, Is this what she really meant? The second problem concerns the continuity of the wish. People tend to accommodate new circumstances – they learn to live with them. Therefore, a now incompetent patient might have changed her opinion on the once fictitious but now actual circumstances. Unfortunately, we are not able to hear this new opinion because of the incompetence. Of course this is all a thought experiment; many incompetent patients are beyond opinions. Nevertheless this experiment teaches us that we can ask a second question: Would she still think of it in the same way?

One could argue, of course, that one need not worry about this second question, because the person who wrote the advance directive consciously took the 'risk' of living (while incompetent) with a nonactual wish. Such a strategy would be very practical, but would not take away the moral problem.

In the absence of advance directives one could ask relatives whether they know of relevant utterances of the patient. If such statements exist, they may be very helpful to determining the right course of action. Nevertheless a third problem is added to the two mentioned above: it is not certain that the patient, when saying what she said, meant to give directives for deciding in case of incompetence.

If no relevant utterances are known, a values history might help; if the patient has always lived by certain values (religious or nonreligious), these should be reflected in the decision. The regulating power of the value history itself will not be very large; some interpretation will be necessary before the general value fits the specific circumstance.

Beyond this not even a shadow of an autonomous wish can be constructed. Then one has to rely on a best-interests judgment. These should be made by the physician and the relatives of the patient together. Their task is to place themselves in the patient's place and decide from her perspective. [. . .] It should be stressed that, however difficult, the decision has to be faced because avoiding it will imply a decision in favor of CPR by default. [. . .]

III. Conclusion

Since in hospitals it is common practice to resuscitate any patient with a cardiac and/or breathing arrest, these phenomena are part of the final, common pathway to death, and resuscitation in itself is a rather violent treatment, thinking about whether or not to resuscitate is very appropriate. Moreover, because do-not-resuscitate decisions are made in advance, when no emergency exists (yet), one has time to weigh burdens and benefits. This makes DNR decisions a paradigm case for describing and regulating the decision-making process in non-treatment decisions.

41

The 'blue-spotted' patient
do-not-resuscitate decisions in the acute surgical wards of an English district general hospital

Basiro Davey

> The other day we had a [cardiac] arrest and we had been talking at the handover only two hours before – 'Is this patient blue-spotted?' and she [nurse giving the handover] said 'I don't know, we ought to find out'. And just as the arrest was taking place *nobody* knew. We contacted the house officer, the house officer came. You know it's a new lot of house officers and of course they're learning and that's of great significance right across the board. But she was a bit panicky because *she* didn't know, *she* couldn't tell us, and she had to ring up the consultant to find out from him. And I think the wording was 'Mrs. So and So, is she for resuscitation?' and the answer was 'No'. And I reckon that the consultants have become used to this sort of question where an anxious voice asks 'Is so and so for resuscitation?'. And they deduce that they *are* being resuscitated and so they say 'No' because they've decided well if they *are* being resuscitated, at least they can stop. *Nurse N32*

The staff nurse in this interview extract gives a potent insight into the potential sources of confusion about 'do-not-resuscitate' (DNR) decisions in British hospital wards. This article aims to illuminate the circumstances in which DNR decisions were taken in two acute surgical wards, by exploring the perceptions of medical and nursing staff. Some reasons why confusions occurred are suggested. In the process, some of the major issues concerning decisions not to attempt to resuscitate patients who suffer a cardiac or respiratory arrest will be reviewed and illustrated. First, the key terms are defined and some historical background is given for current debates.

Referring to a patient as 'blue-spotted' may be unique to nurses on the surgical wards in the study reported here. The term arises from the practice of drawing a blue spot on the nursing notes of patients whom doctors have decided should not be resuscitated if their heart stops beating (cardiac arrest) or if they stop breathing (respiratory arrest). Cardiac and respiratory arrest occurs during all deaths, so doctors are faced with a decision about whether to attempt resuscitation in each case. The doctor's decision to withhold resuscitation is written in the medical notes, where two other coded instructions are frequently recorded – 'Not for CPR' (cardiopulmonary resuscitation), or 'Not for 333', the phone number in this hospital for the specialist resuscitation team. The 'crash team' is called whenever a patient without a written DNR decision arrests or 'crashes' in the jargon of the wards.

Nurses are frequently the only trained staff on hand at the time of a sudden arrest, but junior doctors (pre-registration house officers) may also be present, since they spend the most time on the wards. In the absence of a DNR order, the professional obligation of both nurses and doctors is to commence immediate basic resuscitation procedures (mouth-to-mouth assisted respiration and rhythmic chest compression) and call the emergency resuscitation team. The crash team uses specialist equipment for advanced cardiopulmonary resuscitation, which includes inserting a tube to open the airways and intravenous catheters for drug administration, and attaching a heart monitoring device. Advanced CPR may also involve electric shocks to the chest to restart the heart. These procedures have become familiar to anyone who watches hospital dramas on TV, but the fictional version downplays the inherent violence and invasiveness of advanced CPR (Page, 1999), and the low success rate. Excluding patients in coronary care units, only about 15 per cent of in-patients who arrest in hospital wards survive to be discharged home after CPR (Tunstall-Pedoe et al., 1992; Birtwhistle and Nielsen, 1998).

A brief history of DNR policy guidelines

British doctors have generally believed that DNR decisions could be taken in the patient's best interests without 'potentially painful' discussions with the patient and next of kin (Bayliss, 1982: 1374). But in 1991 a patient's son complained to the Health Service Commissioner after discovering by chance that a DNR decision had been written in his mother's notes by a junior doctor without discussion with him or the consultant in charge. The Commissioner's report to the House of Commons criticized the lack of an agreed DNR policy and the failure of the consultant concerned to brief his junior staff on how and by whom DNR decisions should be made, communicated and reviewed (Health Service Commissioner, 1990–91). The Chief Medical Officer then wrote to all NHS consultants in England drawing attention to the implications 'particularly in respect of the training of junior staff' (Chief Medical Officer, 1991). Another outcome was the publication by the Royal College of Nursing and the British Medical Association of joint guidelines on withholding resuscitation (RCN/BMA, 1993; revised BMA/RCN, 1999).

Four general points emerge from the BMA/RCN guidelines. First, patients for whom a DNR decision is appropriate are clearly identified. If resuscitation is unlikely to be successful, or is likely to be followed by 'a length and quality of life which would not be in the best interests of the patient to sustain', then CPR is withheld on the grounds of *futility*. If the patient has expressed a sustained wish not to be resuscitated and this has been recorded in the medical notes or in an advance directive (a 'living will'), the patient's *autonomy* should be respected by not attempting resuscitation. Not mentioned in the BMA/RCN guidelines, but widely cited in the ethical literature, is the fact that advanced CPR techniques may cause physical injury to the patient, which can include brain damage, broken ribs and skin burns. So unless there is a reasonable chance of success, resuscitation is prohibited by the medical principle of *non-maleficence*, not actively doing harm (Hilberman et al., 1997).

Second, the responsibility for making DNR decisions in hospitals is located firmly with consultants, who should review these decisions regularly. They must explain their DNR policy clearly to all members of their medical team and particularly to junior, temporary or locum staff.

Third, DNR decisions and subsequent reviews should be unambiguously written in the patient's medical notes, together with the reason for withholding resuscitation. Details of key discussions about the decision with other doctors, nurses, the patient and his or her relatives should also be recorded. All staff should be informed that a DNR decision has been taken.

Fourth, the 1999 guidelines state that 'there should be sensitive exploration' by senior experienced doctors, supported by senior nursing colleagues, of the competent patient's wishes regarding resuscitation. This advice has become firmer since the 1993 guidelines, which acknowledged that 'it would not be appropriate in all cases'. If the patient cannot participate, the family or close friends may be asked what they believe to be the patient's views, but they cannot decide *for* the patient.

The Royal College of Physicians made clear that the 1993 RCN/BMA guidelines 'encompass only the broad principles, as it is envisaged that each hospital or unit will require a more detailed policy according to local circumstances and facilities' (Williams, 1993: 139). Although more detailed specification of DNR policies have since been developed (Doyal and Wilsher, 1993, 1994; Florin, 1993; Stewart, 1995; Skerritt and Pitt, 1997; Hayward, 1999), the 1999 BMA/RCN guidelines still advise hospitals to produce their own DNR protocols. In the USA, written DNR policies have been mandatory since 1988. The consequences of a failure to enforce a clearly articulated DNR policy were illuminated by the surgical ward study reported below. However, studies in other British hospitals reveal that even where a written DNR policy exists, compliance may be low (Mello and Jenkinson, 1998; Hayes et al., 1999).

The surgical ward study methods

In 1996–97 a wide-ranging study of medical and nursing communication began in the male and female acute surgical wards of an English district general hospital. The study sought to illuminate the structures, strategies and attitudes affecting communication between and within the two professions and was, in part, a follow-up to an earlier study on the same wards (Davey, 1993). A six-month period of intensive observation on the surgical wards included attending medical and nursing ward rounds, nurse handover reports and staff meetings. Observations, verbatim communication between staff and with patients, and informal conversations were recorded in field notes, and formed the basis for tape-recorded semi-structured private interviews with doctors and nurses after the observation period. Field notes and interview tapes were fully transcribed for analysis. Each staff member is identified in the extracts below by a unique code, which distinguishes them from staff interviewed in previous research at this hospital.

The study was not directed towards DNR decisions. They emerged as one among several other areas of persistently difficult communication identified by staff. Information about their experiences of DNR decisions was given by 12 doctors (seven junior doctors, one senior house officer and four consultant surgeons), 13 registered general nurses (including six senior nurses) and one state enrolled nurse. Incidents relating to DNR decisions were also observed which tended to support the interview accounts.

Concern for the patient's quality of living and dying

Doctors and nurses on the acute surgical wards readily described the sort of patients they thought should be 'blue-spotted'. Their accounts generally reflected the quality of life considerations emphasised in the BMA/RCN guidelines described above.

> Mrs X has got hepatic metastases from a bowel cancer and has had a stroke and she's 83. *Consultant D27*

> He'd had a stroke and pancreatitis and basically his conscious level had deteriorated even further . . . it became obvious that he was going to die in the next few days. *Junior doctor D34*

> She was 96 . . . she had suffered from asthma most of her life so she had chronic airways disease, and she also had a heart condition and she wasn't mobile. *Nurse N41*

> He's living, you know, but his quality of life is such . . . what if he arrested? He's completely dependent on carers. It's what he would be like afterwards. *Nurse N40*

There were no instances of nursing staff questioning the appropriateness of those DNR decisions that had already been taken by doctors. However, the rationale for the *absence* of a DNR decision was not always clear to nursing staff. Several nurses were exasperated by the lack of DNR orders for patients who should not, in their view, be resuscitated if they suffered an arrest.

> I mean we've got a few on [the ward], a few at the moment that I wouldn't consider suitable for resuss. . . . They haven't been blue spotted yet. I mean some of the elderly people that we've got, maybe three or four, who've got cancer, had the operation and found that it was terminal and are quite poorly afterwards. I can't really see the point of resussing someone for an extra couple of weeks. *Nurse N28*

Nurses were unsure in these circumstances whether the absence of a written DNR order meant that doctors had simply not considered the patient's resuscitation status yet, or if doctors disagreed with the nurses' view that resuscitation would be inappropriate. A discrepancy between doctors' and nurses' views on which patients should have DNR orders has been reported in another hospital (Yip and Lenox, 1994). In justifying their anxiety to get doctors to take DNR decisions more quickly, some nurses in the surgical ward study described resuscitation attempts which, in their view, should never have taken place. Accounts of failed resuscitation attempts have also been documented by Page and Meerabeau (1996).

> And there was an instance of that yesterday evening, um, when a lady came back from theatre . . . and she'd had a major operation that really wasn't curative, and she arrested and they went full-blown into the resuscitation procedure. And *I* felt, well, this is not particularly kind, because what are we doing here? *Nurse N23*

> I mean we have had some instances and I can give you one now, a gentleman who was 103 who we had to resuss, who shouldn't have been for active resuss if anything had happened. For one, we broke quite a few ribs when we were resussing him and the resuss team weren't very pleased at coming up to resuss a 103 year old. *Nurse N28*

On average, 20 resuscitation attempts are made on inpatients in every district general hospital in Britain each month (Tunstall-Pedoe et al., 1992), a figure that excludes resuscitation in Accident and Emergency departments. Evidence from medical audits of case notes in other British hospitals suggests that a sizeable minority of these resuscitation attempts are medically futile and could have been prevented by DNR decisions, which were not taken soon enough or were not properly recorded in the notes (Stewart et al., 1990; Aarons and Beeching, 1991; Davies et al., 1993; Jones et al., 1993; Skerritt and Pitt, 1997; Hayes et al., 1999).

Nurses in the surgical wards reported here were particularly upset by instances where (as in the example with which this article began) advanced resuscitation procedures were commenced, only to be called off when clarification about the patient's DNR status was sought from senior medical staff. The dying patient is subjected to a futile, violent and invasive procedure, other patients and staff are needlessly distressed by the sights and sounds of the crash team at work, and emergency services are tied up in a pointless and avoidable exercise. The desire to enable patients to die peacefully was uppermost in nurses' minds:

> Yeah, nurses like you to be very clear cut and they like it to be written in the notes 'Not for 333' or whatever . . . so that we know where we stand, so that we don't impinge on a patient's dignity even further by jumping on their chest and sticking needles and tubes into them when they are, in effect, dying and it just needs to be allowed to happen. *Nurse N23*

None of the doctors interviewed gave spontaneous accounts of patients who were subjected to inappropriate resuscitation attempts. One referred to patients who should, in the doctor's view, have had DNR orders much sooner in their hospital stay.

> People who haven't died here but have been dodgy, have usually gone off to [the local hospice]. So had they died here it would have been a bit of a cock-up in hindsight, because the resuss team would have been called and that would have been a waste of time for them. *Junior doctor D35*

Junior doctors also wanted to protect the quality of the patient's dying, a view that emerged obliquely in their accounts of what they say to relatives:

> If it happens that she gets very poorly and maybe she goes into heart failure or her heart stops, we think it wouldn't be the right thing to do to go into the full emergency resuscitation procedure . . . They can see for themselves that it would be unkind to call the crash team. *Junior doctor D29*

Acute surgical wards are geared towards curing patients, the majority of whom are elective admissions. Deaths occur relatively infrequently, perhaps four or five times a month. Slowness or inconsistency in assigning a DNR status to some terminally ill patients may suggest that doctors on surgical teams may sometimes be reluctant to 'concede defeat', or they may have a low awareness of the need to consider their patients' resuscitation status. Surgical teams are not primarily concerned with the dying patient, who may represent 'matter out of place' in Mary Douglas's memorable phrase (Douglas, 1966). This interpretation has some support from a study using matched case histories, which found that hospital physicians were less likely than geriatricians to take DNR decisions (Davies et al., 1993).

Who takes DNR decisions?

The chain of decision making about DNR orders in the surgical wards was primarily 'bottom-up', rather than the 'top-down' consultant-led model advised by the BMA/RCN guidelines. Nurses reported pushing junior doctors to get a DNR decision taken for patients with very poor quality-of-life prospects.

> We do try and point it out, whatever, mention it, you know, when you feel that the doctors are wavering, or not taking an active decision. *Nurse N25*

The junior doctors in turn usually prompted their immediate superiors, the senior house officers or specialist registrars:

> One way you can do it is to present it to your senior, leaning a particular way. You can say anything, paint any picture you want over the phone and just say 'They shouldn't be for resuss, or should they?' and they go 'No'. *Junior doctor D30*

A recent audit of medical notes in a London teaching hospital found that consultants had been involved in only 9 per cent of DNR decisions, the majority of which had been taken by middle-grade doctors (Hayes et al., 1999). The extent to which DNR decisions originated from or were actually discussed with the consultants in the surgical ward study was unclear, but some consultants seemed remote from it to their junior staff and one acknowledged his own detachment.

> I mean it's something that consultants don't really do actually now. I think it's the middle grades that do it. *Junior doctor D30*

> *Interviewer*: I was trying to work out who talked to whom about when a particular patient was going to be marked 'not for resuss'. Does it reach you?
> *Consultant*: It does sometimes. It should always shouldn't it. *Consultant D27*

Of the other three consultant surgeons in this study, one usually took DNR decisions himself (confirmed by his junior staff), one stated that DNR decisions are 'almost always' discussed with him. The third said DNR decisions should be taken by the most senior doctor available and 'never' by a junior doctor – a policy that his junior doctor (D31) did not know.

> *Interviewer*: In the specific case of where the patient is designated not for resuscitation, who is usually involved in taking that decision?
> *Doctor*: Um, I usually do that myself.
> *Interviewer*: On your own authority?
> *Doctor*: Yes. *Junior doctor D31*

None of the seven junior doctors in this study had been briefed on DNR policy by their consultant:

> Yeah I mean it *is* a pretty woolly area. I'm not actually sure if there is any official guidelines or legal lines. I mean at [previous hospital] we were always told that it's certainly not a house officer's decision, it's something SHOs could do . . . Whereas *here* [pause] I think it's probably the same. *Junior doctor D30*

Of the seven junior doctors interviewed, four had written DNR orders on occasions without prior discussion with senior medical staff.

> Unless it's late at night or somebody who's obviously very poorly, I won't write it down unless I've discussed it with somebody who's a bit above me. Because I don't think we are actually legally allowed to write it on our own judgement as a house officer. But if it's late at night, then I will do it. *Junior doctor D32*

The reference to a DNR decision being taken 'late at night' by a junior doctor tends to support the interpretation that consideration of a patient's resuscitation status was sometimes overlooked by the surgical teams during their regular ward rounds. Another junior doctor gave a graphic example of the consequences:

When I did it [wrote a DNR order] I, you know, you can just see the impending crash five minutes away, and you know I just really didn't feel that I wanted it [CPR] to happen at all, you know. No-one did, and the nurses didn't, and the relatives weren't there, you know. Obviously the patient doesn't know. But I think a few *are* done like that. You see the patient's about to crash and you make the decision *then*, you know. Obviously in a way that's a doctor/nurse decision and the relatives *aren't* informed . . . When *I've* seen it done, usually it's left to the last minute . . . Things are often in the heat of the moment and the patient's died quite quickly afterwards I think, and relatives often aren't around. *Junior doctor D30*

These circumstances are not unique to this hospital; 'delay' in taking DNR decisions has been documented in audits of medical notes elsewhere (e.g. Skerritt and Pitt, 1997; Hayes et al., 1999).

Communicating DNR decisions

Doctors and nurses in other British hospitals commonly use verbal and written codes for 'do-not-resuscitate' decisions, for example: 'DNR', 'Not for 333 (or 222)', 'TLC only' (tender loving care) and 'Not for CPR' (Aarons and Beeching, 1991; Hayes et al., 1999). The truly cryptic 'blue-spotted' code enabled the nurses in this study to communicate a DNR decision to each other covertly, even in front of patients. The 1999 BMA/ RCN guidelines address the potential ambiguity inherent in coded instructions and propose that 'not for cardiopulmonary resuscitation' should be written in the patient's notes. Staff on the surgical wards reported that uncertainty about whether to commence resuscitation on a patient who suddenly arrests was, in at least some cases, due to inadequate recording of the DNR decision in the medical notes. The problem was particularly acute during the night and at weekends.

Well, the problem of course is that the people involved in the patient's care vary from day to day and from hour to hour and that's, I think, where you're picking up that problem, isn't it? Not with my team, who have been round and we have had a discussion about Mrs X's prospects and decided that, you know, we have made that decision. And then perhaps somebody hasn't written it in the notes and Saturday's rolled round and someone else's team is on and nobody can pin it down. *Consultant D27*

And I think we're pretty bad at doing that, actually, I think, um. It needs to be written in the notes and quite frequently it isn't. What usually happens is we see people who are ill and there's a sort of tacit agreement amongst all of us that 'she's not for resuss' type of thing. *Junior doctor D35*

Failure to communicate recent DNR decisions during staff handovers may also contribute to the uncertainty. Junior doctors had no formal mechanism for handing over decisions taken during the night or at weekends, but updated each other 'in passing' on the wards, in corridors or in the off-duty room. And on several occasions DNR decisions were not reported during nurse handovers witnessed in this study. Discrepancies between the actual DNR status of patients and nurses' knowledge of it have been documented in another hospital (Jones et al., 1993).

Seeking views from patients and relatives

In the acute surgical wards of the study hospital the patient's views on resuscitation were rarely sought, despite the BMA/RCN guidelines. One junior doctor and one consultant said that they generally initiate discussion with at least some patients, but they were exceptions. Of the other six junior doctors, three did not think that patients were ever consulted about DNR decisions and three had not come across it at this hospital. One consultant commented:

> I mean nobody actually goes to the patient and says 'If you have a sudden collapse would you like to be resuscitated?' *Consultant D27*

Eight out of 10 nurses said that DNR decisions were 'never' or 'rarely' discussed with the patient, whereas they thought that relatives were consulted 'always', 'usually' or 'sometimes'. However, the doctors gave conflicting views about the extent to which relatives were involved:

> I *do* like to talk to relatives, because *I* may have a perception . . . that it's probably better *not* to resuscitate [the patient] if they suffer a catastrophe, but the relative may have a very firm view about it in the opposite direction. *Consultant D24*

> It's properly discussed with the relatives too. So I mean that's the standing arrangement, but I agree it often happens in a rather vague sort of way. *Consultant D22*

> We don't tell the patient, we don't tell the relatives, we don't tell *anyone* unless they ask. *Junior doctor D34*

D34 had informed a relative of a DNR decision on just one occasion: a wife was so often with her terminally-ill husband that the junior doctor thought it likely she would be there when he died and should know that no attempt would be made to resuscitate him. The wife was so distressed at the news that the junior doctor sought guidance from the consultant.

> And the consultant said 'Well actually on the grounds of futility you wouldn't have to have discussed it with her. You just make that decision as a clinical decision. Because there was no point, he's so unwell, there is no point in trying to resuscitate him and so she needn't have been told' . . . I mean ideally you would discuss it with everyone, but it's quite good in a way having this futility grounds, to get this sort of excuse to wriggle out of having to discuss it with people, in a way. *Junior doctor D34*

Futility is one of the grounds for a DNR decision identified in the BMA/RCN guidelines, but it does not absolve doctors from discussing the decision with either patients or relatives. Several studies at other British hospitals have found that most doctors are very reluctant to discuss DNR decisions with patients and, to a lesser extent, relatives (Davies et al., 1993; Hill et al., 1994; Mello and Jenkinson, 1998; Hayes et al., 1999). But active avoidance of difficult conversations is not the only reason why DNR decisions are so rarely discussed with patients or relatives. As documented earlier, the decision making itself is sometimes left until the patient is close to death and the relatives may not be present. These circumstances are not unique to this hospital, but the underlying attitudes and emotional responses of medical and nursing staff have rarely been explored elsewhere.

An ethical dilemma

Several studies in Britain and the USA have shown substantial discrepancies between the resuscitation status of seriously ill and/or very elderly hospital inpatients and what the patients themselves say they would want to happen if they suffered a sudden arrest. A proportion (varying between 27 and 48 per cent) of patients who say that they do *not* wish to be resuscitated would in fact be given CPR because they do not have DNR orders written in their notes (Hill et al., 1994; Morgan et al., 1994; Hakim et al., 1996). The proportion wanting resuscitation falls if the details of advanced CPR techniques and the low probability of a successful outcome are explained (Liddle et al., 1994; Mead and Turnbull, 1995). Conversely, studies have shown that a proportion (varying between 28 and 73 per cent) of seriously ill patients, including some in hospices, *do* want to be resuscitated if they arrest, but would not be given CPR because they already have a DNR decision written in their notes without their knowledge (Liddle et al., 1994; Meystre et al., 1994; Morgan et al., 1994; Mead and Turnbull, 1995; Bruce-Jones et al., 1996; Hakim et al., 1996).

At first sight, the obvious response to these discrepancies is to advocate discussion about their resuscitation status with all competent patients who seem likely to suffer a cardiorespiratory arrest. Such discussions are required by law in many states in the USA before a DNR order can be written in a patient's notes, and in some states the decision to forego resuscitation requires the patient's signature (Koehler et al., 1999). However, a consequence of doctors' reluctance to conduct these mandatory, difficult conversations with seriously ill patients is that appropriate DNR decisions may be 'under-used' (Wenger et al., 1995; Mello and Jenkinson, 1998). Since CPR is the default position in the absence of a DNR decision, inappropriate and futile attempts at resuscitation will occur and the patient's dying moments will be invaded by the crash team.

Moreover, there is disagreement in the literature about whether patients are psychologically harmed by being 'forced' to discuss their resuscitation status. An influential American case series presented evidence that 'discussions of resuscitation procedures simply add to the agony of the dying process' (Schade and Muslin, 1989: 186). This assertion was challenged by studies showing that a majority of patients were in favour of their views on resuscitation being sought (Hill et al., 1994; Morgan et al., 1994), and few patients were apparently distressed by the discussion. However, a study in a British hospital (Sayers et al., 1997) found that patients who initially appeared calm during doctor-led discussion of their resuscitation status, had become seriously distressed about it two days later and a minority showed signs of psychological harm.

At the start of the new millennium, the debate about respect for the patient's autonomy may be shifting back onto old territory. Is it in the patients' best interests to be involved in decisions about whether to resuscitate them, or should doctors 'exercise their moral imagination' (Ardagh, 1999: 378) and take DNR decisions which reflect what they think the patient would want? In the context of the surgical ward study reported here, consultants also have to attend to 'basic housekeeping' by ensuring that the decision to 'blue-spot' a dying patient is taken by a senior experienced doctor soon enough to prevent a futile resuscitation attempt, and is unambiguously recorded in the medical notes, communicated clearly to other medical and nursing staff and regularly reviewed.

References

Aarons, E.J. and Beeching, N.J. (1991) 'Survey of "Do not resuscitate" orders in a district general hospital', *British Medical Journal*, 303: 1504–6.

Ardagh, M. (1999) 'Resurrecting autonomy during resuscitation – the concept of professional substituted judgement', *Journal of Medical Ethics*, 25: 375–8.

Bayliss, R.I.S. (1982) 'Thou shalt not strive officiously' (editorial), *British Medical Journal*, 285: 1373–5.

Birtwhistle, J. and Nielsen, A. (1998) 'Do not resuscitate: An ethical dilemma for the decision-maker', *British Journal of Nursing*, 7 (9): 543–9.

BMA/RCN (1999) *Decisions Relating to Cardiopulmonary Resuscitation*. A statement from the British Medical Association and the Royal College of Nursing, in association with the Resuscitation Council, UK, May 1999.

Bruce-Jones, P., Roberts, H., Bowker, L. and Cooney, V. (1996) 'Resuscitating the elderly: what do the patients want?', *Journal of Medical Ethics*, 22 (3): 154–9.

Chief Medical Officer (1991) 'Letter to all consultants on resuscitation policy', 20 December 1991, (PL/CMO(91)22). London: Department of Health.

Davey, B. (1993) 'The nurse's dilemma: truth-telling or big white lies?' in D. Dickenson and M. Johnson (eds), *Death, Dying & Bereavement*, 1st edn. London: Sage. pp. 116–23.

Davies, K.N., King, D. and Silas, J.H. (1993) 'Professional attitudes to cardiopulmonary resuscitation in departments of geriatric and general medicine', *Journal of the Royal College of Physicians of London*, 27 (2): 127–30.

Douglas, M. (1966) *Purity and Danger*. London: Routledge and Kegan Paul.

Doyal, L. and Wilsher, D. (1993) 'Withholding cardiopulmonary resuscitation: proposals for formal guidelines', *British Medical Journal*, 306: 1593–6.

Doyal, L. and Wilsher, D. (1994) 'Withholding and withdrawing life sustaining treatment in elderly people: towards formal guidelines', *British Medical Journal*, 308: 1689–92.

Florin, D. (1993) '"Do not resuscitate" orders: the need for a policy', *Journal of the Royal College of Physicians of London*, 27 (2): 135–8.

Hakim, R.B., Teno, J.M., Harrell, F.E., Knaus, W.A., Wenger, N., Phillips, R.S. et al. (1996) 'Factors associated with do-not-resuscitate orders: patients' preferences, prognoses, and physicians' judgements', *Annals of Internal Medicine*, 125 (4): 284–93.

Hayes, S., Henshaw, D., Rai, G.S. and Stewart, K. (1999) 'Audit of resuscitation decisions has little impact on clinical practice', *Journal of Royal College of Physicians of London*, 33 (4): 348–50.

Hayward, M. (1999) 'Cardiopulmonary resuscitation: are practitioners being realistic?' *British Journal of Nursing*, 8 (12): 810–14.

Health Service Commissioner (1990–91) 'Communications surrounding a decision not to resuscitate a patient, Case No. W.258/89 90', in *Third Report for Session 1990–91, Annual Report for 1990–91*, The House of Commons, paper 482, 28 June 1991, London. pp. 50–8.

Hilberman, M., Kutner, J., Parsons, D. and Murphy, D.J. (1997) 'Marginally effective medical care: ethical analysis of issues in cardiopulmonary resuscitation (CPR)', *Journal of Medical Ethics*, 23: 361–7.

Hill, M., MacQuillan, G., Forsyth, M. and Heath, D.A. (1994) 'Cardiopulmonary resuscitation: who makes the decision?', *British Medical Journal*, 308: 1677.

Jones, A., Peckett, W., Clark, E., Sharpe, C., Krimholtz, S., Russell, M. and Goodwin, T. (1993) 'Nurses' knowledge of the resuscitation status of patients and action in the event of a cardiorespiratory arrest', *British Medical Journal*, 306: 1577–8.

Koehler, S., Ramadan, R. and Salter, M. (1999) 'Do not resuscitate (DNR): Analysis of the DNR Act', *Journal of the Oklahoma State Medical Association*, 92 (7): 316–19.

Liddle, J., Gilleard, C. and Neil, A. (1994) 'The views of elderly patients and their relatives on cardiopulmonary resuscitation', *Journal of the Royal College of Physicians of London*, 28: 228–9.

Mead, G.E. and Turnbull, C.J. (1995) 'Cardiopulmonary resuscitation in the elderly: patients' and relatives' views', *Journal of Medical Ethics*, 21: 39–44.

Mello, M. and Jenkinson, C. (1998) 'Comparison of medical and nursing attitudes to resuscitation and patient autonomy between a British and an American teaching hospital', *Social Science & Medicine*, 46 (3): 415–24.

Meystre, C.J.N., Ahmedzai, S. and Burley, N.M.J. (1994) 'Terminally ill patients may want to live', *British Medical Journal*, 309: 409.

Morgan, R., King, D., Prajapati, C. and Rowe, J. (1994) 'Views of elderly patients and their relatives on cardiopulmonary resuscitation', *British Medical Journal*, 308: 1677–8.

Page, S. (1999) 'The power of resuscitation as a cultural event: its limitations as a biomedical practice'. Paper given to the 31st Annual Medical Sociology Conference, 24–26 September 1999, University of York.

Page, S. and Meerabeau, L. (1996) 'Nurses' accounts of cardiopulmonary resuscitation', *Journal of Advanced Nursing*, 24: 317–25.

RCN/BMA (1993) 'Cardiopulmonary resuscitation: A statement from the Royal College of Nursing and the British Medical Association', *Issues in Nursing and Health*, 20, March.

Sayers, G.M., Schofield, I. and Aziz, M. (1997) 'An analysis of CPR decision-making by elderly patients', *Journal of Medical Ethics*, 23 (4): 207–13.

Schade, S.G. and Muslin, H. (1989) 'Do not resuscitate decisions: discussions with patients', *Journal of Medical Ethics*, 15: 186–90.

Skerritt, U. and Pitt, B. (1997) '"Do not resuscitate": How? Why? and When?', *International Journal of Geriatric Psychiatry*, 12: 667–70.

Stewart, K. (1995) 'Discussing cardiopulmonary resuscitation with patients and relatives', *Postgraduate Medical Journal*, 71: 585–9.

Stewart, K., Abel, K. and Rai, G.S. (1990) 'Resuscitation decisions in a general hospital', *British Medical Journal*, 300: 785.

Tunstall-Pedoe, H., Bailey, L., Chamberlain, D.A., Marsden, A.K., Ward, M.E. and Zideman, D.A. (1992) 'Survey of 3765 cardiopulmonary resuscitations in British hospitals (the BRESUS study): methods and overall results', *British Medical Journal*, 304: 1347–51.

Wenger, N.S., Pearson, M.L., Desmond, K.A., Harrison, E.R., Rubenstein, L.V., Rogers, W.H. and Kahn, K.L. (1995) 'Epidemiology of do-not-resuscitate orders', *Archives of Internal Medicine*, 155: 2056–62.

Williams, R. (1993) The "do not resuscitate" decision: guidelines for policy in the adult', *Journal of the Royal College of Physicians*, 27: 139–40.

Yip, B. and Lenox, I.M. (1994) 'Nurses' and doctors' views may differ', *British Medical Journal*, 309: 408.

42

The main tradition

Fiona Randall and R.S. Downie

From the time of Hippocrates until the 1960s medical ethics was seen in terms of doctors' duties to patients. These duties have traditionally been thought of as those of not harming the patient (non-maleficence) and of helping the patient (beneficence). Underlying these two apparently simple types of duty there are, however, complexities. Medical understanding of these duties has been affected by three different currents of thinking. Let us examine these currents, which are discussed by Jonsen (1990).

The first current is the one flowing from the origins of modern medicine in the Greek world. When the Hippocratic Oath requires the physician not to harm but to help, it is against a background of Greek craftsmanship. The art or craft (*techne*) of the carpenter is to work on wood according to the nature of wood. There are bounds or limits concerning what is appropriate for each craft, and to go beyond these bounds is to be guilty of *hubris* or pride. Hence, when the Greek doctor promises not to harm and to do good to the patient what is intended is much the same requirement as that laid on the carpenter when, as a good craftsman, he tries not to damage his material, wood, but rather to bring out its nature as wood. We might term the Hippocratic ethic that of the competent craftsman. The relevant portion of the Hippocratic Oath really indicates that there are constraints on the skill or art of medicine; it does not truly involve beneficence in our modern sense.

But beneficence in our modern sense enters the scene via the Samaritan tradition in medicine. It is known that St Luke was a physician and there is some evidence that the good Samaritan was meant to be a physician – certainly he treats the man fallen by the wayside with an infundation of oil and wine, which was a remedy for wounds in Greek medicine. However that may be, the ideal of the good Samaritan who ministers to the sick despite inconvenience and danger to himself was one which enormously affected the tradition of medicine, and it gave us the ideal of beneficence in something like its modern form.

Yet not completely like its form in modern medicine, for another current also affected medical beneficence. Historians of medicine have debated the origins of this tradition, but it may have been in the religious orders which were founded to care for the sick and wounded during the Crusades. For

Extract from *Palliative Care Ethics: A Good Companion*, Oxford: Oxford University Press, 1996, pp. 3–9.

example, the Order of Knights Hospitallers was founded in the eleventh century to provide hostels for pilgrims to the Holy Land and to care for the sick, and later those wounded at the Crusades. The members of this Order were mainly of noble families and were dedicated to serve 'our lords, the sick' (a favourite phrase). This tradition continued in the religious orders, and it emerged in a different form in the eighteenth century when the status and education of doctors began once again to improve, and the image of the gentleman-physician began to reappear. The opening words of the influential book of medical ethics, written by the British physician Thomas Percival (1803), bear witness in elegant language to the ethic of *noblesse oblige*:

> Physicians and surgeons should minister to the sick, reflecting that the ease, health and lives of those committed to their charge depend on their skills, attention and fidelity. They should study, in their deportment, so to unite tenderness with steadiness, and condescension with authority, as to inspire the minds of their patients with gratitude, respect and confidence.

These words echo the sentiments of the Knights Hospitallers of the Crusades, and they were incorporated into the Code of Ethics of the American Medical Association and stood unchanged from 1847 to 1912; as Jonsen says (p. 66), 'their spirit lived long after that'.

To sum this up, we can say that all doctors would nowadays subscribe to the ethical idea that they have duties not to harm and to do good to their patients, but they may be unaware of the fact that the medical interpretation of these duties has been coloured by (at least) three traditions: the Hippocratic tradition of competent craftsmanship, the Samaritan tradition of helping one's neighbour in all circumstances, and the Knights' Hospitaller tradition of noble service.

This rich medical ethos, which we shall call 'the main tradition', remained largely undisturbed from the Greek world to the end of the 1950s. Since then, however, there have been at least three attacks on it, deriving from three different sets of ideas: the emergence of nursing as an independent profession and along with that the development of a team approach to health care; the rise of patients' rights movements; and the need for rationing following the growth of demand on medical services. These movements overlap in various ways, and all are particular manifestations of broader social changes.

Teams and the nursing profession

The demand for a team approach to health care has been greatly influenced by the rise of nursing to full professional status. Nurses are nowadays very intolerant of the traditional references of doctors to 'my' patients. They are increasingly demanding consultation before important decisions affecting patient care are taken. Hence we have one partial explanation of the

increasing use of teams making joint decisions. Other parts of the explanation – such as the increasingly technical complexity of the decisions which
therefore require a range of specialist opinion – do not concern us here. But
granted that nursing opinion is increasingly important in decisions we find
the beginnings of a new approach to health care which involves more group
decisions. The emergence of group decision making (and the extent of it
varies a great deal) is therefore a challenge to the older ideas of the doctors'
duties. Let us hope that if there can be broad discussion involving not only
different specialists but also different gender perspectives more balanced
decisions may result. Before leaving this topic, however, we should note
that group decision making involves group responsibility. If nursing wishes
as a profession to have equal claim to be heard with doctors then nurses
must be willing to be held responsible for their decisions.

Although the rise of other professional groups and the consequent challenge to (predominantly) male medical supremacy in decision making has
perhaps been psychologically disturbing to the medical profession, there is no
reason why it cannot be assimilated into the traditional approach to patient
care. Instead of thinking of the supremacy of medical duties to patients we
can think of team-based duties and hope that the decisions of a broadly
based team are more compassionate and less 'gung-ho' then they otherwise
might have been. But this is a development and humanizing of the great
tradition rather than an abandonment of it.

Patients' rights and autonomy

A more radical challenge to the tradition may be thought to come from the
appearance of the patients' rights movement. This movement is not uncon-
nected with the rise of nursing as a profession because many nurses see
themselves as what they call 'the patient's advocate', where what they are
advocating is that patients' rights should be observed. But the patients'
rights movement is influenced by many other considerations. One broad
influence has been the general democratization of society in the post-war
period. The public in general terms wish to be involved in decisions which
are going to affect them. This move to more openness, more consultation,
has affected medicine as much as other branches of society. More specifically, within medicine the rise of patients' rights movements was influenced by the exposure of abuses in medical research, when it emerged in the
1960s that in some cases informed consent was not being obtained for
dangerous research. The result was that, first in the US and then in the UK,
research ethics committees were established and this in turn influenced the
medical approach to the doctor–patient relationship.

The concept which has been adopted to encapsulate the idea of the rights
of patients is 'autonomy'. Codes of medical ethics and philosophical discussion from the 1970s increasingly added 'respect for the patient's autonomous decisions' to the duties of non-maleficence and beneficence. Around

the same period the concept of justice was brought into play. This sometimes seemed to mean treating individual patients justly, say by observing their rights, and sometimes that autonomous patients were all equally entitled to equal shares in the distribution of health care. For almost two decades discussions of medical ethics have been conducted in the US and the UK very largely in terms of the four principles of non-maleficence, beneficence, respect for autonomy and justice, and many influential textbooks have been written, and indeed are still being written, using them as the necessary and sufficient principles of humane discussion in medical ethics.

Before going on to 'examine the principle of respect for autonomy in more detail we should perhaps fill out slightly more of the philosophical position. The four principles can be seen, and were seen by the majority of writers, as first-order moral principles, to be used in reaching medical decisions when ethical questions were raised. It is a separate matter, and one for the moral philosopher, how these principles can be justified. Are they each an expression of a single underlying principle or are they each independently valid; and if so, what happens if they clash? These and many related matters are the concern of moral philosophy proper, and we do not intend to pursue them in this book. But it is worth noting, for the terms are often used in ethical debate, that those who think that there is a single underlying principle often identify that principle as the principle of utility – that actions are right if they maximize individual preferences, or in older terminology, if they bring about the greatest happiness of the greatest number. As opposed to the utilitarians, those who hold that the principles can each independently be seen to be valid have been called 'deontologists'. We shall not pursue the interesting debates which have clustered round these theories.

Returning to the principle of respect for the patient's autonomy we shall find that once we look beyond the slogan it is not clear what is meant by 'autonomy'. There are in fact at least two ways of interpreting it. One interpretation is compatible with what we call 'the main tradition' of medical ethics and is an enrichment of it, but the second is not compatible, and indeed it implies a radical change in the doctor–patient relationship.

The idea of 'autonomy', of persons as self-determining, self-governing beings, is first discussed with a proper understanding of what it means by Kant (1785). He assumes that people are essentially rational, although our desires may at times blind us. Decisions which are made as a result of dominant or blinding desires he called 'heteronomous'. They are not truly the desires of the self, for they are caused by the non-rational aspects of human nature.

The Kantian tradition of moral philosophy as it affected medical ethics was modified by the liberal tradition of J. S. Mill (1859). Briefly, Mill argues that we have a right to do whatever we want unless it can be shown that we are harming others. The key difference between Kant's approach to autonomy and Mill's lies in the respective emphases given to rationality and preferences. For Kant, a decision is autonomous if it is rational (whether it expresses our preferences or not). For Mill, an autonomous decision does express our preference, and it is less important whether the decision is rational. These traditions have merged and what has come out is autonomy as the expression of informed preferences or consent to whatever we do or is done to us by others.

This fused Kantian–Millean conception of autonomy, as preference or as informed consent, is one which can be absorbed by what we term the main tradition. No doubt the doctor–patient relationship always involved some sort of consultation and discussion, and we can read the more recent emphasis on autonomy, on obtaining informed consent for all medical decisions, as an extension of and an insistence on that process of consultation. It can be seen as an antidote to the paternalism which was the pathology of the doctor–patient relationship in the past, and as a way of modernizing the relationship, of modifying it in terms of the modern ethos of openness in human relationship. It is important to note, however, that autonomous choice or informed consent in this sense takes place within the context of a professional consultation, with the patient retaining the right of veto to unwanted treatment and the doctor retaining the right of veto to treatment professionally considered useless or harmful. But now let us look at the important difference when preference autonomy becomes consumer autonomy.

To set the scene consider a genuine situation of consumer autonomy. Suppose that a person goes into a shoe shop and asks for a pair of strong shoes for walking along country lanes. He tries on various pairs which do not appeal to him and then his eye lights on a pair of shiny patent leather shoes and he says he wants to buy them. A good salesperson will explain to him that they are not appropriate shoes for his purpose, but if he insists that these are the ones he wants the salesperson has no duty to refuse the sale having advised against it. The customer here is exercising consumer autonomy. Can this idea be carried over into the medical context? Many ethicists think that it can, and indeed the British Government is encouraging the idea of consumer autonomy in health care to the extent that patients are being exhorted to see themselves as customers. Let us look at the ethics literature on this.

Take the situation in which a patient, or relatives of the patient, request treatment which the doctor believes is useless or even harmful. In a study surveying the literature on this, Paris et al. (1993) note that doctors will almost always continue treatment if requested by patients or relatives even if they regard it as futile. They do this because they believe that patient autonomy carries with it the right to whatever treatment the patient requests. Moreover, this view is supported by many US ethicists. For example, Veatch and Spicer (1992) maintain that a physician is obliged to supply requested treatment even if the request 'deviates intolerably' from established standards or is in terms of the doctor's judgement 'grossly inappropriate'.

In discussion of this we should note, first, that Veatch and Spicer, and many other US ethicists who hold this view of patient autonomy, are surely mistaken if they think that it follows from any interpretation of the doctrine of autonomy that people should be given something simply on the grounds that they demand it.

Secondly, we must remember that the principle of respect for autonomy applies not only to the patient but to the doctor, and if in the doctor's professional opinion the requested treatment is 'grossly inappropriate' then the doctor has no duty to provide it; indeed he/she has a duty not to provide it. This position has in fact been supported in the UK by the Court of Appeal. In a case in which a physician had indicated that he would not concur with a family's request to give a dying patient venilatory treatment if that became necessary to sustain the patient's life, Lord Justice Donaldson stated that 'courts should not require a medical practitioner . . . to adopt a course of treatment which in the *bona fide* clinical judgement of the practitioner was contraindicated'. Lord Justice Balcome went further and wrote that he 'could conceive of no situation where it would be proper to order a doctor to treat a patient in a manner contrary to his or her clinical judgement'. In other words, the Court of Appeal is here supporting the professional autonomy of the doctor (Re J. 1992).

Thirdly, let us consider the change in ethos or culture which is leading to the consumer view of autonomy, and the implications of the change for the main tradition of the doctor–patient relationship. It will be remembered that in a true consumer situation the shoe salesperson, having advised me against buying shoes which are 'grossly inappropriate' for my purposes, has no duty to refuse the sale if I insist on buying them. What are the implications of importing these consumer assumptions into the doctor–patient relationship?

The most obvious implication is that medicine will cease to be a profession and will become a service industry. If that happens the ethics of medicine will completely change. Indeed, some might argue that the need for ethics of any kind will vanish because the discipline of the market will replace the need for ethics. But we prefer to say that traditional medical ethics (which have grown up to protect the vulnerable patient against exploitation) will be replaced by the ethics of consumerism. And this is indeed being encouraged by the British Government. Let us look briefly at the ethics of consumerism.

Consumer ethics tend to highlight the following concepts. Consumers must have *access* to the services or goods they require; they must have *choice* of the goods or services they require; and this will involve *competition* between suppliers and a fair balance in the market place between supplier and customer; consumers must have *adequate information* on the goods and services they require, and the information must be expressed in clear language; it must be possible for the customer to obtain *redress* in the event of poor services or goods; the products or services must be *safe and subject to regulation* to ensure safety.

A consumer ethic of this kind underlies the idea of the free market and it is certainly appropriate in some areas of life. The question is whether it is appropriate in health care. It has at least two important implications: health care becomes a commodity like any other in the market, and the carers make up a service industry. It is not possible in this short introduction to discuss the far-reaching implications of such a change in ethos or to evaluate it. We shall simply note in summary that one and the same concept of patient autonomy is open to two different interpretations – and in the case of the second interpretation gives rise to a radically different view of medical practice from the traditional one.

References

Jonsen, A.R. (1990) *The new medicine and the old ethics.* Harvard University Press, Cambridge, Mass.

Kant, I. (1785) *Fundamental principles of the metaphysics of ethics* (ed. H.J. Paton 1948). Hutchinson, London.

Mill, J.S. (1859) *On liberty* (ed. Mary Warnock 1962). Collins, London.

Paris, J.J., Shreiber, M.D., Statter, M., Arensman, R. and Seigler, M. (1993) Sounding board. *New England Journal of Medicine*, 329, no. 5, 354–7.

Percival, T. (1803) *Medical ethics.* (ed. Chauncey Leake 1976), p. 71. Krieger, New York.

Re J. (a minor), (1992) 4 *All England Reports*, 614, For discussion, see 'British judges cannot order doctors to treat'. *Hastings Centre Report* 1992, 22 (4), 3–4.

Veatch, R.M. and Spicer, C.M. (1992) Medically futile care, the role of the physician in setting limits. *American Journal of Law and Medicine*, 18, 15–36.

43

Right to die or duty to live?
The problem of euthanasia

William Grey

Of old, when folk were sick and sorely tried
The doctors gave them physic, and they died;
But here's a happier age, for now we know
Both how to make men sick and keep them so.

(Hilaire Belloc)

1. Introduction

The world's first legal euthanasia death occurred in the Australian city of Darwin on Sunday September 22 1996 when Bob Dent ended his life under the Northern Territory's short-lived Rights of the Terminally Ill Act 1995 (1). It is well known that euthanasia is openly practised in the Netherlands, even though the practice there remains technically in breach of the criminal law (2). The Northern Territory however was the first jurisdiction to boldly legislate where none had gone before.

Dent's death intensified argument about euthanasia in Australia, transforming the debate from a textbook discussion in social ethics into a vigorous and divisive social dispute. Dent's death undermined the view that a *de facto* acceptance of the practice of euthanasia as part of palliative care might provide an avenue for defusing the debate. This may have been a rash suggestion anyway, even though there is evidence that euthanasia is covertly practised in Australia on a scale even greater than its more widely reported occurrence in the Netherlands (3).

2. The classical arguments

The debate about the moral acceptability of the practice of euthanasia embodies a number of quintessentially philosophical elements (4). Several of the crucial concepts need to be articulated carefully to ensure that argument is not vitiated by vagueness and equivocation. Key terms which need careful delineation include 'death', the distinction between 'ordinary' and 'extraordinary' measures in medical treatment, and the distinction

From *Journal of Applied Philosophy*, 1999, 16(1): 19–31 (abridged).

between active and passive killing – the distinction between killing and allowing to die. This important elucidatory task has been ably and extensively addressed elsewhere and I have little to add to it here (5). I will however say something about the taxonomy of acts of dying which these categories help to delineate.

Related to this clarificatory task we must consider several distinct *prima facie* categories of 'persons' (using the term widely to include 'pre-persons' and 'post-persons') for which the practice of euthanasia has been considered or proposed. These include, first, individuals who have descended into a persistent vegetative state, perhaps through injury of pharmacological mishap, who can be sustained by medical technology. Karen Ann Quinlan was a well known exemplar of this category (6).

Secondly there are cases where persons have lapsed into a state of contented dementia, perhaps as a result of accident or the later stages of the 'long goodbye' of Alzheimer's disease. Such individuals may manifest little or no capacity for any significant personal interaction, let alone development or growth. Should someone in such a condition receive treatment for a life-threatening illness?

Suppose that such an individual had earlier, when their faculties were intact, executed a living will requesting that treatment in such circumstances be withheld. Should that earlier decision be decisive? It is certainly not taken as decisive by a large number of physicians. Ruth Fischbach, Assistant Professor of Social Medicine at Harvard Medical School, reported at a recent medical conference that 66 per cent of physicians interviewed felt that there was nothing wrong with overriding a patient's advance directive, even if that directive unambiguously stated the conditions for the withdrawal and withholding of medical treatment (7).

Thirdly there are problematic cases of defective newborns. Cases of anencephalous, or Down's syndrome infants with duodenal atresia (intestinal blockage), are textbook clinical examples which raise vexing problems about permissible treatment, and permissible neglect.

Fourthly and (for present purposes) finally there are cases where a life is one of agonising and unrelenting pain. This is perhaps the strongest category of claimants for the 'right to die' – a right which was eloquently claimed by Bob Dent in a letter to Members of Australian Federal Parliament which Dent dictated to his wife the day before his physician-assisted death (8).

3. Types of euthanasia

The taxonomy of euthanasia includes active and passive and voluntary, non-voluntary and involuntary. These can be depicted in a table [Table 1], including *prima facie* candidates for the different categories.

The non-voluntary and involuntary categories, set out in the two right-hand columns, are often conflated and this is an important source of

Table 1

	Voluntary	Non-voluntary	Involuntary
Passive	Patient refusal of medical treatment	Persistent vegetative state (Karen Quinlan)	Medical rationing (drugs or treatment; organ recipients)
Active	Patient request for termination (Bob Dent)	Persistent vegetative state	Unlawful killing (Nazi 'euthanasia' programme)

confusion and misconception (9). Because they raise significantly different issues it is important to distinguish them carefully. Non-voluntary cases include individuals who are incapable of indicating a preference, or who are not even capable of having preferences at all. The permissible treatment and permissible neglect of those in this category is different from that of those who have indicated a preference about their treatment, as is the case in respect of both the voluntary and involuntary categories.

There is widespread consensus about some of the categories. Passive voluntary euthanasia, the right to refuse treatment, is almost universally accepted. Active involuntary euthanasia, the infamous outcome of the so-called 'euthanasia' program of Nazi Germany, is unanimously condemned, and indeed has done much to raise alarm about permitting euthanasia in any form. One of the principal arguments marshalled by opponents is that sanctioning euthanasia in any of its forms will inexorably slide into an acceptance of acts in this inadmissible category.

The category which is most vigorously contested is active voluntary euthanasia, the category into which Bob Dent fell. What are the arguments for and against this?

4. Arguments for active euthanasia

(a) Autonomy

The strongest argument in favour of active voluntary euthanasia is based on respect for individual autonomy. The argument from autonomy is based on the claim that every person has the right to shape their own life through their choices – and that must include, certainly under the unfavourable circumstances of pain or disability and some would argue more widely, the right to choose the time and circumstances of their death (10). On this view it is a matter of basic human dignity to be given the right to decide about the circumstances of our own lives – and our deaths.

The principle of autonomy is an expression of the essentially Kantian idea that what is of paramount importance for my life is that it consists of my own choices, for good or ill. For Kant, notoriously, it is never permissible to treat persons as a means rather than as ends-in-themselves, even if this involves attempting to use them as a means to their own well-being. Treating someone as a means to their own well-being would involve the dubious paternalistic presumption that someone other than that person might know better than they in what this well-being might consist (11).

J.S. Mill was as resolute a defender as Kant of the right to determine one's own destiny autonomously, and to be free from heteronomous determination by others. This right is implicit in Mill's famous 'harm' principle:

> the only purpose for which power can be rightfully exercised over any member of a civilised community, against their will, is to prevent harm to others. His own good, either physical or moral, is not a sufficient warrant. (12)

> . . . Mankind are greater gainers by suffering each other to live as seems good to themselves than by compelling each to live as seems good to the rest. (13)

Taking autonomy (literally 'self-governance') seriously means acknowledging individual sovereignty over all purely self-regarding acts. Determining the circumstances of one's own death, according to this principle, should be allowed provided that it is a self-regarding act, and if so like other self-regarding acts it should be exempt from the interference of others. Mill, like Kant, thought that other people's taking control of one's life was an intolerable intrusion.

In the spirit of Kant and Mill, Bob Dent clearly regarded Kevin Andrews' (ultimately successful) proposal to limit the freedom of individuals to seek medical assistance to end their intolerable life as an insufferable impertinence. In his last letter, written to the Australian Members of Parliament who were then debating the fate of the Northern Territory's Rights of the Terminally Ill Act, Dent wrote:

> . . . I have no wish for further experimentation by the palliative care people in their efforts to control my pain. My current program involves taking 30 tablets a day! For months I have been on a roller-coaster of pain made worse by the unwanted side-effects of the drugs. Morphine causes constipation – laxatives work erratically. . . . Other drugs given to enhance the pain-relieving effects of the morphine have caused me to feel suicidal to the point that I would have blown my head off if I had had a gun. . . . If I were to keep a pet animal in the same condition I am in, I would be prosecuted. . . . What right has anyone, because of their own religious faith (to which I don't subscribe), to demand that I behave according to their rules until some omniscient doctor decides that I must have had enough and goes ahead and increases my morphine until I die? If you disagree with voluntary euthanasia, then don't use it, but don't deny me the right to use it if and when I want to. I am immensely grateful that I have had the opportunity to use the Rights of the Terminally Ill Act to ask my doctor, Philip Nitschke, to assist me to end this interminable suffering and to end my life in a dignified and compassionate manner. (14)

(b) Beneficence and fairness

There are at least three other important, and related, subsidiary arguments which are used to support a right to determine the circumstances of one's own death. First the golden rule 'do as you would be done by' requires that we provide aid to those in distress and in particular provide appropriate relief from suffering. In cases where palliation is ineffective, again illustrated in the case of Bob Dent, it would be unreasonable (many would say unconscionable) to deny anyone the right to make a dignified end to their suffering.

Secondly, a corollary of the harm principle is that the denial of a right to die is unfair and cruel; no one should be obliged to endure unbearable suffering. The unreasonableness of those who would deny someone's rational choice to end their suffering is a principal concern of Bob Dent's letter. Thirdly, the denial of a right to die amounts to imposing a 'duty to live' – no matter what the abject condition of that life might be. This imposition is presumptuous and intolerable.

5. Arguments against legalizing euthanasia

Not everyone opposed to the legalization of euthanasia is opposed to the practice of euthanasia: we must therefore distinguish arguments against the practice of euthanasia from arguments directed solely against the legalization of the practice. Those who oppose euthanasia in principle will of course oppose its legalization; but there are some who, while supporting euthanasia in principle, have misgivings about its institutionalization. Thus there are some who defend the right of people to choose the time and circumstances of their death but who find the requirement of satisfying a medical bureaucracy that their decision is sound both onerous and offensive. End-of-life decisions, on this view, should be a personal matter between patient and physician. Indeed one of the results of the survey of euthanasia in medical practice in Australia is that ending life by personal arrangement with one's physician is much more widespread than is commonly supposed (15). A significant number of physicians apparently are prepared to assist patients illegally to end their lives.

According to a survey of doctors' attitudes towards, and practice of, euthanasia in New South Wales and the Australian Capital Territory, approximately half the respondents had been asked by a patient to hasten their death, and approximately a third had assisted patients to end their lives (16). These figures were almost identical with the result of an earlier survey of doctors in Victoria (17). Medical practitioners who have included themselves in the substantial minority of doctors who have admitted to helping patients die sooner than they might have include Peter Baume, Professor of Community Medicine at the University of New South Wales and a former Federal Minister for Health, and the present (1997) Federal Minister for Health, Dr Michael Wooldridge.

However, there are problems about tolerating euthanasia as a covert clinical procedure to be allowed to operate outside the law. It is arguable that it is social hypocrisy to advocate in private something which is rejected as a matter of public policy. Moreover it is an unjust policy because its benefits are not equally accessible to all, but depend to a large extent on individual resources, or resourcefulness, or luck.

6. Arguments against the practice of euthanasia

Turning from arguments directed simply against the legalization of euthanasia to objections in principle to the practice of euthanasia, there are three lines of objection which predominate, together with several auxiliary arguments. The three main objections are first the so-called 'slippery slope' or 'wedge' argument, second the worry that the overt practice of euthanasia would change the culture of medicine, and third an objection based on a denial of the claim that a decision to end one's life is purely self-regarding.

The auxiliary arguments include the claim that palliation delivers adequate relief from indignity and pain, uncertainly arguments about the possibility of miraculous cures, the suggestion that people in the grip of a temporary physiological or psychological crisis may make an unwise and irrevocable choice to end their lives, the claim that all human life is sacred, and finally, an attempt to delineate which acts of killing are justified through the doctrine of 'double effect'.

I will discuss each of these in turn and then briefly discuss a claim about power which was raised during the controversy generated by the case of Bob Dent.

(a) Thin end of the wedge

The most commonly articulated worry is that if euthanasia is admitted for deserving cases, such as Dent's, then this will lead to the admission of less deserving or quite inappropriate cases. In time the principle will be progressively extended while the safeguards become diluted and weakened. Soon a policy motivated by compassion will become a vehicle for abuse and monstrous injustice. If we allow a case like that of Bob Dent, it is suggested, then we are on the slippery slope to Auschwitz and Buchenwald (18).

This alarmist rhetoric is unpersuasive. Any overt practice of euthanasia will attract the closest scrutiny and for this reason it is very difficult to imagine safeguards being eroded without vigorous public opposition. The wedge argument is in any case in general uncompelling, and it fares no better here than in its other applications. It is worth quoting F.M. Cornford's droll assessment of 'wedge' arguments in general:

> The Principle of the Wedge is that you should not act justly now for fear of raising expectations that you may act sill more justly in the future – expectations which you are afraid you will not have the courage to satisfy. A little reflection will make it evident that the Wedge argument implies the admission that the persons who use it cannot prove that the action is not just. If they could that

would be the sole and sufficient reason for not doing it, and this argument would be superfluous. (19)

The answer to wedge arguments, here as elsewhere, is not to forbid just practices, but to take careful steps to ensure that proper regulation is maintained so that standards are not eroded. In particular the line which most express fear about crossing is the line between voluntary and non-voluntary.

If it is true that abuses have occurred where the practice is allowed, as has been alleged of the Netherlands, this does not indicate the need for complete prohibition (20). An obvious alternative is to ensure that adequate safeguards are established to prevent abuses. In particular the aim of safe-guards is to ensure that the final responsibility for the decision and its execution rests squarely with the patient, not with the physician or with any other party. It would be crucial to ensure that regulations and safeguards were developed to guarantee that the line between voluntary and non-voluntary acts of euthanasia will not be transgressed. Considerable care was given to this important matter in developing the procedures approved in the Northern Territory.

(b) Culture of medicine

A second argument used by opponents of euthanasia is that it changes the culture of medicine. Instead of sustaining and nurturing life, medical prac-tice would come to include the deliberate killing of patients. Doctors it is said should be healers, not killers. One response to this is to point out first that compassionately-motivated killing has become a surprisingly common part of medical practice (21). What needs to be done is to turn an unregu-lated procedure, whose benefits are now capriciously distributed, into a pattern of practice which is both safe and just.

In an age of sophisticated life-sustaining technology some elements of the Hippocratic oath, such as the injunction to preserve life at all costs, have passed their use-by date (22). Contemporary medical circumstances demand that the physician's duty of care and beneficence is primary and sustaining life needs to be subordinated to this basic aim. It is no longer credible to regard the sustaining of life, regardless of its quality, as the primary and paramount concern of medical practice (23).

(c) Social limits of autonomy

One of the strongest objections to euthanasia is that the autonomy which it is our duty to respect is not enjoyed by everyone. Even if it is granted that respect for individual autonomy is of paramount importance, it nonetheless applies only to socially empowered individuals or groups within society. There may be serious problems with the application of this principle to marginalized groups and especially to individuals who are, or can be, exploited. Legalizing euthanasia, according to some, ignores the social reality of marginalized groups, and persons who might be exploited by unscrupulous relatives, or unscrupulous doctors. This is an essentially utilitarian argument drawing attention to grave social consequences of legalizing the practice.

A fundamental clash of intuitions arises here. On the one hand it is claimed by individualistically-inclined liberals that no one has a right to dictate to them a duty to live. Against this it is argued by those who reject this individualistic conception of society that liberal individualists have no right to damage the social fabric of society by making choices which might lead to the degradation of the value of life within the community. The difference between these fundamentally opposed intuitions hinges on the extent to which acts of self-destruction are purely self-regarding or whether they are significantly social or political in character. We can distinguish individual acts, which primarily affect the agent and which affect others only minimally, from social acts, which significantly affect, and possibly harm, others.

Mill's harm principle explicitly allows for restrictions on an individual's freedom to act in cases where their act harms others. Opponents of euthanasia can claim that individual acts of self-destruction, and the medical assistance for such acts, do in fact affect others and therefore are not purely self-regarding. They affect adversely the attitude of the community to the value of life and undermine the culture of medicine, to the detriment of all. Bob Dent's right to die diminishes the rights of others to live. Attitudes to life are degraded and disregard of its serious value is facilitated. Bob Dent's death, on this view, is not just Bob Dent's business, and we cannot appeal to Mill's principle to privilege his views of the matter.

The dispute about euthanasia on this point resembles another which arises in discussions of pornography and prostitution. Some women claim a right to make commercial use of their bodies as a matter of individual liberty. To this it has been replied that such choices do not affect them alone but help to shape community attitudes about how women are perceived. In allowing themselves to be viewed or used as sex objects, they are fostering degrading attitudes towards all women.

Whether pornography and prostitution involve choices which are purely self-regarding, and how to balance these competing views, are not matters to be addressed here. I want only to note the analogy and to point out its consequences: in particular that those who appeal to the claim that permitting the legalization of killing has adverse social consequences are in effect insisting that Bob Dent had a duty to live for the greater social good, no matter how wretched his circumstances (24).

(d) It is unnecessary: palliative care provides all the comfort needed

A subsidiary and supporting argument frequently used by opponents of euthanasia is the claim that the practice is unnecessary because the relief sought by patients can be adequately provided with palliative care. Perhaps in some cases the end-of-life quality can be improved by the skilful deployment of palliative care, but palliation is not effective in all cases – certainly as far as Bob Dent was concerned it was not good enough (25).

(e) Ignorance and uncertainty objections

Another objection to allowing euthanasia is that this irrevocable step should be avoided because a miraculous cure or spontaneous remission might reverse medical misfortune. Clearly this cannot happen for people who have chosen to end their lives prematurely. This suggestion is fairly unpersuasive when one examines real clinical cases like that of Dent. Nothing was more certain to Dent than the fact that his condition was very bad and would only get worse. He had a strong desire not to be remembered as a pain-wracked incontinent wreck. Dent, and the other three who died under the provisions of the Rights of the Terminally Ill Act, were all terminal cancer patients, and it is from this category that the majority of those seeking medically-assisted death could be expected to come.

(f) Sanctity of life

The final objection to euthanasia I mention is based on the claim that all human life is sacred. As a simple unqualified claim this is much too strong to be taken seriously. If it were accepted then it would provide a powerful objection to passive as well as active acts of euthanasia, and that consequence is widely rejected. It is usually taken for granted that there is no serious moral objection to declining further medical treatment. In general, arguments about sanctity and sacredness need further bolstering with more substantial moral argument.

The related suggestion that ending life is the prerogative of the deity is equally unhelpful precisely because divine prerogatives are conceived so disparately by different religious authorities. It is not helpful to be told that an action transgresses the prerogatives of the deity unless we know what these prerogatives are.

Larue, for example, has recorded an immense diversity of religious opinion both between and within Christian and non-Christian denominations concerning the acceptability of euthanasia or physician-assisted suicide (26). There is in general no unified Christian, Jewish or other denominational position on this issue. The major problem with the claims based on the 'sacredness' of life or of 'playing God' is the danger that they operate as rhetorical devices to obfuscate rather than to illuminate discussion (27).

(g) Double effect

Some opponents of euthanasia nevertheless allow that it is permissible to provide treatment to the terminally ill which hastens death. It is popularly,

though not unanimously, believed that aggressive doses of morphine short-
ens life in many cases (28). When a patient's condition becomes sufficiently
wretched it is permissible, on one view, for a doctor to end the misery with
a lethal overdose of a pain killer, but this must be administered with
the primary intention of alleviating pain – even though there is also the
foreseen but unintended consequence of killing the patient.

The principle behind this view is the doctrine of double effect which
draws a sharp moral line between what is intended and what is merely
foreseen but which is not intended (29). Those who apply the principle
usually have a robust confidence about its application. It is a confidence
however which is not universally shared. It rests in particular on a dubious
assumption that in analysing a complex act with multiple consequences
(such as death and the alleviation of pain) we can identify which of these
consequences are intended and which are not intended but merely foreseen.

But how are we to distinguish, in any given act with complex or multiple
consequences (relieving pain and killing a patient), what is intended from
what is not intended but nevertheless foreseen? While the doctrine of
double effect appears to provide a plausible reason for drawing a distinction in some cases there are many others where it delivers no unambiguous
or unproblematic answer. Philippa Foot has suggested that the morally
relevant distinction operating in cases in which the doctrine of double effect
appears to provide guidance is actually the quite different distinction
between negative duties not to harm others and the less stringent positive
duties to give others aid. One does not in general have the same duty to
help people as one does to refrain from injuring them (30).

The distinction between what is really intended and what is merely
foreseen, to which the doctrine of double effect appeals, was mercilessly
lampooned by Pascal in his dazzling attack on some disreputable uses of
casuistry (31). Pascal's attack on the methods of casuistry (moral reasoning
through the use of cases) as an instrument of moral reasoning is an intellectual *tour de force* of such magnitude that it has taken more than three
centuries for a serious attempt at its revival (32).

7. The issue of power

A significant point raised by Bob Dent's physician, Philip Nitschke, is that
a pivotal and underlying issue in the debate is the empowering of patients.
The Northern Territory legislation, according to Nitschke, embodied a shift
of power from the medical profession to the patient, and according to
Nitschke the medical profession does not welcome any such shift of power.
There is a clear insinuation in Dent's letter that physicians are prepared to
help their patients put an end to their misery – but the timing of the lethal
overdose is to remain squarely in medical hands (33).

There is evidence that unwillingness to give up power exercised over
patients is a widespread feature of medical practice. Earlier we noted

evidence from a recent medical conference of the propensity of physicians to disregard the advance directives of patients, indicating the reluctance of physicians to relinquish the power which they exercise over their patients. Another study which examined the views and experiences of physicians at a major Canadian teaching hospital regarding the use of advance directives in clinical care found that 40 per cent of the physicians questioned chose a level of care different from that requested in advance by patients who subsequently became incompetent. The physicians interviewed indicated that they would only follow a patient's advance directive if it was consistent with their own clinical judgment and indicated that they wanted to reserve the right to make clinical judgments about treatment regardless of a patient's request (34).

Nevertheless, sometimes it seems not so much a case of an autonomous doctor exercising sovereignty over the disempowered patient as a doctor being as much a victim of the social and cultural circumstances in which the medical treatment of the patient takes place. This appears to be the case for example in the relief reported by a specialist upon learning of objections of family members to futile surgery which he had proposed, because he felt that in the absence of such objection he was ethically bound to proceed (35).

This suggests that there may be cases in which physicians are acting against both their own wishes and against the wishes of patients and their families, because the parties are too reticent to express their preferences, and too prepared to submit to what they take to be conventional expectation. Perhaps such cases are instances of so-called 'defensive medicine' – the overzealous or excessive provision of medical treatment to preclude any possible (moral or legal) charge of negligence. Whatever the reason, the complex and still unresolved issues surrounding the euthanasia debate point once again to the paramount importance of the effective communication of patients' hopes, values and aspirations to the health professionals who provide their medical care (36). [. . .]

Notes

(1) The Northern Territory's Rights of the Terminally Ill Act 1995 was passed by the Northern Territory Legislative Assembly on March 25 1995. The bold social experiment was terminated two years later when a private member's bill, sponsored by Victorian Liberal backbench member of the House of Representatives Kevin Andrews, was passed by the Australian Federal Parliament. Under the Australian Constitution the Federal parliament is empowered to override the law of territories, but not states. Andrews' bill was approved by the House of Representatives on December 10 1996 and by the Senate on March 25 1997. Four people died under the provisions of the Rights of the Terminally Ill Act 1995 during the period of its enactment. As well as Bob Dent, Janet Mills died under its provisions on January 2 1997 and two unnamed persons died on January 20 and March 1 1997. They were all terminal cancer victims.

(2) In the Netherlands there is a high level of public support for euthanasia and the Dutch Parliament has indicated that providing doctors comply with certain guidelines they will not be

prosecuted; see G. van der Wal and R.J.M. Dillmann (1994) Euthanasia in the Netherlands, *British Medical Journal*, 308, pp. 1346–49.

(3) Helga Kuhse, Peter Singer et al. (1997) End-of-life decisions in Australian medical practice, *Medical Journal of Australia*, 166, pp. 191–6. Published on the internet by the *Medical Journal of Australia* <http://www.library.usyd.edu.au/MJA/

(4) A preliminary definition of euthanasia is: a deliberate act aimed at ending a person's life, or hastening their death, for that person's benefit. Passive euthanasia is withholding or withdrawing life-sustaining treatment. Active euthanasia involves a deliberate act to terminate life. Voluntary euthanasia is the termination of a life at the request of the patient concerned.

(5) See Thomas L. Beauchamp and J.F. Childress (1994) *Principles of Biomedical Ethics*, 4th edn (New York, Oxford University Press); Diane Collinson and Robert Campbell (1988) *Ending Lives* (Oxford, Basil Blackwell); Ronald Dworkin (1993) *Life's Dominion: An Argument about Abortion and Euthanasia* (London, Harper-Collins); Jonathan Glover (1987) *Causing Death and Saving Lives* (Hamondsworth, Penguin); James Rachels (1987) *The End of Life: Euthanasia and Morality* (Oxford, Oxford University Press); Peter Singer (1993) *Practical Ethics*, 2nd edn (Cambridge, Cambridge University Press).

(6) Quinlan became permanently comatose in April 1975 and died 10 years later on June 11 1985 at the age of 31.

(7) Mary D. Clement (1996) Care near the end of life. Report on conference sponsored by the Division of Medical Ethics, Harvard Medical School. Published on the internet <http://www.efn.org/~ergo/wfn27.3.html boston

(8) Bob Dent (1996) Why I wanted to die: Bob Dent's last words, *The Courier-Mail* (Brisbane, Friday, September 27), pp. 1, 6. Dent dictated this letter to his wife because he was by then too weak to write. [. . .]

(9) Since discussion understandably centres on active voluntary euthanasia (AVE) it might be thought to be tendentious to include the 'non-voluntary' and 'involuntary' categories in the taxonomy. In the Netherlands 'euthanasia' is narrowly construed as AVE and other cases of active termination of life would not be described as euthanasia at all. However the wider interpretation provides a way of depicting some of the principal objections to the practice, in particular the so-called 'slippery slope' objections to euthanasia.

(10) Dramatic cases of 'heroic' suicide – such as the sensational ritual suicide of the complex and tormented Japanese novelist Yukio Mishima on November 25 1970   provide a vivid expression of this view.

(11) For Kant, equally notoriously, this principle did not extend to acts of self-annihilation, seen by some as ultimate expressions of self-determination and by others, including Kant, as their denial. Whether Kant's well-known advocacy of individual autonomy can be reconciled with his opposition to suicide is a matter which I will not pursue here. The question of suicide is discussed in Immanuel Kant (1979 [1930]) *Lectures on Ethics*, 3rd edn (trans) L. Infield and J. Macmurray (London, Methuen), pp. 147–57.

(12) John Stuart Mill (1956 [1859] *On Liberty* (ed.) C.V. Shields (Indianapolis: Bobs-Merrill Co.), p. 13.

(13) Mill, op. cit., p. 17.

(14) Dent, op. cit.

(15) Kuhse et al., op. cit.

(16) Peter Baume and E. O'Malley (1994) Euthanasia: attitudes and practices of medical practitioners, *Medical Journal of Australia*, 161, pp. 137–44.

(17) Helga Kuhse and Peter Singer (1988) Doctors' practices and attitudes regarding voluntary euthanasia, *Medical Journal of Australia*, 148, pp. 623–27.

(18) For an excellent discussion of this strategy see Thomas Cavanaugh (1997) The *Nazi!* accusation and current US proposals, *Bioethics*, 11, pp. 291–7.

(19) F.M. Cornford (1953) *Microcosmographia Academica: Being a Guide for the Young Academic Politician*, 5th edn (Cambridge, Bowes and Bowes), p. 15. Cornford's presentation of the wedge argument is a little mischievous in that he points to its use to block further 'more deserving cases', whereas the objectors' worry of course concerns 'less deserving cases'.

However, Cornford's main point, viz. that the wedge argument is used to side-step the question of justice in the case immediately under consideration is perfectly fair.

(20) For an alarmist account of the erosion of standards of practice of euthanasia in the Netherlands see Rita Marker (1993) *Deadly Compassion: The Death of Ann Humphry and the Truth About Euthanasia* (New York, William Morrow and Company, Inc.).

(21) Kuhse et al. (1997).

(22) Other elements of the Hippocratic oath – such as the requirement to look after one's medical teachers and their families and not 'cutting for the stone' – have of course long since been abandoned.

(23) The costs of sustaining life are already enormous. Already 50 per cent of the health budget in Australia is spent on the last two years of life, and large teaching hospitals spend up to 70 per cent of their budgets on the last six months of life and up to 50 per cent on the last six weeks. I offer no opinion about whether this proportion of expenditure is or is not appropriate, but clearly it poses a case of diminishing returns on investment. Doubling the budget on intensive care would not result in any significant extension of lives of quality.

(24) Stephen Clark pointed out to me that it is not odd – or even unusual – for someone to be required to do something personally unpleasant for the common good. (Paying income tax according to some might fall in this category.) However, arguably there are limits on the level of sacrifice which can be reasonably required of individuals for the common good, and intuitively the requirements should not be too heroic. While it is not obvious that anyone 'owns' their own life (as Clark also pointed out) it is not clear either that anyone *else* should have an overriding say in determining its denouement.

(25) The ability of palliative care to provide adequate relief has been repeatedly challenged. Terminally ill Max Bell travelled to the Northern Territory several months before Bob Dent died, seeking a dignified medically assisted death. Bell had similar reservations to Dent about the efficacy of palliation: 'They fill you up with pills and give you morphine. Is that living? Would you say that was an alternative to having a nice long sleep? Of course it's not', Kerry O'Brien (1996) Interview with Philip Nitschke and Kevin Andrews; including contributions from Genevieve Hussey, Max Bell, Peter Wiese and Ted Collins, 7:30 Report (Australian Broadcasting Corporation TV, September 26). The three doctors' signatures Bell needed in order to comply with the Northern Territory law could not be procured and Bell had to return to his home in Broken Hill, in New South Wales, where he died 12 days later.

(26) Gerald A. Larue (1996) *Playing God: Fifty Religious' Views on Your Right to Die* (West Wakefield, R.I., Moyer Bell).

(27) William Grey (1998) Playing God, in Ruth Chadwick (ed.) *Encyclopedia of Applied Ethics* (San Diego, Academic Press), Vol. 3, pp. 525–30.

(28) Even large doses of morphine (or other opiods) are not however a reliable way of ending lives in an easy, comfortable, and controllable manner; see Michael Ashby (1987) The fallacies of death causation in palliative care, *Medical Journal of Australia*, 166, pp. 176–7.

(29) Such consequences are sometimes misleadingly said to be merely 'indirectly' intended.

(30) Philippa Foot (1967) The problem of abortion and the doctrine of double effect, in *Viruses and Vices* (Oxford, Blackwell, 1978), pp. 19–32. Judith Thompson has added to this the important proviso that in a number of important applications of this principle there must be parity among the claimants for a benefit or against a harm, see J.J. Thompson (1976) Killing, letting die, and the trolley problem, *The Monist*, 59, pp. 204–17.

(31) Blaise Pascal, *Provincial Letters*, see Peter Singer (ed.) (1994) *Ethics. Oxford Readings in Philosophy* (Oxford, Oxford University Press), pp. 265–70. Pascal witheringly exposes the device of 'directing' (or 'deflecting') intentions, used for example to provide spurious justification for duelling and killing by stealth.

(32) Albert R. Jonsen and Stephen Toulmin (1988) *The Abuse of Casuistry: a History of Moral Reasoning* (Berkeley, University of California Press).

(33) Dent was clearly indignant about what he perceived as this imbalance of power when he wrote: 'What right has anyone to demand that I behave according to their rules until some omniscient doctor decides that I have had enough and goes ahead and increases my morphine

until I die?' Dent believed that the timing of his death should not be determined solely by the clinical judgment of the physician.

(34) Clement, op. cit.

(35) Marie Coleman (1996) Right of choice in final exit, *The Canberra Times*, September 28, p. 10.

(36) I would like to thank Stephen Clark, Helen Grey, Roger Lamb, Mal Parker and Eric Shaw for suggestions and comments on an earlier draft of this paper.

44

Euthanasia and assisted suicide
seven reasons why they should not be legalized

Luke Gormally

1. The 'justification' of voluntary euthanasia involves rejection of a tenet fundamental to a just framework of laws in society

Voluntary euthanasia is the killing of a patient at his or her request in the belief that death would be a benefit to the patient and that the killing is for that reason justified. The mere fact that someone says, in an uncoerced fashion, that he or she wants to be killed does not in itself provide a doctor with a reason for thinking death would be a benefit to that patient. No doctor would accede to an apparently naked request to be killed, however seemingly uncoerced, if he thought the patient had prospects of a worthwhile life. A request to be killed appears to be a ground for euthanasiast killing only if the doctor believes that the patient does not have a worthwhile life.

Now, to say that the ongoing life of a person lacks value amounts to denying value or worth to that person, since the reality of a person is not something distinct from his or her ongoing life. What underpins euthanasiast killing are judgements on the overall worth of certain human lives.

It would be contrary to any legal system which purports to protect and enforce a just social order to legalize killing which rests for its justification on the belief that certain lives lack worth. Why? Because justice in society itself requires a non-arbitrary and non-discriminatory way of identifying who are the subjects of justice. But the only way of avoiding arbitrariness in identifying the subjects of justice is to assume that all human beings, simply in virtue of being human, are entitled to be treated justly and are the subjects of certain basic human rights. In other words the basic human dignity and worth which are recognized in respecting human rights must be seen as attaching to our humanity. Basic dignity and worth would not, however, be a title to just treatment if human beings were thought capable of losing them. They are, so to speak, ineliminable features of our humanity.

Euthanasiast killing, even when it is voluntary, involves denial of the ongoing worth of the lives of those reckoned to be candidates for euthanasia.

This article is an edited version of a submission made in 1997 by Luke Gormally to the Senate Legal and Constitutional Legislation Committee prior to the senate vote which overturned the Rights of the Terminally Ill Act. This Act had permitted euthanasia in Australia's Northern Territory.

It is a type of killing, therefore, which cannot be accommodated in a legal system for which belief in the worth and dignity of every human being is foundational.

It is of critical importance to every state to maintain a body of laws *consistent with* respect for the dignity and worth of every human being. In particular, it is important not to legalize killing of the innocent. For it is the fundamental task of civil authority to protect the innocent. But if the claim that a person lacks a worthwhile life is held to make killing lawful, then the state has ceased to recognize the innocent as having binding claims to protection. If the state treats these claims as null, then what claim has it to that authority which derives precisely from the need of citizens for protection from unjust attack?

2. To legalize assistance in suicide is also inconsistent with the same fundamental tenet of a just legal system

The decriminalization of suicide (and attempted suicide, therefore) makes sense if we contemplate the plight of people having to face criminal proceedings after failed suicide attempts. Decriminalization motivated by the desire to ease the plight of such people does not, however, imply that the law takes a neutral view of the choice to carry out suicide. Those who attempt suicide are clearly moved by the (at least transient) belief that their lives are no longer worthwhile. Since just legal arrangements rest on a belief in the ineliminable worth of every human life, the law must reject the reasonableness of a choice which is so motivated.

Hence the law must also refuse to accommodate the behaviour of those who effectively endorse the choice of the suicide: for they too are acting on the view that the person they are helping no longer has a worthwhile life. Their behaviour would not be sufficiently explained if one were to say that they were acting 'out of friendship' or 'out of compassion'. For how could the motives of the person assisting in suicide be described as 'friendship' or 'compassion' if they were not informed by the thought that the person intending to kill himself would be better off dead? If one thought this person could continue to have a worthwhile life it would hardly be an act of friendship, for example, to help him kill himself.

So there is reason to resist the legalization of assisted suicide as fundamental as the first reason given for resisting the legalization of euthanasia.

3. If voluntary euthanasia is legalized then the most compelling reason for opposing the legalization of non-voluntary euthanasia has been abandoned

Many of those who support the legalization of voluntary euthanasia are opposed to the legalization of non-voluntary euthanasia. But if we cannot make sense of the claim that euthanasia is a benefit to the person to be killed without relying on the thought that that person no longer has a worthwhile life, then supporters of voluntary euthanasia are buying into a larger package-deal than they perhaps realize. For if one can be benefited by being killed, is it reasonable to deprive people of that benefit simply because they are incapable of asking to be killed? And if we are puzzled (rightly) by the claim that someone might be benefited by having his life ended, we might nonetheless accept the claim that a person cannot be harmed by having his worthless life ended.

In fact the most active and clear-sighted advocates of the legalization of voluntary euthanasia are also advocates of the legalization of non-voluntary euthanasia. They promote the view that many human beings lack the 'moral standing' (what is here called 'basic dignity') in virtue of which they enjoy basic human rights; so they cannot be wronged even if the motive for killing them is merely the convenience of those human beings who do have 'moral standing'. The whole exercise of drawing a line between human beings who do and those who do not possess 'moral standing' is utterly arbitrary.

4. Legalization of voluntary euthanasia would also encourage the practice of non-voluntary euthanasia without benefit of legalization

This would happen in two ways:

- firstly, it has proved to be the case that those who begin by saying they wish to confine the practice of euthanasia to *voluntary* euthanasia come to think that, if *that* is allowed, no good reason remains for disallowing non-voluntary euthanasia, so they begin to plan for the systematic practice of non-voluntary euthanasia. This phenomenon can be seen, for example, in the behaviour of The Royal Dutch Medical Association over the past 15 years. Having worked for the acceptance of what purported to be the 'strictly controlled' practice of voluntary euthanasia only, they are now working for the acceptance of the practice of non-voluntary euthanasia.
- secondly, because the criteria for delimiting the practice of euthanasia to killing at the request of the patient prove to be *irremediably imprecise*. The Dutch experience has demonstrated the truth of what critics said about any legal accommodation of voluntary euthanasia (whether by statute law or by judicial decision), namely, that it would lead to the extensive practice of non-voluntary euthanasia. The available data show, on a conservative estimate, that about 1 in 12 deaths in Holland in 1990 were euthanasia deaths (10,558 cases) and more than half of these were without explicit request.

5. Euthanasia undermines the dispositions we require in doctors and is therefore destructive of the practice of medicine

The practice of medicine cannot flourish unless doctors are so disposed that they inspire trust in patients many of whom are extremely vulnerable. Doctors will not inspire trust unless patients are confident that doctors

- are for *no* reasons disposed to kill them;
- have no inclination to ask whether a patient is worth caring for or treating, rather than asking what care or treatment might benefit the patient.

But the practice of euthanasia systematically undermines both of the required dispositions. For it disposes doctors to kill certain of their patients, and it inculcates a disposition to think of some patients as not having worthwhile lives. Since there are no non-arbitrary criteria for determining who has and who has not a worthwhile life, the temptation to categorize the difficult and the unappealing as not having worthwhile lives is very strong for the person who has failed to eschew such discriminatory thinking as a matter of principle.

It is an important part of the duty of the state to maintain a framework of law which is conducive to an essential profession such as medicine functioning well in the interests of citizens. The state would fail in that duty were the law to permit behaviour on the part of doctors which was corrosive of the doctor-patient relationship.

6. The legalization of euthanasia undermines the impetus to develop truly compassionate approaches to the care of the suffering and the dying

The proper expression of compassion is care motivated by a more or less strong sense of sympathy with the affliction of the person suffering. But one cannot care for people by killing them.

It is very important to bear in mind that a key element in the context of contemporary debates about legalizing euthanasia is the drive to reduce health care costs. One of the conspicuous dangers of legalization is that, before long, euthanasia would be seen as a convenient 'solution' to the heavy demands on care made by certain types of patient. Medicine would thereby be robbed of the incentive to find genuinely compassionate solutions to the difficulties presented by such patients. The kind of humane impulses which have sustained the development of hospice medicine and care would be undermined because too many would think euthanasia a cheaper and less personally demanding solution.

7. Three Committees established by English-speaking legislatures to consider proposals to legalize euthanasia have recommended that it not be legalized

The years 1994–95 saw the publication of Reports of Committees established by the House of Lords of the UK Parliament, by the New York State Task Force on Life and the Law, and by the Senate of the Canadian Parliament. All these Committees were composed of people with different views on the intrinsic morality of euthanasia, yet they were clear in opposing its legalization. For example, the House of Lords' Select Committee had among its members many who were on record as advocates of euthanasia. And yet after a year of hearing and reading an extensive body of evidence and debating the issues among themselves, they decided *unanimously* to recommend that euthanasia should not be legalized.

There is much in all three Reports that is worthy of the attention of the Legal and Constitutional Legislation Committee of the Senate of the Australian Federal Parliament. Let the following quotation from the House of Lords' Select Committee Report stand as the epitome of the collective wisdom of these Committees:

> [S]ociety's prohibition of intentional killing . . . is the cornerstone of law and social relationships. It protects each of us impartially, embodying the belief that all are equal. We do not wish that protection to be diminished and we therefore recommend that there should be no change in the law to permit euthanasia. . . . The death of a person affects the lives of others, often in ways and to an extent which cannot be foreseen. We believe that the issue of euthanasia is one in which the interest of the individual cannot be separated from the interest of society as a whole.

It is the hope of the present writer that the members of the Legal and Constitutional Legislation Committee will, after due consideration, associate themselves with the moral and political wisdom exhibited in this statement.

45

A student's story

Anonymous

During my third year of training in a large city training hospital, I elected to do the obstetric module. I was placed on the special care baby unit (SCBU) for a period of about four weeks. On my second or third day on the unit, I was on a 'late shift', i.e. 12.25 p.m.–9 p.m.

During the day a very premature baby, estimated to be about twenty-eight weeks' gestation, was brought to the unit from the labour ward.

He was extremely tiny, I had never seen such a small baby before. There were three or four other babies nursed in cots on the unit and only this tiny premature baby was in an incubator.

During the afternoon I gradually became aware that I would be the only nurse on duty between 5 p.m. and 9 p.m. that evening. I was naturally terrified at the prospect of being left alone with this tiny baby and refused to tube feed him.

He was having hourly tube feeds of minute quantities.

It was arranged that the sister from the antenatal ward next door would come and feed him at 6 p.m. I was to continue his routine observations of respiratory rate, apex beat, etc. I had never measured a baby's apex beat before, but I was instructed during the afternoon how to do this.

Needless to say I hovered above the incubator watching him constantly and doing his observations far more frequently than instructed.

Six o'clock eventually came, but there was no sign of the sister who was to tube feed him. The minutes ticked by endlessly and by 6.10 p.m. I went to the antenatal ward to remind her. She assured me she hadn't forgotten and would be along in a minute, she still hadn't appeared at 6.15 p.m.

The baby appeared to change colour slightly and I felt he didn't look well. I took his apex beat and it had fallen quite dramatically. I was really frightened now, so I ran to get the sister.

She came in promptly, laughed at me saying he looked fine, but he certainly didn't to me. I asked her to check his heart rate, which she did very briefly and said it was quite normal and she promptly left without feeding him.

From G. Fairbairn and D. Mead, 'Ethics and the loss of innocence', *Paediatric Nursing*, June 1990: 22–3. This extract is taken from an article discussing ethical dilemmas in nursing and the ways in which the effects such dilemmas have on nurses can be viewed as being akin to bereavement. It was written during a workshop on ethics. The authors of the article express their gratitude to the nurse who shared this experience with them.

I was now terrified. He looked ghastly to me, so I did his observations again. His apex beat was now down to 60. I knew I was right, but I obviously couldn't get her back again, so I just ran into the corridor, grabbed a doctor and dragged her into the unit to look at the baby.

She immediately demanded resuscitation equipment. I hadn't a clue where it was kept. I frantically started searching cupboards, she was shouting, I was terrified. The baby died before I could find anything.

I reported the death to the senior sister on the labour ward and was instructed to prepare the baby for the mortuary.

Nobody came to see me or to help me, so I did what I thought was right. I found a little nightdress that appeared to be a shroud and I washed him and dressed him in the shroud and reported to the sister that he was ready to be checked before going to the mortuary.

When she came to the unit and found that I had neither weighed him nor checked his head circumference, she really laid into me.

I had no idea that preparing a baby would be different from an adult. She handled the baby quite roughly, removing his nightdress, weighing and measuring him, I found her actions very disturbing, and she really upset me. I was made to feel worse than useless.

I already felt the baby had died because of my actions. If I had known where the resuscitation equipment was kept he may have lived.

Perhaps I did his observations too often, and caused him to be cold. I felt responsible for his death for years.

This all happened sixteen years ago but I can remember it as if it happened yesterday. One thing that strikes me particularly about it all, is that even now when I remember and think about it, I can smell the unit. It had a very distinctive sort of smell about it.

46

Betting your life
an argument against certain advance directives

Christopher James Ryan

A long tome ago, in a country far far away, there lived a very wise old king. The king was a very ethical man and his subjects were very happy. Everyone lived together in perfect harmony and times were generally regarded as good.

One day the king introduced a new law. The law allowed his subjects to enter into a mysterious wager. Those who won the wager would receive a rich reward, but those who lost would be put to death. Entry into the wager was entirely voluntary and despite the dire consequences of losing many took up the challenge. To win, a contestant had only correctly to answer an apparently straightforward question. The question was known to all participants before they entered and all who took up the challenge were sure that they knew the answer and could not lose. Strangely, even the king's ethicists had no objection to the introduction of the law and in fact praised the king for his wisdom and progressiveness. The ethicists also believed that the answer to the question was obvious and focused only on the rich reward.

Unfortunately, however, many contestants got the answer wrong. They lost the wager and were put to an early and needless death. The question, that caused so much difficulty, was this: 'Even though you are now well and healthy, imagine yourself in a situation where you have a terminal illness and are temporarily confused or unconscious. Imagine that whilst you are in this state your doctors give you a choice; either they will treat you to the best of their ability and you may recover some of your health for some undefined period, or they will treat you conservatively and, though they will ensure that you are in no pain, they will not attempt to save your life. If you were in this situation what would you want the doctors to do?'

Advance directives or living wills frequently require their users to undertake the kind of task set out above; that is, to imagine themselves in a situation where they are required to make a decision about whether or not they should receive active treatment but are incompetent to do so. These have become increasingly popular over the last decade. Legislation giving statutory status to these directives has been enacted in many parts of the

Western world and planned in many others. In places where no such legislation exists living wills are thought to have increasing weight in common law.[1-3]

In this paper I oppose a common form of advance directive on ethical grounds. The basis of my argument is my contention that, like the citizens of the country above, many people who take out advance directives do so under the belief that they know the answer to the question above, when in fact they do not. In order to support my position I will first provide evidence which supports this contention and then demonstrate the ethical difficulties this creates for advocates of living wills.

I do not intent to provide opposition to all forms of advance directives, but will restrict my discussion to a fairly narrow but not uncommon set of criteria. I will examine only cases where an advance directive demands that the user receive only conservative or palliative care in a situation where he or she is incompetent to consent to such treatment but where that incompetence is potentially reversible.

Getting the answer wrong

My argument hinges on the notion that people are likely grossly to underestimate their desire to have medical intervention should they become ill; I will therefore explain why this is likely to be so on theoretical grounds and then provide some empirical evidence that suggests that this actually occurs.

Denial is a strong and largely successful mechanism for dealing with the stressors of everyday life. For the healthy person considering a terminal illness it involves the subconscious decision to reject the possibility that one will suffer in the way one might be expected to if one were to succumb to such an illness. There are two standard ways of going about this. The first is simply to tell yourself that terminal illnesses are things that happen to other people and that they will not happen to you. This method works reasonably well whilst one is still young and all, or most, of the people that get such illnesses are not like you at all. It starts to lose its power, however, as you grow older and terminal illnesses begin to befall your peers. Now the other people begin to look a lot like you and the only-happens-to-others strategy looks increasingly anaemic.

The second option is to use denial in a slightly more complicated manner and when confronted by the suffering of another in the midst of a terminal illness to say that this would not happen to you because, if you were in that situation, you would kill yourself before the suffering became too great. Here you have traded the real and very distressing possibility that you may develop, and suffer at the hands of, a terminal illness for the hypothetical notion of a future early death. As a hypothetical abstract your early death is unpleasant but much more bearable than the realization that you could become so ill.

Of course once you have developed a terminal illness, this coping strategy will no longer be successful. Now the possibility of your death is no longer hypothetical and you are faced with balancing real dying with the possibility of real suffering. While there is no doubt that some individuals now decide that they would still be better off dead, I believe that the vast majority of people now decide to battle it out. Most people with terminal illnesses do not want to die and are prepared to put up with a certain amount of suffering in order to live a little longer. Now that death is no longer a hypothetical it holds little appeal and frequently denial is used again, this time to maintain hope that a cure will be found.[4]

Human beings are, I suggest, very poor at determining their attitudes to treatment for some hypothetical future terminal illness and very frequently grossly underestimate their future desire to go on living.

Though based on psychological theorizing, there is some evidence to support this contention. The first piece of evidence is admittedly anecdotal but none the less quite powerful. Healthy people frequently believe that if they were suffering a terminal illness and required various forms of medical intervention they would rather be allowed to slip away. This view is so common among healthy people that it can be regarded as perfectly normal. Among terminally ill people, however, the sustained expression of a preference not to receive treatment is very rare. Most palliative care specialists will readily recall one or two patients who persistently requested that they be allowed to die. Some will recall several. However, palliative care physicians do not report that this sustained desire is very common and certainly do not report that it is the norm. This strongly suggests that many people who, when healthy, predict they would refuse treatment in the future, will change their mind when they develop a terminal illness.

This anecdotal evidence is supported by a number of studies in the psychiatric literature. One such study by Owen et al. found that among patients with cancer the strongest interest in euthanasia was among those patients being offered potentially curative treatment. Patients with poorer prognoses, who were only being offered palliative care, tended to reject the idea of euthanasia as a future option ($p < 0.05$).[5] Similarly, a 1994 study by Danis et al., which examined the stability of future treatment preferences, found that while preferences for most remained stable over the study's two-year duration, people that had been hospitalized, had an accident or had become immobile were likely to change their health care preferences to opt for more intervention.[6] Both studies suggest that having had an episode of serious illness or a deterioration of an existing illness may make people more likely to want more intervention.

Seale and Addington-Hall asked relatives and friends of people who had died whether the dead person would have benefited from an earlier death. They found that respondents, who were not spouses, were frequently willing to say that an earlier death would have been better for the person even though the person who had died had not expressed a desire to die sooner. That is, the healthy relatives and friends were keener on euthanasia than the terminally ill patient had been. This again suggests that healthy people may view euthanasia differently from terminally ill people or at least that it is hard to empathize with the position of the terminally ill.[7]

Though it is not possible directly to equate suicide with a desire for euthanasia, one might expect that if terminally ill people increasingly wanted to die as they became sicker and sicker then suicide among patients with terminal illness would peak towards the end of their illnesses. This would be the time when pain and suffering was at its worst and when there was little to look forward to. In fact, however, completed suicide is most common in the first year after diagnosis in the terminally ill.[8] It may be that in this situation suicide more often represents an irrational reaction to the crisis of diagnosis than a reasoned decision that life has become intolerable.

Further evidence that a desire for euthanasia is uncommon in the terminally ill comes from a study by Brown and co-workers who found that among 44 terminally ill patients, the only patients who had experienced a desire for an early death were those who were suffering from a clinical depressive illness.[9]

Arguments in support of advance directives

Advocates of this form of advance directive argue for the documents along two lines. Firstly, they take a deontological position that the directives maximize the affected person's autonomy by allowing her some control over her medical management. They argue that since maximization of autonomy is a legitimate aim and since living wills seem to facilitate the maximization of autonomy, then living wills are not only ethically justified but beneficial.[10–12] Second, advocates may take a utilitarian line and argue that the directives help to facilitate the death of people who believe they would be better off dead than alive. By facilitating these deaths the directives not only end people's suffering, but spare them an undignified death. In addition the directive may ease the burden on medical staff and family of the ill individual who may find making these decisions painful. Through all these means, they argue, the directive increases the net utility of the community.[10]

Opponents of this form of advance directive usually base their opposition upon an opposition to euthanasia.[13] However, since most living will legislation throughout the world facilitates only passive euthanasia and since passive euthanasia is rarely objected to, there has been little solid opposition to this form of advance directive legislation.

My objections to these advance directives do not rely on an objection to either active or passive euthanasia. Rather my objections are based on the proposition that these living wills do not necessarily increase the user's autonomy nor society's net utility in the unproblematic way they are imagined to do, because people are much more likely to refuse treatment when faced with a future hypothetical scenario then when faced with a real here and now choice. If this contention is accepted it has a number of consequences for arguments used in support of living wills.

Consequences for the argument from autonomy

The principle of a right to autonomy holds that adult human beings have the right to make decisions about their lives and so direct the course of their own fate. The right to autonomy is a powerful maxim. It is the right to autonomy that underlies the notions of consent, the right to freedom and democracy itself. By grounding their support for directives in this principle proponents of living wills set up a strong case.

It is an accepted part of the principle, however, that one cannot properly exercise one's autonomy if one is not in possession of all available information that might influence one's decisions. A patient's consent to a procedure, for example, is only valid if she has been informed of all the risks and consequences. If the psychological reasoning and empirical evidence above is accepted, then a person currently using a living will does not have access to a vital piece of information that may radically alter her decision. Specifically, she does not know that it is highly likely that her decision, made now, that she would rather die if faced with a hypothetical future scenario is not what her decision would have been if she were actually faced with that scenario.

Almost everyone assumes that he knows his own mind and that he would know the choices he would make in the event of a crisis. While there is little doubt that the individual alone is in the best position to know how he would act and it is also true that some people must correctly guess how they would act, nevertheless evidence strongly suggests that many people simply get it wrong. They believe they would not opt for treatment in a hypothetical future circumstance but were they actually to face the circumstance they would opt for treatment. Most people have no experience of their reactions to a life-threatening illness, they can only guess at their reaction and they frequently guess wrong. More importantly for my argument, people do not believe in, or even know of the possibility of, an inaccurate guess. If users of advance directives do not know of the distinct possibility that their choices may be inaccurate, they lack a vital piece of information and that lack prohibits a fully informed and autonomous choice.

Consequences for the utilitarian argument

The possibility that a large number of people are dying when they would not have wanted to because of the introduction of advance directives, directly threatens the utilitarian argument offered in support of these directives.

The utilitarian argument draws its strength from the hope that the existence of advance directives will end the suffering of people with terminal illnesses who have decided that they would be better off dead. It is assumed that they have come to this opinion by weighing up the benefits of their continued existence with the pain and suffering of their terminal illness. There is an additional hidden assumption that the affected individuals can accurately estimate this balance from the safety of health and happiness prior to their illness. If this additional assumption is unjustified then the utilitarian argument is undermined.

Conclusions regarding living wills

With the argument from autonomy and the utilitarian argument both undermined, ethical support for living wills of this sort is seriously diminished. The effect this diminution will have upon one's attitudes to living wills will depend on both the seriousness with which one takes the evidence for the inaccuracy of people's choices and one's beliefs about how well this inaccuracy can be addressed through changes to legislation and education.

At a minimum one should require significant changes in legislation to address users' ignorance of their likelihood of wrong decisions. The principle of autonomy demands that the individual making the choice be given all available relevant information, therefore those making living wills must be informed of the apparent likelihood that their decision to refuse treatment now may not accurately reflect the decision they would make in the future, were they competent at the time. To my knowledge, no piece of living will legislation currently refers to this likelihood. Though there are numerous published advance directive forms and more publications to assist in filling them in, none of them inform the potential user of the likely inaccuracy of their current decision.[10][11][14][15]

While such a change may satisfy strong advocates of advance directives that autonomy is now again maximized, I would remain dubious that this were the case. The logistics of giving such warnings to all people filling in living wills will necessarily mean that the warnings will be scant and superficial. The belief that one knows one's own mind now and in the future is understandably held with some vehemence by most of the community. The psychological needs met by the belief that one would rather be dead in a future tragic situation are strong and deeply ingrained. An insignificant warning is unlikely to have any impact upon this belief and many people will continue falsely to believe they definitely know what they would want in the hypothetical scenario.

This kind of reasoning leads me to believe that it will be practically impossible to allow people to make an autonomous choice about this kind of advance directive and therefore on the grounds that such directives will neither increase autonomy nor increase the community's level of utility I believe that this type of living will should be abolished.

It is important to note that this line of argument will not demand the abandonment of all varieties of advance directive. It will not, for example, apply to advance directives where the ability to consent to treatment is irreversibly lost. In this situation there will be no possibility of the person recovering to give carers a more accurate report of her current desire for treatment. Carers would then be justified in taking their best guess as to the affected individual's preferences, no matter how inaccurate it is likely to be. Moreover, this best guess will be substantially improved if the person has taken out a living will. Neither will it affect advance directives made by people who are already critically ill and who are, for example, giving instruction that they should not be resuscitated in the event of cardiac arrest. These people are already critically ill and therefore are able correctly to determine their preferences for what is essentially their current situation.

The argument applies only to advance directives made by essentially healthy individuals who opt for withdrawal of active care in a situation where their inability to consent is potentially reversible. In these situations, patients should be resuscitated and their opinions regarding future treatment sought again now that they are in the scenario that they had previously only imagined. For some no doubt this will lead to considerable hardship, as they must again state their preference that they would rather be allowed to die, but for others, perhaps the majority, it will provide a safety net and a chance to reconsider their decision with all available information.

Those who would have wished to see the King's wager abolished because of the needless deaths it seemed to cause must be similarly troubled by this form of living will.

References

1 Mendelson D. The Medical Treatment (Enduring Power of Attorney) Act and assisted suicide: the legal position in Victoria. *Bioethics News* 1993; 12: 34–42.
2 Stern K. Living wills in English law. *Palliative Medicine*, 1993; 7: 283–8.
3 Greco PJ, Schulman KA, Lavizzo-Mourey R, Hansen-Flaschen J. The Patient Self-Determination Act and the future of advance directives. *Annals of Internal Medicine*, 1991; 115: 639–43.
4 Kübler-Ross E. *On death and dying*. New York: Macmillan, 1969.
5 Owen C, Tennant C, Levis J, Jones M. Suicide and euthanasia: patient attitudes in the context of cancer. *Psycho-Oncology*, 1992; 1: 79–88.
6 Danis M, Garrett J, Harris R, Patrick DL. Stability of choices about life-sustaining treatments. *Annals of Internal Medicine*, 1994; 120: 567–73.
7 Dillner L. Relatives keener on euthanasia than patients. *British Medical Journal*, 1994; 309: 1107.
8 Alleback P, Bolund C, Ringback G. Increased suicide rate in cancer patients. *Journal of Clinical Epidemiology*, 1989; 42: 611–6.
9 Brown JH, Henteleff P, Barakat S, Rowe CJ. Is it normal for terminally ill patients to desire death? *American Journal of Psychiatry*, 1986; 143: 208–11.
10 Molloy W, Mepham V, Clarnette R. *Let me decide*. Melbourne: Penguin, 1993.

11   Quill TE. *Death and dignity. Making choices and taking charge.* New York: WW Norton, 1993.
12   Charlesworth M. A good death. In: Kuhse H, ed. *Willing to listen – waiting to die.* Melbourne: Penguin, 1994: 203–16.
13   Marker R. *Deadly compassion. The death of Ann Humphry and the case against euthanasia.* London: Harper Collins, 1994.
14   Humphry D. *Dying with dignity: understanding euthanasia.* New York: Birch Lane Press, 1992.
15   Kennedy L. *Euthanasia.* London: Chatto & Windus, 1990.

47

Palliative care and the doctrine of double effect

Stephen Wilkinson

What is the doctrine of double effect?

Although frequently criticized by moral philosophers and others, the doctrine of double effect is widely accepted by health care professionals and by various religious groups (most notably, the Catholic Church) and many (though not all) academic lawyers believe that it is part of UK law (Beauchamp and Childress, 1994: 206–11; Brazier, 1992: 447; Gillon, 1986: 133–9; Glover, 1977: 86–91; Harris, 1985: 43–5; McHale et al., 1997: 822–3; Mackie, 1977: 160–8; McMahan, 1994: 201–12; Randall and Downie, 1996: 71–3). The main idea behind the doctrine is that, provided certain conditions are met, one is not fully responsible for *all* the effects of one's actions, but only for those which are *intended*. It is normally applied therefore to cases in which an action (for example, administering a drug) has both a good effect (for example, pain relief) and a bad effect (for example, adverse side-effects, including perhaps shortening life).

What the doctrine of double effect says about such cases is roughly the following. Provided that the good effect is what was intended and the bad effect is a *foreseen but unintended* side-effect, then the action is ethically acceptable. Although most commonly discussed in the health care setting, the doctrine is meant to capture a general ethical truth (i.e. one which is applicable to everyone, not just health care workers) and, as such, has been used, for example, in attempts to differentiate the 'strategic bombing' of military targets (which is supposed to be acceptable – at least sometimes – because the civilian deaths involved are foreseen but unintended side-effects) from the 'terrorist bombing' of non-combatants (which is supposed to be morally indefensible because the civilian deaths involved are the *intended* means of achieving political or other objectives).

Here is a more precise account of the doctrine: an action is morally acceptable provided that all of the following conditions are met (Beauchamp and Childress, 1994: 207).

(a) The action is not *intrinsically* wrong (i.e. wrong considered apart from its effects).
(b) The person acting is aiming to do something good (for example, to relieve pain).
(c) The bad effects are *not* aimed at and are *not* means of achieving the good effects.

(d) The good effects are sufficiently good to outweigh the bad effects. (This is sometimes referred to as the 'proportionality criterion'.)

Why is the doctrine of double effect relevant to palliative care?

The doctrine of double effect is often illustrated by reference to the use of diamorphine. Take the case of a weak, terminally-ill patient who is in pain. In order to alleviate the pain, a doctor administers diamorphine, which (in the case in question) causes depressed respiration and hastens the patient's death. Why isn't this (either morally or legally) a case of murder? The short answer is that the doctor didn't have the relevant intention, since (let's assume) her intention was to relieve the patient's pain, not to kill her.

A fuller answer can be provided using the doctrine of double effect. Assuming that the administration of diamorphine is not intrinsically wrong (wrong independently of its effects) we need to ask three questions, corresponding to parts (b)–(d) of the doctrine in order to see whether it would classify the action as permissible.

First, was the intended end (pain relief) good? Almost certainly 'yes': relieving pain seems uncontroversially to be a good thing. Second, was the bad effect (hastened death) aimed at and was it a means of achieving the good effect (pain relief)? Again, almost certainly 'no' (to both parts of the question). The doctor did not intend death (on the contrary, she would probably prefer the patient to survive) and death was not the means of causing pain relief. Rather, death and pain relief were both effects of the same cause: the administration of diamorphine. Finally, is the good effect (pain relief) sufficiently good to outweigh the bad effect (hastened death)?

This last question is much harder and the answer will vary depending on the details of the case. To take one extreme, if the pain in question was minor and the patient lost 10 years of life, then many of us would say that the 'proportionality criterion' clearly had *not* been met. In other words, the patient would be better off keeping both the pain and the extra 10 years, rather than losing both. At the other extreme, if the pain was intolerable and the patient only lost a few minutes of life then many of us would say that the patient had benefited overall from the administration of diamorphine – in spite of its hastening her death. In between these two extremes there is, unfortunately, an enormous grey area in which 'quality of life' must be weighed against 'quantity of life'. And to complicate matters still further there may also be cases in which the patient is judged to have a *negative* quality of life: cases in which, because quality of life is so poor, death is seen as benefiting (or at least as not harming) her.

It may seem as if the doctrine of double effect sanctions some forms of euthanasia, since I have started to talk in terms of patients benefiting from having their lives shortened. However, it should be stressed that the doctrine is *not* supposed to be a way of justifying euthanasia. It is rather an attempt to establish that there is a morally significant difference between those cases where death is a foreseen but unintended side-effect of an intervention, and those in which it is intended, either as an end in itself, or as a means of achieving pain relief. Only cases like the latter can be cases of euthanasia, since *euthanasia is the intentional killing of a patient*, performed by someone who believes death to be in the patient's best interests. Euthanasia, therefore, is not sanctioned by the doctrine, since it (by definition) involves intentional killing.

Before moving on to consider briefly some of the problems with the doctrine, one further point of clarification needs to be made. Some health professionals argue that effective pain management never, or at least hardly ever, requires us to give life-shortening doses. Twycross (1999: 639) for example, suggests that 'when correctly used, morphine and other strong opioids are safe – safer than non-steroidal anti inflammatory drugs, which are prescribed with impunity'. Whether this is actually true is not something that can be considered here. What *can* be considered here though is this question: what ethical implications would there be *if* it were true?

The main implication is that the idea of 'double effect' would become almost totally irrelevant as far as palliative care is concerned. For, if life-shortening interventions are never required, what reason could there be for a person to give patients drugs which shorten life? There are two main possibilities. Either she does so because she *wants* to cause death – in which case we have a case of *intentional* killing and the doctrine of double effect doesn't apply. Or she does so accidentally and/or negligently and does not foresee the lethal side-effect – in which case the doctrine again doesn't apply because death isn't even a foreseen side-effect (since it's not foreseen). (Of course, we may, in certain circumstances, wish to condemn the doctor in such a case for being negligent and incompetent but that is another matter.) For these reasons, then, the doctrine only has relevance to palliative care if it is true that good palliative care sometimes necessarily involves interventions with life-shortening side-effects.

A problem with the doctrine of double effect

When applying the doctrine, we need often to make very difficult judgements about which effects are intended and which are not. But (and this is the main problem) *how do we know* what is intended and what is not? This question can arise from two different perspectives. First, from the 'first person' perspective, if a doctor administers diamorphine to relieve pain, but at the same time would be glad if the patient's death was hastened (perhaps because she believes that the patient would be 'better off dead') she may not be sure herself which effects she intends and which she doesn't. Second, from the 'third person' perspective, how are other professionals, relatives and the public to know what was going on 'in the doctor's head' when she administered the drug? How are they to know what she intends? This problem may render the doctrine unworkable in practice. Furthermore, it also opens up the possibility of health carers abusing the doctrine and using it as a way of 'smuggling in euthanasia by the back door'. In other words, the acceptance of the doctrine might make it possible to kill patients intentionally while *pretending* that their death is an unintended side-effect.

Conclusions

The doctrine of double effect is a potentially useful tool for distinguishing *intentional* killings (such as euthanasia) from cases in which hastened death is only an *unintended* side-effect. Practitioners, however, should remain aware that there are both practical and theoretical problems (including several that have not been discussed here) with the doctrine and that it should not be accepted or applied uncritically.

References

Beauchamp, T. and Childress, J. (1994) *Principles of Biomedical Ethics*, 4th edn. Oxford: Oxford University Press.

Brazier, M. (1992) *Medicine, Patients and the Law*, 2nd edn. Harmondsworth: Penguin.

Gillon, R. (1986) *Philosophical Medical Ethics*. Chichester: John Wiley & Sons.

Glover, J. (1977) *Causing Death and Saving Lives*. Harmondsworth: Penguin.

Harris, J. (1985) *The Value of Life*. London: Routledge.

McHale, J., Fox, M. and Murphy, J. (1997) *Health Care Law*. London: Sweet & Maxwell.

Mackie, J. (1977) *Ethics*. Harmondsworth: Penguin/

McMahan, J. (1994) 'Revising the doctrine of double effect', *Journal of Applied Philosophy*, 11 (2): 201–12.

Randall, F. and Downie, R. (1996) *Palliative Care Ethics: A Good Companion*. Oxford: Oxford University Press.

Twycross, R. (1999) 'Palliative care physicians always have their patients' best interests in mind', *British Medical Journal*, 319 (4 September 1999), http://www.bmj.com/cgi/content/full/319/7210/63.

48

Palliative care and the ethics of resource allocation

Eve Garrard

There are never enough resources for health care. Everyone agrees on this, and everyone sees that decisions have to be taken, sometimes very hard decisions, on how to divide up the resources that are available. This is the complex and difficult problem of resource allocation.

Why is this issue an ethical problem? Why can it not be settled by medical experts or economists, or perhaps teams of both? Of course, both medical experts and economists have a great deal to say which is of great importance to questions of resource allocation. There is a reason why they cannot decide these matters entirely on their own. When scarce resources are being divided, fairness seems to be a necessary feature of any satisfactory allocation, and issues of fairness are moral issues on which everyone, at least potentially, has something to say, and on which there are no experts with ultimate authority.

Fair division of resources

The problem of finding a fair division of health-care resources is a particularly pressing one for palliative care. The reason for this is that, where there is a choice between alleviating one person's distressing symptoms and actually saving another person's life, the strong moral intuition is to concentrate on saving life. Whatever harm is done to the person whose symptoms are left untreated, it seems that it cannot be as great as the harm done to the person whose life is lost. Life is good, we feel, and being alive is a necessary condition for experiencing good things. Nothing can compensate people for the loss of their lives (since they will not be there to be compensated), and so life-saving procedures must always have first claim on scarce resources.

However, if this line of thought is correct, then it will be extremely difficult to justify allocating resources to palliative care, which does not aim to save lives at all. Since there will always be people whose lives could be saved by pouring resources into doing so, it is hard to see why these resources should be diverted into treating people whose terminal illnesses

From *International Journal of Palliative Nursing*, 1996, 2 (2): 91–4.

cannot be cured. It is also hard to justify putting resources into the treatment of illnesses which are not life threatening at all.

Nevertheless, large amounts of resources are commonly allocated to such treatments, and it seems to be morally right to do this. If a patient is in acute pain from a disease which is not life threatening, and if it is known how to alleviate the pain, it seems wrong to leave the pain untreated, even if that means that scarce resources are diverted from life-saving procedures. It appears that saving life is not always the most important aim for health carers. The duty to alleviate distress is, at least sometimes, just as important as the duty to try and save lives, and make just as strong a claim on resources, i.e. the quality of people's lives is as morally significant as the number of lives which can be saved. If this is the case, then there is no special difficulty in justifying the allocation of resources to palliative care.

This service, like many other aspects of health care, aims to improve quality rather than quantity of life. In a catastrophic situation – the kind of circumstances calling for triage – we generally treat the saving of lives as the overriding moral priority, whereas in non-emergency situations we are, at least some of the time, prepared to give quality of life interventions a high, or higher, priority. Significant ethical issues that are beyond the remit of this article lie behind this difference.

It is still necessary, however, to establish some way of deciding how scarce resources can be fairly allocated between the various elements of health care, and between the different individuals who ultimately receive the treatments. These decisions are difficult, partly because fairness is itself a complex concept and partly because there is often disagreement on what fairness actually amounts to, especially in the health-care context.

Equal division

A natural starting point on this issue is the thought that a fair division of resources is an equal division. Sometimes, equality is indeed a fair principle of allocation, but in the health-care context, equal division of resources rapidly comes to seem very unfair. One resource that is always scarce is professional time: but there is nothing fair in requiring a doctor or a nurse to divide his/her time equally between a patient with a sore finger and a patient with suspected meningitis (which is not to say, of course, that the sore finger should be entirely neglected). Similarly, it would not be fair, to say the least, to divide the analgesics equally between a patient with a slight headache and a patient with bone cancer.

Examples such as these suggest the need to look at a wider range of considerations than equality alone, if a fair method of allocating resources is to be established. Features that have often been thought to be relevant to fair distribution include:

- The patient's level of need
- The patient's degree of merit

- The extent of the patient's contribution to society
- The likelihood of the treatment's success with a particular patient.

Not all of these features stand up to close consideration. At first sight it might seem plausible to think that resources ought to go to those who most deserve it, or who make the greatest contribution to society. Why should those who give more not receive more? However, any attempt to apply this thought as a principle of resource allocation comes up against a problem: who should decide, and on what basis, which patients are the most deserving and which are the most valuable to society? Who are the experts in these matters? The answer is not immediately obvious. Furthermore, what about people who, perhaps through serious congenital disability, are not in a position to make a major contribution to society? It does not seem fair to deny them medical resources because of something over which they have no control.

Apart from these problems, many people find the thought of allocating resources on the basis of merit, or desert, deeply unattractive. People's need for health care is so basic and universal that allocating it according to moral (or any other) achievement seems to run counter to the recognition of our common humanity and its common needs. Even the least deserving, or the least useful, among us has the same need for the relief of pain and the treatment of illness, and it is that need which seems to make a moral claim on the distribution of health-care resources.

So the patient's need for the treatment is beginning to look like the most relevant feature for fair allocation of resources. But what is it that people actually need? A patient in acute pain needs an analgesic – so much is uncontentious. But does a man who dislikes the shape of his nose need plastic surgery? Does a woman who would prefer not to be pregnant need an abortion? The answers here are less clear-cut, and are more likely to vary from case to case.

Furthermore, patient need cannot be the sole criterion for allocating scarce resources. Consider two patients who both have the same level of need for a very limited resource: one of them has a condition which will respond very well to treatment, whereas the other would probably receive very little benefit because the treatment has a low success rate in his type of case. If the resource is so limited that only one person can be treated, many people would think that the treatment should be given where it is most likely to be successful.

It seems plausible therefore to think that the features most relevant to a fair allocation of health-care resources are:

- The needs of the patient (if it can be established what these are)
- The (likely) success of the treatment.

Scarce resources should be allocated by giving more to those who need more, and for whom it is more likely to be successful. If a way can be found of combining these two features so that treatments can be assessed in terms of how successfully they meet patients' genuine needs, then this may constitute a satisfactory (because it is fair) method of deciding how to allocate scarce health-care resources among different types of treatment, and ultimately among different patients in need.

Quality Adjusted Life Years

One well known way of doing this is to appeal to Quality Adjusted Life Years (QALYs). The idea behind QALYs is that a patient's state, as a result of taking a particular treatment, can be assessed in terms of three factors:

1.   The amount of pain (or distress) the patient suffers
2.   The extent of the patient's disability
3.   The number of extra years of life the patient may reasonably look forward to as a result of taking the treatment.

The background assumption, a very plausible one, is that we all have a genuine need to be free of pain, disability, and the threat of imminent death. Therefore, a treatment which leaves the patient virtually pain free, mobile, and with a long life-expectancy will have a high QALY rating, and a treatment which leaves the patient in pain, bed-bound and with only a few months or weeks to live will have a very low QALY rating. These ratings can then be combined with the cost of the different treatments, and the resultant figure will show how many QALYs each procedure will produce and cost.

The enormous advantage of using QALYs is that they provide a rational way of comparing different medical procedures. For example, in taking the decision whether to allocate resources to heart transplants or to intensive care for neonates, it can be established how many QALYs per patient each procedure will produce and how much each QALY will cost. If there are two treatments, each of which generates the same number of QALYs but where one is much more expensive than the other, then it seems reasonable to prefer the cheaper treatment.

In fact, there are serious ethical problems associated with accepting this way of allocating resources. Because the increased life expectancy provided by a treatment is taken into account by QALYs, treatments for the diseases of old age always do badly in QALY calculations.

Discrimination against the elderly

Elderly people have relatively few years left to them, and no treatment, however successful, can give them an enormously increased life expectancy.

Therefore, relying on QALY calculations to settle resource allocation problems will effectively discriminate against the elderly. Some philosophers, most notably Harris (1985), have argued forcefully that such discrimination is unfair as elderly people place the same value on living out the rest of their lives, however long or short that may be, as younger people. 'The rest of our lives' is of equal value to each one of us and resources should be allocated so that we each have an equal opportunity to live it out.

Discrimination in favour of the young

It must be acknowledged, however, that other philosophers (and non-philosophers) have argued that resources should be disproportionately channelled towards younger rather than older patients. The argument here is that elderly people have had a 'fair innings', or at least a fairer innings than young patients suffering from life-threatening diseases. This argument breaks down when the age gaps are relatively small. It is not persuasive to assert that a 20-year-old has a stronger claim on our resources than a 21-year-old because he/she has had less of a 'fair innings' in life.

QALYs and palliative care

For similar reasons, palliative care does not come out well on QALY calculations, since it does not even aim at increasing life expectancy. However, as we saw earlier, extending life is not the only thing of value in health care. It is also valuable to free people from pain and anxiety, especially in the last part of their lives. In fact, it might be claimed that palliative care is very high in value indeed, second only in importance to life saving, and so it should perhaps take priority over routine treatments. The reason for this is that delays and inadequacies in routine treatments can sometimes be compensated for, but for those in need of palliative care who do not receive it, no compensation is possible. In palliative care, we are dealing with the whole of the rest of the patient's life, and the provision of adequate care is of correspondingly great importance.

Indeed, it has recently been argued that the importance of the last part of life and, in particular, the manner of dying, goes well beyond the immediate confines of these final months or weeks, and in fact makes a difference to the significance of the whole of the person's life (Dworkin, 1993). People's lives have a certain individual shape, determined, at least in part, by how they choose to live them. The endings of these lives can fit, or alternatively distort, that overall shape. In the light of this thought, there is an overall need for palliative care to maintain, as far as possible, the shape and integrity of the individual life, and where this is sadly not possible, there is a special need to pay attention to the patients' views on what treatments, and even what care, they should or should not undergo.

Funding issues

Finally, there is one other type of allocation decision to be considered in the field of palliative care. This is the decision about what aspects of palliative care should receive the greatest funding. Should the aim be to provide the best possible service for a limited number of patients, or should there be a focus on, for example, excellent pain and symptom control for everyone, even if this means that there are insufficient resources left to deal with *all* the fears and anxieties which patients may be experiencing?

People often feel pulled in opposing directions. They want to give whatever they can to the patient presently with them, whatever is needed to alleviate their suffering. On the other hand, they know that the vividness of the needs of the patient presently with them may make it difficult to consider the needs of the next patient, the one who has not managed to get access to the services that are provided. These patients may be invisible to us but, nevertheless they are still in need. In this situation it might be argued that, in the case of palliative care, an essential component of fairness in resource allocation is equality of treatment for those who are equally in need (Farsides and Garrard, 1997). If this is so, then we should be aiming at a provision of palliative care which is more egalitarian and more accessible to everyone in need than is currently the case, even if this means that we cannot provide the resources for a 'Rolls Royce' service for anyone, much as we would like this to be the case.

This choice, between funding what is best for the patient who manages to get access to our services, and funding a more basic service which is available to all in need of it, is one that has to be faced in many health-care contexts. It is perhaps the most pressing, and the most contentious, resource allocation problem facing palliative care today.

Note

The author would like to thank Bobbie Farsides and David McNaughton for helpful discussion of these issues.

References

Dworkin R. (1993) *Life's Dominion*. Harper Collins, London.
Farsides C., Garrard E. (1997) 'Euthanasia, palliative care and resource allocation'. In: Clark D., Ahmedzai S., Hockley J. eds. *Themes in Palliative Care*. Open University Press, Buckingham (in print).
Harris J. (1985) *The Value of Life*. Routledge, London.

49

On withholding nutrition and hydration in the terminally ill
has palliative medicine gone too far?

Gillian M. Craig

Introduction

From time to time in the professional life of a doctor incidents occur which cause one to stop and think hard. There are times when two doctors, each with the best interests of the patient at heart, would treat in diametrically opposite ways. There are widely divergent opinions on what is correct and morally acceptable when it comes to the management of patients who are, or appear to be, terminally ill and unable to maintain their own nutrition and hydration. This inability to eat and drink may be a consequence of the illness or of the treatment, for example heavy sedation. Differences in opinion about management may be voiced by relatives, by nurses and by doctors who may or may not be directly or professionally involved in the care of the patient. Particularly difficult management problems may arise if the dissenting relative is a nurse, doctor or paramedic, and great care must be taken to ensure that his or her views are taken into account and discussed openly, and that the management adopted is acceptable to all parties, if this is humanly and legally possible.

Ethical dilemmas in the field of hydration and nutrition cover a wide spectrum, from dehydration due to dysphagia of various aetiologies, through terminal cancer with intestinal obstruction, to the persistent vegetative state, terminal Alzheimer's disease patients who are unable to eat, and patients with anorexia nervosa or elderly depressives who deliberately refuse nourishment to the point of self-annihilation. The main issue highlighted by this paper is the use of sedation without hydration or nourishment in the terminally ill. This raises ethical issues which require debate by the profession and the public.

The need for an open mind about intravenous hydration in terminal care

Palliative medicine is a relatively new and growing specialty and the hospice movement is held in high esteem by the public. Some doctors, however,

From *Journal of Medical Ethics*, 1994, 20: 139–43.

have reservations. There are dangers in grouping patients labelled 'terminal' in institutions, because diagnoses can be wrong (1). There is a risk that if all the staff in an institution are orientated towards death and dying and non-intervention, treatable illness may be overlooked. Not everyone who is referred for terminal care proves to be terminally ill, and no physician should accept such a diagnosis without reviewing the evidence personally.

Certain policies that are practised in palliative medicine would be dangerous if applied without due care and thought. In particular the view that in the terminal phase of disease 'no form of artificial hydration or alimentation is undertaken, all measures not required for comfort are withdrawn, and no treatment-related toxicity is acceptable' (2). It is not uncommon for the elderly to be admitted to hospital in a seriously dehydrated condition, looking terminally ill. A treatment-orientated physician will rehydrate these patients energetically, often with dramatic results, in order to buy time in which to assess the situation carefully. A therapeutically inactive doctor would lose many patients for the sake of avoiding a drip. Two examples from my personal experience will illustrate this point.

Case 1

An elderly man was sent to hospital for terminal care with a diagnosis of carcinoma of the pancreas. He had indeed had a stent inserted at another hospital to relieve bilary obstruction due to tumour. However, his 'terminal' illness was due to a small stroke and uncontrolled diabetes mellitus. He recovered with insulin and intravenous rehydration and lived happily for several weeks more.

Case 2

An elderly man was admitted for terminal care but the geriatrician felt the diagnosis of cancer was not well established. The main problem was severe dehydration with ischaemic feet and severe pressure sores on the heels. With intravenous rehydration and intensive nursing he recovered and went home for 18 months.

It is important for the public to realize that most patients with terminal illness can continue to eat and drink as and when they wish. Only in the last days may they be too weak or tired to bother, in which case the lack of food and drink will not contribute to death. If dehydration develops under these circumstances it is a natural consequence of irreversible disease, and artificial hydration would not be appropriate.

The use of sedation

There are times in the care of the dying 'when it is necessary to use benzodiazepines, phenothiazines and barbiturates to sedate a patient in order to relieve intolerable distress where dying is complicated by an agitated delirium or tracheal obstruction' (3). In skilled hands no person should die in pain, whatever the cause of the illness. As a last resort some people advocate use of high-dose analgesia and induction of sleep with continuous intravenous midazolam (4). Whatever the underlying pathology 'the cardinal ethical principle remains that the treatment goal must be achieved with the least risk to the patient's life' (3). I would add – and in a manner that is acceptable to the patient's closest relatives.

Having decided that sedation is needed, the doctor must try to find a drug regime that relieves distress but does not prevent the patient from taking fluid and nourishment, does not prevent verbal communication with friends and relatives, and does not lead to toxic side-effects, or expedite death. Unfortunately currently available therapeutic options are not ideal in all these respects. Even light sedation can cause drowsiness that may prevent a person from taking enough fluid to maintain hydration. Heavy sedation may render an alert person incapable of swallowing within minutes, depending on the drug regime used.

If death is imminent few people would feel it essential to put up a drip but ethical problems arise if sedation is continued for more than one or two days, without hydration, as the patient will become dehydrated. Dehydration can result in circulatory collapse, renal failure, anuria and death. I do not think it is morally acceptable to leave a sedated patient for long without hydration. Others would dissent from this view using words such as 'meddlesome' and 'unethical' if intravenous fluids are suggested under such circumstances. However, in my opinion, if it is not possible to reduce sedation to a level that enables the patient to drink, the question of hydration must be addressed to everyone's satisfaction.

Particular problems may arise if the patient has a primary mental disorder such as chronic schizophrenia or depression. In such people the stress of the physical illness may make the mental state worse. Great skill may be needed to distinguish a potentially treatable psychotic reaction from an untreatable, terminal agitated delirium. In cases of difficulty expert psychiatric help should be obtained as the distinction may be vital. If the diagnosis is a psychotic reaction, hydration must be maintained and the patient observed in the hope that sedation can be reduced. If the diagnosis is a terminal agitated delirium, those with experience advise against reducing sedation, and argue against giving intravenous fluids as this would prolong dying.

To take a decision to sedate a person, without hydration, until he/she dies is a very dangerous policy medically, ethically and legally. No doctor's judgement is infallible when it comes to predicting how close a patient is to death. To say that it is a matter of days, and to treat by this method, is to make the prediction self-fulfilling. I know of a patient who died after at least seven days of sedation without hydration – how much longer would he have survived with hydration? Diagnostic errors can also occur. A reversible psychosis or confusional state can be mistaken for terminal delirium, aspiration pneumonia for tracheal obstruction, obstruction due to faecal impaction for something more sinister, and so on. The only way to ensure that life will not be shortened is to maintain hydration during sedation in all cases where inability to eat and drink is a direct consequence of sedation, unless the relatives request no further intervention, or the patient has made his/her wishes known to this effect. If naturally or artificially administered hydration and nutrition is withheld, the responsible medical staff must face the fact that prolonged sedation without hydration or nutrition will end in death, whatever the underlying pathology. Even a fit Bedu tribesman riding in the desert in cool weather, can only survive for seven days without food or water (5).

The legal question

The Institute of Medical Ethics working party on the ethics of prolonging life and assisting death has argued the case for withdrawing food and water from patients in a persistent vegetative state (6). Such patients are unaware of their surroundings as a result of severe brain damage. Recent reports indicate that 'persistent' does not necessarily mean 'permanent' (7) and it is essential to ensure that the prognosis is hopeless before considering withdrawing treatment (8).

A key issue in English law in such patients has been 'whether artificial feeding counts as medical treatment – which can lawfully be discontinued if the patient is receiving no benefit – or is simply the means of sustaining life, which if withdrawn could lay a doctor open to a charge of murder' (8). This argument is largely semantic since in patients with a persistent vegetative state this treatment sustains life. The key issue surely is whether it benefits the patient to be alive rather than dead. Those who advocate withdrawing food and water from these patients have been warned by medical defence organizations that such a policy may result in a charge of manslaughter by neglect (9). This risk has been reduced but not eliminated by the Bland case ruling (10) which has clarified the legal position in England and Wales. The legal position in Scotland remains unclear but is being actively reviewed by the Lord Advocate following the judgement in the Bland case.

The case of Airedale NHS Trust v Bland

In the final judgement or declaratory statement made in the House of Lords in February 1993, it was ruled that the responsible attending physicians could lawfully discontinue all life-sustaining treatment and medical supportive measures designed to keep the patient (Mr Bland) alive in his persistent vegetative state, including the termination of ventilation, nutrition and hydration by artificial means (10). In coming to this judgement, the Law Lords accepted as responsible medical opinion, a paper prepared by the British Medical Association (BMA) medical ethics committee (11). Referring to this the judges highlighted four safeguards which should be observed before discontinuing life support in a patient with a persistent vegetative state – namely: 1. Every effort should be made at rehabilitation for at least six months after injury; 2. The diagnosis of irreversible persistent vegetative state should not be considered confirmed until at least 12 months after injury; 3. The diagnosis should be agreed by at least two other independent doctors; and 4. Generally the wishes of the patient's immediate family should be given great weight.

Lord Goff pointed out that to discontinue artificial feeding might be categorized as an omission, which if deemed to constitute a breach of duty to the patient is unlawful (10). However, in the case of Mr Bland, he argued that the patient was incapable of swallowing and therefore of eating and drinking in the normal sense of these words. Artificial feeding via a nasogastric tube was therefore a form of life support, and could be discontinued if treatment was futile and no longer in the best interests of the patient.

It must be emphasized that the case of Airedale NHS Trust v Bland does not give doctors freedom to withdraw treatment from all patients in a persistent vegetative state. For the foreseeable future doctors in England and Wales must apply to the family division of the High Court for a declaration in each case as to the legality of any proposed discontinuance of life support, where there is no valid consent on the part of the patient. There has not been a rush of applications to date. Moreover a civil court ruling is no guarantee against subsequent prosecution in a criminal court, since a declaration as to the lawfulness or otherwise of future conduct is 'no bar to a criminal prosecution, no matter the authority of the court which grants it' (12).

The judgement regarding hydration and nutrition in the Bland case was clearly swayed by the patient's irreversible brain damage, although the law as to killing is unaffected by the victim's mental state (13). It would be extremely dangerous to extrapolate the legal decision made in this case to other clinical situations. The legality or otherwise of withholding hydration and nutrition from the dying has not been tested in the courts in the United Kingdom (13).

Despite the differences in mental state, pathology and life expectation between a terminally ill sedated patient and one with a persistent vegetative state, the key issues are similar. Are you, by withholding fluid and nourishment, withholding the means of sustaining life? In short are you killing the patient? The answer I fear in some cases could be *YES*. In some terminally ill patients, especially those who are rendered unable to swallow by heavy sedation, failure to hydrate and nourish artificially could be judged an unlawful omission. The question of intent is important and the principle of double effect, and other medico-legal issues are relevant (13). However, doctors who deliberately speed death could face the prospect of life imprisonment (13). Clearly the legality of prolonged sedation without hydration is highly debatable yet this treatment is regarded as ethical and compassionate by senior and respected specialists in palliative medicine. If a dying patient is treated in this way there may be reasonable grounds for doubt as to whether the patient died of the treatment or the disease. It is our duty and our privilege as doctors to sustain life, not to shorten it. Euthanasia must remain illegal, and practices that seem tantamount to euthanasia must be exposed.

The risk of inappropriate sedation

Clearly a policy of sedation without hydration or nutrition in terminal care is a drastic solution to a difficult problem. Those who take such action no doubt do so thinking that they have the patient's best interests at heart. They may also be influenced by subconscious fears. As Main said:

> Perhaps many of the desperate treatments in medicine can be justified by expediency, but history has an awkward habit of judging some as fashions, more helpful to the therapist than the patient. Patients tend to be sedated when the carers have reached the limit of their resources, and are no longer able to stand the patient's problems without anxiety, impatience, guilt, anger or despair. A sedative will alter the situation and produce a patient who if not dead, is at least quiet. (14)

The case of the Winchester rheumatologist who was convicted of attempted murder demonstrates what can happen when doctor and patient reach the end of their tether (15, 16).

The importance of comfort

The guiding principle in the care of the dying is that 'everything in the terminal phase of an irreversible illness should be clearly decided on the basis of whether it will make the patient more comfortable and whether it will honour his/her wishes' (17). 'Comfort' is a state of conscious physical and mental well-being. It is debatable therefore whether the word can be applied to a heavily sedated, dehydrated patient. However, most would agree that it is preferable to be comfortable and conscious or semi-conscious without pain, than uncomfortable, distraught and fully awake.

The therapeutic ideal would be to have a patient who is calm, clear-headed and pain-free. Unfortunately there are times when this cannot be achieved with the drugs at our disposal.

The consensus in the hospice movement seems to be that rehydration and intravenous fluids are inappropriate in terminal care (2, 18, 19). Dehydration is even considered to be beneficial in patients with incontinence (18)! This is a weak argument to justify withholding intravenous fluids. Therapeutic anuria may be the ultimate cure for incontinence but the side-effect is death. Those who have coped with incontinence without a catheter in the past can be nursed without a catheter to the end, if that is their wish. Rehydration should not influence this aspect of care. Hospice staff also argue that a drip makes it more difficult to turn a dying patient in bed, yet they are happy to give analgesics by subcutaneous infusion when necessary, and occasionally use a drip inpatients with hypercalcaemia. To those of us who use drips frequently on acute medical, surgical and geriatric wards, these arguments do not carry much weight. Setting up a drip or a subcutaneous infusion is a simple and straightforward procedure that rarely causes the patient discomfort or distress. Many dehydrated patients look and feel a lot better when they are rehydrated. If the staff in hospices used drips more, they would not have to find so many reasons for avoiding them.

The question of thirst

If hydration and nutrition are withheld, the attendant staff must be sensitive to the effect this may have on the family and friends (17). Some say that a patient should be comatose, so as not to experience thirst, before it is morally acceptable to withhold or withdraw intravenous fluids (20). It is widely assumed that a terminally ill patient is not troubled by hunger or thirst but this is difficult to substantiate as few people return from the grave to complain. Thirst may or may not bother the patient. Concern about thirst undoubtedly bothers relatives. They will long to give their loved one a drink. They may sit by the bed furtively drinking cups of tea, taking care to make no sound lest the clink of china is torture to the patient. Anyone who has starved for hours before an anaesthetic will sympathize with dying patients who seem to thirst and starve for days. Nurses are taught that moistening the patient's mouth with a damp sponge is all that is necessary to prevent thirst. Relatives may not be convinced. It way well be that sedation relieves the sensation of hunger and thirst. If there is evidence to this effect it would be helpful for the relatives of dying patients to be told about it.

The role of the family

It has been said that the family must request no further medical procedures before treatment can be withheld and that the previously expressed wishes of the patient or current family must predominate over those of staff (20). Staff who believe strongly that intravenous fluids are inappropriate should not impose their views on knowledgeable or distressed relatives who request that a dying patient be given intravenous fluids to prevent dehydration or thirst. To overrule such a request is, in my view, ethically wrong. The only proviso would be if the patient had, when *compos mentis*, specifically said that he/she did not want a drip under any circumstances.

No relatives should be forced to watch a loved one die while medical staff insist on withholding hydration. This has happened to my knowledge. Such an experience is deeply disturbing and could haunt a person forever. Is all this agony worth it for the sake of avoiding a drip? I think not.

The converse also applies. There will be occasions when the medical staff who are professionally involved would like to use a drip, but a knowledgeable relative requests no intervention. In this situation, the medical team will need to make a carefully balanced judgement as to whether intervention is essential or not. If the scales are not heavily weighted in favour of intervention the wise doctor will compromise and stand back in the interests of the peace of mind of the relative.

A doctor cannot be obliged to act contrary to his or her own conscience but equally doctors should bear in mind that relatives also have consciences, and should not be forced to accept for their loved ones treatment that they consider to be unethical. It is inevitable that terminally ill patients will die and that their relatives will be sad. Care must be taken to ensure that the burden of bereavement is not loaded heavily by distress about patient management in the terminal phase. In the care of the dying, both patients and their relatives must be treated with compassion.

Final comments

The question of hydration and nutrition in terminal care is one that generates strong views. It is probably inevitable that sooner or later those working in the field of palliative medicine will meet colleagues working in different fields of medicine who are used to adopting a more active approach to management. Those who don't believe in using intravenous fluids will encounter those who do. Faced with this situation it is essential that both parties sit down together to discuss the issues. They must reach a compromise that takes into account the expressed or probable wishes of the patient concerned and the views of the closest relatives. No one individual has right entirely on his/her side. The ethically correct solution may prove to be somewhere in the middle, and it must be found.

Where opinions differ on the management of an individual case, further discussion may throw light on the situation, firmly held opinions may prove to be wrong, diagnoses may need to be revised and factors that had not been considered before may soften entrenched attitudes. If the issue is the futility or otherwise of intervention, or doubt about the patient's views or best interest, there may be room for manoeuvre in any given situation. The underlying reasons for sedation and the cause of the patient's inability to eat and drink are obviously of critical importance. What is essential in the final analysis is that all parties should feel comfortable with the clinical management strategy adopted. If this is not the case the strategy is probably not ethically sound. Somewhere between the poles of opposing opinion there must be some morally acceptable common ground. If after further discussion a mutually acceptable management policy cannot be agreed, it is no solution to the dilemma for a hospice team to tell the relatives to take the dying patient elsewhere. Where for example can you take a dying man, in the middle of winter, in an ambulance strike? However strong your ethical position, it is unacceptable to seek to silence dissent in this way. Where time permits, a second consultant opinion should be sought, or help from some other appropriate independent source.

As Rabbi Lionel Blue said recently of theology: 'Even more important than your views is the kindness with which you hold them, and the courtesy with which you treat those who oppose you'. The same could be said of the issues explored in this paper. People who hold strong views in this difficult and emotive area of palliative medicine should hold them kindly and with sensitivity. At the end of the day there should not be the slightest grounds for suspicion that death was due to anything but the disease. Unless this can be guaranteed, the public's faith in doctors in general, and in the hospice movement in particular, will be ill founded.

References

(1) Kamisar Y. In: Downing A, ed. *Euthanasia and the right to death.* London: Peter Owen, 1969: 100–1.
(2) Ashby M, Stoffell B. Therapeutic ratio and defined phases: proposal of ethical framework and palliative care. *British medical journal,* 1991; 302: 1322–4.
(3) Twycross RG. Assisted death: a reply. *Lancet,* 1990; 336: 796–8.
(4) Tapsfield W, Amis P. [letter]. *British medical journal,* 1992; 305: 951.
(5) Thesiger W. *Arabian sands.* London: Readers' Union, Longmans, Green & Co, 1960: 87.
(6) Institute of Medical Ethics working party on the ethics of prolonging life and assisting death. Withdrawal of life support from patients in a persistent vegetative state. *Lancet,* 1991; 337: 96–8.
(7) Andrews K. Managing the persistent vegetative state. *British medical journal,* 1992; 305: 486–7.
(8) Dyer C. BMA examines the persistent vegetative state. *British medical journal,* 1992; 305: 853–4.
(9) Baron JH [letter]. *Lancet,* 1991; 337: 639.
(10) House of Lords. Law Report. Withdrawal of medical treatment from hopeless case not unlawful. *The Times* 1993 Feb 5: 8.
(11) Medical ethics committee of the British Medical Association. *Discussion paper on treatment of patients in persistent vegetative state.* London: BMA, 1992.
(12) See reference (10): Viscount Dilhorne in Imperial Tobacco Ltd v Attorney General 1981. AC 718 741 Quoted by Lord Goff.
(13) Mason JK, McCall Smith RA. *Law and medical ethics* [3rd edn]. London: Butterworths, 1991: 317–43.
(14) Main TF. The ailment. *British journal of medical psychology,* 1957; 30: 129–45.
(15) Dyer C. Rheumatologist convicted of attempted murder. *British medical journal,* 1992; 305: 731.
(16) Illidge TM, Kirkham SR [letter]. *British medical journal,* 1992; 305: 1225.

(17) Wanzer SH, Adelstein SJ, Cranford RE et al. The physician's responsibility toward hopelessly ill patients. *New England journal of medicine*, 1984; 310: 955–9.

(18) Sykes N. The last 48 hours of life: caring for patient, family and doctor. *Geriatric medicine*, 1990; 20, 9: 22–4.

(19) Belcher NG. Pulling out the drip: an ethical decision in the terminally ill. *Geriatric medicine*, 1990; 20, 6: 22–3.

(20) Micetich KC, Steinecker PH, Thomasma DC et al. Are intravenous fluids morally required for a dying patient? *Archives of internal medicine*, 1983; 143: 975–8.

50

On withholding nutrition and hydration in the terminally ill

has palliative medicine gone too far? A reply

R.J. Dunlop, J.E. Ellershaw, M.J. Baines, N. Sykes and C.M. Saunders

The issues surrounding the management of fluid and nutritional status in the terminally ill were brought sharply into focus by Dr Craig (1). She rightly pointed out the dangers of automatically withholding fluid replacement therapy. Palliative care never has been, and never should be, an excuse for bad medicine. The need for careful clinical assessment and diagnosis of every problem is a central premise of palliative care. Reversible conditions such as hypercalcaemia may cause dehydration in cancer patients who are not imminently dying. If rehydration is not carried out, the patient will deteriorate rapidly. The gaunt appearance and altered state will mimic the effects of advanced cancer.

It is important to distinguish those patients for whom fluid replacement is medically indicated. A distinction can often be made on clinical grounds. Dying patients have a longer history (weeks or months) of gradual deterioration with increasing weakness, fatigue, weight loss and drowsiness. Dehydration will cause a more rapid deterioration, usually over days, in the setting of a precipitating cause suggested by the history (for example, polyuria, polydipsia with hypercalcaemia, or vomiting from bowel obstruction) clinical examination and appropriate laboratory findings. The acute change will cause considerable distress both to the patient and the family. Such distress should be used as a further prompt to search for a reversible problem. It should be borne in mind that some people deny the previous history of gradual decline and then 'suddenly' become distressed when the patient finally stops swallowing. When there is doubt, a therapeutic trial of fluids and other appropriate treatments may well be warranted so long as the wishes of the patient are not contravened.

On the other hand, most terminally ill cancer patients reach a point during their gradual physical decline when they first stop eating and then subsequently stop drinking. This occurs even in patients who are not taking medications and as Dr Craig pointed out, this situation arouses considerable distress for the relatives. Dr Gillon discussed the principles which should be followed when conflict arises between patient proxies and staff (2). However, conflict may be prevented by anticipatory dialogue

From *Journal of Medical Ethics*, 1995, 21: 141–3.

based on the evidence for the risks and benefits of giving versus withholding treatment.

Nutritional support should be considered as a separate issue from hydration. The administration of conventional dextrose solutions via peripheral veins does not constitute nutritional support. This can only be achieved by enteral feeding (nasogastric tube or gastrostomy) or by parenteral administration into a central vein. Although patients with advanced cancer appear to be malnourished, the metabolic abnormalities are quite different from starvation in an otherwise healthy person. There is no evidence that in patients with advanced cancer, aggressive nutritional support, either enteral or parenteral, prolongs life or even significantly alters the metabolic abnormalities (3). Indeed there is evidence that cancer growth may be accelerated, thereby increasing local symptoms from the cancer (4). Nutritional support may be helpful for the small number of patients who have local disease causing swallowing difficulties but who are not yet dying from widely disseminated endstage cancer, for example, those with head and neck cancers.

Dehydration results from an intake of water below the minimum required to maintain homeostasis. In someone who is otherwise healthy, the symptoms are thirst, dry mouth, headache, fatigue, then cognitive impairment followed by the sequelae described by Dr Craig: circulatory collapse, renal failure, anuria and death. The first clue suggesting that the situation in cancer patients is not equivalent to acute dehydration came from clinical observations in dying patients who were not taking any medications and who did not have correctable causes for their deterioration. In such patients systemic symptoms such as fatigue and drowsiness usually precede the cessation of fluid intake by several days or weeks. Even though these patients may be very drowsy at the time they stop drinking, they can rouse and respond to questions from family, for example.

Analysis of blood and urine chemistry in terminally ill patients has failed to disclose evidence of the expected changes from dehydration (5, 6). In a recent prospective study of dying cancer patients (median time to death, two days) the symptoms of dry mouth and thirst were not correlated with the level of hydration (6). These findings support the work of Burge who investigated dehydration symptoms in 51 cancer patients with an estimated prognosis of less than six weeks. He found no significant association between biochemical markers of dehydration (serum osmolality, urea and sodium) and the symptom of thirst (7). Therefore giving additional fluid to dying patients in order to alleviate the symptoms of dry mouth and thirst may well be futile.

In the same way that hunger is not a feature of the anorexia-cachexia syndrome, thirst is not associated with decreasing fluid intake in those close to death. It is possible that the normal homeostatic mechanisms controlling fluid intake and fluid balance are altered in the dying process. Further evidence for this hypothesis derives from studies of patients given fluids intravenously. Waller et al. compared 55 patients treated with oral fluids with 13 patients who received IV fluids (8). They found no difference in the biochemical parameters and state of consciousness between the two groups.

It seems reasonable to conclude from these observations that nutritional or fluid supplementation cannot be automatically justified on medical grounds for patients dying of advanced cancer. Is fluid therapy harmful? To our knowledge, no studies have demonstrated any adverse effects from fluid therapy. Intravenous cannulae can pose a problem to patient comfort if the arm needs splinting. This can be overcome by using the subcutaneous route. Terminally ill patients have lower albumin levels (6) which may cause problems when crystalloid solutions are administered. Albumin is the plasma protein which is largely responsible for maintaining colloid osmotic pressure. This pressure counteracts the forces which tend to move fluid out of the blood vessels. The authors have seen patients develop pulmonary oedema, rapidly increasing ascites, and unsightly peripheral oedema involving conjunctivae and the hands when given intravenous fluids in acute hospital wards, particularly if the serum albumin is below 26 g/l.

Dr Craig drew attention to the use of sedation in terminal care. Once again, a careful history and examination is necessary to distinguish terminal agitation from a reversible problem in someone who is not actually dying. Terminal agitation must be treated aggressively, otherwise the distress of the patient will become extreme. Even when incremental doses of sedatives are given, it is rarely possible to achieve a balance between relief of agitation and alertness. All palliative care practitioners would echo the experience of Dr Wilkes who described the problems of trying to reduce the dose of sedatives when the patient is settled (9).

When sedation is required in a patient who is not actually dying, we rarely find that it is necessary to render the patient unconscious. Nursing staff can still feed the patient and maintain hydration. The dose of tranquillisers is always reduced to the lowest dose necessary to control the symptoms. We would seek the advice of a consultant psychiatrist in treating such cases.

Given that there is no clear evidence of symptomatic benefit from nutritional or fluid therapy in cancer patients who are dying and that there is potential for harm if there is severe hypoalbuminaemia, we do not recommend the routine use of intravenous or subcutaneous fluids. When discussing these issues with a family, it is important not to argue from some philosophical standpoint, but it is important to present the facts carefully. On most occasions, families will be reassured and their sense of helplessness can be assuaged by encouraging them to perform mouthcare. Some families (particularly from some cultural and religious backgrounds) may not be satisfied. In these circumstances, so long as no contrary opinion has been expressed by the patient, we give subcutaneous fluids for the sake of the family. This situation only arises two to three times per 1,000 admissions per year at St Christopher's Hospice. The volume is kept to no more than one litre per 24 hours to avoid overload. The use of a local anaesthetic cream will prevent pain from the cannula insertion. The infusion is usually given overnight; the subcutaneous line is capped and left in-site during the day so that the patient is not subjected to multiple needle pricks. By giving the infusion intermittently, it is easier for the family to make the decision to discontinue therapy.

References

(1) Craig G.M. On withholding nutrition and hydration in the terminally ill: has palliative medicine gone too far? *Journal of medical ethics*, 1994, 20: 139–43.

(2) Gillon R. Palliative care ethics: non-provision of artificial nutrition and hydration to terminally ill sedated patients. *Journal of medical ethics*, 1994; 20: 131–2, 187.

(3)   Brennan M.F. Total parenteral nutrition in the cancer patient. *New England journal of medicine*, 1981; 305: 373–5.

(4) Rice M.I, Van Rij A.M. Parenteral nutrition and tumour growth in the patient with complicated abdominal cancer. *Australia and New Zealand journal of surgery*, 1987; 57: 375–9.

(5) Oliver D. Terminal dehydration. *Lancet*, 1984; 2: 631.

(6) Ellershaw J.E, Sutcliffe J.M, Saunders C.M. Dehydration and the dying patient. *Journal of pain and symptom management* (in press).

(7) Burge F.I. Dehydration symptoms of palliative care cancer patients. *Journal of pain and symptom management*, 1993; 8, 7: 454–64.

(8) Waller A, Adunski A, Hershkowitz M. Terminal dehydration and intravenous fluids. *Lancet*, 1991; 337: 745.

(9) Wilkes E. On withholding nutrition and hydration in the terminally ill: has palliative medicine gone too far? A commentary. *Journal of medical ethics*, 1994; 20: 144–5.

PART 4

BEREAVEMENT: PRIVATE GRIEF, COLLECTIVE RESPONSIBILITY

Introduction

This final part of the Reader contains first-person accounts, poetry, imaginative literature and practitioners' stories along with more conventionally academic articles. Throughout, the theme is responding to the needs of bereaved people in a direct and open-minded manner.

This part begins with a classic exposition of reaction to loss. 'Bereavement as a psychosocial transition' by Colin Murray Parkes. Parkes extends the frequent explanation of why loss affects us deeply – John Bowlby's assertion that it throws us back into the profoundly disturbing separation anxiety which we first experienced as children – by adding that we must also consider how loss shakes the entire worldview of the bereaved person. This is the idea of loss as a 'psychosocial transition', one which typically affects many areas of the bereaved person's life. Loss is one aspect of the psychosocial transition, the psychological change that takes place whenever people are forced to change their assumptions about the world. Refusing to recognize change and other defence mechanisms against the transition may be temporarily useful, Parkes argues, but ultimately the transition must be made.

This view is balanced by an article which focuses on the social factors determining grief as well as the psychological ones: Lindsay Prior's 'The social distribution of sentiments'. Prior argues that the psychological approach alone is too individualistic: we must also understand grief in terms of what responses each society permits or encourages. In our own multi-cultural society, carers need to understand the bereavement practices of many communities, and in order to help them do this we have included the updated article by Shirley Firth, 'Cross-cultural perspectives on bereavement', specially commissioned for the first edition of this Reader. Her article informs the reader in relation to a range of rituals adopted by Asian immigrants in the UK. Her article like others in this part emphasizes the need for non-judgemental listening based on acceptance of our own unresolved pain. This idea is carried forward in other articles which urge practitioners not to impose set ideas of normality in bereavement or to expect standard stages and patterns of griefwork. These accounts are particularly moving when they come from bereaved practitioners whose personal grief has enabled them to see shortcomings in their own practice. Sheila Awooner-Renner's 'I desperately needed to see my son' describes what happened to her following the accidental death of her 17-year-old son. Another first-person account, Evelyn Gillis's story of the death of her 22-year-old daughter ('A single parent confronting the loss of an only child') is followed by a brief epitaph about another early death: the inscription from the tomb of Libby Dickinson, 1798–1818.

Changes in hospital practice in relation to the deaths of babies before the legal age of viability are detailed in Nancy Kohner's 'Pregnancy loss and the death of a baby', which is a new version written for this Reader. Management of stillbirth after the legal age of viability (currently 24 weeks) has changed radically, Kohner notes, from a sense that parents should minimize the experience to emphasis on allowing the parents to hold the baby and on providing respectful burial or cremation. Kohner in this version questions whether contemporary practices of encouraging bereaved parents to talk and to do things with their deceased babies are as restrictive and inflexible as previous practices which denied the experience. A first-person account by one such parent, Gavin Fairbairn ('When a baby dies – a father's view'), reflects on the treatment which he and his wife Susan received following the death one hour after birth of their daughter Hesther Frances.

Another area of change is in relation to gay and lesbian bereavement, the subject of another article written and then updated for this edition of the Reader by Dudley Cave of the Gay Bereavement Project. The particular needs of bereaved gay and lesbian partners are considered, particularly following the AIDS pandemic. He notes the complications of dealing with the family of origin – who may well be estranged from the surviving partner, or even unaware of his or her existence. The special needs of people with learning difficulties, another group whose feelings are sometimes ignored, are the subject of an article by Maureen Oswin: 'The grief that does not speak'. Using case studies illustrating the tendency to equate disturbed behaviour after bereavement with the ordinary effects of learning disability, Oswin argues eloquently for a better response.

In encouraging reflective practice, the Reader articles do not ignore the stress on professional carers dealing with death and dying. Tom Heller's 'Personal and medical memories from Hillsborough' is a poignant account of one GP's experience at the scene of the catastrophe. Heller, also a member of the School of Health and Social Welfare at the Open University, which produced this Reader, was one of the first doctors on the terrible scene. The subject of bereavement through violent death, accidental in the Hillsborough disaster, is extended to the case of murder in Lesley Moreland's 'Ruth: death by murder'. Her thoughts and experience following the murder of her daughter provide insight into a peculiarly traumatic form of sudden death.

The final pieces concern ways of remembering the dead: William Wordsworth's 'Essays upon epitaphs', from which we include excerpts, and 'December' one of the sequence of poems which Douglas Dunn wrote after the death of his wife.

51

Bereavement as a psychosocial transition
processes of adaptation to change

Colin Murray Parkes

People are fascinating because of their individuality; no two problems are alike because no two people are alike. This tempts some people to reject theories of human behaviour. There are none that can be expected to predict or explain more than part of a person, and it seems mechanistic to attempt to force people into preconceived models. Yet we must have some frame of reference if we are to be of use to those who cannot cope with life's vicissitudes. It is not enough for us to stay close and to open our hearts to another person's suffering; valuable though this sympathy may sometimes be, we must have some way of stepping aside from the maze of emotion and sensation if we are to make sense of it.

One might say that our central nervous system has been designed to enable us to do just that. Human beings, to a greater extent than other species, have the capacity to organize the most complex impressions into internal models of the world, which enable us to recognize and understand the world that we experience and to predict the outcome of our own and others' behaviour. Psychological theories are one way of doing this, and the measure of their success is their usefulness.

This article describes a theory that the writer has found useful in explaining certain aspects of the human reaction to loss. Other theories are useful in explaining other aspects; these include theories about the nature of attachments, anxiety, family dynamics and the psychophysiology of stress. Each of these adds something to our understanding of loss, and *they do not conflict* with each other.

Reactions to life events

Bereavement by death is often a major psychological trauma but there are some bereavements that are not a cause for grief and many griefs that have causes other than bereavement by death.

What then, defines a loss? How can we distinguish grief from the other emotions that arise in the face of life events? Why is it that some life events menace our sanity while others are an unmitigated blessing? These questions are more easily asked than answered.

Originally published in *Journal of Social Issues*, 1988, 44 (3): 53–65 (abridged and revised).

Grief is essentially an emotion that draws us toward something or someone that is missing. It arises from awareness of a discrepancy between the world that is and the world that 'should be'. This raises a problem for researchers because, though it is not difficult to discover the world that is, the world that should be is an internal construct; hence each person's experience of grief is individual and unique. Two women who have lost husbands are not the same. One may miss her husband greatly, while the other's grief may arise less from her wish to have her husband back (for she never did like him as a person) than from loss of the status and power that she achieved in marrying an important man. Clearly, grief is not a unitary phenomenon. [. . .]

Psychosocial transitions

Studies of the life events that commonly precede the onset of mental illness (Brown and Harris, 1978; Caplan, 1961; Rahe, 1979) suggest that the most dangerous life-change events are those that (a) require people to undertake a major revision of their assumptions about the world, (b) are lasting in their implications rather than transient, and (c) take place over a relatively short period of time so that there is little opportunity for preparation. These three criteria are the defining characteristics for events that can be termed 'psychosocial transitions' (PSTs) and that provide us with boundaries for a reasonably discrete area of study (Parkes, 1971). They exclude events that may threaten but do not result in any lasting change (e.g. exposure to terrifying situations over short periods of time) because these seem essentially different in their psychological implications. Insofar as these latter events cause psychiatric problems (such as anxiety reactions or post-traumatic neuroses), these are likely to be different from the disorders associated with PSTs. The criteria also exclude gradual changes, such as those associated with maturation, unless these are associated with more rapid changes that 'bring home' implications of the more gradual change. Thus the physical changes associated with sexual maturation do not constitute a PST, but they may bring about rapid attachments or disappointments that are PSTs. [. . .]

The assumptive world

The internal world that must change in the course of a PST consists of all those expectations and assumptions invalidated by the change in our life space (this is, the part of the world that impinges upon us – Lewin, 1935). These expectations constitute part of an organized schema or 'assumptive world', which contains everything that we assume to be true on the basis of our previous experience. It is this internal model of the world that we are constantly matching against incoming sensory data in order to orient ourselves, recognize what is happening and plan our behaviour accordingly.

Waking in the morning, we can put on the light, get out of bed and walk to the bathroom because we have an assumptive world that includes assumptions about the presence and layout of the doors, windows, light switches and rooms in our home, and assumptions about the parts of the body that we must use in turning the light on, getting out of bed, walking across the floor, etc. If as a result of some life event we lose a limb, go blind, lose our memory, move to a new house or have the electricity cut off, we must revise our assumptive world in order to cope with the numerous discrepancies that arise.

The death of a spouse invalidates assumptions that penetrate many aspects of life, from the moment of rising to going to sleep in an empty bed. Habits of action (setting the table for two) and thought ('I must ask my husband about that') must be revised if the survivor is to live as a widow.

The pain of change

Such changes are easier said than done, for not only does a major PST require us to revise a great number of assumptions about the world, but most of these assumptions have become habits of thought and behaviour that are now virtually automatic. The amputee knows very well that he has lost a limb, but this knowledge does not prevent him from leaping out of bed in the morning and sprawling on the floor because he has tried to stand on a leg that is not there. Likewise, the blind person 'looks' toward a sudden noise, and the widow 'hears' her husband's key in the lock. Each is operating on a set of assumptions that have become habitual over many years. Grief following bereavement by death is aggravated if the person lost is the person to whom one would turn in times of trouble. Faced with the biggest trouble she has ever had, the widow repeatedly finds herself turning toward a person who is not there.

These examples begin to explain why PSTs are so painful and take so much time and energy. For a long time it is necessary to take care in everything we think, say or do; nothing can be taken for granted any more. The familiar world suddenly seems to have become unfamiliar, habits of thought and behaviour let us down, and we lose confidence in our own internal world.

Freud (1917) called the process of reviewing the internal world after bereavement 'the work of mourning', and in many ways each PST is a job of work that must be done if a person is to adapt to the requirements of the real world. But the mind that is doing the reviewing is also the object that is being reviewed. A person is literally lost in his or her own grief, and the more disorganized one's thinking the more difficult it is to step aside from the disorganization and to see clearly what is lost and what remains.

Since we rely on having an accurate assumptive world to keep us safe, people who have lost confidence in their world model feel very unsafe. And because anxiety and fear cloud our judgement and impair concentration and memory, our attempts to make sense of what has happened are likely to be fitful, poorly directed and inadequate.

Coping and defence

Of course, people are not completely helpless when the level of anxiety becomes disorganizing. We have a number of coping mechanisms that usually reduce the level of tension or at least prevent it from rising any higher. Hence people in transition often withdraw from the challenges of the outside world, shut themselves up at home and restrict their social contacts to a small group of trusted people. They may avoid situations and chains of thought that will bring home the discrepancies between inside and outside worlds; they may fill their lives with distracting activities, or deny the full reality of what has happened. The complete range of psychological defence mechanisms can be called into play to protect someone from too painful a realization of a loss. These defences will often succeed in preventing anxiety from becoming disorganizing, but they are also likely to delay the relearning process.

Taking stock

The magnitude of a PST is such that it includes simultaneous dysfunctions in several areas of functioning. Thus the loss of a spouse may produce any or all of the following: (1) loss of sexual partner, (2) loss of protection from danger, (3) loss of reassurance of worth, (4) loss of job, (5) loss of companionship, (6) loss of income, (7) loss of recreational partner, (8) loss of status, (9) loss of expectations, (10) loss of self-confidence, (11) loss of a home, (12) loss of a parent for one's children, and many other losses. It may also produce (a) relief from responsibilities, (b) entitlement to the care of others, (c) sympathy from others and an increase in tenderness (or at least inhibition of hostility and competition), (d) attributions of heroism, (e) financial gains, and (f) freedom to realize potentialities that have been inhibited. These latter consequences, too, involve change in the life space and require that assumptions be modified, but since they also serve to assist those modifications (e.g. by providing time and opportunity for introspection, and by keeping people safe from threat during that time), they are more likely to facilitate than to impair the transition.

PSTs thus emerge as a complex interweaving of psychological and social processes, whose implications are far from clear to the person who undergoes them and even less clear to the would-be helper. Only in the most general terms can anyone else be said to 'understand'. But this does not mean we cannot help. By encouraging those who are in transition to help us understand, by talking about their situation, we help them take stock, review and relearn their assumptive world.

Resistance to change

Although minor changes are often embraced, major changes are more usually resisted. Resistance to change is seen as an obstacle by planners, but it is not always so irrational or so harmful as it seems. We can bring to the appraisal of new situations only the assumptions that arise out of old situations. Our old model of the world may be imperfect, but it is the best we have, and if we abandon it we have nothing left. Our first effort, in the face of change, must therefore be to interpret the change in the light of our old assumptions. To throw over old models of the world the moment they appear discrepant with the new is dangerous and often unnecessary. Closer scrutiny will sometimes reveal that our initial appraisal of the situation was incorrect and that the discrepancy was more apparent than real. Thus, a person who is told by a doctor that he has a terminal illness may be wise to ask for a second opinion before preparing himself to die.

Refusing to accept change also gives us time to begin rehearsing in our minds the implication of the change, should it come about. Thus, the patient who refuses surgery may need time to talk through its implications with his doctor and his family before changing his mind. While he does this, he is preparing a new model of the world, which will help ensure that the transition proceeds smoothly when, eventually, it comes about.

On the other hand, there may come a time when it is more dangerous to resist change than to accept it. Because the person in transition has no models of thought and behaviour to meet the new situation, he or she will eventually feel helpless and in danger. Three things are needed: emotional support, protection through the period of helplessness, and assistance in discovering new models of the world appropriate to the emergent situation. The first two of these may need to be provided before the person can begin to feel safe enough to accept the third. Thus, people whose sight has failed often refuse to learn blind skills until they have been supported in their helplessness and reached a point where they feel safe enough to accept the help of guide dogs, white canes and all the other means by which blind people can rebuild their model of the world. [. . .]

Implications of transition theory for bereavement

The death of a loved person evokes a characteristic emotion – pining for the lost person (or 'separation anxiety') – which is largely independent of the magnitude of the life change that will result. Thus, the death of a child may lead to very little change in the mother's model of the world, whereas the death of a spouse inevitably leads to a major upheaval. Yet it has been claimed that the emotional reaction of a mother to the death of a child is as great or greater than the typical reaction to the loss of a spouse (Fulton and Owen, 1971). This suggests that it is the nature and quality of the attachment that determines the intensity of grief, rather than the magnitude of the psychosocial transition that results. This does not mean that the PST is unimportant, but it does seem overshadowed, during the early phase of bereavement, by the pangs of grief, which are more easily explained in terms of attachment theory than transition theory. John Bowlby (1982) has shown how the bonds between human beings arise out of deep-seated innate mechanisms, which have evolved in order to ensure survival. The child's tie to the mother and the mother's tie to the child are biologically determined, and their very strength is a reflection of their survival value. Although derived from an inborn tendency, the child's attachment to its mother is influenced by its experience of its parents, and thus attachments may become secure or insecure. Basic trust arises out of these early attachments and then influences all later attachments, including those the child will make to his or her own children in years to come.

From this point of view, it is reasonable to suppose one's reaction to loss of a person will be determined as much by the biological significance of that person as by the magnitude of the life change resulting from the loss. In other respects, however, loss of a person resembles other losses such as that of a limb. [. . .]

Conclusion

Societies have always had their elders, doctors, shamans, priests and counsellors. Most of these have a dual role – to provide wise counsel and to perform rituals. The rituals mark the rites of passage (Van Gennep, 1909). They identify people in transition, induct them into a temporary status (as 'client', 'mourner', 'initiate', 'patient', etc.), and then, after sufficient time has elapsed, mark the end of the transition to a new identity (as 'widow', 'adult', 'disabled person', etc.). The rites performed by doctors include the provision of sickness certificates, prescriptions and a range of other procedures (some of them bloody) through which patients pass on the way to their new life.

The success of scientific medicine in finding cures for many diseases has distracted many members of the caring professions from their traditional responsibility to care for people in transition. As a result, medicine and its allied professions find themselves faced with the need to change, to face a psychosocial transition of their own, whose implications penetrate all aspects of our work. We can expect similar difficulties in revising our models of the world, to those experienced by the bereaved, the disabled and the dying when faced with irreversible changes in their lives. The implications of this model for members of the health care professions are spelt out in a recent book *Coping with Loss* (Parkes and Markus, 1998). Social workers and counsellors are likely to find it less difficult than medical personnel to make use of a theory of transition because much of their existing work is carried out from a similar viewpoint. Consequently, they may need to take the lead in educating doctors, nurses and other health care workers. It is hoped that the theory presented here will facilitate this transition.

References

Bowlby, J. (1982) *Attachment and Loss: Vol. 1 Attachment*. London: Hogarth.

Brown, G.W. and Harris, T. (1978) *Social Origins of Depression: A Study of Psychiatric Disorder in Women*. London: Tavistock.

Caplan, G. (1961) *An Approach to Community Mental Health*. London: Tavistock.

Freud, S. (1917) 'Mourning and melancholia', in *Standard Edition of the Complete Psychological Works of Sigmund Freud, Vol. 14*, ed. J. Strachey. New York: Norton, 1957.

Fulton, R. and Owen, G. (1971, October) *Adjustment to Loss through Death: A Sociological Analysis*. Center for Death Education and Research: University of Minnesota.

Lewin, K. (1935) *A Dynamic Theory of Personality*. New York: McGraw-Hill.

Parkes, C.M. (1971) 'Psycho-social transition: a field for study', *Social Science & Medicine*, 5: 101–5.

Parkes, C.M. and Markus, A. (eds) (1998) *Coping with Loss*. London: BMJ Books.

Rahe, R.H. (1979) 'Life events, mental illness: an overview', *Journal of Human Stress*, 5 (3): 2–10.

Van Gennep, A. (1909) *Les rites de passage*. (English translation, *The Rites of Passage*. London: Routledge & Kegan Paul, 1960.)

52

The social distribution of sentiments

Lindsay Prior

Mourning is not the spontaneous expression of individual emotions.

(Durkheim, 1968: 567)

[. . .] In this [article] I intend to do [two] things. The first is to trace the routes by which grief and sorrow were normalized and medicalized during the twentieth century. The second is to examine the evidence for the claim that human grief is socially patterned and socially channelled. [. . .]

The normalization of grief

[. . .] Grief in the twentieth century is primarily understood and 'managed' on the basis of principles which were first elaborated within the context of a normalizing psychology. The starting point of normalization rests in Freud's 1917 essay on mourning and melancholia in which he drew distinctions between normal and pathological responses to loss. This theme of pathology was extended in 1940 by Klein who asserted that all grief is in a sense pathological insofar as it apes the manic-depressive state – though for most people the phase is transitory. Now, these ideas contrast quite markedly with those of the nineteenth century in which grief, although it was sometimes viewed as a cause of insanity, was never interpreted as itself pathological. Grief, if anything, was a condition of the human spirit or soul rather than of the body and in that sense it could be neither normalized nor medicalized. The work of the psychoanalysts, however, was only the first in a series of processes which sought to medicalize grief. The second stage was represented in the work of Lindemann (1944).

Lindemann's work was the first to place the study of grief on an empirical footing and the first to establish a 'symptomatology of grief'. His work was based on the reactions of 101 bereaved 'patients' and included a number of subjects involved with the notorious Cocoanut Grove fire. His primary aim was to establish the symptomatology of grief and the secondary aim was to discuss the management of grief. The symptomatology was drawn in terms of five or six factors and the general conclusion which Lindemann arrived at was:

Extract from *The Social Organization of Death*, London: Macmillan, 1989, pp. 133–52 (abridged).

> Acute grief is a definite syndrome with psychological and somatic [bodily] symptomatology. (Lindemann, 1944: 141)

Furthermore, and in addition to reducing grief to a somatic state. Lindemann sought to measure it, and he did so by dividing his patients into those who suffered from normal and those who suffered from morbid grief. The two variables along which such normalization was assessed were those of intensity and duration, and he further argued that the management of grief should be related to these forms and factors. Needless to say, grief management was discussed in terms of the principles of clinical medicine alone.

The 'pathological' features of grief were emphasized in a somewhat disturbing article by Anderson (1949), entitled, 'Aspects of pathological grief and mourning', but the most forceful attempt to reduce grief to a somatically sited disease was that proposed by Engel (1961) in his paper 'Is grief a disease?', in which he directly compares grief to pathogenic bacteria Further developments in the attempt to characterize grief as a (double-edged) disease occurred with the publication of Parkes's work in the 1960s and 1970s, though, as the following quotations illustrate, the symptomatology of the proposed disease remains somewhat ambiguous.

> Of all the functional mental disorders almost the only one whose cause is known, whose symptomatology is stereotyped and whose outcome is usually predictable is grief. That grief is a mental disorder there can be no doubt, since it is associated with all the discomfort and loss of function which characterizes such disorders. (Parkes, 1965: 1)

By 1972 [sic], however, the blanket assessment that grief is a mental disorder was somewhat modified and now only the abnormal forms took this symptomatology.

> On the whole, grief resembles a physical injury more closely than any other type of illness. . . . But occasionally . . . abnormal forms arise, which may even be complicated by the onset of other types of illness. (Parkes, 1975: 19)

For all of these authors and investigators, then, grief was something in the body which could be measured and assessed. The intensity and duration of grief were factors whose origins could be located in the biochemistry of the body or in the infantile history of the subject, and the context in which grief was analysed was viewed in medical terms, or at best in psychotherapeutic terms. Furthermore, the medicalization and normalization of grief took place within a theory of developmental stages. [. . .] In this view, human behaviour is seen to involve an unfolding of human potential towards an ultimate stage of stability or 'reintegration'. This theme has dominated the study of many and varied facets of death. Kübler-Ross (1970), for example, analyses the responses of the dying in terms of five stages: denial and isolation, anger, bargaining, depression and acceptance. And Backer et al. (1982) invoke the concept of stages in order to account for attitudes to death among children and therapeutic responses of hospital staff, as well as the responses of the terminally ill. In like manner, most of those who discuss grief also use the developmental metaphor. Thus Parkes (1975) talks of phases of yearning and phases of despair. Backer et al. (1982) list three stages: yearning, anger and guilt, and disorganization. Kavanaugh (1972) lists seven stages: shock, disorganization, volatile emotions, loss, loneliness, relief and re-establishment. Attempts to categorize grief as it occurs in specific age groups and populations have also been made and probably the most notable of these was that of Bowlby (1961) in his study of bereaved children. Broadly speaking, however, it is in terms of stages and timescales that the normal is assessed and it is within this context that grief is seen to unfold within the human psyche.

Despite the fact that both Lindemann and Bowlby gave a hesitant nod in the direction of social factors when they were assessing the impact of grief on the bereaved individual, most authors seem to have remained quite ignorant of the work of Durkheim and Hertz. The Durkheimians [. . .] had sought, very early on in the twentieth century, to discuss and explore the fact that the intensity of grief was not the product of some inner unfolding, but of social processes which tended to channel grief in some directions whilst deflecting it away from others. The structural distribution of grief seems to have been more or less ignored until the publication of Peter Marris's work on widows (1958) and Gorer's work on the bereaved (1965), and though both of the latter authors continued to assess grief in terms of the 'normal', 'stages' and timetables, they did supplement the study of grief with the missing link of social structure.

Broadly speaking, however, it is clear that psychology and anthropology adopted incommensurable standpoints on the study of grief, so that whilst the first concentrated on the subjective experience of grief in different populations, the second concentrated on the outward expression of grief and utilized that outward expression as an indicator of inner sentiment. In Western culture, it was psychology which therefore dominated the study of grief and bereavement during the twentieth century and, overall, the problem of grief, like death before it, became medicalized and individualized and subsequently fell under the control of medical personnel. Thus, the priest was ousted from the aftermath of death in favour of the doctor and grief was treated (in all senses of that word) as a private and segmented emotion. It was this segmentation and individualization of grief which prompted Gorer to carry out his study of the phenomenon, and it was on the basis of that study that he theorized about the denial of death in Western culture. [. . .]

Sentiments and social structure

The attempts to normalize grief, in terms of the assumptions and theories of psychology, took a new turn, as we have seen, in the analysis undertaken by

Lindemann. And this concern to trace out the nature and limits of grief in empirical populations was further developed in the work of Marris (1958) and Gorer (1965). Marris's work was based on a study of 72 London widows, whilst Gorer's work encompassed a far wider range of bereaved individuals drawn from a number of age, sex, class and regional groupings. In both cases the intensity and duration of grief were studied empirically and some estimate of the normal and the abnormal was made. Neither study, however, explored the Durkheimian hypothesis that grief is socially distributed and socially controlled. In fact, Gorer, an avowed anthropologist, reached the somewhat curious conclusion that contemporary mourning practices are marked by a total lack of ritual – the consequence of which is 'maladaptive behaviour'. In the England of the 1960s, he concluded, 'The most typical reaction [to death] is . . . the denial of mourning' (1965: 113). Marris's work also rested on many of the prevailing assumptions of psychological theory, though he did recognize that sociological factors impinged on the intensity and duration of grief. Thus, in his 1974 work he asserted that:

> The severity of grief depends, then, on the degree of [social] disruption: and it can be at least crudely predicted from the emphasis which a society places upon different relationships. (Marris, 1974: 38)

In that sense, the loss of infants and of the old is, for example, less disruptive than the loss of those in the economically active age groups, or of the married.

The claim that grief is controlled and distributed in terms of social ritual, as I have suggested, can be traced back to the work of Durkheim and Hertz. Both men argued that the intensity of grief expended by any individual or group was dependent on a socially constructed formula, rather than on innate or natural feeling. Thus, the mourning of infants or strangers was always cursory, whilst the mourning of healthy and active adults was not. [. . .]

One of the strongest adaptations of the Durkheimian thesis was that advanced by Monica Wilson in her (1957) study of the Nyakyusa. This study had its precursor in Godfrey Wilson's (1939) analysis of Nyakyusa burial rites which emphasized a number of issues which are worth noting here. Most important from our point of view was his claim that a 'normal' emotional response could not be assessed in purely statistical terms but only in terms of what is regarded as obligatory by any given group. To obey the constraints of the group is normal, to ignore them is abnormal. Normality was, therefore, socially imposed.

Secondly, the emotions which were so imposed were often socially differentiated. Thus, whilst Nyakyusa burial 'is a lively event', there were still marked differences between the reactions of males and females. Broadly speaking 'the women wail and the men dance', and the funerary ritual emphasized male strength and courage as against female fear and trembling. The women wept all of the time; the chief mourners wept only once or twice and, according to Wilson, the latter were *obliged* to show grief. Finally, he noted that the length of the mourning period depended on the status of the deceased: high status, extended mourning; low status, truncated mourning. The clearest expression of such sociologism, however, was that given by Monica Wilson in her discussion of Nyakyusa *rites de passage*:

> The rituals heighten the emotions and canalize them. They both teach men to feel, and teach them what it is proper to feel. (Wilson, 1957: 232)

Other observations on this funerary theme have been provided by Goody (1962) in his study of the LoDagaa. Goody claimed two things in this connection. First, that different social relationships demanded different expressions of grief, and second, that the amount of grief displayed varied according to the social status of the deceased. Thus, he noted that among the LoDagaa physical restraint was used on the bereaved (either sym-bolically or physically), and that the differences in standardized restraints indicated a diminution of the grief expected in the three classes of kinsfolk affected by bereavement. Hence, conjugal and parental roles demanded the sharpest display, followed by siblings, followed in turn by those who fulfilled filial roles. Furthermore, he often implied that the elaborateness of the funerary ritual was a direct function of the amount of wealth to be redistributed at death, though that was not the only source of differ-entiation, and it was equally clear from the study that this was also dependent on the existence of a social personality. Thus, 'The LoDagaa display no public grief at the death of an unweaned child, for it is not yet accorded human status' (1962: 149). [. . .]

The most adventurous claims of social anthropology on this theme of public displays of sorrow, however, are undoubtedly those made by Radcliffe-Brown in his study of the Andaman Islanders (1922). In that work Radcliffe-Brown offered a theory of weeping. He noted that in Andamanese society there were seven occasions for ceremonial weeping, three of which involved reciprocal (interactive) weeping and four of which involved one-sided weeping (as, for example, in weeping for a dead person). In keeping with his broad functionalist position he sought to discover the purposes of such weeping both for the individuals involved and for the social structure as a whole. He concluded that for individuals, ceremonial weeping served to release emotional tension, but its wider, social purpose was more interesting and more fundamental. Thus, of weeping, he stated:

> The purpose of the rite is to affirm the existence of a social bond between two or more persons. (Radcliffe-Brown, 1922: 240)

Social bonds were therefore asserted and emphasized in public declarations. Consequently, without the bond there could be no weeping. Thus, in

Andamanese society children, who had not yet been awarded a social personality, were 'little mourned' and, 'a stranger who dies or is killed is buried unceremoniously or is cast into the sea' (1922: 109).

My purpose in citing these various cases of anthropological and historical investigation is solely to illustrate the point that grief, at least in its public manifestations, is socially variable and that the social location of a deceased person has much to do with the manner in which grief is expressed. [. . .] It is enough to show that grief is distributed according to social principles and to suggest that the experience of grief is, in some part, reflected in its public expression. [. . .] All public expressions of grief act as a mirror in which private feelings are reflected, and as the public expressions wax and wane so does the social base of the sentiments behind them.

References

Anderson, C. (1949) 'Aspects of pathological grief and mourning', *International Journal of Psychoanalysis*, 30: 48–55.

Backer, B.A., Hannon, N. and Russell, N.A. (1982) *Death and Dying: Individuals and Institutions*. New York: Wiley.

Bowlby, J. (1961) 'Processes of mourning', *International Journal of Psychoanalysis*, 42: 4–5, 317–40.

Durkheim, E. (1968) *Les formes élémentaires de la vie religieuse*. Paris: PUF.

Engel, G. (1961) 'Is grief a disease?', *Psychosomatic Medicine*, 23: 18–22.

Freud, S. (1917) 'Mourning and melancholia', in *Standard Edition of the Complete Psychological Works of Sigmund Freud, Vol. 14*, ed. J. Strachey. London: Hogarth, 1957.

Goody, J. (1962) *Death, Property and the Ancestors: A Study of the Mortuary Customs of the LoDagaa of West Africa*. Stanford, CA: Stanford University Press.

Gorer, G. (1965) *Death, Grief and Mourning in Contemporary Britain*. London: Cresset.

Kavanaugh, R. (1972) *Facing Death*. Baltimore, MD: Penguin.

Klein, M. (1940) 'Mourning and its relationship to manic depressive states', *International Journal of Psycho-Analysis*, 21: 125–53.

Kübler-Ross, E. (1970) *On Death and Dying*. London: Tavistock.

Lindemann, E. (1944) 'Symptomatology and management of acute grief', *American Journal of Psychiatry*, 101: 141–8.

Marris, P. (1958) *Widows and their Families*. London: Routledge & Kegan Paul.

Marris, P. (1974) *Loss and Change*. London: Routledge & Kegan Paul.

Parkes, C.M. (1965) 'Bereavement and mental illness', *British Journal of Medical Psychology*, 38: 1–12.

Parkes, C.M. (1975) *Bereavement*. Harmondsworth: Penguin.

Radcliffe-Brown, A.R. (1922) *The Andaman Islanders*. Cambridge: Cambridge University Press.

Wilson, G. (1939) 'Nyakyusa conventions of burial', *Bantu Studies*, 13: 1–31.

Wilson, M. (1957) *Rituals of Kinship among the Nyakyusa*. London: Oxford University Press.

53

Cross-cultural perspectives on bereavement

Shirley Firth

Religious and cultural rituals

Religious and cultural rituals invest death with meaning from religious, psychological and social perspectives. All the major religions of the world teach that there is some sort of continuity or survival after death. They also comfort and re-assure the mourners by helping to make sense of death and personal loss. Thirdly, they provide shape and meaning to the process of mourning, which lasts for a clearly defined period in many cultures, providing 'milestones' during the period of mourning, allowing the bereaved a gradual time to let go of the deceased and adjust to the changes in their lives psychologically, as well as to changes of status socially. Buddhists, Hindus, Muslims and Sikhs may come from very different religious traditions, yet they all believe in some form of continuity after death and the importance of dying well. In their countries of origin they share some common presuppositions about the nature of family life and marriage, and the role of the wider community. In Britain most have come from the Indian subcontinent although many South Asians, particularly Hindus and Sikhs migrated from East Africa. They tend to live in extended families and maintain closely knit communities, although this may change as new generations move elsewhere to find work.

It is important for carers to understand the religious beliefs and cultural traditions of members of these communities, and be aware of the problems they face when they are unable to follow them because of changes in medical practice, bureaucracy or lack of adequate religious or social support.

Preparing the body

For most cultures the laying-out of the body is an important part of the final care of the deceased person (cf. David Clark, 'Death in Staithes', in Part 1 of this Reader, pp. 4–9). Hindus have caste and family traditions concerning the washing and dressing procedures, which are done by relatives of the same sex. Ganges water is usually used to purify the body. A

I would like to acknowledge my gratitude to the following who helped in preparing this paper: Rahim Bashir, Parveen Damani, Ven. Vajiragnana, Piara Singh Sambhi, and members of the Indian community who shared their experiences with me.

man is dressed in the type of clothes he normally wears, and a woman in a sari, or *salvar kameze*. If she predeceases her husband she will wear a wedding sari. Sikhs follow similar procedures, dressing the deceased in the five Ks as in life (cf. Shirley Firth, 'Approaches to Death in Hindu and Sikh Communities in Britain' in Part 1 of this Reader, pp. 28–34. The body is then placed in a coffin and taken by hearse to the family home.

Among Buddhists family members wash the body, sometimes using scented lotions, dress it in traditional clothes, which may either be what is normally worn, or in white, the colour of mourning, and place it in the coffin. Flowers are not used normally in Sri Lanka. Some Vietnamese cover the face with white cloth or paper to provide a symbolic barrier between the living and the dead (Pearson, 1982: 480).

Muslims prepare the body in the local mosque if there are suitable facilities, or at the local undertakers, according to strict rules. This should be done immediately after death, because until it is done the body is impure, and those performing the ablutions will not be able to say their prayers until they too have bathed. The body has to be washed three times, the first two times with soap and water, and finally with camphor or scented materials, starting with the parts of the body which have to be washed before prayer, carefully observing the modesty of the person at all times. It is then placed in a shroud, or *kafan*, and now the family can have their last viewing. The strict rule which applies in life to the mingling of the sexes still applies in death; a woman who belongs to one of the prohibited relationships for social contact may attend the funeral but cannot look upon the face of the deceased, if male, and vice versa.

Funerals

On the Indian subcontinent Hindus and Sikhs dispose of the body of the deceased within 24 hours. In Britain there may be delays of seven days or more waiting for space in the crematorium, and longer if a post-mortem is required. This causes major disruption in the mourning patterns, which would normally begin immediately after the body has been disposed of and in Britain has to begin before. For Hindus, because of the limited space and time in the crematorium, part of the service which would normally take place at the pyre in India, is shortened and adapted in the home. While the *pandit* (priest) chants from the scriptures the chief mourner (normally the eldest son) performs the rituals according to caste and family traditions. Herbs, sandalwood, clarified butter (which purifies the body and helps it burn) and flowers may be placed on the body. Ganges water and *tulsi* (basil) are put in the mouth, along with a coin, symbolizing payment of the ferryman crossing the river of death. Then the family and mourners circumambulate the coffin to bid farewell. The coffin is closed and taken to the crematorium. All the friends, neighbours and community members follow except for some Gujarati women. After a few prayers and a homily by the pandit or a senior community member, the eldest son or sons go down into the crematorium and press the button, or may push the coffin in.

Mourners and friends then return to the deceased's home, and sit quietly with the family. The principal mourners may bathe at a friend's house before returning home. Panjabi members of the Arya Samaj sect return to the house for a *havan*, the sacred fire ceremony, followed by the giving of a *pagri*, turban, to the eldest son to signify that he is now head of the household.

Children are not normally cremated under the age of three or four, as they have unformed personalities and are too pure to require the ritual purification of fire. They do not have a normal funeral and may be buried with little ceremony in a special corner of the cemetery, or with a pandit saying some prayers.

Sikhs follow a similar pattern to Hindus, although the content of ritual is different and much simpler (Kalsi, 1996). The body is usually brought back to the house for a last viewing, and the *granthi* may attend and say prayers. The family and friends circumambulate the coffin which is then taken to the *gurdwara* (place of worship) where the *granthi* says prayers, and the family, male friends and neighbours walk around the coffin. At the crematorium there is a short service with prayers, and a homily. The evening hymn, *Kirtan Sohila*, is sung before concluding with prayers. The mourners return to the *gurdwara* for a service with a eulogy and prayers, and then return to the family home for a meal. Many Sikhs traditionally bury children, although according to Cole and Sambhi (1978: 177), infants should be cremated where the facilities exist. Sikh infants have a simplified ceremony but no meal is offered afterwards.

Muslims must bury the dead immediately, according to the *Hadith* (the traditional sayings of the Prophet Mohammed). This is often impossible in Britain because of local bureaucracy over the registration of deaths and grave digging. The body, in a coffin, is carried on the shoulders of male relatives or friends either to the mosque or directly to the cemetery, where the funeral prayer (*salat-ul-janazah*) is said. (Women are not allowed to go.) In the mosque it is placed in front of the Imam, who faces Mecca. Prayers are said without the bowing and prostration accompanying normal prayer (Prickett, 1980: 95).

At the cemetery the body is addressed by a reciter who

> addresses him by name, gently shaking the shoulders, and reminds him of the fundamental beliefs of the faith. The underlying philosophy is that the person is not dead but merely in transition to the hereafter. (Bashir Rahim, personal communication)

The body should be buried in a deep grave facing Mecca. The Imam or a leading community member recites verses from the Qur'an, including Surah 20:55: 'From the [earth] did We create you, and into it shall We return you, and from it shall We bring you out once again'. In some cities there are special areas for Muslim burials, and in some they are permitted to bury the shrouded body without a coffin.

Buddhist teaching is directed towards a recognition that death comes to everybody and is part of the changing flux and continuity of existence (cf. Neuberger, 1987: 44). The time for the burial or cremation depends on the tradition of the country of origin. The service may take place in the house prior to going to the cemetery or crematorium. Monks are invited to remind the mourners of the impermanence and fleeting nature of life. Then one monk will make a funeral oration explaining Buddhist teaching and talk about the deceased, his or her family and achievements. The whole funeral is geared towards the comforting and education of the mourners.

Mourning

All four religions discourage too much weeping. Hindus say weeping creates a river which the soul has to cross. Sikh Gurus discourage excessive grief, because the deceased has gone to God. The *Hadith* says that weeping is permitted for three days and wailing is forbidden. However, it still occurs in all three communities on the Indian subcontinent. The expression of grief is often less inhibited than among native Britons and there may also be emotional outbursts at funerals in Britain. One young Muslim woman who was reminded that wailing was forbidden pointed out that if she did not wail the rest of the community would criticize her for not having enough feeling.

For Hindus the period of mourning lasts for 10 to 16 days. The family are regarded as extremely impure, and no other Hindu will receive food or drink from them, although this is changing. Furniture is removed from the living room, white sheets spread on the floor, and friends and neighbours drop in throughout the day to condole and listen to the readings from the *Bhagavad Gita* or other books, and to sing hymns. The family live austerely on simple food, without radio or television. On the 10th to 12th days a series of rituals enable the soul (*atman*) to form a new 'celestial' body and join the ancestors, although these are usually done on the same day, and are considered by many Hindus to be the most important rituals they can do for the deceased. Gifts of money, food and clothing, which the deceased would normally need, are given to the Brahmin priests or to charity.

There are further rituals at one, three and six months. Widows used to be in mourning for at least a year, but here it is reduced to three months, after which they can go out and gradually resume normal life. In addition there is an annual ceremony, called *shraddha*, in which further offerings are made to the deceased relatives on the anniversary of the death and to all the ancestors during a period in the autumn called *pitr paksha*, maintaining a continuous link between the living and the dead. Gifts are made to Brahmins and to charity.

Sikhs follow a similar pattern in the home, without the severe restrictions of Hindus. It is the custom to read the holy book, the *Guru Granth Sahib*, either continuously for three days (*akhand path*) or over 8 to 10 days (*sadharan path*). This should normally begin after the funeral, but if there is a long delay, perhaps because of an inquest, it may be started sooner. At the conclusion of the reading and prayers, if the deceased was head of the household, there is a ceremony offering a turban (*pagri*) to his heir, followed by a feast in celebration of a long life if the deceased was elderly.

Islamic law requires friends and relatives to feed mourners for three days. After this the family should return to normal, and no one should talk about death or the deceased, unless the family is grieving too much or brings the subject up. The only greeting given at this time is 'From God we come, to God we return'. Unofficial mourning often continues until the 40th day with Qur'anic readings. At the end of this period the family may call their relatives and friends and have further readings and a meal to signal the end of mourning. At the end of Ramadan, during the festival of Eid, graves are visited.

Among Sri Lankan Buddhists mourners may return to work in three or four days. There are no religious restrictions for widows, although they may withdraw from social life for a time. Chinese Vietnamese Buddhists call the monks again on the seventh day to give the spirit a 'send-off', when all the relatives and friends come, and money is given to the temple. Other Vietnamese have a series of rituals which enable the spirit of the deceased to join the realm of the ancestors, and they will be especially honoured during the anniversary of the death and the lunar new year. Mourning lasts for 100 days, during which time no one wears bright colours or flowers. A man's wife and children must mourn for three years, but the immediate family only mourns for one year on the death of a woman (Pearson, 1982: 480).

Finding meaning

Hindus believe that after death most people are reborn in a better or worse state, depending on how they have fulfilled their *dharma* (cf. Firth, Chapter 4 above). A common explanation for premature or untimely death is *karma*. The death of a child may be seen as either the parent's or child's *karma*, or both, as one Hindu explained:

> The child has a certain period fixed with you. [Understanding this] helps the parents to come to terms with the death . . . the only way you can explain to the mother is that this child was only going to live with you for five years, and you have to accept it, because now the child has gone for its betterment.

Sikhs also accept the concept of *karma* and rebirth, but believe these are under God's control. Physical death is not to be feared – only spiritual death – and those who are close to God will be united with God after death.

Buddhists also believe in rebirth, although it is not the soul that is reborn, but a collection of five aggregates containing patterns created by *karma*. At popular level this may be understood as fate, so that if a person dies young it is seen as being ordained. Buddhist teaching emphasizes the ephemeral nature of life and provides the way to overcome the suffering inherent in it.

Muslims believe that everything that happens is the will of Allah [God]. At death the soul awaits the Day of Judgement, when the righteous will be resurrected and go to heaven and the wicked and unbelievers will go to hell. The belief that everything is in the hands of God brings great comfort at the time of bereavement. A Muslim woman who lost a much-wanted baby boy prematurely said that she found great comfort from her faith and from a visit to Mecca:

> We have three days' strict mourning, when the neighbours and friends come to help with food, and you talk about the death, and read the Qur'an, and you remember that this is God's will, that everything that happens, happens according to His will. He is gracious and merciful, and never sends you a trial that you can't handle. He always gives you the strength you need. And because I know it was God's will, I feel I can cope, I have made a good adjustment, even though I miss my son, because I know he and I are in God's hands.

Problems of change

With hospital deaths in the United Kingdom several problems can arise. Muslims do not want anyone of a different faith – or of the opposite sex – to touch a body, although some will accept medical staff touching it if there is no one else to do it and rubber gloves are worn. No non-Muslim can give the ritual bath. A Muslim nurse pointed out that discretion must be used:

> I went to see this young Muslim who had died vomiting a lot of stale blood and had been left with his face in it. You need to have common sense. Can you imagine coming in to see your father or husband like that and remembering it for the rest of your life? Generally people don't mind having the tubes removed and the body straightened, but the important thing is to communicate with the family so that you know beforehand what you can do.

Great distress may be caused if a post-mortem is needed, especially for Muslims, whose belief in resurrection of the body makes the idea of mutilation abhorrent. (It also means that amputated limbs or organs or aborted foetuses must be buried and not disposed of in any other way.) To open the body to find out why death occurred seems to deny that death is God's will. The thought of the head being opened is particularly horrifying, and the Muslim insistence on modestly covering the private parts will also be violated, especially if passages have to be blocked. It is believed that the body still has a level of consciousness that enables the person to feel pain and to know what is happening.

Delays in timing before burial or cremation can also cause problems, as there are religious as well as practical reasons why disposal should be immediate in the countries of origin. For Muslims, burial should take place where the person has died so the custom of returning the body to the country of origin is a matter of recent tradition – a need to return to one's roots, to ensure the burial is properly done, and to allow relatives to visit the grave.

Buddhists are less concerned about timing. Tibetan Buddhists believe that consciousness may remain for as long as three days and even longer for accomplished meditators. To cremate prematurely before the loss of consciousness is absolutely certain, is tantamount to murder.

For Hindus, delay in cremating the body could, in theory, disturb the proper progress of the soul and prevent it from becoming an ancestor or being reborn. It also upsets the mourning procedures which normally begins immediately after the funeral, but which, if there is a delay, have to be set in motion beforehand. Eisenbruch (1984b) shows that 'When it is impossible to carry out traditional rituals that have great meaning and serve to comfort the bereaved, the stress of bereavement is amplified'.

The notion of professional people who are paid to arrange things for them is regarded by some Asians as a complete denial of the community aspect they are used to, even though funeral directors are often perceived to be more sympathetic than some medical staff. A Sikh man said:

> Whoever heard of funeral directors in the Punjab? Here funerals are administered by third parties who take money for this purpose, whereas in the Punjab a funeral is very properly a community affair.

He spoke of his shock, when his little boy died in England, at having to carry the little coffin by hearse instead of on his own shoulder, as he would have done in India (cf. Kalsi, 1996).

Young Asians who have been brought up in Britain may never experience a death in the family until their late teens, and may be expected to mourn for relatives in India or East Africa whom they have rarely or never met. Even if it is a close relative who has died, young people may have difficulty coping with the expectations of relatives or other community members. One young girl said:

> They used to cry loudly, so loudly, but what they were doing really was impressing everybody around them that they were feeling the grief, but what you really feel inside is something different.

Traditional family structures are changing in Britain with Westernized education, social and geographic mobility. This may mean that close relatives may not be at hand at the time of a death, although delays do allow them to get to the funeral. Fragmentation of the family may create problems when widowed elders come to live with younger members who have established a nuclear family.

Conclusion

As can be seen, Asians bring with them a rich heritage of religious and cultural traditions, which can be disrupted by bureaucratic requirements over disposal. The changes are perhaps the most radical for Hindus because the lengthy rituals depend on specialist priests, and there is neither the time nor, often, the expertise readily available in Britain. However, provided that they can preserve those traditions which are really important, such as being present at the death, giving Ganges water and performing the *shraddha*, Hindus are pragmatic about the changes.

It is at the time of death that communal solidarity is strongest, and members from all communities support one another, which is perceived to be of very real help and comfort despite the pressure of visitors. Legitimated weeping is a valuable expression of grief, and the alternation between talking about the dead person, weeping and scripture readings provides a gradual period of adjustment to his/her absence. The regular gatherings of family and friends reinforce social and religious bonds. The psychological value of the mourning period warrants close attention, as the absence of proper mourning procedures, rituals and an acceptable way of dealing with grief may make adjustments more difficult. In the Asian communities, it is at the time of crisis that the great strengths of the community appear; cultural and religious beliefs give help and support and prove of great value.

Bibliography

Berger, Arthur et al. (eds) (1989) *Perspectives on Death and Dying: Cross-Cultural and Multi-Disciplinary Views*. Philadelphia: Charles Press.

Cole, W.O. and Sambhi, P.S. (1978) *The Sikhs, their Religious Beliefs and Practices*. London: Routledge and Kegan Paul.

Eisenbruch, Maurice (1984a) 'Cross-cultural aspects of bereavement I: a conceptual framework for comparative analysis', *Culture, Medicine and Psychiatry*, 8 (3), September: 283–309.

Eisenbruch, Maurice (1984b) 'Cross-cultural aspects of bereavement II: ethnic and cultural variations in the development of bereavement practices', *Culture, Medicine and Psychiatry*, 8 (4), December: 315–37.

Gardner, Katy (1996) 'Death and burial amongst Bengali Muslims in Tower Hamlets, East London', paper given at the conference, A Comparative Study of the South Asian Diaspora Religious Experience in Britain, Canada and USA. School of Oriental and African Studies, November, 1996.

Kalsi, Sewa Singh (1996) 'Change and continuity in the funeral rituals of Sikhs in Britain', in Howarth Glennys and Peter C. Jupp (eds), *Contemporary Issues in the Sociology of Death, Dying and Disposal*. Basingstoke: Macmillan. pp. 30–43.

Knappert, Jan (1989) 'The concept of death and the afterlife in Islam', in A. Berger et al. (eds), pp. 55–64.

Muwahidi, Ahmad Anisuzzaman (1989) 'Islamic perspectives on death and dying', in A. Berger et al. (eds), pp. 38–54.

Neuberger, J. (1987) *Caring for Dying People of Different Faiths*. London: Lisa Sainsbury.

Pearson, R. (1982) 'Understanding the Vietnamese in Britain, Part II: Marriage, Death and Religion', *Health Visitor*, Vol. 55 (Sept.).

Prickett, J. (ed.) (1980) *Death in Living Faiths Series*. London and Guildford: Lutterworth Educational.

Sogyal Rinpoche (1992) *The Tibetan Book of Living and Dying*. London: Random House.

54

I desperately needed to see my son

Sheila Awoonor-Renner

Recently my child was killed in a road accident. He was 17. The journey had begun at 1 p.m. and he died at 3.28 p.m. I was told at 7.10 p.m. I couldn't quite understand why they had travelled such a short distance in six hours. My mind must have thought that it happened just before I was told. As the policeman who came to tell me of my son's death said that they were unable to take me to the hospital it took me some time to find someone to take me to him. The police at first seemed relieved that I had a car and could drive, but in the circumstances that was impossible. They were then anxious for me to find a relative to take me, and when I failed then a friend. I failed at friends, too. By now they were getting desperate – what about neighbours? I didn't know them either. In fact, there was a huge gulf between my reality and their understanding. My reality was that I needed someone close enough to be able to reveal myself safely who would not take over and do the right thing and say the right words and with whom I would have to behave as they were projecting I should behave. The people I needed are rare and were away. Therefore what I wanted was someone impersonal, a stranger – someone with no expectations of me. The police would have done nicely. I also needed someone with a good reliable car and without children who could just drop everything to take me to a place 50 to 60 miles away in the middle of an ordinary evening. Eventually, though shocked and barely able to function, I found somebody able to take me. The police were to tell the hospital of our intended arrival.

On arrival at the hospital just after 10.15 p.m. no one was expecting us. 'Everybody has gone now, and I should have gone too by now,' a social worker said. My friend and I were put in a small anteroom and the door was closed. We had been put in a box with the lid closed to spare us the sight of panicky people rushing to and fro, telephone calls being made, etc., while the system was being re-assembled for us. I wouldn't have that. I behaved myself for three to four minutes, then I opened the door. I still couldn't see anything but felt better. What would have made me feel much better was to have seen and shared the panic. That would have been human: being put in a small, quiet, impersonal room behind a closed door was not.

Eventually the system assembled itself again. It seemed that I had not after all come to see my son but to identify him. The hospital manager was

From *British Medical Journal*, 1991, 302: 356.

kind and caring with a woman's warmth. She knew what I needed or nearly knew. What I desperately needed was to see my son. But it was explained that I couldn't see him until I had been interviewed by the coroner's officer, who, not knowing I was to arrive, was somewhere else. Eventually he arrived. By now I was getting nicely institutionalized. I was behaving myself. I put him at his ease when he asked his questions – well, I tried to. He, poor man, knew the formula and knew each question had to be put with a sympathetic preamble. He was unctuous. He was sorrowful. And I wanted to see my son. He knew what to do with grieving relatives. He knew the formula, so he did it – to the end. He had no idea who, in reality, I was. I said that I wanted to see my son alone – no, I asked permission to see my son alone. Permission was granted on condition that I 'didn't do anything silly'.

With no idea what 'anything silly' was I acquiesced, imagining he meant 'don't touch and don't disturb anything'. He disappeared. Apparently there was great rushing about preparing Timothy for viewing. Putting a piece of gauze over a graze on his forehead was regarded as important so that I should not be offended or frightened or disgusted. We walked along a corridor. We arrived at a door. It was opened. No more hope; no more thinking it might not be Timothy. Incredibly, it was my Timothy. It was him, my lovely boy.

He was lying on an altar covered by a purple cloth, which was edged with gold braid and tassels. Only his head was visible. Such was the atmosphere of constraint I either asked permission or was given permission to enter. I can't remember. I entered, alone. The others stayed watching through the open door. I reached him and stroked his cheek. He was cold.

Timothy was my child; he had not ceased to be my child. I desperately needed to hold him, to look at him, to find out where he was hurting. These instincts don't die immediately with the child. The instinct to comfort and cuddle, to examine and inspect the wounds, to try to understand, most of all, to hold. But I had been told 'not to do anything silly'. And they were watching me to see that I didn't. So I couldn't move the purple cloth. I couldn't find his hand by lifting the cloth. I couldn't do anything. I betrayed my instincts and my son by standing there 'not doing anything silly'. Because I knew that if I did my watchers would come in immediately, constrain me, and lead me away.

Why did they do this? No doubt they thought that they were acting for the best. We, as a society, have lost contact with our most basic instincts. The instincts we share with other mammals. We marvel at cats washing and caring for their kittens. We admire the protection an elephant gives to her sick calf, and we are tearful and sympathetic when she refuses to leave her offspring when he dies, when she examines him, and nuzzles him, and wills him to breathe again. And we have forgotten that that is exactly what the human mother's most basic instinct tells her to do. And we deny her. If a human mother is not able to examine, hold and nuzzle her child she is being denied her motherhood when *in extremis*.

We have come to think that we are protecting her when we are really protecting ourselves. We have forgotten that this is the mother who has cleaned up the vomit, who has washed his nappies, who has dealt with and cleared away his diarrhoea. She has cleaned the blood from his wounds, she has kissed him better, and she has held him in his distress. She has done all of this since the day he was born. If he has been a patient in hospital she has possibly fed him by tube, she may have changed his dressings, she may have given him his injections. She will certainly have washed him and helped him to dress and combed his hair. And she will have held him.

Again I ask, who are we protecting when we deny her this last service which she can do for her child? We are not protecting the child. There is nothing she can do to harm her child. We are not protecting her: the fact of her child's death is not altered by the denial of her instincts.

Having nursed my mother through her last illness at home I was privileged to bathe her after death, to redress her wounds with clean dressings, to remove her catheter and drainage. It was a tearful and loving last service that my sister and I were privileged to perform for her. And it helped to heal our grief.

But my lovely boy was draped on an altar, covered with a purple robe, and all expressions of love and care which I had were denied to me. And I don't know when that wound will heal.

The time has come when we in the caring services should think again about how we serve the bereaved. A cup of tea and an aseptic look at the body does not serve. If it is their wish and instinct to wash the body, to hold the body, and to talk to the dead loved one then they should be helped to do this. They will be distressed and they may frequently need to stop to wipe the tears. But they will be helped in their healing. How ironic that we will have to retrain ourselves to help in this most basic service, but this is something which we must do.

55

A single parent confronting the loss of an only child

Evelyn Gillis

My daughter, Lorena Mary Main, age 22,
died with my sister, Mary, in an auto accident,
April 26, 1981.

Good night, sweet Lorena.
I'll see you in the morning.
Mom.

The word 'alone' screams at a single parent. Those of us who become single parents – either through death or divorce – find most physical, emotional and financial support severed. We must learn to accept independence from our spouse and assume full responsibility for our child. Daily life for our broken family must be maintained and sustained. It becomes necessary to live as normal a family lifestyle as possible.

After we recover from the emotional trauma of death or divorce, we create a new family unit of parent and child. As the child ages, and if we do not remarry, our relationship evolves beyond that of parent and child. Our lives become closely entwined. The child becomes a companion and help-mate. All of our parental love and caring is given to this one child.

Upon the death of the child, we face the absence of support from another adult who would share the same feelings of loss and grief. After being told of the child's death, we alone carry the responsibility of the funeral arrangements. Even when help is offered by friends and family, we must face those difficult final decisions alone.

After the funeral, when other people return to their own homes and families, we are left to face the reality of the child's death, alone in a house that offers nothing but silence. In the first few months we may charge into a whirlwind of activity. Dinner invitations, nights of visiting, weekends away, and even a movie alone – we'll try anything to get away from the emptiness and silence at home. Eventually, physical exhaustion limits such activity. And what is left? Nights alone in a silent house.

We cry out to have another person alongside who knows, really knows, what the death of the child means, someone who shares those special memories of how our family once was. And that person could be anyone.

From *Parental Loss of a Child*, ed. A.T. Rando, Glencoe, IL: Research Press Co., 1986, pp. 315–19.

We reach out to family, friends, and sometimes even strangers, only to find that it isn't enough. They did not know the child as we did. They cannot understand and return the depth of feeling. They cannot because they do not feel it. We are alone, trying to cope with the insane madness of grief and unable to share our emotions or remembrances with another. During those terrible times when we lose control of our mind and body there is no one to touch us, hold us, and re-assure us that we are not crazy. In the midst of this madness there is just silence. From somewhere we have to find the strength to regain self-control. We are totally responsible for ourselves.

Within a week or two after the death we must return to our job and profession. For eight hours a day or more we are confined with co-workers who expect us to produce and be as normal as possible. During these hours we must suppress our intense feelings of sadness, anger, hate, despair and fear, for society will not accept our expressing such negative emotions. And we ourselves consider this unacceptable public behaviour. These emotions are intense. When they grab hold of the body, most of us cannot control our reactions. The flowing tears, the shaking, nausea, vomiting, and the inexplicable pain through the body erupt as though they had a will of their own.

Conditions in the home change as well. There is no desire to clean house, shop for and cook food, entertain. Doing these things for one person is not enough. What does it matter if the refrigerator's bare insides all but echo? Food sustains life, and life is now a burden. Within us, a storm of fear and self-doubt rages. Why am I unable to function? Why can't I maintain my job and home? Why did my child die? Was it my fault? Am I a bad person? Am I being punished? Who will help me in all of this? No one. We must totally shoulder the feelings of doubt, guilt and blame. If we had custody of the child, we may be blamed by the other parent, thereby increasing the feeling 'I am to blame'. An ugliness and hatred for the other parent may grow, especially if that parent has remarried and has other children. At night, at home, the hours crawl until it is time to sleep.

Perhaps we have one glass of wine to help us sleep. Sleep does not come. One more glass. Still sleep eludes us, as exhausted as we are, and we are alone. Be it one glass of wine or enough wine to bring us to the point of insensibility, hoping to deaden the pain, there is no one to help. There is no one to say, 'You don't need that', 'Come to bed', or 'We can talk.' And most times there is not even the strength to make a phone call to ask for help. And who to call at this time of night? Friends and family would understand a call for help once or twice, but certainly not for the many months that these conditions exist. We are part of an exclusive club that all members wish they had never joined.

After hours of raging pain perhaps there is some sleep, but sleep, in its lack of mercy, does not last long. There are nights when we awake screaming from nightmares and we are in the dark alone, too frightened to try to return to sleep for fear the nightmare will return. In the morning, in this condition, we must present ourselves at our place of business, knowing that we must maintain the standards of our profession. Anything less may put us in jeopardy of losing our income, and this cannot happen because we are responsible for ourselves.

Having been responsible single parents and realizing that we are no longer can be devastating. Our need to be comforted by another adult is great. This realization takes time. It could be months before we are aware we are not coping as well as we could. For this reason we must not always be alone. We must reach out to family and friends. Best of all we should join a self-help group of bereaved parents. They alone will be there for us in the many months and perhaps years that are needed to learn to cope with the death of a child. We need understanding adult companionship to help us become strong, secure, childless, single adults.

Our children are our roots of family. With the death of an only child we know that this is the end of any family life. One day we were parenting, the next – nothing. We will never again hear those words 'Hi, Mom'; we no longer have a person who is truly ours. Where once was a happy family now exists a solitary person. What was once 'we' is now 'I'. In a family-oriented society we find ourself personless, with no one to share the joys and sorrows of life as do a child and parent. We feel the absence in our homes of any activity concerning children. There is nothing to do for our child; we are no longer needed. We begin to feel a sense of aloneness. How different this feeling is from feeling lonesome or lonely. Those feelings can be corrected just by being social with family or friends. I became so affected by this feeling of aloneness that when ordering carry-out food from a restaurant I was unable to order just one dinner, I had to order at least two. A feeling would come over me that if I ordered one dinner everyone in the restaurant would know that I was truly alone. It is difficult to be a family of one.

Gone are the graduations, birthday parties, proms and the dream of my child's wedding. Those once wonderful holidays, Thanksgiving and Christmas, will never be celebrated again as a family, if indeed celebrated at all. The thought of Christmas in my home with a tree, decorations, gifts and a turkey, without this precious person, is unbearable. My grief on normal days was so intense that with the approach of these holidays I feared for my sanity. How would I ever pass these days without becoming insane? Not having other children for whom a pretence of holidays would have to be made, my home was barren at Christmas. I also was unable to accept invitations from family and friends to share these holidays in their homes. I could not face being in the presence of their children knowing that my child was dead.

I will never become a grandparent, never see my family grow through my daughter and her family, never have anyone to whom I can pass on my family china. What will happen to me as I grow old? Who will come to me on holidays? If I become ill or infirm, who will care about and for me? Yes, I know there are people who care for me, but I also know they have families of their own, and that makes the difference. All these things and more contribute to that feeling of aloneness. Never again in social situations will I be able to say 'This is my daughter, Lorena' and know the love and pride I felt in having her. Instead, when asked that cruellest of questions, 'How many children do you have?' I know the answer: 'I had a daughter; she's deceased.' Before the death of my daughter I did not realize how much that question was part of life. Being childless, learning to answer that question became one of the most difficult adjustments. And saying it reinforced that feeling of aloneness.

My visits to the cemetery were overly long. Sometimes I sat by her grave for five to six hours. Although I knew I should leave, being alone, I could not find the strength to go to my car and drive away. Nor did I want to. This became the place where I felt I belonged. I would trace my fingers along the indentations in the newly laid grass, digging little holes to see how far down into the earth I could dig, all the while telling Lorena, 'Don't be afraid, I'll get you out of here. I'll take you home with me.' During this period my thoughts of suicide surfaced. At first it was just a strong urge to follow her. I could not accept on blind faith that she was safe and free from harm. I had loved and protected her in life and I wanted to love and protect her in death. Some spark of self-preservation brought me to a suicide counsellor. She called me daily. Hour after hour she would listen to me talk about Lorena, how agonizing the pain was and how I could not bear it one more minute. She helped me to understand I really did not want to die. I just wanted the pain to stop, and suicide seemed the way to become free from this pain. It is because of her day-after-day patience and under-standing that I am alive today.

For my life to change, I had to give to someone the love and caring I had for my child. But I felt it was better not to love, not to give, to protect myself from pain. It was many months before I could reach out to others. Later I became the chapter leader of a sibling group in the Compassionate Friends' organization. If I had not learned to love and give again, I would always have had that feeling of aloneness.

Epitaph of Libby Dickinson, 1798–1818

Anonymous

Uncertain life, how swift it flies –
Dream of an hour, how brief our bloom –
Like the gay verdure soon we rise
Cut down ere night to fill the tomb.

From an abandoned graveyard in Avon, Connecticut.

Pregnancy loss and the death of a baby
parents' choices

Nancy Kohner

Dramatic changes have taken place in the care professionals give when a pregnancy ends or a baby dies. Within the space of some 20 years, views have changed so radically that some procedures have actually been reversed. For example, a woman who has a stillbirth today is likely to be encouraged to hold and spend time with her baby; her mother or grandmother would almost certainly have been as actively discouraged.

It is worth reflecting on the fact that the 'least said soonest mended' approach of the mid-twentieth century was almost certainly as well intentioned as present practice. Professionals who can remember that era of maternity care often say regretfully, 'We were told it was for the best'. Their instincts may have told them otherwise, but generally they were convinced and led by what they believed to be expert advice.

The interesting question is whether we can now claim that we have got it right. Could it be that because rapid, radical and much needed change has been achieved, and because care is demonstrably improved, there is a danger of self-satisfaction? And could this satisfaction have caused us to cease to question the quality of the care and support that is given? Could we perhaps, as Leon (1992) argues, have created a new orthodoxy to replace the old? Are we wedded to that orthodoxy for the same reasons that impeded us before – namely that giving care when a baby dies is stressful and sad, so we seek safety in procedures that we have been told are 'for the best'? And could this even lead us to consider parents whose responses and requests do not fit with the present orthodoxy to be in some way difficult or even abnormal and perhaps in need of particular help?

From Freud onwards, loss and grief have been theoretically shaped and reshaped with varying degrees of success. The loss of a baby and the grief of bereaved parents have been no exception. And while the effort to understand is helpful, the associated impulse to control and organize is often less so. Bereaved parents are sometimes bewildered to find that their experience of grief does not fit the models they are offered. They may even begin to think that they are 'abnormal' because their feelings do not lessen or resolve in the way or in the time predicted. Professionals who have entered health care in order to help, care and cure, may find it hard to accept that grief is incurable. Yet the truth is that many parents experience grief as never-ending, although not endlessly painful. One mother writes:

For the days around the anniversary of Jemma's death, and her birth ten days later, all the pain comes flooding back, and I know it will always be that way. But day to day, she is now peaceful and safe inside. I carry her always. She is wholly mine, my private sadness but also my perfect, secret joy. (Kohner and Henley, 1995: 75)

This experience of a continuing bond with the person who has died is recognized in comparatively recent models of grieving (Klass et al., 1996). However, all models, being a tidying up of untidy human experience, run the risk of betraying that experience. And in the same way, professional care, which may use these models, runs the risk of presumption.

What form might this presumption take when a baby dies? It may masquerade as good practice and confusingly, for some bereaved parents, it may be exactly that. For others, the very approach or procedure which is thought to be correct may be precisely what they do not want.

One example of this is the well-established idea that talking helps. A central tenet of the support professionals offer when a pregnancy ends or a baby dies is that parents should be enabled (even encouraged) to express their feelings (Walter, 1994). And it is true that for many parents, one of the most important and helpful roles that the professional supporter can fulfil is that of skilled listener. However, there are also parents, many of whom are men, who do not wish to talk. They may not wish to talk to a stranger, or to talk at that time, or they may not wish to talk at all. They may quite simply wish to be alone.

One experienced midwife, who admits that her practice had been based on the notion that 'it's good to talk', tells the following story. She was caring for a woman whose baby was stillborn and was disconcerted to find that the woman did not want to talk. She was clear about her needs, rebuffed the midwife's offers to sit with her and said firmly that she simply wanted to be alone with her baby. She said little, shed few tears and left hospital at the earliest possible opportunity. The midwife felt she had not done enough for this woman and was anxious that her lack of words might mean she was not grieving. She was relieved when the woman said to her as she was leaving, 'Thank you for leaving me alone. It was what I needed'. For the midwife, the inactivity and holding back had been hard. It is easier to be an active problem-solver than be passively supportive and facilitative, and health care professionals are generally more used to the problem-solving role.

Orthodox procedures can too easily become part of a bereavement 'package'. For example, many hospitals now offer bereaved parents a custom-made memento card designed to hold a small lock of their baby's hair, a photo, hand and foot prints. These cards are appreciated and treasured by many parents – but for some, they are not appropriate. A woman who had an emergency Caesarean and whose baby died shortly afterwards was surprised to be given one of these cards complete with mementoes of her baby. Far from being touched and appreciative as her midwife expected, she was distressed and offended. She felt angry that these things had been done without her permission while she was recovering from her operation. She would have wanted to have done them herself, in her own way. And although the hospital memento card was tasteful enough, it was not her style.

It is not protocols, procedures and facilities that make up good care but the flexibility with which protocols are implemented, the extent of parental involvement and the degree to which autonomy is respected and individual wishes met. It is, above all, the principle of choice which is at the centre of good practice and, with it, the acceptance and accommodation of women's and parents' choices by professional caregivers.

Giving choice, and supporting and accepting the choices that parents make, are perhaps the hardest tasks professionals face when a pregnancy ends or a baby dies. If giving choice is regarded as offering a predetermined range of options, if choosing is the process of selecting from these options, and if all the options are regarded by the choice-giver as reasonable, then supporting and empowering parents in this way is not so hard. But if giving choice entails, as it surely should, enabling bereaved parents to decide freely what they would like to happen and what they would like to do, and if professionals, by participating in this process, are committing themselves to helping parents make their choices a reality, then we are entering an area of uncertainty and risk where many professionals feel understandably anxious. What might bereaved parents choose to do? Is anything and everything (this side of the law) acceptable? If not, then where, how and by whom should boundaries be drawn?

There are no clear answers to these questions. Take, for example, this story told by a senior midwife. She was caring for a young couple whose first and very much wanted baby had been stillborn. The baby's father explained to her that as a boy he had been especially close to his own father and that he treasured memories of being taken by his dad to a shallow place on the river where they could skim stones across the water. He had promised his unborn baby that he would be as good a father as his dad had been to him . . . and that he too would take him to skim stones. Now, he said, he would never be able to do this. If only he could take his baby son, just once, to this special place. . . . The midwife suggested that maybe he could do this. He and his wife accepted the suggestion and he returned to the hospital with his baby son a couple of hours later. He brought with him a pebble he had chosen to keep in memory of his son.

This midwife was practising at the edge of what many would regard as acceptable practice and outside the area covered by hospital protocol. Certainly she, and her manager (who supported her), took a risk. Yet she had enabled this couple to do something that was immensely significant and helpful for them.

Those who are involved in supporting women who miscarry or who undergo a termination of pregnancy may find it more difficult to know what they should offer. In these areas of care it is still more essential that professionals listen to and allow themselves to be guided by parents themselves. An early miscarriage may not be significant for some, but for others, and maybe unpredictably, it will hold a meaning which is unknown to an outsider. Assumptions can be too easily made. The manager of an abortion clinic was contacted by a young woman some years after she had chosen to have an abortion. She was sad and unsettled: she couldn't stop thinking about the baby she had lost. She had not had the opportunity to see the baby, find out its sex, choose the way the body would be disposed of. At the time she had felt she did not want this involvement and now it was too late. The clinic manager listened carefully to the woman then asked her tentatively whether she would like to spend some time in the room where her abortion had taken place. The suggestion was welcomed. The woman was able to sit for some time alone in the room and left the clinic feeling calmer.

Stories like these challenge our ideas of good practice. While they may be unusual, they should not be regarded as extreme. Not many parents will want to take their baby out for a walk but many do wish to take their baby's body home – a practice which would have been regarded as a matter of course in the past and is certainly accepted as normal in other cultures. Yet at the time of writing it is probably only a minority of UK hospitals which have procedures in place to enable this to happen. Professionals often feel anxious about handing over responsibility to parents in this way. Even after a miscarriage, when there is no legal requirement to bury or cremate and professionals may therefore feel less anxious, they may still discourage women from taking home their baby's body or remains.

When a pregnancy miscarries or is terminated, or when a baby dies, parents are affected differently and grieve in different ways. For some, the loss will be more disastrous than for others. But whatever their experience of loss and grief, very few of these parents will be unaffected and most will remember their loss and carry their grief with them into their future lives (Rosenblatt, 1996). In contrast, professionals involved in caring for and supporting bereaved parents need to be aware that their interventions are necessarily brief and, as the word intervention suggests, not integrated into people's lives. Their care may be crucial and may have long-term consequences for either good or ill, but is only a small part of a much larger pattern. In this situation it is surely disrespectful for professionals to do anything other than follow parents' own lead. Many parents will be bewildered and not know what to do and professionals have a vital role to play in helping them to work out what will feel right. If that involves a visit to the local river, maybe that's what should happen.

References

Klass, D., Silverman, P.R. and Nickman, S.L. (eds) (1996) *Continuing Bonds. New Understandings of Grief.* Washington DC and London: Taylor and Francis.

Kohner, N. and Henley, A. (1995) *When a Baby Dies. The Experience of Late Miscarriage, Stillbirth and Neonatal Death*. London: Harper Collins.

Leon, I.G. (1992) 'Providing versus packaging support for bereaved parents after perinatal loss', *Birth*, 19 (2): 89–91.

Rosenblatt, P.C. (1996) 'Grief that does not end', in D. Klass, P.R. Silverman and S.L. Nickman (eds), *Continuing Bonds. New Understandings of Grief*. Washington DC and London: Taylor and Francis.

Walter, T. (1994) *The Revival of Death*. London: Routledge.

58

When a baby dies – a father's view

Gavin Fairbairn

When my wife had our baby girl, Hesther Frances, by caesarian section, I was told pretty soon that she was unlikely to live. The paediatrician who was sticking tubes down her throat in an effort to help her breathe asked me whether I wanted him to continue doing so, or whether I would rather that he stopped, since it was unlikely to do any good. He explained that he was sure that Hesther was suffering from a chromosomal disorder called Edward's syndrome which made it very unlikely that she could live. I decided that he should stop and that we should allow Hesther to die rather than continuing this undignified attempt to make her live for a few extra hours.

They took Hesther out of her special care cot and gave her to me. I was in great emotional upheaval. This was my first child and I had agreed that she should be allowed to die. I had taken the word of the paediatric senior registrar that my child was unlikely to live and agreed that he should stop trying to make her live.

I was left holding Hesther while people, as it seemed to me, backed off into the corners of the room. I spoke to her and cried with her. As I welcomed her into the world and said I was sorry she would not be able to stay with us, I held out my hand towards the retreating figures and asked for help. They retreated further and further away. They seemed to vanish into every available corner of the special care room and into the adjoining office – safe behind psychological or glass partitions, able to deceive themselves into thinking that what I wanted was to be left alone with my baby, able to ignore my outstretched hands and eyes. These caring and committed professionals abandoned me when I needed them to stay with me and help me to be with my child.

Very soon I remembered Susan, whose emergency caesarian had come after an attempt to induce labour because of pre-eclampsia: rupturing the membranes at the neck of her cervix had resulted in a cord prolapse. I

From *Nursing Practice*, 1986 1: 167–8 (slightly abridged).

wanted to take Hesther to her. I wanted to know that she was going to be all right: I wanted us to be a family for a while before Hesther died.

I went to Susan and showed Hesther to her: I told her she was very beautiful but she was not going to live, the doctors had told me so. Susan was very dozy, although she managed to come through the fog briefly to say hello to our daughter. It was a very sad time for us. It was a turbulent time for me – what to do? – stay with my wife or stay with my baby? In my mixed-up state it did not occur to me that I could stay with both.

After a few minutes I took Hesther back to the special care room and left her to die in a cot. I went back to Susan: I had begun to believe that she too would die and I wanted to be with her if she was going to do so. She was my love, she was my long-standing friend, she and I shared the world together. I left my baby to die with people who would not hold my hand while I cried and I went to be with my wife.

My continuing concern, my guilt, my regret, is that I left my baby to die with strangers and went and sat with my wife. I remember now how I admired my father many years ago when he sat and held his dog while the vet 'put her to sleep' and I wondered what possessed me to let my baby die in a room full of strangers while I ran off and hid from her.

The paediatrician who looked after Hesther during her few minutes of life after birth said two things to me before she died. The first was that he asked whether I wanted him to continue trying to get her to breathe properly. The second was a request that I give him permission to do a post-mortem. How was it possible that he could ask me such a thing while my baby was still alive in the next room? How was it possible that he could think it appropriate to back off from me in my anguish and yet ask me that minutes later? How was it possible that it could be an important part of his job to be aware of the 'need' to gain permission to perform a post-mortem, while failing to be aware of the need to care for parents in their bereavement, of the need that I had to have someone to be my friend while my baby died?

During the days that followed Hesther's death, Susan and I received very kind and caring nursing from the nurses and midwives at the hospital. They became important figures in our lives as we began to get to know one another in our grief. But during the 10 days or so that she stayed and became gradually physically stronger again very few people with whom we came in contact ever actually referred to the fact that Susan was in hospital to have a baby who had died, rather than because she had had an operation the after-effects of which she was still suffering. Perhaps it was good that she suffered from high blood pressure and Bell's Palsy for a long time after Hesther's death – it gave the nurses and doctors something to worry about other than the fact that she and I were grieving the death of our baby.

Several good things happened in our grief. One occurred when we asked a few days after Hesther's death whether Susan could go to the mortuary to see her. She could not remember what Hesther looked like and needed to see her. At first she was told that she was very ill, that she was not well enough to go downstairs. Then someone came up with a solution – if Susan could not go to Hesther, why not bring Hesther to Susan. She was brought up in a carrycot and we sat and cried together with our baby. The second good thing that happened was that one day a student midwife asked Susan whether the photograph by her bedside was her baby, could she look and what was its name? The third was when the mortuary attendant apologized because he was aware enough to notice me wince when he referred to my child as 'it': he was a nice man – at least he referred to her, at least he acknowledged her existence.

Folk who have babies who die at birth, or are born dead or who die shortly after birth, are parents. They have lived with the idea, and the reality, of their baby for a long time. Perhaps they lived with the idea of their child for many years before it was conceived. Like the parents of babies who survive, they have, in all probability, laid plans. They have probably bought baby clothes and carrycots and nappies and all the other paraphernalia that babies require. They have probably given their baby a variety of names to choose from depending on its sex. They have carried it in their bodies and minds and hearts and souls since conception and perhaps for a good time before that. Because of this they need to be treated as bereaved parents. Women who have given birth to babies who are dead, or who die, need to be treated as mothers who have lost a baby, not as patients who have suffered a physical illness. Men whose babies are born dead or die after birth need to be treated as fathers who have lost a baby, not as men whose womenfolk are a bit unwell just now. All of this is true also for men and women who lose babies through miscarriage – they also are parents, they also are bereaved. [. . .]

Postscript. Hesther Frances lived for one hour in 1983. Her brother Thomas was born in 1986.

59

Gay and lesbian bereavement

Dudley Cave

At the turn of the nineteenth century Oscar Wilde's plays were taken off when he was convicted of homosexual acts; in 1961 Sir Roger Casement was executed, opposition to his execution having melted away when it was revealed that he was homosexual, and it is said that King George, about a homosexual, said 'I thought fellows like that shot themselves'. In 1998 when George Michael was convicted of committing a 'lewd act' in a public lavatory, it made little difference to his popularity and after Sir Elton John, who has made no secret of his sexuality, played the piano in Westminster Abbey at the funeral of Princess Diana sales of that piece of music broke all records. Today the subject is often discussed on radio and television and there are gay characters in most soap operas and many plays. Each year thousands of lesbians and gay men join the annual Pride marches in London and elsewhere, with banners proclaiming their sexual orientation, unworried by the presence of television cameras and happy to be with so many others of the same mind. However they, like me, are part of the minority of homosexuals who are able to come out and speak out. There is still prejudice, prejudice which can wreck lives.

Estimating the number of gay women and men is not easy, it depends on the definitions adopted, on persuading an adequate sample to tell the truth to investigators and the proper interpretation being made of their replies. Kinsey, Pomeroy and Martin in 1948 estimated that 4 per cent of American men were totally, exclusively homosexual and 34 per cent had had homosexual experience to orgasm at least once in their adult lives. These findings were probably flawed by poor sampling, with too many men who were in prison being included in the sample. My personal, informed, guess is that between 4 and 5 per cent of the population identify as lesbians or gay men although some, in fact, will be bisexual. Geographically this figure will vary as most will leave small towns and villages, where everyone knows them, for the cities where they will be anonymous, where there will be a gay social life and there are better chances of meeting partners.

Although most educated people accept homosexuality as, at least, a fact of life, *coming out*, that is being visibly gay, still can damage career prospects and most lesbians and gay men keep their heads down, stay in the closet, live a lie and pray that the secret will remain safe. Staying in the closet isn't just a matter of not coming out; it requires a programme of deceit, of finding suitable escorts for functions, of inventing a convincing opposite-sex partner and keeping secret all gay associations and even, perhaps, laughing at queer jokes.

Some lesbians and gay men play the field but most settle into relationships which are as loving, stable and long-lasting as any marriage (my partner, Bernard, and I lived and loved together until he died just two days after our fortieth anniversary). For those who love in secret, the tangled web of necessary lies will cause problems and when one partner dies, there will be even greater problems. There can be difficulties with inheritance, there will be no talking about the loss with colleagues or neighbours and there won't be any of those kind letters of sympathy, which mean so much (I got over a hundred and they were a comfort, showing that other people cared for Bernard too). We even heard of one man whose cover was so good that the neighbours' only reaction to the death was to ask if he had a vacancy for another flat-mate. If there is no will, blood relatives will inherit and the surviving partner may well not only lose a lover but lose home and shared possessions and have no say in the funeral arrangements. Those who love in secret will surely mourn alone.

A funeral should be a springboard for good grief, but can be a disaster for the survivor of a same-sex couple who, if not excluded by the blood relatives, can be at the back shrouded in personal grief, while all the sympathy is being directed to the family at the front. Even when the relationship is known and the surviving partner is executor or executrix, and able to determine the manner of the funeral, there can still be problems. Clergy (or lay officials) conducting the funeral must be aware of the relationship. They must not have negative feelings about same-sex love because such feelings will probably be perceived by the mourners even if they do not go as far as one priest who prayed for forgiveness of the deceased's deviant lifestyle. Even when the relationship is fairly open and the parents appear to regard the partner as another son or daughter, they may want the relationship concealed at the funeral and even ask the partner not to attend or to act as an acquaintance only – because 'the neighbours would not understand'. Wherever possible the partner should be named at some point in the service, if not in the eulogy, possibly in prayer: 'We pray for those most affected by grief and sorrow: his parents, George and Mary, his sister Elizabeth, and Henry, his partner for many years'. If the survivor is not out, the officiant can make a discreet reference to the friendship. The survivor must be part of the service, not a spectator. An inadequate funeral is a poor start for healing grief.

Lazare (1979) tells us that complicated grief can be expected when the loss is socially unacceptable, socially negated or if there is not an adequate support network. I would also add that where the death is 'out of order', that is the child dying before the parents or the younger partner before the older. All four situations can often be found in same-sex loss.

Nearly all bereavement services will offer support to lesbians and gay men but this is not generally realized; the Lesbian and Gay Bereavement Project also offers telephone support, someone to talk to, someone to turn to. However, if the bereaved partner does not know the Project, they cannot help. Sadly most older people do not read the gay press, go to gay clubs or other meetings and, all too often, 'keep themselves to themselves' and mourn in isolation.

The Lesbian and Gay Bereavement Project arose from a Unitarian church bereavement initiative. It started as a self-help group of bereaved lesbians and gay men meeting to support each other. It was publicized in the gay and local press and people rang to talk and to seek advice. They expressed their anger, worries and fears but few came to meetings and it was soon realized that what people really wanted was someone to talk to, someone who would understand their grief, absorb some of their anger, rather than organized meetings in a church hall. So the group changed to a Samaritan-type telephone service and now has a volunteer on duty every evening of the year.

From listening to bereaved lesbians and gay men, Project members found that many doctors, nurses, clergy and others dealing with death and dying, seemed unaware that same-sex partners would be as bereaved as spouses or families. It had just not struck them. To help in that area of concern the Project started offering speakers to talk to groups of such people. Most of the speaking has been to nurses on English Nursing Board courses and to members of Cruse and other bereavement services.

They also found that many lesbians and gay men were dying intestate, the surviving partner often losing their home and shared possessions on the death of a partner. A printed will form, naming the partner as executor or executrix and sole beneficiary, was prepared and made available to anyone asking for a copy. A letter of advice sent with the will form suggests that wills are best written by lawyers. However there remains a reluctance to write wills. 'I've nothing to leave but my UB40' and 'I'm too young to die' being popular reasons given, but it is probably the superstitious fear that, by writing a will, one is inviting death.

Although AIDS is not confined to gay men, most cases in the UK and USA are in that section of the population and there are those who still perceive it as a 'gay plague'. In the early days diagnosis was followed shortly by death but, as knowledge increased, and drugs used in combinations, many are able to live full lives rather than die in their thirties. Undoubtedly AIDS has added another dimension to loss, new infections still occur and gay men see their friends die, not just one but one after another. Cho and Cassidy (1994) pointed out that multiple losses differ from single losses, the confrontation is extensive, progressive, accumulative and traumatic. The tasks of mourning are interrupted by new losses. Death, especially early death, is not easy to cope with and serial bereavements are harder as the numbers increase.

Funerals can be difficult. People with AIDS may not want the family to know they are ill, or even gay, and the family often try to conceal the cause of death. On two occasions I have conducted funerals for people with AIDS whose parents were not even aware that their son was gay or ill until a few weeks before the death. Both families lived far from London which ruled out pastoral visits and, because of the necessary confidentiality, it was not even possible to refer them to local bereavement services.

The Lesbian and Gay Bereavement Project is small but has a member on call from seven to midnight, every evening, including Christmas Day, ready to listen and advise. The volunteers work from their own homes, calls being automatically transferred from the contact number. However, volunteers are not alone and they are encouraged to share 'heavy' calls with another volunteer and have regular case conferences and in-service training sessions. The office staff is salaried and volunteers can claim out-of-pocket expenses.

The Project has three main aims:

- To help and advise lesbians and gay men bereaved by the death of a life partner
- To educate all who deal with death and dying to the particular problems of same-sex loss
- To educate lesbians and gay men to the facts of death – that, like it or not, we and those we love, are mortal and all people should make wills

However the Project will help anyone bereaved by the death of a lesbian or gay man and any lesbian or gay man bereaved by the death of anyone.

The help-line is on 020 8455 8894 and there is a volunteer on duty from 7pm to midnight every evening, including Christmas.

References

Cho, C. and Cassidy, D. (1994) 'Parallel processes for workers and their clients in chronic bereavement resulting from HIV', *Death Studies*, 18: 273–92.

Kinsey, A.C., Pomeroy, W.B. and Martin, C.E. (1948) *Sexual Behaviour in the Human Male*. Philadelphia, PA and London: W.G. Saunders & Co.

Lazare, A. (1979) 'Unresolved grief', in A. Lazare (ed.), *Outpatient Psychiatry, Diagnosis and Treatment*. Baltimore, MD: Williams and Wilkins. pp. 498–512.

60

The grief that does not speak

Maureen Oswin

An art therapist working in one of the old-style long-stay mental handicap hospitals became concerned when one of the residents attending her class seemed very depressed. He then suddenly said he was worried because his parents, who usually came each Sunday, had not visited him for several weeks. The therapist went up to his ward but could not find anyone on the staff to give her any information, so she looked in his case notes for any clues to explain why his parents' visits had ceased.

She discovered that his father had died. This meant that his frail mother, who was unable to use public transport, could no longer visit him. Nobody had told the young man what had happened. All that was recorded in his case notes was the bare fact of his father's death.

No recommendation was made that anything should be done about breaking the news of the death to him, let alone helping him with his bereavement or arranging that he should be in contact with his mother. Nobody had made a deliberate decision not to tell him; but everyone on the staff had somehow assumed that he knew, that somebody had told him. In that impersonal institution, the bereaved resident as a sensitive, worried son had been quietly forgotten.

* * *

Thirty-year old Miss A had very severe learning disabilities and additional physical disabilities, she had always lived at home. She could not walk or speak. She needed help with all ordinary tasks such as dressing, eating, washing, going to the lavatory. Her father had died when she was in her twenties but her mother had continued to care for her on her own. Once a week Miss A went to a local day centre. She also had outings when her mother and a neighbour pushed her round the park or to the supermarket in her wheelchair.

When her very robust mother suddenly died, Miss A lost everything – not only her mother and her mother's loving care, but every vestige of

From *Search* (Rowntree), Winter 1990, 4: 5–7 (abridged and revised).

family life and routine and the security of her home and the neighbourhood where she had lived all her life. The same day that her mother died the social services department arranged that Miss A should go into the care of a mental handicap hospital where she was lifted, washed and fed and clothed by strangers who knew nothing about her or her previous life. She was unable to ask questions because she could not speak. Without speech it was almost impossible for her to relate to the strangers who were now caring for her, especially when she was also grief-stricken for her mother.

For many months Miss A pined and grieved. The kindly staff worried about her wan condition and deterioration: 'We feel so helpless when people as handicapped as her come into hospital after a parent dies: we don't know them, they don't know us, and they must feel so unhappy'.

* * *

After Mrs Z was widowed, the doctor advised: 'Don't tell your son, you have enough problems and he might make more problems for you, and anyway he won't understand'. Acting on his advice Mrs Z kept the death of her husband a secret for several months and merely told her son with learning disabilities that father had 'gone away'. It was a dreadful strain for her, grieving for her husband and at the same time having to keep the death a secret from her adult son who was sharing the same house.

When she did finally tell him, she discovered that he had known for some weeks and felt very resentful that she had not talked to him about it before. He had somehow found out from things he had overheard at his day centre. The doctor's advice to his mother had set the widow and her son apart at a time when they had both needed to be emotionally close and supporting each other.

Why did he give such crazy advice? Was it because he did not know any people with learning disabilities and had a stereotyped image of them as being disruptive and troublesome, and not having any emotional needs? It is sometimes said by thoughtless professionals working in the health services that 'people with learning disabilities don't have the same feelings as other people'.

* * *

The majority of professionals are not callous or insensitive: so how do these things happen? Perhaps, in the grey area of emotions and grief, with the double taboo of death and a learning disability, it is very easy for bereaved people to be lost in a muddle of misconceptions and a panic of re-organizing their lives – so that their needs as grieving people are quite forgotten.

People with learning disabilities have a right to grieve; they need opportunities to mourn, they need time to recover, and sensitive support as they go through the normal reactions of grief such as anger, weeping and depression. Their emotional care is just as important as their need for continuing care at home or appropriate residential care, and any plans made for them should consider their emotional needs as grieving people. Unfortunately, when people with learning disabilities do react in normal ways to loss, some professionals perceive the reaction only in terms of the primary learning disabilities.

For example, a young man who was usually quiet and placid began to get into very angry tempers at his day centre during the months following his father's death. The staff knew that he was bereaved but saw his behaviour only as part of his learning disability; they did not recognize that he was reacting normally to his loss; they did not allow that he needed time to recover from his father's death and that he wanted to express his grief in anger, nor that he required support and understanding in the same way as any other grieving person. After having a staff meeting to discuss his 'problem behaviour' they called in a psychologist to put him onto a behaviour modification programme. Their failure to recognize his needs as a grieving person was partly because nobody on the staff understood normal grief; their training had largely been concentrated on looking for abnormalities amongst persons with learning disabilities.

Nobody intends to be deliberately unkind to people with learning disabilities when they are bereaved, but unkindness seems to creep in because of the way that services are organized, or because of shortcomings in staff training. One young man, on being told that his father had died, asked: 'Am I allowed to cry?' His tentative question sums up how vulnerable some people with learning difficulties feel when they are bereaved. It is also a question about the quality of services organized for such people and the attitudes of some people providing them. If social policy does not allow for tears, then what sort of services do we have?

A local support service for bereaved people with learning disabilities might help to prevent some of the sadness and misunderstanding described here. It would not require elaborate organization. Its members might be interested professionals already working with people with learning difficulties, and representatives of parent groups. One of its functions might be to alert other local professionals to instances of bereavement amongst people with learning disabilities and to help in the planning of sensitive and appropriate services for them in the months following the bereavement. Another function might be to draw staff attention to the norms of bereavement, so that people with learning disabilities would have their grief reactions recognized as normal and be given opportunities to grieve.

Three issues should be of concern to all people who have an interest in bereavement problems.

First, *forward planning*: when a single carer dies, leaving a severely multiply handicapped person like Miss A, that person should not be removed from her home immediately. Somebody could stay with her for a few days or weeks until she can be carefully introduced to a residential care placement which is appropriate for her. She should feel that she has some choice about her future, a chance to grieve for the dead parent in her own home and a chance to say her last good-byes to that home.

Second, *honesty*: people with learning disabilities ought to be kept in the picture all the time about a death having occurred, whether within their own family or amongst their friends. This might mean making sure that somebody is named as being responsible for breaking bad news and then helping the bereaved person through the following months. Honesty also means giving the person an opportunity to attend the funeral if they wish to, listening to them when they want to talk about what has happened, ensuring that they have momentoes of the dead person, letting them know what has happened to the house, their belongings, any pets, clothes and books. In other words, keeping the person with a learning disability in the picture the whole time and respecting their need to be a normal grieving person.

Third, *in-service training courses* on bereavement could be arranged for all staff working with people who have learning disabilities, in day centres, schools, in residential care and as field social workers. Such courses would cover normal grief reactions to a death in the family or the death of a close friend, and would alert staff at all levels to what they might expect with regard to supporting bereaved people.

* * *

The above article (1990) came from the author's notes made during research, funded by the Joseph Rowntree Foundation, which aimed to discover what was happening to bereaved people who had learning disabilities. The full research was published by Souvenir Press in 1991 (reprinted 2000), as the book *Am I Allowed to Cry?* It described a huge gap in bereavement support for people with learning disabilities and made recommendations for improving services. Since 1991, various support schemes have developed and there is an awareness that even people who have major communication problems may be helped with their grief. Bereavement services may not be confined to only giving help with grief caused by a death. Major changes in lifestyle may also create immense sadness. For example, the closure of institutions where many people with learning disabilities have lived all their lives, may cause overwhelming feelings of loss through breaking up friendships and reactivating the severe distress they experienced when admitted to the institutions in childhood.

In Staffordshire a bereavement support scheme called SHOULDER won the 1996 Community Care Award. The award money was to establish a base of helpful materials, information and the production of life-story books.

The main centre for studies of bereavement and learning disability is St George's Hospital Medical School, Department of the Psychiatry of Disability. The staff there have produced helpful books and papers, amongst them being *When Mum Died* and *When Dad Died* (1994) by S. Hollins and L. Sireling (Gaskell Press). In 2000 a training pack called *Understanding Grief*, by S. Hollins and L. Sireling, will be published by Pavilion (London).

61

Personal and medical memories from Hillsborough

Tom Heller

Outside every public house and on every verge on my way home there were relaxed groups of young men chatting and joking in their 'uniforms' of tight faded jeans, off colour teeshirts, and something red and white. Were these the people whom later I saw laid out on the floor with life just pushed out of them? There were so many I didn't dare count them. They looked as they had in life, not disfigured; they were just lying there, not quite the right colour. Not much to identify them on that sports hall floor. Who were they? What had gone wrong? Who was to blame for all this?

Call for help

I was on call for a practice adjacent to the Hillsborough ground for the weekend of Saturday 15 April. On Saturdays when there is a home match at the stadium I avoid passing the ground when crowds are coming and going. My home is one side of the ground and the practice is on the other. On the 15th the atmosphere was special for the semi-final; people were parking their cars miles away from the stadium and walking to the ground many hours earlier than the crowds usually do for home games. I remember being especially cheerful (despite being on duty) and proud that Sheffield was the centre of the sporting world that day. The snooker world championship was on just down the road, and at Hillsborough the semi-final that many people thought should have been the final of the FA Cup was being held. Both sets of supporters wear red and white; I wonder who was who on those verges and which of them now live to tell their tale of the day when such a terrible tragedy happened out of a relaxed and gentle sunny moment?

I switched on the television just after 3 p.m. and saw the coverage of the snooker being interrupted by scenes from Hillsborough. Like almost everyone else, I imagine, I thought that there had been a pitch invasion and worried about how this might affect the chances of English clubs being allowed back into Europe. I then got into my car and took my daughter to a party that she was due to attend. At about 3.30 p.m. I heard on Radio Sheffield the call for doctors to go to Hillsborough, so I hurried to drop off

From *British Medical Journal*, 1989, 299: 1596–8.

my daughter and go to the ground. The party was about 2 km from Hillsborough, and on my way to the ground I followed a fire engine with flashing lights and siren that was going through red traffic lights and on the wrong side of keep left signs. I kept my car glued to the back of the fire engine and was at the ground within a few minutes of hearing the announcement. I parked in Leppings Lane, about 20 m from the blue gate that became such a focus of attention later. I had no notion of the significance of the gate at the time.

As I was parking on the forecourt of a garage that fitted tyres I was approached by some policemen. I told them that there had been a call for doctors on the radio. One of them immediately used his radio to find out where doctors were being asked to go, and we set off, running through the corridors, round the stadium, and towards the sports hall. The stadium was familiar to me as I had often been to matches there. The concrete beneath the grandstands is unusual: it is stained grey, cold and unyielding; the light is always poor beneath the stands, even on sunny afternoons like that one. As we rushed along the atmosphere was all wrong: there were lots of people but there was no noise. We got to the sports hall in about two minutes, and I entered by stepping through a cordon of police officers who were holding back people who were crowding around the outside of the door.

Bodies everywhere

Nothing could have prepared me for the scenes inside. I had thought vaguely that there might be a couple of members of St John Ambulance standing over a man with his head between his knees, telling him to take deep breaths. I had thought that they might have been overwhelmed because four people fainting was more than they could cope with and that I'd join in their exhortations and be back at my daughter's party in time for the second round of the Marmite sandwiches. This was not normal though. There were bodies everywhere. Who was alive and who was dead? They couldn't all be dead. It had to be a mistake; this just didn't happen on sunny afternoons. Blotchy faces against the floor, not disfigured but apparently peaceful. Bodies higgledy-piggledy just inside the door, the line stretching over to the far wall. I asked a policeman what was to be done. Thankfully he pointed away from the bodies to a section of the hall that was separated from them by a long, low screen of the type used to divide sports halls when two different sports are being played at the same time. There were more bodies here though. My God, what could I do? Who was going to tell me what to do?

Without directions I ran along the line of crumpled bodies. At least this lot were alive. I stopped between two bodies, took out my stethoscope, and lifted up a teeshirt and listened, grateful to have the time at last to do something that I knew how to do. I often use 'stethoscope on the chest time' to think during consultations. It's a good ploy really; the patient thinks that I am being ever so thoughtful and thorough, and I have time to think about what the hell to do next. Panic overtook me on this occasion. How could I be sure that this person was the one who needed help most? What was going to happen to all of the others if I stayed with this bloke? I could hear his heartbeat and breath sounds. For some reason I took my stethoscope out of my ears and crawled up to his face.

'What's your name, mate?' I asked.

'Terry' was the reply.

'OK Terry. How are you feeling?'

No answer. Silly question really.

How could I help?

His leg was at the wrong angle somehow, and so was one of his arms; he looked terrible, and where I had rested my stethoscope earlier was obviously not all right at all: it was moving wrongly and was not the right colour either. Although I could hear breath sounds, they were hard to interpret. I think I was just panicking. I remembered how to do a tracheotomy with a Biro. Would this be my opportunity? I turned him over on to his side and pushed my fingers on to the top of his tongue to establish an airway. This seemed to help, and his breathing started again. I had pulled him over on to his bad leg though – there didn't seem much alternative. His face was against the floor, so I reached out and found a leather jacket on the floor and picked up his head and rested it on the jacket. What medical equipment could enable this man to survive? If only someone would arrive who knew what to do. What did I know about anything? I turned around and looked at the man behind me; he was immobile and a terrible blue-grey colour . . . and so it went on.

I had taken my bags full of the equipment and drugs that I usually use. Not much call for antibiotics or infant paracetamol this afternoon. After some time – how long? – I became aware of a friend of mine going between the bodies doing the same as I was. Another general practitioner. We had worked together in the past but not on anything like this, nor are we likely to again. A smile of recognition. I wonder if I looked as lost as he did.

The first large-scale equipment arrived, and we started working together, putting up drips on everyone. We intubated as many patients and established as many airways as we possibly could. We needed scissors to cut through clothes. Why didn't I carry them in my bags? We started giving intravenous diamorphine, and some sort of routine and organization began to be established. I'm quite proud in a funny sort of way to be able to put up so many intravenous drips so quickly without missing a vein. More doctors had arrived by now, and around every body there was a little huddle of workers. Someone said that he was an anaesthetist – gold dust. Come over here and look at Terry for me, mate. He's still alive, but he keeps stopping breathing. 'Hang on, Terry.' The anaesthetist took out the airway, and it was blocked with blood. Not a good sign. One rib seemed to be almost through the chest and was certainly at the wrong angle. The ambulance stretchers arrived, and we put in a passionate bid for Terry to be taken off first. By now six people were around him, holding the drip bottle, his head, and his legs, which were at all angles. He was rested on to a low trolley. I checked that the ambulance was waiting and could get through to the hospital. The anaesthetist went with Terry to the ambulance. Thank God for anaesthetists. I'll never tell an anti-anaesthetist joke again.

Comradeship amid the horror

Now that I had no one to work on I wandered around and could see the dead bodies again at the other side of the sports hall. Among the doctors I recognized many of my friends and colleagues who had also answered the call of duty. One of them gave me a hug, bless him – a friend for life after what we went through that day. The police were much in evidence, but nobody was in charge of the medical tasks. What should I do next? Where would I be most useful? I decided to use my newly refound skills to put up drips on everybody who was going to be transferred to hospital. I somehow remembered that this was the thing to do in case the patients suffered more collapse on the way to hospital. It was also a sign to the hospital doctors that we general practitioners could do something right after all. I used up all of my diamorphine on those in need. By this time the routines were more established. Someone was writing down the obvious major damage to each person and what he or she had received in the way of drugs, etc. Then suddenly there was nobody left in the hall who was in need of attention and who wasn't dead.

I noticed a close friend crouching over amid the sea of dead faces. He was comforting someone who was leaning over a body. I stepped over some bodies to speak to him and offer some help; there weren't any words, just a look of rare empathy and comradeship.

Not knowing how to react

The doctors in the hall grouped together, almost silent, all wondering what to do next. I left the hall and walked through the silent crowds back to my car. I went home stunned and numbed. My children were playing in the garden; it was all so lovely and normal. Sandpits and skipping ropes. I had not known any of the dead or injured. Why is a major disaster so important for the people who participate as helpers? I meet death almost every day of my working life. Was this worse or was it just larger numbers? Everyone sort of expects that an event like this will be upsetting. But why is it that more attention is focused on the feelings of helpers in such disasters than on those of people concerned with upsetting events that happen every day? For me it seems to have been a major shock to my system in a general sort of way. I was grumpy, washed out and flat for a couple of weeks. Passing Hillsborough shocked me again for a long while afterwards when I had nearly rebuilt my professional defences.

All of us general practitioners who were there met a few times to talk about our experiences and to support each other. Why are all the others so articulate about how they are feeling whereas I'm just sort of non-specifically upset? I can't remember what I felt like at the ground and can't describe to the helpful counsellor how I'm feeling during the group sessions. I know all the theory, but I can't get it together for myself – the plight of the modern professional. It's three weeks since the disaster now, and I'm feeling OK again; I make jokes at work and have lots to be thankful for. I've been enormously well supported through all this by family, friends and colleagues. Time has passed and lessons to be learnt are being thought about. Perhaps British football has changed because of these events, and perhaps major disasters will be better dealt with in the future.

I'd like to tell the official inquiry in a systematic way what I think went right with the medical response that day and what I think could be done better next time. I don't know what training should be given to general practitioners and why none of us took charge of the medical happenings in the sports hall and was prepared to be the coordinator. I've got strong views about the counselling that is necessary and appropriate after the event for helpers at disasters. I'd like to do physical damage to the person who took the pictures for the *Daily Mirror* and reserve a special act of aggression for the person who allowed them to be published. But most of all I'd like to find out what happened to Terry.

62

Ruth
Death by murder

Lesley Moreland

As the New Year 1990 started our family life seemed to have entered on a new and welcome stage. Our eldest daughter had married happily and moved to Knebworth in 1988 when she was 24 and our youngest daughter, then 22, had moved to share a rented house with friends in Enfield in the same year.

I had left my job as Director of the Stillbirth and Neonatal Death Society (SANDS) early in 1989 and had taken a big leap into working freelance, partly as a management consultant in the voluntary sector and also starting a very small business in holding craft workshops. We felt, maybe somewhat smugly, pride in our daughters and that our relationship with them and with each other was strong and loving and life looked very good indeed.

On 2 February, just as we had finished eating our evening meal, the doorbell rang. What happened after that was like a nightmare except that it was real. The callers were police officers who came to let us know that our youngest daughter, Ruth, was dead. She had been murdered and a young man was held in custody. The police were and have remained very certain that he is the person who killed her. We had never heard his name before Ruth died. Her 24th birthday was on 6 February and we had been expecting to see her over the weekend.

My years at SANDS had given me a wider than average background in the theory of bereavement and a great deal of contact with people in the various stages of grieving. In some ways this was helpful, in others it seemed to hamper the free expression of feelings.

Forgiveness

The Greek philosopher Aristotle said that there was one loss from which a person could never recover, and that was the loss of a child. It struck too deeply, he thought, at the foundations of a life for there ever to be a chance of rebuilding.

Since Ruth died there has been a constant struggle to survive rather than become a victim of her loss. I have always been aware that the issue of forgiveness of the person who killed her would need to be faced but this was difficult to even begin as our family had never even heard the name of the young man who was charged with her murder until after her death.

Many people asked how I felt about him and I found it impossible to answer, although I had no problem with how I felt about what he had done.

Ralph Hetherington wrote a commentary about forgiveness in *The Friend* in January 1991 which was published in the week before the trial of the young man charged with Ruth's murder. The article considered whether repentance was a prerequisite for forgiveness and stressed the need to recognize the dangers of judging people who have harmed us. It seems to me that passing judgement on others is difficult partly because we cannot understand why someone has behaved in a way which has hurt us or those we love and partly because we have to recognize our own failings in our behaviour towards other people.

I was shocked that the evidence given during the trial seemed to reveal no remorse or insight into the suffering caused to Ruth and all those who loved her. One of my nieces, who also attended the trial, said 'I needed to see that he was sorry and he wasn't'.

But life takes many unexpected turns. When the trial was over I contacted a friend who is a probation officer. It hadn't occurred to me that the young man would be sent to the prison where she works. With our agreement, she saw him and he asked that a message should be sent to us to say how sorry he was, how much he admired and respected Ruth and that she had always been very kind to him. I was also able to send a message to him in which I hoped that he would accept any help offered to him to help him understand why he had done what he had done, to use any opportunities to extend his skills and education and to resolve to use the rest of his life in positive ways both for himself and for others. However, I couldn't bring myself to send a message of forgiveness.

Those affected and involved in the aftermath of murder

A month after Ruth was murdered her employers held a gathering of her colleagues and many of the people who had attended the courses that she had arranged for women returners. The event was guided by a man who described those present in terms of having been affected by an 'earthquake' and spoke of those in Ruth's family as being at the 'epicentre'.

Figure 62.1 is not intended to make distinctions between the depth of people's feelings – we were very aware that many who were involved professionally were also emotionally affected. Rather it is intended to give Victim Support volunteers a framework so that they can be aware of the numbers and kinds of people who are affected or involved in the aftermath of a murder.

Those included in the Figure will vary with each murder. We were spared any direct press or media involvement; for other families this will be a major aspect.

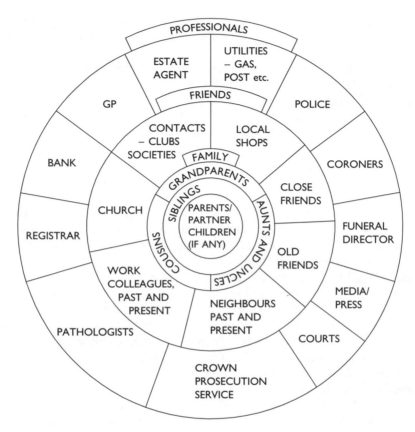

Figure 62.1 *Circles of support. Based on work done by Birmingham and Surrey SANDS, 1987.*

Reference

Hetherington, R. (1991) 'Commentary', *The Friend*, 149 (3): 67–8.

63

Essays upon epitaphs

William Wordsworth

Yet even these bones from insult to protect
Some frail memorial still erected nigh,
With uncouth rhymes and shapeless sculpture deck'd,
Implores the passing tribute of a sigh.

Their name, their years, spelt by the unletter'd Muse,
The place of fame and elegy supply,
And many a holy text around she strews,
That teach the rustic moralist to die.

When a Stranger has walked round a Country Church-yard and glanced his
eye over so many brief Chronicles, as the tomb-stones usually contain, of
faithful Wives, tender Husbands, dutiful Children, and good Men of all
classes; he will be tempted to exclaim, in the language of one of the Characters of a modern Tale in a similar situation, 'Where are all the *bad* People
buried?' He may smile to himself an answer to this question, and may regret
that it has intruded upon him so soon. For my own part such has been my
lot. And, indeed, a Man, who is in the habit of suffering his mind to be
carried passively towards truth as well as of going with conscious effort in
search of it, may be forgiven, if he has sometimes insensibly yielded to the
delusion of those flattering recitals, and found a pleasure in believing that
the prospect of real life had been as fair as it was in that picture represented.
And such a transitory oversight will without difficulty be forgiven by those
who have observed a trivial fact in daily life, namely, how apt, in a series of
calm weather, we are to forget that rain and storms have been, and will
return, to interrupt any scheme of business or pleasure which our minds are
occupied in arranging. Amid the quiet of a Church-yard thus decorated as it
seemed by the hand of Memory, and shining, if I may so say, in the light of
love, I have been affected by sensations akin to those which have risen in my
mind while I have been standing by the side of a smooth Sea, on a Summer's
day. It is such a happiness to have, in an unkind World, one Enclosure
where the voice of detraction is not heard; where the traces of evil inclina-
tions are unknown; where contentment prevails, and there is no jarring tone
in the peaceful Concert of amity and gratitude. I have been rouzed from this
reverie by a consciousness, suddenly flashing upon me, of the anxieties, the
perturbations, and, in many instances, the vices and rancorous dispositions,

Extracts from 'Essays upon epitaphs', in *Prose Works of William Wordsworth*, ed. W.J.B.
Owen and Jane Worthington Smyser, Oxford: Clarendon Press, 1971, pp. 63–7, 93.

by which the hearts of those who lie under so smooth a surface and so fair an outside must have been agitated. The image of an unruffled Sea has still remained; but my fancy has penetrated into the depths of that Sea – with accompanying thoughts of Shipwreck, of the destruction of the Mariner's hopes, the bones of drowned Men heaped together, monsters of the deep, and all the hideous and confused sights which Clarence saw in his Dream [in Shakespeare's *Richard III*]!

Nevertheless, I have been able to return, (and who may not?) to a steady contemplation of the benign influence of such a favourable Register lying open to the eyes of all. Without being so far lulled as to imagine I saw in a Village Church-yard the eye or central point of a rural Arcadia, I have felt that with all the vague and general expressions of love, gratitude, and praise with which it is usually crowded, it is a far more faithful representation of homely life as existing among a Community in which circumstances have not been untoward, than any report which might be made by a rigorous observer deficient in that spirit of forbearance and those kindly prepossessions, without which human life can in no condition be profitably looked at or described. For we must remember that it is the nature of Vice to force itself upon notice, both in the act and by its consequences. Drunkenness, cruelty, brutal manners, sensuality, impiety, thoughtless prodigality, and idleness, are obstreperous while they are in the height and heyday of their enjoyment; and, when that is passed away, long and obtrusive is the train of misery which they draw after them. But, on the contrary, the virtues, especially those of humble life, are retired; and many of the highest must be sought for or they will be overlooked. Industry, oeconomy, temperance, and cleanliness, are indeed made obvious by flourishing fields, rosy complexions, and smiling countenances; but how few know anything of the trials to which Men in a lowly condition are subject, or of the steady and triumphant manner in which those trials are often sustained, but they themselves! The afflictions which Peasants and rural Artizans have to struggle with are for the most part secret; the tears which they wipe away, and the signs which they stifle, – this is all a labour of privacy. [. . .] The encomiastic language of rural Tomb-stones does not so far exceed reality as might lightly be supposed. Doubtless, an inattentive or ill-disposed Observer, who should apply to the surrounding Cottages the knowledge which he may possess of any rural neighbourhood, would upon the first impulse confidently report that there was little in their living Inhabitants which reflected the concord and the virtue there dwelt upon so fondly. [. . .] Besides, to slight the uniform language of these memorials as on that account not trustworthy would obviously be unjustifiable. Enter a Church-yard by the Sea-coast, and you will be almost sure to find the Tomb-stones crowded with metaphors taken from the Sea and a Sea-faring life. These are uniformly in the same strain; but surely we ought not thence to infer that the words are used of course without any heart-felt sense of their propriety. Would not the contrary conclusion be right? [. . .] We learn from the Statistical account of Scotland that, in some districts, a general transfer of Inhabitants has taken place; and that a great majority of those who live, and labour, and attend public worship in one part of the Country, are buried in another. Strong and inconquerable still continues to be the desire of all, that their bones should rest by the side of their forefathers, and very poor Persons provide that their bodies should be conveyed if necessary to a great distance to obtain that last satisfaction. Nor can I refrain from saying that this natural interchange by which the living Inhabitants of a Parish have small knowledge of the dead who are buried in their Church-yards is grievously to be lamented whereso-ever it exists. For it cannot fail to preclude not merely much but the best part of the wholesome influence of that communion between living and dead which the conjunction in rural districts of the place of burial and place of worship tends so effectually to promote. [. . .]

An experienced and well-regulated mind will not, therefore, be insensible to this monotonous language of sorrow and affectionate admiration; but will find under that veil a substance of individual truth. Yet, upon all Men, and upon such a mind in particular, an Epitaph must strike with a gleam of pleasure, when the expression is of that kind which carries conviction to the heart at once that the Author was a sincere mourner, and that the Inhabit-ant of the Grave deserved to be so lamented. This may be done sometimes by a naked ejaculation; as in an instance which a friend of mine met with in a Church-yard in Germany; thus literally translated. 'Ah! they have laid in the Grave a brave Man – he was to me more than many!'

> Ach! sie haben
> Einen Braven
> Mann begraben
> Mir war er mehr als viele.

An effect as pleasing is often produced by the recital of an affliction endured with fortitude, or of a privation submitted to with contentment; or by a grateful display of the temporal blessings with which Providence had favoured the Deceased, and the happy course of life through which he had passed. And where these individualities are untouched upon it may still happen that the estate of man in his helplessness, in his dependence upon his Maker or some other inherent of his nature shall be movingly and profitably expressed. Every Reader will be able to supply from his own observation instances of all these kinds, and it will be more pleasing for him to refer to his memory than to have the page crowded with unnecessary Quotations. [. . .]

In an obscure corner of a Country Church-yard I once espied, half-overgrown with Hemlock and Nettles, a very small Stone laid upon the ground, bearing nothing more than the name of the Deceased with the date of birth and death, importing that it was an Infant which had been born one day and died the following. I know not how far the Reader may be in sympathy with me, but more awful thoughts of rights conferred, of hopes awakened, of remembrances stealing away or vanishing were imparted to my mind by that Inscription there before my eyes than by any other that it has ever been my lot to meet with upon a Tomb-stone.

December

Douglas Dunn

'No, don't stop writing your grievous poetry.
It will do you good, this work of your grief.
Keep writing until there is nothing left.
It will take time, and the years will go by.'
Ours was a gentle generation, pacific,
In love with music, art and restaurants,
And he with she, strolling among the canvases,
And she with him, at concerts, coats on their laps.
Almost all of us were shy when we were young.
No friend of ours had ever been to war.
So many telephone numbers, remembered addresses;
So many things to remember.
The red sun hangs in a black tree, a moist
Exploded zero, bleeding into the trees
Praying from the earth upward, a psalm
In wood and light, in sky, earth and water.
These bars of birdsong come from another world;
They ring in the air like little doorbells.
They go by quickly, our best florescent selves
As good as summer and in love with being.
Reality, I remember you as her soft kiss
At morning. You were her presence beside me.
The red sun drips its molten dusk. Wet fires
Embrace the barren orchards, these gardens in
A city of cold slumbers. I am trapped in it.
It is December. The town is part of my mourning
And I, too, am part of whatever it grieves for.
Whose tears are these, pooled on this cellophane?

From *Elegies*, London: Faber & Faber, 1985, p. 53.

Index